ESSENTIAL LAW TEXTS

Criminal Law

Essential Law Texts—The Series

Essential Law Texts series from Round Hall provides students of Irish Law with a thorough introduction to core subject areas. Each title in the series covers the fundamentals of the subject and is specially written with undergraduate courses in mind.

- The Law of Tort by Philip Burke & Val Corbett
- Administrative Law—2nd edition by Gerard Coffey
- Criminal Law by Gerard Coffey
- Civil Practice and Procedure by Melody Buckley
- Company Law by Sinead McGrath
- Competition Law by Anna-Louise Hinds
- Constitutional Law by Fergus Ryan
- Contract Law in an E-Commerce Age by Simon Haigh
- Succession Law by Albert Keating

Visit *www.roundhall.ie* to check for the latest editions.

ESSENTIAL LAW TEXTS

Criminal Law

by

Dr Gerard Coffey PhD

ROUND HALL  THOMSON REUTERS

Published in 2010 by
Thomson Reuters (Professional) Ireland Limited
(Registered in Ireland, Company No. 80867. Registered Office
and address for service 43 Fitzwilliam Place, Dublin 2)
trading as Round Hall

Typeset by Carrigboy Typesetting Services

Printed by ColourBooks, Dublin

ISBN 978–1–85800–587–4

A catalogue record for this book is available from the British Library.

All rights reserved. No part of this publication may be reproduced or transmitted in any form or by any means, or stored in any retrieval system of any nature without prior written permission. Such written permission must also be obtained before any part of this publication is stored in a retrieval system of any nature.

Thomson Reuters and the Thomson Reuters Logo are trademarks of Thomson Reuters. Round Hall is a registered trademark of Thomson Reuters (Professional) Ireland Limited.

© Thomson Reuters (Professional) Ireland Limited, 2010

Preface

Criminal law is a complex subject which students will find both fascinating and challenging. The complexity is largely a result of the uncertainty created by the Superior Courts in most common law jurisdictions pertaining to the fundamental principles of criminal law. Consequently, students may find the subject as frustrating as it is challenging.

Textbooks on criminal law have conventionally provided much more detail than students require, which may add to the complexity of the subject. The aim of this book is to state clearly the core principles of criminal liability and areas of the criminal law typically covered by diploma and degree courses, including the areas covered by the entrance examinations for the Law Society of Ireland and The Honorable Society of King's Inns. This introductory book provides a systematic account of the essential topics on undergraduate criminal law courses in an easily comprehensible manner. Each chapter is structured to explain the law in the best order to facilitate a thorough understanding of the subject. Chapters have clear headings in order to navigate the reader through the text, which facilitates progression with confidence to a sound understanding of the core principles and policies of Irish criminal law. Each chapter includes suggestions for supplementary reading which provides direction for further investigation and study. Due to the dearth of authority in this jurisdiction, reference is made to developments on cognate jurisdictions. The text pays special attention to recent legislative developments and the Law Reform Commission's proposals for reform, such as the reform of the law relating to defences in criminal law.

The book takes the format of the Round Hall Essential Law Texts series and is designed to provide a clear explanation of the key principles and concepts for students, lawyers and others who require an understanding of the essentials of the subject, drawing on comparative law from cognate jurisdictions. The aim of this text is to explain the material clearly in an easily comprehensible manner. Each chapter is structured with the intention that the material is presented in a systematic order for the purposes of learning and revision. Clear sub-headings make specific points easy to locate. This introductory book covers the essential topics on undergraduate criminal law courses. It is easily comprehensible and includes extracts from leading cases.

Criminal Law will assist students in meeting the intellectual challenges that the study of the subject represents and to negotiate the student through a typical undergraduate criminal law course. In a book of this size it is impossible to cover the entire criminal law but I have set out the main topics on a typical undergraduate course on substantive criminal law.

I would like to express my gratitude to Frieda Donohue (Commissioning Editor) for her guidance and support on this project, Catherine Bermingham–Thomas (Editor), and the staff at Round Hall for their courteous efficiency and the very professional way in which they have dealt with the production and publication of this book. I also wish to acknowledge the assistance from my colleague, Philip Smyth, PhD. in Law Candidate in the Centre for Criminal Justice, School of Law, University of Limerick, for his most helpful comments and suggestions on draft chapters of this book. Naturally, any errors or omissions are mine alone.

I have endeavoured to state the law as of June 30, 2010.

Gerard Coffey
School of Law
University of Limerick
June 30, 2010

Contents

Preface v
Table of Cases xiii
Table of Legislation xxv

1 Introduction to Criminal Law 1
   Introduction 1
   Distinction between Public and Private Law 1
   Functions of Criminal Law 1
   Morality and Criminal Law 4
   Indicia of Criminal Offences 6
   Sources of Criminal Law 8
   Burden of Proof 13
   Standard of Proof 13
   Punishment 14
   Criminal Law Jurisdiction of the Courts 19
   Principle of Legality 24
   Constitutional Considerations in Criminal Law 26
   Classification of Criminal Offences 31

2 Actus Reus 36
   Introduction 36
   Categories of Criminal Offences 36
   Status Offences 38
   Voluntary Conduct 39
   Possession 43
   Criminal Liability for Omissions 51
   Causation 58

3 Mens Rea 70
   Introduction 70
   Motive and Mens Rea 70
   Intention 71
   Recklessness 82
   Criminal Negligence 88
   Knowledge and Belief 88
   Transferred Malice 89
   Principle of Double Effect 91

4	Coincidence of Actus Reus and Mens Rea	93
	Introduction	93
	Fault Element Must Coincide with the Prohibited Conduct	93
	Coincidence in Law	94
	Coincidence in Time	94
	Continuing Act	96
5	**Strict Liability**	99
	Introduction	99
	Classification of Strict Liability Offences	99
	Strict and Absolute Liability	99
	Rationale for Strict Liability Offences	100
	Strict Liability in Context	101
	General Principles	102
	Strict Liability Offences at Common Law	104
	Statutory Offences and Mens Rea	106
	Criteria	108
	Defence of Due Diligence	113
	Impact of the ECHR	114
	Constitutionality of Strict Liability Offences	114
6	**Introduction to Defences**	116
	Introduction	116
	Justification and Excuse	116
	Burden of Proof	117
	Proposed Law Reform	118
7	**Infancy**	119
	Introduction	119
	Age of Criminal Responsibility	119
	Duty of Gardaí in Relation to Under-Age Children	120
8	**Insanity and Diminished Responsibility**	121
	Introduction	121
	Fitness to be Tried	122
	Verdict and Disposition	122
	Appeals	122
	Diminished responsibility	123
	Mental Health (Criminal Law) Review Board	123
	Review of Detention	123
	Temporary Release and Transfer of Prisoners	124
	Criminal Law (Insanity) Bill 2010	124

9 Automatism ... 126
Introduction ... 126
Definition ... 126
Internal and External Factors ... 128
Degree of Consciousness ... 129
Automatism and Insanity ... 130

10 Intoxication ... 135
Introduction ... 135
Offences of Specific and Basic Intent ... 135
Voluntary Intoxication ... 137
Involuntary Intoxication ... 137
Intoxication and Dutch Courage ... 138
Proposed Law Reform ... 139

11 Duress and Necessity ... 141
Introduction ... 141
Duress ... 141
Necessity ... 150
Proposed Law Reform ... 154

12 Self-Defence and Defence of Others ... 155
Introduction ... 155
Imminence ... 156
Preparation ... 156
Requirement to Retreat ... 157
Mistake ... 158
Subjective or Objective Test? ... 159
Use of Excessive Force ... 159
Self-Defence in the Home ... 161
Proposed Law reform ... 162
Criminal Law (Defence and the Dwelling) Bill 2010 ... 163

13 Provocation ... 165
Introduction ... 165
Meaning of Provocation ... 165
Provocative Words or Conduct ... 166
Provocation in Irish Criminal Law ... 166
Evidence of Provocation ... 167
Third-Party Provocation ... 168
Self-Induced Provocation ... 169
Subjective Test ... 169

	Cumulative Provocation	171
	Proposed Law Reform	173
14	**Secondary Participation**	**174**
	Introduction	174
	Accessories	174
	Doctrine of Common Design	186
	Duty to Report Criminal Activity	193
15	**Inchoate Offences**	**194**
	Introduction	194
	Attempt	194
	Conspiracy	206
	Incitement	212
	Proposed Law Reform	216
16	**Homicide**	**218**
	Introduction	218
	Murder	218
	Manslaughter	222
	Merging the Offences of Murder and Manslaughter	230
	Infanticide	230
	Assisted Suicide	232
	Absence of a Victim	236
	Unworthiness to Succeed	237
	Proposed Law Reform	237
17	**Non-Fatal Offences Against the Person**	**239**
	Introduction	239
	Omission of a Saving Clause	239
	Assault	240
	Assault Causing Harm	242
	Causing Serious Harm	243
	Threats to Kill or Cause Serious Harm	244
	Syringe Attacks	244
	Possession and Abandonment of Syringes	245
	Placing or Abandoning Syringes	246
	Coercion	247
	Harassment	247
	Demands for Payment of Debt	249
	Poisoning	249
	Endangerment	250

Endangering Traffic	250
False Imprisonment	251
Abduction of Children by Parents	251
Abduction of Children by Other Persons	252
Justifiable Use of Force	253
Justifiable Use of Force in Effecting or Assisting Lawful Arrest	254
Meaning of "Force"	254
Amendment of the Criminal Damage Act 1991	255
General Defences	255
Consent by Minors to Surgical, Medical and Dental Treatment	255
Abolition of Corporal Punishment	255
Evidential Value of Certificates Signed by Medical Practitioners	255

18 Sexual Offences — 257

Introduction	257
Rape	257
Section 4 Rape	261
Sexual Assault	262
Sexual Offences against Children	266
Incest	268
Sexual Offences against People with Disabilities	271
Consent	272
Reckless Endangerment of Children	279
Child Trafficking and Pornography	279

19 Theft and Fraud Offences — 282

Introduction	282
Overview of the Criminal Justice (Theft and Fraud Offences) Act 2001	282
Repeals and Transitional Provision	283
Theft and Related Offences	284
Handling Stolen Property and Other Proceeds of Crime	292
Forgery and Related Offences	295
Counterfeiting and Related Offences	297
Convention on Protection of European Communities' Financial Interests	298
Investigation of Offences	300
Trial of Offences	302
Miscellaneous Matters	304

20 Public Order Offences ... 307
Introduction ... 307
Meaning of a Public Place ... 307
Intoxication in a Public Place ... 307
Disorderly Conduct in a Public Place ... 308
Threatening, Abusive or Insulting Behaviour in a Public Place ... 309
Distribution or Display of Threatening, Abusive, Insulting or Obscene Material ... 309
Failure to Comply with the Direction of a Garda ... 310
Wilful Obstruction ... 310
Entering a Building with Intent to Commit an Offence ... 311
Trespass on a Building ... 311
Riot ... 312
Violent Disorder ... 312
Affray ... 313
Blackmail, Extortion and Demanding Money with Menaces ... 314
Assault with Intent ... 315
Assault or Obstruction of a Peace Officer ... 315
Crowd Control at Public Events ... 316
Garda Powers of Arrest without Warrant ... 317
Exclusion and Closure Orders ... 319
Begging in Public ... 319
Impact of the Constitution ... 320
Adult Cautioning Scheme ... 320

Index ... 323

Table of Cases

IRELAND

A v The Governor of Arbour Hill Prison [2006] 4 I.R. 88 266
A Ward of Court, Re (Withdrawal of Medical Treatment No. 2) [1996] 2 I.R. 79 ... 235
Attorney General v Oldridge [2000] 4 I.R. 593 211
Attorney General v Whelan [1934] I.R. 518 .... 141, 147
Attorney General v X [1992] 1 I.R. 1 .... 10, 153
Attorney General (SPUC) v Open Door Counselling Ltd [1988] I.R. 593 208

B v DPP [1997] 2 I.L.R.M. 18 30
Burns v Governor and Company of the Bank of Ireland [2008] 1 I.R. 762 294

CC v Ireland [2006] 4 I.R. 1 .... 28, 114, 266
Clifford v DPP [2008] IEHC 322 309
Conroy v AG [1965] I.R. 411 33
Cummins v McCartan [2005] 3 I.R. 559 240
CW Shipping Co Ltd v Limerick Harbour Commissioners [1989] I.L.R.M. 416 ... 24

Dillon v DPP [2008] 1 I.R. 383 .... 29, 319
Dowman v Ireland [1986] I.L.R.M. 111 254
Doyle v Wicklow County Council [1974] I.R. 55 123
DPP (Ryan) v Mulligan [2009] 1 I.R. 794 318
DPP (Travers) v Brennan [1998] 4 I.R. 67 316
DS v Judges of the Cork Circuit and the DPP [2008] 4 I.R. 379 30
Duncan v Gleeson [1969] I.R. 116 107

Emergency Powers Bill 1976, Re [1977] I.R. 159 251
Enright v Ireland [2003] 2 I.R. 321 .... 11, 18

Gilligan v Criminal Assets Bureau [1998] 3 I.R. 185 19
Glynn, Martin, the Goods of, In Re [1992] I.L.R.M. 582 237
Grealish v DPP [2001] 3 I.R. 144 240

Halnon v Fleming [1981] 1 I.R. 489 88
Hardy v Ireland [1994] 2 I.R. 550 .... 27, 30, 245
Heaney v Ireland [1996] 1 I.R. 580 (SC); [1994] 3 I.R. 593 (HC) 27

JM v St. Vincent's Hospital [2003] 1 I.R. 321 235
JR v Minister for Justice, Equality and Law Reform [2007] 2 I.R. 748 57

K (Ward of Court), In Re [2001] 1 I.R. 338 235
Kiberd v Hamilton [1992] 2 I.R. 257 317
King v Attorney General [1981] I.R. 233 .... 28, 319, 320
Kane v The Governor of Mountjoy Prison [1988] 1 I.R. 757 251

Lynch v Fitzgerald (No. 2) [1938] I.R. 382 254

M'Adam v Dublin United Tramways Company Ltd [1929] I.R. 327 107
Magee v O'Dea [1994] 1 I.R. 500 30
Maguire v Shannon Regional Fisheries Board [1994] 3 I.R. 581 ..... 109, 111, 112
Mallon v Minister for Agriculture, Food and Forestry [1996] 1 I.R. 517 33
McGee v AG [1974] I.R. 587 29
Melling v O Mathghamhna [1962] I.R. 1 .... 7, 8, 32
Minister for Posts and Telegraphs v Campbell [1966] I.R. 69 .... 44, 47
Mullins v Harnett [1998] 4 I.R. 426 239
Murphy v DPP [2004] 1 I.R. 65 309

National Irish Bank, Re [1999] 1 I.R. 145 27
Norris v AG [1984] I.R. 36 30
North Western Health Board v HW [2001] 3 I.R. 622 235

O'Brien v Parker [1997] 2 I.L.R.M. 170 129
O'Keeffe v Ferris [1993] 3 I.R. 165 8
O'Leary v Attorney General [1993] 1 I.R. 102 .... 27, 30, 245

People (AG) v Ball (1936) 70 I.L.T.R. 202 236
People (AG) v Byrne [1974] I.R. 1 14
People (AG) v Cadden (1957) 91 I.L.T.R. 97 236
People (AG) v Capaldi [1949] 1 Frewen 95 214
People (AG) v Crosbie and Meehan [1966] I.R. 426 225
People (AG) v Dermody [1956] I.R. 307 257
People (AG) v Dunleavy [1948] I.R. 95 .... 88, 227, 228
People (AG) v Dwyer [1972] I.R. 416 .... 158, 159, 161, 253
People (AG) v Edge [1943] I.R. 115 252
People (AG) v England [1947] 1 Frewen 81 .... 195, 200
People (AG) v Grey [1944] I.R. 326 286
People (AG) v Keatley [1954] I.R. 12 .... 155, 253
People (AG) v Kelly [1982] I.L.R.M. 1 30
People (AG) v Kelly and Robinson [1953] 1 Frewen 147 46
People (AG) v McGrath [1960] 1 Frewen 267 64
People (AG) v Mesitt [1972] I.R. 204 30
People (AG) v Nugent and Byrne (1964) 98 I.L.T.R. 139 47
People (AG) v O'Callaghan [1966] I.R. 502 27
People (AG) v Quinn [1965] I.R. 366 116
People (AG) v Ryan [1966] 1 Frewen 304 187
People (AG) v Sullivan [1964] I.R. 169 .... 200, 206
People (AG) v Singer [1975] I.R. 408 30
People (AG) v Thornton [1952] I.R. 91 196
People (DPP) v Barnes [2007] 3 I.R. 130 162
People (DPP) v Bartley, unreported, High Court, June 13, 1997 57
People (DPP) v Clarke [1994] 3 I.R. 289 161

People (DPP) v Conroy (No. 2) [1989] I.R. 160 230
People (DPP) v Cullagh, unreported, Court of Criminal Appeal,
 March 15, 1999 228
People (DPP) v Cullen, unreported, Central Criminal Court,
 November 17, 1982 220
People (DPP) v Davis [2001] 1 I.R. 146 166
People (DPP) v Doohan [2002] 4 I.R. 463 188
People (DPP) v Douglas and Hayes [1985] I.L.R.M. 25 .... 78, 79, 203
People (DPP) v Eccles (1986) 3 Frewen 36 187
People (DPP) v Egan [1989] I.R. 681 184
People (DPP) v Finnerty [1999] 4 I.R. 364 27
People (DPP) v Foley [1995] 1 I.R. 267 47
People (DPP) v Gilligan, unreported, Special Criminal Court, March 15, 2001 ... 174
People (DPP) v Hull, unreported, Court of Criminal Appeal, July 8, 1996 .... 79, 80
People (DPP) v Kavanagh, unreported, Special Criminal Court,
 October 29, 1997 239
People (DPP) v Kelly (No.2) [1983] I.R. 1 251
People (DPP) v Kelly [2000] 2 I.R. 1 .... 167, 170
People (DPP) v Kelly, Circuit Court, October 29, 2004; December 2, 2004 70
People (DPP) v Kelso [1984] I.L.R.M. 329 157
People (DPP) v M [1994] 3 I.R. 306 .... 13, 30
People (DPP) v MacEoin [1978] I.R. 27 .... 87, 144, 167, 169, 170
People (DPP) v Madden [1977] I.R. 336 184
People (DPP) v McBride [1996] 1 I.R. 312 .... 79, 240
People (DPP) v McCormack [2004] 4 I.R. 333 253
People (DPP) v McDonagh [1996] 1 I.R. 565 260
People (DPP) v McDonagh [2001] 3 I.R. 201 167
People (DPP) v McGinty, unreported, Court of Criminal Appeal, April 3, 2006 159
People (DPP) v McGrath and Cagney [2008] 2 I.R. 111 .... 87, 250
People (DPP) v Meehan, unreported, Special Criminal Court, July 29, 1999 ... 174
People (DPP) v Mullane, unreported, Court of Criminal Appeal,
 March 11, 1997 170
People (DPP) v Murray [1977] I.R. 360 .... 23, 77, 86, 87,
 110, 187, 209, 248, 254, 261
People (DPP) v Nally [2007] 4 I.R. 145 .... 14, 161
People (DPP) v Noonan [1998] 2 I.R. 439 170
People (DPP) v O'Donoghue [2007] 2 I.R. 336 223
People (DPP) v O'Loughlin [1979] I.R. 85 286
People (DPP) v O'Reilly [1991] 1 I.R. 77 176
People (DPP) v O'Reilly, unreported, Court of Criminal Appeal, July 30, 2004 159
People (DPP) v Pringle [1981] 2 Frewen 57 187
People (DPP) v Pringle [1997] 2 I.R. 225 22
People (DPP) v Quilligan [1986] I.R. 495 22
People (DPP) v Ramachandran [2000] 2 I.R. 307 248
People (DPP) v Reid [1993] 2 I.R. 186 274
People (DPP) v Reid and Kirwan [2004] 1 I.R. 392 314

People (DPP) v Reilly [2005] 3 I.R. 111 .... 131, 136
People (DPP) v Shortt (No.2) [2002] 2 I.R. 696 22
People (DPP) v Wall, unreported, Court of Criminal Appeal,
  December 16, 2005 22
People (DPP) v Ward, unreported, Special Criminal Court,
  November 27, 1998 174
People (DPP) v Ward, unreported, Court of Criminal Appeal,
  March 22, 2002 174
People (DPP) v WM [1995] 1 I.R. 226 271
PSS v JAS, unreported, High Court, May 22, 1995 87

Quinlivan v Governor of Portlaoise Prison [1998] 2 I.R. 113 239

R v Dee (1884) 15 Cox C.C. 579 .... 272, 274
R v Hehir [1895] 2 I.R. 709 93
Ryan v DPP [1989] I.R. 399 27

Savage and McOwen v DPP [1982] I.L.R.M. 385 22
Shannon Regional Fisheries Board v Cavan County Council
  [1996] 3 I.R. 267 .... 111, 114
State (Buchan) v Coyne (1936) 70 I.L.T.R. 185 30
State (Clancy) v Wine [1980] I.R. 228 316
State (Coughlan) v Minister for Justice [1968] I.L.T.R. 177 122
State (Harrington) v Garvey, unreported, High Court, December 14, 1976 251
State (O'Connell) v Fawsitt [1986] I.R. 362 30
State (O'Hagan) v Delap [1982] I.R. 213 316

Thorpe v DPP [2007] 1 I.R. 502 309

Ward of Court (Withdrawal of Medical Treatment), In Re [1996] 2 I.R. 79 .... 235, 236

ENGLAND

A, Re (Children) (conjoined twins) [2001] 2 W.L.R. 480 153
Abbott v R [1977] 1 A.C. 755 148
Adler v George [1964] 2 Q.B. 7 311
Airedale N.H.S. Trust v Bland [1993] 1 A.C. 789 .... 51, 91, 235
Alphacell Ltd v Woodward [1972] A.C. 824 .... 100, 111
Andrews v DPP [1937] A.C. 576 .... 226, 227
Attorney-General v Able [1984] Q.B. 795 .... 182, 233
Attorney General for Northern Ireland v Gallagher [1963] A.C. 349 138
Attorney General's Reference (No.1 of 1975) [1975] Q.B. 773 .... 175, 177
Attorney General's Reference (No.2 of 1983) [1984] Q.B. 456 157
Attorney General's Reference (No.2 of 1992) [1994] Q.B. 91 .... 129, 203
Attorney General's Reference (No.3 of 1994) [1998] A.C. 245 90
Attorney General's Reference (No.3 of 2003) [2005] Q.B. 73 86

TABLE OF CASES

B (A Minor) v DPP [2000] 2 A.C. 428 105
Beckford v R [1988] A.C. 130 158
Blakely and Sutton v DPP [1991] Crim. L.R. 763 .... 182, 183
Bratty v Attorney General for Northern Ireland [1963] A.C. 386 127
Brown v Dyerson [1969] 1 Q.B. 45 150
Buckoke v Greater London Council [1971] 1 Ch. 655 151
Cartledge v Allen [1973] Crim. L. R. 530 243
Chang Wing-Siu v The Queen [1985] A.C. 168 188
Chief Constable of Avon v Shimmen (1987) 84 Cr. App. R 7 85
Chlemsford Justices, Re; ex parte Amos [1973] Crim. L.R. 437 215
Cundy v Le Cocq (1884) 13 Q.B.D. 207 102

Davey v Lee [1968] 1 Q.B. 366 196
DPP v Beard [1920] A.C. 471 135
DPP v Daley [1979] 2 W.L.R. 239 67
DPP v Majewski [1976] 2 All E.R. 142 .... 135, 137
DPP v Morgan [1976] A.C. 182 259
DPP v Newbury and Jones [1977] A.C. 500 223
DPP v Nock [1978] A.C. 979 .... 205, 212, 216
DPP v Shannon [1975] A.C. 717 211
DPP v Smith [1961] A.C. 290 .... 72, 77
DPP v Stonehouse [1978] A.C. 55 198
DPP for Northern Ireland v Lynch [1975] A.C. 653 .... 144, 148
Dunbar v Plant [1997] 3 W.L.R. 1261 233

Elliot v C (A Minor) [1983] 1 W.L.R. 939 .... 84, 85
Environment Agency v Empress Car Co (Abertillery) Ltd [1997] 2 A.C. 22 105

Fagan v Metropolitan Police Commissioner [1969] 1 Q.B. 439 .... 96, 279
Fairclough v Whipp [1951] 2 All E.R. 834 264
Faulkner v Talbot [1981] 1 W.L.R. 1528 263

Gammon v Attorney General of Hong Kong [1985] A.C. 1 ...... 105, 108, 109, 112
Gillick v West Norfolk and Wisbech Area Health Authority
    [1986] 1 A.C. 112 .... 178, 181

Hargreaves v Diddams (1875) L.R. 10 Q. B. 582 99
Haughton v Smith [1975] A.C. 476 .... 199, 204, 205, 206
Hill v Baxter [1958] 1 Q.B. 277 41
Hyam v DPP [1975] A.C. 55 .... 72, 74, 79, 230

Invicta Plastics Ltd v Clare [1976] Crim. L.R. 131 215

James & Son Ltd v Smee [1955] 1 Q.B. 78 110
Jones v Brooks and Brooks (1968) 52 Cr. App. R. 614 201

Kaitamaki v R [1985] A.C. 147 .... 98, 272, 278, 279
Knuller v DPP [1973] A.C. 435; Shaw v DPP [1962] A.C. 221 208

Lawrence v Commissioner of Metropolitan Police [1972] A.C. 626 .... 285, 286
Leicester v Pearson [1952] 2 Q.B. 668 40
Lim Chin Aik v R [1963] A.C. 160 .... 103, 111

Mawji v R [1957] A.C. 126 209
Mee v Cruikshank (1902) 20 Cox C.C. 210 251
Metropolitan Police Commissioner v Caldwell
 [1981] 1 All E.R. 901 .... 82. 83, 84, 85,86
Miller v Minister for Pensions [1947] All E.R. 372 14

National Coal Board v Gamble [1959] 1 Q.B. 11 181

Partington v Williams (1975) 62 Cr. App. R. 220 .... 204, 205
Pharmaceutical Society of Great Britain v Storkwain Ltd. [1986] 1 W.L.R. 903 102
R v Adams [1957] Crim. L.R. 365 60
R v Adomako [1995] 1 A.C. 171 226
R v Ahluwalia (1993) 96 Cr. App. R. 133 172
R v Ali [1995] Crim. L.R. 303 147
R v Allen [1988] Crim L.R. 698 138
R v Anderson and Morris [1966] 2 Q.B. 110 186
R v Bainbridge [1960] 1 Q.B. 129 183
R v Batemen (1925) 19 Cr. App. R. 8 226
R v Becerra; R v Cooper (1976) 62 Cr. App. R. 212 .... 190, 191, 192
R v Blaue [1975] 1 W.L.R. 1411 66
R v Bland [1988] Crim. L.R. 41 180
R v Bolton [1991] Crim. L.R. 57 210
R v Bourne [1939] 1 K.B. 687 153
R v Bourne (1952) 36 Cr. App. R. 125 185
R v Bowen [1996] Crim L.R. 577 144
R v Bree [2007] E.W.C.A. Crim. 256 276
R v Brown [1985] Crim. L.R. 212 291
R v Brown [1994] 1 A.C. 212 241
R v Buck and Buck (1960) 44 Cr. App. R. 213 178
R v Bullock [1955] 1 W.L.R. 1 180
R v Burgess [1991] 2 Q.B. 92 .... 130, 131
R v Calhaem [1985] 1 Q.B. 808 176
R v Campbell [1991] Crim. L.R. 268 197
R v Camplin (1845) 1 Cox C.C. 22 276
R v Carmichael [1940] 1 K.B. 630 270
R v Cato [1976] 1 W.L.R. 110 59
R v Cheshire [1991] 1 W.L.R. 844 63
R v Church [1966] 1 Q.B. 59 96
R v Clarence (1888) 22 Q.B.D. 23 273

R v Clarke [1991] Crim L.R. 383 168
R v Clarkson [1971] 1 W.L.R. 1402 179
R v Cocker [1989] Crim. L.R. 740 167
R v Cogan and Leak [1976] Q.B. 217 185
R v Coles [1995] 1 Cr. App. R. 157 .... 84, 142, 150
R v Coney (1882) 8 Q.B.D. 534 178
R v Conway [1989] Q.B. 290 151
R v Cooper and Schaub [1994] Crim. L.R. 531 279
R v Cope (1921) 16 Cr. App. R. 77 200
R v Corbett [1996] Crim. L.R. 596 66
R v Coughlan (1976) 64 Cr. App. R. 11 211
R v Court [1989] A.C. 28 .... 263, 264
R v Cuerrier [1998] 2 S.C.R. 371 278
R v Cunningham [1957] 2 Q.B. 396 .... 82, 83
R v Cunningham [1982] A.C. 566 219
R v D [2004] E.W.C.A. Crim. 1391 76
R v Deller (1952) 36 Cr. App. Rep. 184 37
R v Dias (2002) 2 Cr. App. R. 96 67
R v Donovan [1934] 2 K.B. 498 242
R v Doughty (1986) 83 Cr. App. R. 319 166
R v Dudley & Stephens (1884) Cox C.C. 624 .... 149, 152, 153
R v Duffy [1949] 1 All E.R. 932 .... 165, 166
R v Dyson [1908] 2 K.B. 454 218
R v Dytham [1979] Q.B. 722 .... 56, 57, 178
R v Eagleton (1855) 6 Cox C.C. 559 .... 195, 196, 198
R v EB [2006] E.W.C.A. Crim. 2945 .... 243, 278
R v Elbekkay [1995] Crim. L.R. 163 275
R v Evans (Gemma) [2009] EWCA Crim. 650 .... 68, 69
R v Fennell [1971] 1 Q.B. 428 254
R v Firth (1990) 91 Cr. App. R. 217 58
R v Fitzmaurice [1983] Q.B. 1083 .... 213, 215
R v Flattery (1877) 2 Q.B.D. 410 275
R v Fletcher (1859) 8 Cox C.C. 131 276
R v G [2004] 1 A.C. 1034 .... 85, 86
R v G (Secretary of State for the Home Department) [2009] 1 A.C. 92 86
R v Gardner (1993) 14 Cr. App. R. (S) 364 168
R v Ghosh [1982] Q.B. 1053 287
R v Gianetto (1997) 1 Cr. App. R. 1 .... 176, 178
R v Gibbins & Proctor (1918) 13 Cr. App. Rep. 134 53
R v Gibson [1990] 2 Q.B. 619 208
R v Gomez [1993] A.C. 442 286
R v Gotts [1992] 2 A.C. 412 .... 148, 149
R v Graham [1982] 1 W.L.R. 294 143
R v Griffiths [1966] 1 Q.B. 589 208
R v Grundy [1977] Crim. L.R. 543 191
R v Hancock and Shankland [1986] A.C. 455 .... 73, 76

R v Hardie [1984] 1 W.L.R. 64 137
R v Hayward (1908) 21 Cox C.C. 692 .... 65, 229
R v Hegarty [1994] Crim L.R. 353 144
R v Hibbert (1869) L.R. 1 C.C.R. 184 101
R v Hibbert (1875) 13 Cox 82 247
R v Hinks [2001] 2 A.C. 241 .... 5, 286
R v Horne [1994] Crim L.R. 584 144
R v Howard (1833) 172 E.R. 1188 166
R v Howe [1987] A.C. 417 .... 143, 148, 149, 153, 175
R v Hudson and Taylor [1971] 2 Q.B. 202 145
R v Humphreys [1996] Crim. L.R. 431 172
R v Ilyas (1983) 78 Cr. App. R. 17 198
R v Instan (1893) 1 Q.B. 450 53
R v Ireland; R v Burstow [1998] A.C. 147 243
R v Jakeman (1983) 76 Cr. App. R. 223 94
R v Johnson (1989) 89 Cr. App. R. 148 169
R v Jones [1990] 1 W.L.R. 1057 201
R v Jordan (1956) 40 Cr. App. R. 152 .... 61, 62
R v K [2002] 1 A.C. 462 107
R v Kamara [1974] A.C. 104 207
R v Kennedy (No. 2) [2008] 1 A.C. 269 68
R v Kilbourne [1972] 1 W.L.R. 1365 265
R v Kingston [1995] 2 A.C. 355 .... 138, 139
R v Kumar [2005] Crim. L.R. 470 108
R v Lang (1975) 62 Cr. App. R. 50 276
R v Larkin (1942) 29 Cr. App. R.18 225
R v Larsonneur (1933) 29 Cox C.C. 673 .... 38, 43, 100
R v Latimer (1886) 17 Q.B.D. 359 .... 89, 94
R v Lawrence [1981] A.C. 510 .... 83, 86
R v Le Brun [1992] 1 Q.B. 61 96
R v Lemon and Gay News Ltd [1979] A.C. 617 106
R v Lewis (1988) 87 Cr. App. R. 270 47
R v Linekar [1995] 1 Q.B. 340 275
R v Lipman [1970] 1 Q.B. 152 137
R v Lomas (1914) 9 Cr. App. R. 220 180
R v Lowe [1973] Q.B. 702 54
R v Mackie (1973) 57 Cr. App. R. 453 67
R v Malcherek; R v Steel [1981] 1 W.L.R. 690 62
R v Marriott [1971] 1 W.L.R. 187 108
R v Martin (1832) 5 C&P 123 65
R v Martin (1881) 8 Q.B.D. 54 243
R v Martin (1989) 88 Cr. App. R. 343 151
R v Martindale [1986] 1 W.L.R. 1042 50
R v Matthews and Alleyn (2003) 2 Cr. App. R. 30 76
R v Mayes (1872) 12 Cox C.C. 311 276
R v McInnes [1971] 1 W.L.R. 1600 .... 157, 254

R v McNamara (1988) 87 Cr. App. R. 246 49
R v Merrick (1996) 1 Cr. App. R. 130 85
R v Miller [1983] 2 A.C. 161 56
R v Mills [1963] 2 W.L.R. 137 209
R v Miskell [1954] 1 Q.B.D. 137 195
R v Mitchell [1983] 1 Q.B. 741 .... 94, 226
R v Mitchell; R v King [1999] Crim. L.R. 497 191
R v Mohan [1976] 1 Q.B. 1 195
R v Moloney [1985] A.C. 905 .... 73, 74, 76
R v Morris [1984] A.C. 320 .... 285, 286
R v Most (1881) 14 Cox CC 583 215
R v Mulcahy (1868) L.R. 3 H.L. 306 207
R v Nedrick [1986] 1 W.L.R. 1025 .... 74, 75
R v Nicholls (1874) 13 Cox C.C. 75 53
R v O'Donoghue (1927) 28 Cox C.C. 461 231
R v O'Flaherty, Ryan and Toussaint (2004) 2 Cr App. R. 20 191
R v Olugboja [1982] Q.B. 320 273
R v Pagett (1983) 76 Cr. App.R. 279 .... 64, 226
R v Parnell (1881) 14 Cox C.C. 508 .... 207, 210
R v Pearson [1992] Crim L.R. 193 168
R v Pembliton (1874) L.R. 2 C.C.R. 119 .... 89, 94
R v Perman (1996) 1 Cr. App. R. 24 191
R v Pittwood (1902) 19 T.L.R. 37 52
R v Pommell [1995] 2 Cr. App. R. 607 152
R v Poulton (1832) 5 C&P. 329 219
R v Powell; R v English [1999] 1 A.C. 1 188
R v Prince (1875) L.R. 2 C.C.R.154 102
R v Quick [1973] 1 Q.B. 910 42
R v R (Stephen Malcolm) (1984) Cr. App. R. 334 .... 84, 85
R v Rahman (Islamur) [2009] 1 A.C. 129 184
R v Rahman (1985) 81 Cr. App. R. 349 251
R v Reeves (1839) 9 C&P 25 219
R v Roberts (1971) 56 Cr. App. R. 95 65
R v Robinson [1915] 2 K.B. 342 198
R v Rogers [2003] 1 W.L.R. 1374 68
R v Rolfe (1952) 36 Cr. App. R. 4 264
R v Rook [1993] 1 W.L.R. 1005 192
R v Satnam and Kewel (1984) 78 Cr. App. R. 149 260
R v Scalley [1995] Crim. L.R. 504 76
R v Scarlett (1993) 98 Cr. App. R. 290 224
R v Selton (1871) 11 Cox C.C. 674 166
R v Senior (1899) 1 Q.B. 283 52
R v Seymour [1983] 2 A.C. 493 84
R v Sharp [1987] 1 Q.B. 853 .... 146, 147
R v Shepard (1987) 86 Cr. App. R. 47 146
R v Sleep (1861) Le & Co. 44 45

R v Smith [1959] 2 Q.B. 35 .... 61, 62, 63
R v Spratt [1990] 1 W.L.R. 1073 240
R v Steane [1947] 1 K.B. 997 148
R v Stephens (1866) L.R. 1 Q.B. 702 99
R v Stone & Dobinson [1977] 2 Q.B. 354 54
R v Sullivan [1984] A.C. 156 130
R v T [1990] Crim L.R. 256 1278
R v Taaffe [1984] A.C. 539 .... 203, 205
R v Taylor (1875) 13 Cox C.C. 68 178
R v Thornton (1993) 96 Cr. App. R. 12 .... 171, 172
R v Thornton (No. 2) [1996] 1 W.L.R. 1174 172
R v Tyrell, [1894] 1 Q.B. 710 215
R v Vickers [1957] 2 Q.B. 664 219
R v Walker [1962] Crim. L.R. 458 215
R v Walker; R v Hayles (1990) 90 Cr. App. R. 226 75
R v White [1910] 2 K.B. 124 .... 59, 205
R v Whitefield (1984) 79 Cr. App. R. 36 191
R v Whitehouse [1977] Q.B. 868 .... 215, 270
R v Whybrow (1951) 35 Cr. App. R. 141 202
R v Wild (1837) 2 Lew 214 225
R v Venna [1976] Q.B. 421 240
R v Willer (1986) 83 Cr. App. R. 225 152
R v Williams [1923] 1 K.B. 340 275
R v Williams (1984) 78 Cr. App. R. 276 158
R v Woods (1931) 22 Cr. App. R. 41 200
R v Woolin [1999] 1 A.C. 82 .... 75, 76, 82
R v Z [2005] 2 A.C. 467 147
R (Pretty) v DPP [2002] 1 A.C. 800 .... 91, 234
R (Purdy) v DPP [2010] 1 A.C. 345 234
Race Relations Board v Applin [1973] Q.B. 815 214
Roberts v Egerton (1874) L.R. 9 Q.B. 494 99

Shaw v DPP [1962] A.C. 220 24
Sherras v De Rutzen [1895] 1 Q.B. 918 .... 99, 103, 109, 111
Sullivan v Earl of Caithness [1976] Q.B. 966 43
Sweet v Parsley [1970] A.C. 132 .... 104, 105, 110

Thabo Meli v R [1954] 1 W.L.R. 228 .... 95, 96
Thorne v Motor Trade Association [1937] A.C. 797 314
Thornton v Mitchell [1940] 1 All E.R. 339 185
Tuck v Robson [1970] 1 W.L.R. 741 180

Ward, Lock & Co v Operative Printers' Assistants' Society
   (1906) 22 T.L.R. 327 247
Warner v Metropolitan Police Commissioner
   [1969] 2 A.C. 256 .... 43, 48, 49, 100, 108

Wilcox v Jeffery [1951] 1 All E.R. 464 178
Winzar v Chief Constable of Kent, *The Times*, March 28, 1983 .... 38, 100
Woolmington v DPP [1935] A.C. 435 13

NORTHERN IRELAND

Devlin v Armstrong [1971] N.I. 17 .... 155, 156

R v Browne [1973] N.I. 96 254
R v Clinton [2001] N.I. 207 157
R v Fegan [1972] N.I. 80 156
R v Fitzpatrick [1977] N.I. 20 .... 146, 147
R v Maxwell [1978] N.I. 42 183
R v Murphy, Lillis and Burns [1971] N.I. 193 .... 46, 47
R v Porter [1980] N.I. 18 .... 210, 211
R v Whelan [1972] N.I. 153 .... 47, 48

SCOTLAND

HM Advocate v Ritchie (1926) SC (J) 45 42

AUSTRALIA

Giorgianni v R (1985) 58 A.L.R. 641 .... 182, 183

Jiminez v The Queen [1992] 173 C.L.R. 572 42

Papadimitropoulos v R [1957] 98 C.L.R. 249 .... 275, 277

R v Falconer (1990) 50 A. Crim. R. 244 .... 126, 133
R v Holzer [1968] V.R. 481 228
R v Hurley [1967] V.R. 526 142
R v O'Connor (1980) 29 A.L.R. 449 136
R v Orton [1922] V.L.R. 469 211
R v Radford (1985) 42 S.A.S.R. 266 132
R v Tait [1976] V.R 151 129
R v Taktak [1988] 14 N.S.W.L.R. 226 55
Ryan v The Queen [1967] 121 C.L.R. 205 129

Williams v Douglas [1949] 78 C.L.R. 521 45

NEW ZEALAND

Kilbride v Lake [1962] N.Z.L.R. 590 39

Millar v Ministry for Transport [1986] 1 N.Z.L.R. 660 .... 109, 113

R v Baker [1924] N.Z.L.R. 865 201

The Queen v Strawbridge [1970] N.Z.L.R. 909 .... 111, 112

CANADA

Leary v The Queen [1978] 1 S.C.R. 29 137

Miller v The Queen [1977] 2 S.C.R. 680 190

R v Barnier (1980) 51 CCC (2d) 193 264
R v Bernard [1988] 2 S.C.R. 833 137
R v City of Sault Ste Marie (1978) 85 D.L.R. (3d) 161 .... 113, 114
R v K (1970) 3 C.C.C. (2d) 84 126
R v Parks [1992] 95 D.L.R. (4th) 27 .... 130, 131
Rabey v R [1980] 2 S.C.R. 513 .... 127, 132, 134
R v Whitehouse (1941) 1 W.W.R. 112 .... 189, 190

SOUTH AFRICA

Nkosiyana 1966 (4) SA 655 212

S v Goliath (1972) (3) S.A. 1 148

HONG KONG

HSKAR v Paul Y-ITC Construction Ltd [1998] 3 H.K.C. 189 109

UNITED STATES

United States v Holmes (1842) 26 Fed. Cas. 360 153

EUROPEAN COURT OF HUMAN RIGHTS

Müller v Switzerland (1991) 13 E.H.R.R. 212 309
Murray v United Kingdom (1996) 22 E.H.R.R. 29 27

Norris v Ireland (1991) 13 E.H.R.R. 186 30

Salabiaku v France (1991) 13 E.H.R.R. 379 114

Table of Legislation

THE IRISH CONSTITUTION

Art.5 10
Art.13.6 220
Art.15.2.1° 9, 10, 11
Art.15.5.1° 9, 11, 24, 26
Art.15.5.2° 218
Art.34 22
Art.34.3.4° 20
Art.34.4.1° 23
Art.38.1 .... 19, 26, 27, 28, 115, 245
Art.38.2 .... 20, 32
Art.40 319
Art.40.1 .... 15, 28
Art.40.3 28
Art.40.3.1 .... 28, 162
Art.40.3.2 162
Art.40.4.1° 27, 28
Art.40.6 27
Art.40.6.1°(ii) 316, 320
Art.41 210

IRISH STATUTES

Accessories and Abettors Act 1861 175

Bail Act 1997 33
   s.2(1) 27
   s.4 14

Censorship of Publications Act 1929
   s.10 19
Child Trafficking and Pornography Act 1998 279
Children Act 2001 120
   s.52 119
   s.53 120
Coinage Offences Act 1861 283
Companies Act 1963
   s.297 8
   s.297(1) 8
   s.297(3) 8
Conspiracy and Protection of Property Act 1875
   s.7 247

Court and Court Officers Act 1995
    s.4 23
Courts (Establishment and Constitution) Act 1961 23
Courts of Justice Act 1924 23
Criminal Damage Act 1851 94
Criminal Damage Act 1991 .... 3, 21
    s.5 290
    s.6(2) 255
Criminal Justice Act 1951
    s.2 32
    s.23 221
    Schedule 20, 32
Criminal Justice Act 1964 160
    s.4 .... 77, 91, 160
    s.4(1) 219
    s.4(2) 77, 80
Criminal Justice Act 1984 27
    s.11 .... 14, 31
Criminal Justice Act 1990
    s.1 .... 218, 221
    s.2 .... 15, 123, 165, 220
    s.3 .... 221, 234
    s.4 221
Criminal Justice Act 1993 22
    s.6 19
Criminal Justice Act 1994 295
    s.31 .... 294, 295
    s.56A 295
    s.57 295
    s.57A 295
Criminal Justice Act 1999
    s.38 218
Criminal Justice Act 2006 .... 15, 21
    s.21 23
    s.101 18
    s.102 18
    s.129 119
    s.130 120
    s.176 279
    s.176(2) 279
    s.176(3) 279
    s.176(4) 279
    s.184 308
    s.185 316
Criminal Justice Act 2007 27
    s.33 15

Criminal Justice (Community Service) Act 1983 16
Criminal Justice (Drug Trafficking) Act 1996 27
Criminal Justice (Public Order) Act 1994 ... 3, 17, 18, 307, 314, 315, 316, 317, 319
   s.3 307
   s.4 .... 16, 307, 308, 310, 317, 319, 320
   s.4(3) 308
   s.5 .... 16, 308, 310, 319, 320
   s.5(1) 308
   s.5(3) 308
   s.6 .... 16, 19, 307, 308, 309, 310, 317, 319, 320
   s.6(1) 309
   s.6(2) 309, 320
   s.7 .... 16, 310, 317, 319
   s.7(1) 309
   s.7(2) 310
   s.8 .... 16, 19, 310, 317, 319, 320
   s.8(1) 310
   s.8(3) 310
   s.9 .... 16, 310, 319, 320
   s.11 .... 19, 311, 317, 320
   s.11(1) 311
   s.11(2) 311
   s.13 .... 19, 317
   s.13(1) 311
   s.13(2) 311
   s.13(3)(a) 311
   s.13(3)(b) 312
   s.14 .... 32, 317
   s.14(1) 312
   s.14(2) 312
   s.14(3) 312
   s.14(4) 312
   s.15 317
   s.15(1) 312
   s.15(3) 313
   s.15(4) 313
   s.16 .... 19, 317
   s.16(1) 313
   s.16(1)(c) 314
   s.16(4) 314
   s.16(5) 314
   s.17(1) 314
   s.17(2) 314
   s.17(3) 315
   s.18 .... 315, 318
   s.18(1) 315

s.18(2) 315
s.19 .... 314, 318
s.19(1) 315
s.19(1)(a) 316
s.19(2) 316
s.19(3) 316
s.19(4) 316
s.19(6) 316
s.21(1) 316
s.21(2) 317
s.21(3) 317
s.21(4) 317
s.21(5) 317
s.22 320
s.22(1) 317
s.22(2) 317
s.22(3) 317
s.22(4) 317
s.23A 308
s.23B 308
s.24 318
s.24(1) 317
s.24(2) 318
s.24(3) 318
s.24(4) 318
s.25 311
Criminal Justice (Public Order) Act 2003 .... 3, 17, 307, 319
   s.3(1) 319
   s.3(2) 319
   s.3(4) 319
   s.4(1) 319
   s.5(2) 319
Criminal Justice (Surveillance) Act 2009 .... 212, 248
Criminal Justice (Theft and Fraud Offences) Act 2001 .... 3, 9, 20, 32, 37,
                                      43, 93, 282, 283, 294, 300, 301, 302, 303, 304, 305
   s.2 .... 283, 284
   s.2(1) 284
   s.3(1) 283
   s.3(2) 283
   s.3(2) 284
   s.4 .... 284, 287
   s.4(1) 284
   s.4(2) 284
   s.4(3) 284
   s.4(4) 284
   s.4(5) 284

TABLE OF LEGISLATION

s.4(6) 284
s.5 288
s.5(1) 287
s.5(2) 287
s.5(3) 287
s.5(4) 287
s.5(5) 287
s.6 .... 288, 302
s.7 302
s.7(1) 289
s.7(4) 289
s.8(1) 289
s.8(2) 289
s.8(3) 289
s.8(4) 289
s.8(5) 289
s.8(6) 289
s.8(7) 289
s.9 302
s.9(1) 290
s.9(2) 290
s.10 .... 290, 302
s.10(3) 290
s.11 .... 290, 302
s.11(1) 290
s.11(2) 290
s.11(3) 290
s.11(4) 291
s.12(1) 291
s.12(3) 291
s.13 291
s.13(3) 291
s.14(1) 291
s.14(2) 292
s.15(1) 292
s.15(2) 292
s.15(3) 292
s.15(4) 292
s.15(5) 292
s.16(1) 292
s.17(1) 292
s.17(2) 292
s.17(3) 293
s.17(4) 293
s.18(1) 293
s.18(2) 293

s.18(3)	293
s.18(4)	293
s.19(1)	293
s.19(2)	294
s.19(3)	294
s.19(4)	294
s.20	294
s.20(3)	294
s.21	294
s.22	295
s.23	295
s.24	295
s.25(1)	295
s.25(2)	295
s.26(1)	295
s.26(2)	295
s.27(1)	295
s.27(2)	296
s.28(1)	296
s.28(2)	296
s.29(1)	296
s.29(2)	296
s.29(3)	296
s.29(4)	296
s.29(5)	296
s.29(6)	296
s.30	296
s.31	297
s.32	297
s.33(1)	297
s.33(2)	297
s.34(1)	297
s.34(2)	297
s.35(1)	297, 298
s.35(2)	297, 298
s.36(1)	298
s.36(2)	298
s.36(3)	298
s.37(1)	298
s.38	300
s.40(1)	298
s.40(2)	298
s.41	298
s.42	299
s.42(1)	299
s.43	299

s.44	299
s.45	304
s.45(1)	299
s.45(2)	299
s.45(3)	299
s.46(1)	299
s.46(2)	300
s.46(3)	300
s.46(4)	300
s.47	300
s.48	300, 301
s.48(2)	300
s.48(3)	300
s.48(4)	300
s.48(5)	300
s.48(6)	300
s.49(1)	300
s.49(2)	301
s.50(1)	301
s.50(2)	301
s.50(3)	301
s.50(4)	301
s.51(1)	301
s.51(2)	301
s.51(3)	301
s.52	301
s.52(1)	301
s.52(2)	301
s.52(3)	301
s.52(4)	301, 302
s.52(5)	302
s.52(6)	302
s.52(7)	302
s.52(8)	302
s.53	302
s.54(1)	302
s.54(2)	302
s.54(3)	302
s.54(5)	303
s.54(6)	303
s.54(7)	303
s.55(1)	303
s.55(2)	303
s.56(1)	303
s.56(2)	303
s.56(3)	303

s.56(4) 303
s.57(1) 303
s.57(3) 303
s.58(1) 304
s.58(2) 304
s.59(1) 304
s.59(4) 304
s.60(1) 304
s.60(2) 304
s.61 304
s.62 305
s.65 305
Sch.1 283
Criminal Justice (United Nations Conventions Against Torture) Act 2000 12
Criminal Law Act 1997 .... 32, 33, 175, 186, 188, 194
 s.2 194
 s.2(1) 291
 s.3 58
 s.4 33
 s.7 235
 s.7(1) 174, 175, 213
 s.7(2) 186
 s.9(1) 222
Criminal Law Amendment Act 1885 274
 s.3 277
 s.11 30
Criminal Law (Amendment) Act 1935 .... 266, 274
 s.1(1) 28, 266
 s.1(2) 114
 s.12 269
Criminal Law (Amendment) Act 1936
 s.17 28
Criminal Law (Incest Proceedings) Act 1995 .... 3, 268, 270
 s.2 271
 s.3 271
Criminal Law (Insanity) Act 2006 .... 121, 122, 124, 125, 232
 s.1 121
 s.4 122
 s.6 123
 s.6(3) 232
 s.8(1) 122
 s.8(6) 122
 s.11 123
 s.11(2) 123
 s.13 .... 123, 124

s.13(2)	123
s.14	124
Criminal Law (Jurisdiction) Act 1976	305
Criminal Law (Rape) Act 1981	3, 257
s.2	257
s.2(1)	257, 260, 261
s.2(1)(b)	258
s.2(2)	259, 260
Criminal Law (Rape)(Amendment) Act 1990	3, 21, 32, 257, 272
s.2	258, 262
s.2(1)	262
s.2(2)	262
s.2(3)	262
s.3	265
s.3(1)	262, 265
s.3(2)	262, 265
s.3(3)	265
s.4	119, 261
s.4(1)(a)	261
s.4(1)(b)	261
s.4(2)	261
s.4(3)	261
s.5(1)	258
s.5(2)	258
s.8	261
s.9	272
Criminal Law (Sexual Offences) Act 1993	5, 30
s.2(2)	272
s.5(1)	271
s.5(3)	272
s.5(4)	272
s.5(5)	272
Criminal Law (Sexual Offences) Act 2006	3, 266
s.2	267
s.2(1)	267
s.2(2)	267
s.2(3)	267
s.2(4)	267
s.2(5)	267
s.3	267
s.3(1)	267, 268
s.3(2)	267, 268
s.3(3)	268
s.3(4)	268
s.3(5)	268

s.3(6) 268
s.3(7) 268
s.3(9) 268
s.3(10) 268
Criminal Law (Sexual Offences) (Amendment) Act 2007 3
   s.5 267
   s.6 279
Criminal Law (Suicide) Act 1993 233
   s.2(1) 233, 235
   s.2(2) 233, 234, 235
   s.2(3) 234
   s.2(4) 234
Criminal Procedure Act 1967
   s.34 23
Customs (Consolidation) Act 1876 6
   s.186 7

Defence Act 1954
   s.156 305
Dublin Carriage Act 1853
   s.50 107

European Convention on Human Rights Act 2003 12
   s.2 12
   s.4 12
   s.5 12
Explosive Substances Act 1883 22
Extradition Act 1965 300
   s.38 300

Falsification of Accounts Act 1875 .... 282, 283
Firearms Act 1925–2006 22
Fisheries (Consolidation) Act 1959
   s.171(1)(b) 111
Forgery Act 1861 .... 282, 283
Forgery Act 1913 .... 282, 283

Geneva Conventions Act 1962 000
Genocide Act 1973 21

Harbours Act 1946
   s.53(1) 26

Industrial Relations Act 1990
   s.11 247

Infanticide Act 1949 232
   s.1(1) 231
   s.1(2) 232
   s.1(3) 232
International Criminal Court Act 2006 12
Intoxicating Liquor Act 2008 308

Larceny Act 1861 .... 9, 93, 282, 283
Larceny Act 1916 .... 37, 282, 283, 285
   s.1 286
Larceny Act 1990 282
Licensing Act 1872 .... 39, 102, 103
   s.13 102
   s.16(2) 103, 109
Litter Pollution Act 1997 6

Married Women's Status Act 1957
   s.9(1) 305
   s.9(2) 305
   s.9(3) 305
Mental Health Act 2001 121
Misuse of Drugs Act 1977
   s.15A 15
   s.27 15

Non-Fatal Offences Against the Person Act 1997 ..... 3, 9, 18, 155, 239, 262, 315
   s.1 .... 242, 243
   s.2 .... 19, 240, 242, 243, 250, 263
   s.2(1) 240, 242
   s.2(2) 242, 249
   s.2(3) 242
   s.3 .... 19, 242, 243
   s.3(1) 242
   s.3(2)(a) 242
   s.3(2)(b) 242
   s.4 .... 31, 242, 243, 249, 278
   s.4(1) 243
   s.4(2) 244
   s.4(4) 242
   s.5(1) 244
   s.5(2) 244
   s.6 91
   s.6(1) 244, 245
   s.6(2) 245
   s.6(3) 245

s.6(4)	245
s.6(5)	245
s.7	245
s.7(1)	246
s.7(2)	246
s.7(3)	246
s.7(5)	246
s.8(1)	246, 247
s.8(2)	247
s.9	19, 247
s.9(2)	247
s.10	19, 247
s.10(1)	248
s.10(2)(a)	248
s.10(3)	248
s.10(5)	248
s.11	249
s.12	249, 277
s.12(1)	249
s.13	250
s.14	250
s.15	251
s.15(1)	251
s.15(2)	251
s.15(3)	251
s.16	252
s.16(3)	252
s.16(4)	252
s.16(5)	252
s.17	252
s.17(1)	252
s.17(2)	252
s.17(3)	252
s.18	155, 158, 240, 251, 253, 255
s.18(1)	253, 254
s.18(3)	254
s.18(5)	254
s.18(6)	254
s.18(7)	254
s.19	155, 251, 253, 254
s.20	155, 242, 251, 253
s.20(4)	155, 254
s.21	255
s.22	243, 255
s.23	255

```
s.24 .................................................... 255
s.25 .................................................... 255
s.28(1) ...................................... 239, 240, 315

Offences Against the Person Act 1861 ........................ 239, 249
    s.14 .................................................... 220
    s.20 ................................................ 241, 243
    s.23 ..................................................... 82
    s.34 ..................................................... 52
    s.47 ...................................... 158, 241, 242, 243
    s.55 ................................................ 101, 102
    s.58 .................................................... 153
    s.61 ..................................................... 30
    s.62 ..................................................... 30
Offences Against the State Act 1939 ................... 21, 22, 27, 221
    s.9 ...................................................... 58
    s.9(1) .................................................. 193

Petty Sessions (Ireland) Act 1851
    s.22 ................................................ 174, 213
Probation of Offenders Act 1907 ................................ 17
Proceeds of Crime Act 1996 .................................... 19
Prohibition of Incitement to Hatred Act 1989 .................. 213
Protection of the Environment 2003 ............................. 6
Punishment of Incest Act 1908 ......................... 268, 269, 270
    s.1 .................................................... 270
    s.1(1) ................................................. 269
    s.1(2) ................................................. 269
    s.2 .................................................... 269
    s.3 ............................................... 269, 270
    s.4(3) ................................................. 269
    s.5 .................................................... 271

Sex Offenders Act 2001 ........................................ 18
Succession Act 1965
    s.120 .................................................. 237

Vagrancy Act 1824
    s.4 ..................................................... 28
Vagrancy (Ireland) Act 1847
    s.3 ................................................ 29, 319

Waste Management (Amendment) Act 2001 .......................... 6
```

ENGLISH STATUTES

Aliens Act 1920 38

Children Act 1960 105
Criminal Justice Act 1967 72
Criminal Law Act 1977
    s.2 209

Dangerous Drugs Act 1965
    s.5 104
Drugs (Prevention of Misuse) Act 1964
    s.1 100
    s.1(1) 48

Homicide Act 1957
    s.4(1) 234

Infanticide Act 1922 231
Infanticide Act 1938 231

Law Reform (Year and a Day Rule) Act 1996
    s.1 218
Malicious Damage Act 1861
    s.51 90

Misuse of Drugs Act 1971
    s.5(2) 50

Rivers (Prevention of Pollution) Act 1951 111
    s.2 100

Sexual Offences Act 1955
    s.20 101
Sexual Offences Act 1956
    s.14 107
Sexual Offences (Amendment) Act 1976 259
Suicide Act 1961 233

Theft Act 1968 .... 58, 283, 285, 287

Wireless Telegraphy Act 1949
    s.1(1) 215

Australian Statutes

Gold Buyers Act 1921
    s.36 45

European Convention on Human Rights

    art.2 12
    art.3 12
    art.5 .... 12, 125
    art.6 12
    art.6(1) 27
    art.6(2) 27, 114
    art.7 12
    art.8 12
    art.9 12
    art.10 12
    art.11 12

European Directives

Directive 2008/99/EC 12

1. Introduction to Criminal Law

INTRODUCTION

This book provides a comprehensive introduction to substantive criminal law. To that end, it offers a critical evaluation of the law that determines whether an act, or sometimes an omission, constitutes a criminal offence and whether the defendant has a defence that may exculpate or reduce his criminal liability. A broader study of the criminal justice system would include an analysis of related subjects that are fields of study in themselves. Criminology is the study of crime with an emphasis on the sociological, as opposed to, the legal perspective. Criminal procedure evaluates the processes governing the investigation, prosecution and trial of offenders, including the appellate process. Criminal justice is concerned with the formal response of the criminal justice system to the occurrence of crime in society. This includes a wide range of issues such as policing, prosecution policies, imprisonment and other matters pertaining to the overall administration of the criminal justice system.

DISTINCTION BETWEEN PUBLIC AND PRIVATE LAW

In the study of criminal law it is important for the student to be aware of the legal dichotomy between public law and private law. Public law governs the legal relationship between the citizen and the State (vertical legal relationship), which incorporates constitutional law, criminal law and administrative law. In the context of criminal law, the State regulates socially unacceptable behaviour. The involvement of the State in the prosecution of offenders is justified because of the seriousness of the proscribed conduct and actual or potential harm caused to person or property. Public law is distinguished from private law which governs the interrelationship between citizens *inter se* (horizontal legal relationship), and includes the law of torts, family law, labour law, contract law, land law, and company law. As a general rule, the State is not a party to civil disputes between individuals.

FUNCTIONS OF CRIMINAL LAW

In liberal democratic states people are free to engage in whatever type of conduct they choose, so long as their behaviour does not infringe on the constitutional and legal rights of other members of society. This is the gist of the arguments put forward by John Stuart Mill (*On Liberty* (London: John W.

Parker and Son, 1859)) that supported the moral and economic freedom of individuals from the State. As a consequence of the social component that is inherent in criminal law, it is the State that prosecutes offenders on behalf of society. In this context, a criminal offence is conduct that society deems to be socially unacceptable and, therefore, is prosecuted by the State on behalf of society. In a prosecution for serious or indictable criminal offences, the first-named party is the Director of Public Prosecutions (the "DPP") representing the State. Minor offences are prosecuted by a member of An Garda Síochána, or State agencies such as the Revenue Commissioners or the Environmental Protection Agency for regulatory or quasi-criminal offences.

Conduct that is deemed unacceptable in society is regulated by various modes of compliance in accordance with accepted social standards, for instance, social norms and customs, religious beliefs and the laws of the State. In order to maintain a peaceful, just and ordered society, as mandated by the preamble to the Constitution, it is necessary for the State to curtail socially unacceptable behaviour. The State endeavours to achieve social control through criminal law accompanied by criminal sanctions, which are outlined below. The predominant issue as to how we as a society conceptualise the functions of the criminal law is not just a matter of theoretical interest for legal academics; it also has significant practical effects. Legal scholars, legislators, policy makers, and others with a genuine concern about the occurrence of crime in society ought to be concerned about the way in which we distinguish the various rules of criminal law and define their interrelation.

Criminal law serves to regulate human behaviour and to preserve the proper functioning of liberal democratic societies. Devlin (*The Enforcement of Morals* (Oxford: Oxford University Press, 1965), p.22) succinctly describes the function of criminal law in the following terms:

> "... the criminal law exists for the protection of individuals ... But the true principle is that the law exists for the protection of society. It does not discharge its function by protecting the individual from injury, annoyance, corruption, and exploitation; the law must protect also the institutions and the community of ideas, political and moral, without which people cannot live together."

The true measure of any liberal democratic society is how it treats and protects its most vulnerable members from harm caused by others.

MAINTAINS ORDER IN SOCIETY

Criminal law provides for the efficient functioning of society. It also ensures predictability in accordance with the rule of law, in that people know what to expect from others and without criminal law there would be chaos and uncertainty in society. Social contract theory describes the process by which people vest authority in the State in order to maintain social order. The concept implies that people conditionally surrender their sovereignty to government or other legal authority in order to receive or maintain social order in accordance with the rule of law. In essence, social contract theory is an agreement by the governed pertaining a set of prescribed rules by which people are governed. Consequently, the legitimate authority of the State must be derived from the consent of the governed. Social contract theorists have propounded various rationales for, and benefits of, citizens electing to voluntarily surrender their natural state of freedom in exchange for the benefits of political order. The foremost philosophers of social contractarianism are Thomas Hobbes, *Leviathan* (1651), John Locke, *Two Treatises of Government* (1689), Jean-Jacques Rousseau, *The Social Contract* (1762), who drew different conclusions from social contract theory: Hobbes' theory advocated an authoritarian monarchy; Locke advocated a liberal monarchy; and Rousseau advocated liberal republicanism. In criminal law, social contract theory stipulates that members of society have conditionally surrendered their sovereignty to government authority and, in return, the government and State agencies will endeavour, through the criminal justice system, to protect members of society from wrongdoers and will prosecute and punish offenders for harm caused to others.

PROTECTS INDIVIDUALS AND PROPERTY

The criminal law serves to protect members of society and their property by prosecuting and punishing offenders in accordance with the rule of law. The Non-Fatal Offences Against the Person Act 1997 provides for various types of non-fatal offences. Murder and manslaughter are common law offences. Sexual offences are prohibited by several pieces of legislation, including the Criminal Law (Rape) Act 1981, Criminal Law (Rape) (Amendment) Act 1990, Criminal Law (Sexual Offences) Act 1993, Criminal Law (Incest Proceedings) Act 1995, Criminal Law (Sexual Offences) Act 2006, and the Criminal Law (Sexual Offences) (Amendment) Act 2007. Offences against property are provided for by the Criminal Justice (Theft and Fraud Offences) Act 2001 and the Criminal Damage Act 1991. Public order offences are provided for by the Criminal Justice (Public Order) Act 1994, and the Criminal Justice (Public Order) Act 2003.

RESOLVES DISPUTES

At common law, disputes between individuals were resolved by crude measures, for instance the blood feud and trial by battle. Holmes, O.W. Jr.,

The Common Law (New York: Dover Publications, 1991), Lecture I, "Early Forms of Liability", pp.2-3, writes:

"It is commonly known that the early forms of legal procedure were grounded in vengeance. Modern writers have thought that Roman law started from the blood feud, and all the authorities agree that the German law begun in that way."

Conflicts and disputes between individuals can be resolved in accordance with the ethos of a liberal democratic state in contemporary society. To that end, the criminal law provides a peaceful and orderly way to resolve grievances between individuals.

MORALITY AND CRIMINAL LAW

Should criminal law be used to enforce widely-shared standards of morality, even if a violation of those standards does not cause any tangible harm to anyone other than the person who engaged in such conduct? Alternatively, should criminal law concentrate instead on the more narrow and neutral task of dealing with behaviour which, in the words of John Stuart Mill (*On Liberty* (London: John W. Parker and Son, 1859)), "causes harm to others"? Mill postulated the view that there must remain in society a realm of private morality and immorality which is not the concern of the civil law of the State. This is the gist of the distinguished Hart-Devlin debate that followed the publication of the Wolfenden Report (*Report of the Committee on Homosexual Offences and Prostitution* (Cmnd. 247) (London: HMSO, 1957)), which recommended that homosexual conduct between consenting males should no longer be treated as a criminal offence, and also advocated a liberalisation of the laws prohibiting prostitution. The Report recommended that homosexuality should be decriminalised on the basis of freedom of choice and privacy of morality.

In the 1960s, there was a heated debate on the issue of morality and criminal law in the aftermath of the publication of the Wolfenden Report. This debate on the theoretical basis of decision-making in cases where there is a conflict between individual moral freedom and social control took place between H.L.A. Hart (*Law, Liberty and Morality* (Oxford: Oxford University Press, 1963)) one of the most important legal philosophers of the twentieth century, and Lord Devlin (*The Enforcement of Morals* (Oxford: Oxford University Press, 1965)). Devlin's position was that law without morality "destroys freedom of conscience and is the paved road to tyranny", and appealed to the idea of society's "moral fabric". Accordingly, criminal law must respect and reinforce the moral norms of society in order to keep social order from unravelling. Conversely, Hart warned against the dangers of "populism" and questioned whether the conventional morality of a few members of society could be a justification for preventing people from doing what they want. This essentially reiterated John Stuart Mill's "harm principle" referred to above. Both Hart and Devlin raised important jurisprudential issues pertaining to the scope of criminal law. Devlin's view is more pragmatic and focused on the majority rule, while Hart's approach is more humanistic.

Throughout the development of common law, only the most heinous acts, such as murder or rape, were considered to be criminal and the link between law and morality was clear. However, in contemporary society, criminal laws have become more complex and the link between law and morality is somewhat tenuous. While most people in contemporary society would agree that murder is morally wrong and should be a serious criminal offence, some members of society would consider parking on a yellow line to be immoral. Furthermore, certain acts, such as homosexual behaviour between two consenting adults in private, might be considered by some individuals to be immoral but these acts are, nevertheless, not illegal (Criminal Law (Sexual Offences) Act 1993). These and other related issues present a dilemma for linking law and morality, both in theory and in practice, in the construction of criminal liability.

Despite the fact that most people might agree that certain behaviour is wrong, this will not automatically render that conduct unlawful. In *R v Hinks* [2001] 2 A.C. 241, Lord Hobhouse opined:

> "An essential function of the criminal law is to define the boundary between what conduct is criminal and what merely immoral. Both are the subject of the disapprobation of ordinary right-thinking citizens and the distinction is liable to be arbitrary or at least strongly influenced by considerations subjective to the individual members of the tribunal. To treat otherwise lawful conduct as criminal merely because it is open to such disapprobation would be contrary to principle and open to the objection that it fails to achieve the objective and transparent certainty required of the criminal law by the principles basic to human rights."
> [2001] 2 A.C. 241 at 262

If the scope of criminal law was limited to moral beliefs, this would present a dilemma with regard to the definition of criminal offences. Language can be an imprecise tool and when legislation is drafted, it is possible that a broad approach to defining the criminal offence will not only encourage desired behaviour, but may also encourage undesirable behaviour. Conversely, a narrow definition of a statutory offence might result in people following the letter of the law whilst avoiding the intent of the legislation. Consequently, an attempt to legislate in a way that demands compliance with moral behaviour, even if that were the theoretical aim and that one set of common morals could be decided upon, would render effective criminal law legislation virtually impossible to achieve.

INDICIA OF CRIMINAL OFFENCES

The nature of a criminal offence has proven to be a difficult concept to define. Many offences are classified as *mala in se*, which means they are inherently wrong in any civilised society, e.g. murder, manslaughter, and sexual offences. Other offences are classified as *mala prohibita* in that they are prohibited by criminal law more for the sake of efficiency rather than the inherent seriousness of the offence, for example, parking offences, pollution offences, and strict liability offences. A crime, or what is now generally referred to as a criminal offence, is a legal wrong for which the response is the investigation, prosecution and punishment of the offender at the instance of the State.

Most people would generally endeavour to define criminal offences in terms of morality, harm to person and property, and such-like. However, there are certain types of conduct that may cause harm but are not criminal offences, such as harm to one's good name, which is dealt with under the private law of torts. Offences against the person would exclude harm to society, such as offences against the environment. In this context, dropping a single piece of litter in a public place would not cause a great deal of harm to society, however, this offence carries an on-the-spot fine of €150 or a maximum penalty of €3,000 on conviction in the District Court under the Litter Pollution Act 1997, as amended by the Waste Management (Amendment) Act 2001 and the Protection of the Environment Act 2003. If littering and pollution offences are excluded from the range of criminal offences, what then of the multinational company that intentionally dumps environmental waste into rivers polluting them and killing wildlife? If the focus is on morality, this presents a dilemma as to whose morals such issues are decided upon. If the dominant religion in the State is used as a basic moral guide, then sex outside marriage would be deemed an offence, as would the use of contraception, homosexuality and other such "immoral" behaviour. It is for these reasons that contemporary legislation defines criminal offences on the basis of their identifying characteristics, that is, in terms of the conduct that the offence was designed to prohibit, in addition to the characteristics typically associated with a criminal trial.

The identifying characteristics of criminal offences were considered by the Supreme Court in *Melling v O'Mathghamhna* [1962] I.R. 1. The issue for determination was whether smuggling, contrary to s.186 of the Customs (Consolidation) Act 1876, was a criminal offence. This provision stipulated a fine treble the value of the goods, and s.232 provided that, in default of paying the fine, the defendant would be sentenced to a period of imprisonment of up to 12 months. Lavery J. considered the procedural aspects in determining whether the impugned conduct was a serious criminal offence:

> "... a proceeding, the course of which permits the detention of the person concerned, the bringing of him in custody to a Garda Station, the entry of a charge in all respects in the terms appropriate to the charge of a criminal offence, the searching of the person detained and the examination of papers and other things found upon him, the bringing of him before a District Justice in custody, the admission to bail to stand his trial and the detention in custody if bail be not granted or is not forthcoming, the imposition of a pecuniary penalty with the liability to imprisonment if the penalty is not paid has all the *indicia* of a criminal charge." [1962] I.R. 1 at 9

Accordingly, powers of arrest, detention in custody and search and seizure by the police are procedural issues which clearly indicate that the suspect has (allegedly) committed a criminal offence. Kingsmill Moore J. offered a broader definition of the indicia of criminal offences by defining proscribed conduct as an offence against society and punishable by the State:

> "What is a crime? The anomalies which still exist in the criminal law and the diversity of expression in statutes make a comprehensive definition almost impossible to frame. 'The criminal quality of an act cannot be discerned by intuition; nor can it be discovered by reference to any standard but one: Is the act prohibited with penal consequences?'..." [1962] I.R. 1 at 24

Kingsmill Moore J. then went on to identify the characteristics that would indicate whether a provision created a criminal offence. It should be an offence against society at large; the sanction should be of a punitive nature rather than discretionary; and the performance of the illegal act should generally require proof of a guilty state of mind or mens rea. Thus, there are two principal elements of criminal offences. First, what must be considered is the substance of the offence itself in that it should be an offence against society and require proof of mens rea. Secondly, there should be a procedure whereby once the offence has been committed, the defendant is punished in accordance with the fundamental principle of proportionality in the sentencing process.

The Superior Courts will occasionally examine the wording of the statutory provision to determine whether the impugned conduct is a criminal offence.

In *O'Keeffe v Ferris* [1993] 3 I.R. 165, the issue for determination pertained to whether fraudulent trading was a criminal offence under s.297 of the Companies Act 1963 (the "1963 Act"). The High Court invoked the indicia outlined in *Melling* to determine whether the statutory provision provided for a criminal offence. Murphy J. stated:

> "Of the *indicia* of a criminal offence identified in the judgments of the Supreme Court in the *Melling* case some are not present at all in [the statutory provision] and those that are present are ambiguous." [1993] 3 I.R. 165 at 172

The court noted that the section under consideration did not identify the State as being responsible for commencing proceedings. Furthermore, the party injured was not the State and the words used in the section were not particularly criminal in nature. Although the section did use the term "with intent to defraud creditors", hence requiring proof of mens rea, Murphy J. stated:

> "In the instant case this wider examination shows an extraordinary dearth of terms which one would expect to find in a subsection dealing with a criminal offence. Ordinarily one would expect to find words such as 'conviction', 'imprisonment', 'fine', 'summary proceedings', and/or 'indictment'. Not only do such words not occur and their absence cast doubt on the argument put forward on behalf of the plaintiff but there is the marked and extraordinary contrast between sub-s. 1 and sub-s. 3 of s. 297, where the Oireachtas demonstrates clearly how (in modern legislation at any rate) the State identifies a criminal offence and provides for the manner and extent to which it is to be punished." [1993] 3 I.R. 165 at 172–173

The court also noted that fraud within the meaning of s.297 of the 1963 Act was only punishable on liquidation and that, if it were a criminal offence, it should be punishable regardless of whether liquidation had occurred. Accordingly, the court held that the section did not create a criminal offence but rather a civil wrong.

SOURCES OF CRIMINAL LAW

The foundations of criminal liability are derived from a variety of legal sources, thus reflecting the development of criminal law at common law. The primary sources of criminal law are legislative provisions and the common law. It is important to note, however, that sources of law are subject to the provisions of the Constitution, which are outlined below.

Legislation

Statute law, legislation, or what is otherwise referred to as Acts of the Oireachtas are a primary source of criminal law. Article 15.2.1° of the Constitution provides that:

> The sole and exclusive power of making laws for the State is hereby vested in the Oireachtas: no other legislative authority has power to make laws for the State.

This is subject to the proviso that the Oireachtas shall not enact legislation that conflicts with the provisions of the Constitution. Furthermore, legislation creating a criminal offence is prospective only and will be deemed unconstitutional if purported to have retrospective effect (Art.15. 5.1° of the Constitution).

Criminal law is comprised of an assortment of statutes, many of which date back to the 19th century and earlier. In view of this, the Department of Justice, Equality and Law Reform is currently working towards the proposed codification of the criminal law into a Crimes Act, which is imperative in view of the existing fragmented nature of Irish criminal law.

Legislation may be enacted to create new offences or to codify and enhance common law rules. The sole and exclusive power of the Oireachtas to make laws for the State, including the creation of criminal offences, can be problematic. Criminal offences are sometimes created in response to a public outcry regarding the commission of heinous criminal offences, typically against the most vulnerable members of society. This public outcry can sometimes be partly influenced by graphic or sensationalist media coverage of particular crimes. Consequently, the creation of criminal offences by legislation can be ill thought-out, imperfectly phrased and occasionally unnecessary. An example of this occurrence is the creation of syringe offences under the Non-Fatal Offences Against the Person Act 1997. These offences were apparently created for political reasons as opposed to remedying a lacuna in criminal law to deal with this type of criminal behaviour. However, this could have been adequately dealt with under the offence of robbery (under the Larceny Act 1861), and with the new definition of robbery under the Criminal Justice (Theft and Fraud) Offences Act 2001. A person found guilty of robbery under the 2001 Act is liable on conviction on indictment to imprisonment for life. The maximum sentence available to the court under the provisions of the 1997 Act for syringe offences ranges from 12 months to 10 years, and even to life imprisonment. It is important to take into consideration that criminal offences created by legislative provisions are not always the product of sustained research and debate into the necessity of creating new offences.

Criminal offences created by legislation may provide for new offences to deal with new or novel forms of conduct not previously provided for under the criminal law. Statutory offences may also codify common law offences or simply complement existing common law offences. The obvious advantage with this process is that in order to create a new criminal offence, a democratic process is followed in accordance with the constitutional mandate under Art.5 that, "Ireland is a sovereign, independent, democratic State." A major disadvantage with this process is that, if the Oireachtas is unwilling—typically for politically sensitive reasons—to legislate for a particular issue, the result is that a lacuna remains in criminal law. A clear example of this dilemma is the controversial and politically sensitive issue of abortion. Notwithstanding a constitutional amendment (Eighth Amendment of the Constitution, October 7, 1983), which "acknowledged the right to life of the unborn, with due regard to the equal right to life of the mother" and, subsequently, the "X case" (*Attorney General v X* [1992] 1 I.R. 1), the Oireachtas has to date failed to legislate for the circumstances in which abortion is legal within the jurisdiction of the Irish State.

COMMON LAW

Judge-made law is generally referred to as common law, as developed and expounded by the decisions of the Superior Courts before the foundation of the State. The common law courts had for centuries exercised their inherent and residual power to declare certain behaviour illegal without having any statutory basis for doing so. However, as stated above, Art.15.2.1° of the Constitution stipulates that the Oireachtas is vested with the sole and exclusive power to make laws in the State. Notwithstanding the fact that judges of the Superior Courts are no longer permitted to create new offences, which is the exclusive function of the Oireachtas, the judiciary retain the inherent power to declare and to expand upon existing common law rules, and to interpret and apply the meaning of words used by legislative drafters (officials in the Office of the Parliamentary Counsel to the Government) in the statutory provision creating a criminal offence.

Frequently in the study of Irish law, and in particular criminal law, reference is made to the decisions of the Superior Courts in other major common law jurisdictions, typically the UK, the US, Canada, Australia and New Zealand. The decisions of the Superior Courts in cognate jurisdictions, while not binding per se in this jurisdiction, may nevertheless offer persuasive authority where there is a lacuna in Irish law, or in the interpretation or meaning of Irish legislation (which often contain similar provisions to legislation in other common law jurisdictions), or common law principles.

Constitution of Ireland

The Constitution is the primary source of law and is generally referred to as the fundamental and basic law of the State. Hence, any legislative enactment or common law rules are susceptible to being struck down on grounds of unconstitutionality. Consequently, any other laws that conflict with the provisions of the Constitution are deemed void ab initio. The relevant provisions of the Constitution provide a framework within which the criminal justice system operates. As already noted above, the Constitution provides that the sole and exclusive power of making laws for the State is now vested in the Oireachtas under Art.15.2.1°. The Constitution also prohibits the creation of offences with retrospective effect. If an individual engages in conduct that is subsequently declared a criminal offence by legislative provision, that individual cannot subsequently be charged and prosecuted because the conduct was lawful at the time it was committed, in accordance with the provisions of Art.15.5.1° (see e.g. *Enright v Ireland* [2003] 2 I.R. 321).

Institutional Writers

Occasionally when the courts are interpreting specific legal rules, it may be necessary to trace the development of the offence at common law so as to discover its true nature and extent. In this context, the Superior Courts will often refer to commentaries on the early development of common law such as Coke, *Institutes of the Laws of England; 4 volumes, 1628–1644* (Charleston, South Carolina: BiblioBazaar, 2010); Hale, *The History of the Pleas of the Crown 2 volumes, 1736* (Charleston, South Carolina: BiblioBazaar, 2010); and Blackstone, *Commentaries on the Laws of England; 4 volumes, 1765–1769* (Charleston, South Carolina: Forgotten Books, 2010). These commentaries were accorded a status similar to that of judicial decisions and occasionally assist the courts when determining the meaning of common law offences.

Scholarly Writings

In recent decades there has been a substantial increase in the volume of academic publications and legal writings, including legal encyclopaedias, case notes and articles in seminal law journals. However, unlike the aforementioned commentaries, scholarly writings only offer persuasive authority and the courts are free to form their own conclusions on the points of law under consideration in any particular case.

European Union Law

As a result of Ireland's accession to the (now) European Union and the associated constitutional amendments to the Constitution, all laws, acts and measures adopted by the EU institutions become part of the Irish domestic legal system. This is in accordance with the (now) Treaty on the Functioning of the European Union. For instance, to provide for the implementation and enforcement of EU environmental law the European Parliament and Council adopted a directive on the protection of the environment through criminal law (Directive 2008/99/EC).

INTERNATIONAL LAW

Due to the fact that the Irish State has signed and ratified certain international agreements, the State is under a legal obligation to incorporate these agreements into national law. For instance, as a result of the State's ratification of the United Nations Convention against Torture, it was necessary to enact the Criminal Justice (United Nations Convention against Torture) Act 2000. Likewise, as a result of the 23rd Amendment to the Constitution, which allowed the Irish State to ratify the Rome Statute of the International Criminal Court, the International Criminal Court Act 2006 was enacted.

EUROPEAN CONVENTION ON HUMAN RIGHTS

The European Convention on Human Rights was designed to protect human rights and fundamental freedoms. The Convention established the European Court of Human Rights with the result that citizens of State parties who assert that a State or an emanation of the State has infringed their rights under the ECHR, may petition the ECtHR for redress. Also, since the enactment of the European Convention on Human Rights Act 2003, individuals who claim that the State or emanation of the State has infringed their fundamental rights under the European Convention on Human Rights, may petition the ECtHR for redress. The jurisprudence of the ECtHR has had greater purchase in domestic proceedings with the result that Irish courts are now required to take judicial notice of declarations, decisions, advisory opinions and judgments of the ECtHR and to take "due account" of the principles established by those instruments (s.4). The Irish Superior Courts are enjoined, where possible, to interpret domestic law in a manner that is compatible with the ECHR (s.2) and the Superior Courts are authorised to issue a declaration of incompatibility where a national law is deemed to have infringed the applicant's rights under the ECHR (s.5). The provisions of the ECHR that are most pertinent to criminal law include: the right to life (art.2), prohibition of torture (art.3), the right to liberty and security (art.5), the right to a fair trial (art.6), no punishment without law (art.7), the right to respect for private life (art.8), freedom of religion (art.9), freedom of expression (art.10), and freedom of assembly (art.11).

Burden of Proof

In a criminal trial the defendant enjoys the presumption of innocence. The onus or burden of proof is on the prosecution to prove all the elements of the criminal offence "beyond reasonable doubt". In a criminal trial, the onus or burden of proof rests with the prosecution, that is, the DPP for indictable criminal offences, members of An Garda Síochána for summary offences, and regulatory agencies such as the Environmental Protection Agency for quasi-criminal offences. The defendant is never required to prove his innocence and is always entitled to remain silent and force the prosecution to prove his guilt. The leading common law authority on this fundamental rule of law is *Woolmington v DPP* [1935] A.C. 462, where the House of Lords per Lord Sankey explained:

> "Throughout the web of the English Criminal Law one golden thread is always to be seen, that it is the duty of the prosecution to prove the prisoner's guilt subject to what I have already said as to the defence of insanity and subject also to any statutory exception. If, at the end of and on the whole of the case, there is a reasonable doubt, created by the evidence given by either the prosecution or the prisoner, as to whether the prisoner killed the deceased with a malicious intention, the prosecution has not made out the case and the prisoner is entitled to an acquittal. No matter what the charge or where the trial, the principle that the prosecution must prove the guilt of the prisoner is part of the common law of England and no attempt to whittle it down can be entertained." [1935] A.C. 462 at 481–482

This means that the prosecution must prove to the satisfaction of the jury, or the court in the case of a non-jury trial, the mens rea or requisite state of mind and the actus reus consisting of the factual circumstances or prohibited behaviour constituting the criminal offence. An exception to this general rule is where the defendant raises the defence of insanity. In these circumstances he must prove that he was suffering from a mental disorder when the offence was committed, or before the trial commences.

Standard of Proof

The standard of proof in criminal cases is "beyond a reasonable doubt" and it places a very high onus on the prosecution authorities to prove that a defendant is guilty of the offence charged. This is a much higher standard than that required in civil cases, in which the plaintiff must prove the case only on the balance of probabilities. The jury must acquit the defendant if there is reasonable doubt as to his guilt, despite other evidence tendered by the prosecution during the criminal trial suggesting the defendant's guilt (*People (AG) v Byrne* [1974] I.R. 1; *Miller v Minister for Pensions* [1947] 2 All E.R. 372). However, juries occasionally might also engage in so-called "jury nullification", where the jury effectively acquits against the evidence (cf. *People (DPP) v Nally* [2007] 4 I.R. 145). Where the burden of proof shifts to the defendant as, for instance, where the defendant raises the issue of insanity, then this burden must be discharged on the balance of probabilities.

Punishment

Once a defendant is convicted, he is sentenced in accordance with the centrality of proportionality in Irish sentencing policy, which means that the punishment imposed by the court must be *proportionate* to the personal circumstances of the defendant and also to the offence for which the defendant has been convicted (*People (DPP) v M* [1994] 3 I.R. 306). The type of punishment imposed by the trial court may be a custodial or non-custodial sentence depending on the nature of the offence and the personal circumstances of the offender. The court will also have regard to aggravating factors (such as the use of violence against the victim of rape) and mitigating factors (such as an early plea of guilty in sexual offence cases) and will adjust the sentence accordingly. Typically, a term of imprisonment and/or a pecuniary penalty is imposed. However, in recent years, legislative provisions have provided for alternative modes of punishment for less serious criminal offences. There is a wide measure of discretion vested in the courts when deciding on the sentence to be imposed in any particular case. Depending on the seriousness of the offence for which the defendant has been convicted, secondary non-custodial sanctions may be appropriate, including disqualification, confiscation and compensation. In circumstances where a defendant has been convicted of multiple offences, the sentences imposed will run concurrently. However, offences committed while the defendant was on bail will run consecutively (s.11 of the Criminal Justice Act 1984, as amended by s.10 of the Bail Act 1997).

Imprisonment and Pecuniary Fines

Statutory provisions creating criminal offences stipulate a maximum term of imprisonment and/or a pecuniary fine at the discretion of the trial judge. The imposition of a pecuniary fine may be in addition to, or instead of, a custodial sentence. The problematic, and often controversial, feature of the maximum sentence available to the sentencing judge is the absence of a framework for structuring judicial sentencing discretion in the Irish criminal justice process.

The consequence of this is a perceived disparity in the Irish sentencing process, whereby defendants convicted of the same offence with similar factual circumstances receive disparate sentences that are clearly disproportionate. This could infringe the equality guarantee as mandated by Art.40.1 of the Constitution.

Maximum sentence

Maximum sentences as stipulated for in the statutory provision creating the offence which specify the maximum period of imprisonment available to the sentencing court. Trial judges have a wide measure of discretion in the sentencing process and can impose any sentence up to and including the maximum sentence.

Mandatory sentence

A mandatory sentence is one which must be imposed on conviction for certain offences, for instance, murder, which carries a mandatory life sentence (Criminal Justice Act 1990, s.2). The trial court has no discretion other than imposing the mandatory sentence. In other words, the trial judge cannot take into consideration any other relevant circumstances of the offender, such as relevant mitigating factors.

Mandatory minimum sentence

A mandatory minimum sentence stipulates that the trial judge must impose a minimum sentence provided for in the legislative provision creating the offence. For instance, where a defendant has been convicted of possessing drugs with a value greater than €13,000 under s.15A of the Misuse of Drugs Act 1977 (see s.27 of the 1977 Act, as amended by s.33 of the Criminal Justice Act 2007), a mandatory minimum sentence of 10 years' imprisonment must be imposed.

Likewise, the Criminal Justice Act 2006 introduced several new firearms offences that carry a minimum sentence where the defendant is convicted on indictment. If it is the defendant's first offence, the trial judge has discretion to impose a lesser sentence, having regard to mitigating factors such as a guilty plea or assistance provided to the Gardaí in the investigation of related offences. If, however, it is the defendant's second or subsequent drugs or firearms conviction, then the minimum sentence will be imposed.

Suspended sentence

A suspended sentence is where the trial judge imposes a prison sentence, but it is suspended, provided that the defendant complies with the conditions of the suspended sentence. This means that the defendant is not deprived of his liberty, notwithstanding a conviction for what is often a very serious offence, including manslaughter. Typically, a suspended sentence is subject to the condition that the defendant keeps the peace, is of good behaviour and undergoes specific treatment, especially where the defendant had alcohol or drug abuse problems. However, if the defendant fails to comply with the conditions of the suspended sentence during a period specified by the trial court, the sentence will be activated and the defendant will serve the term of imprisonment originally imposed by the court.

Community service order

Under the provisions of the Criminal Justice (Community Service) Act 1983, a court (other than the Special Criminal Court) instead of imposing a prison sentence may impose a community service order on the defendant, which essentially involves unpaid work in the community. In order to be considered for this programme, a defendant must be 16 years of age or over and the judge may impose a community order of between 40 and 240 hours' work. The aim of this scheme is for the defendant to make a positive contribution to the community for the damage caused by his offending. Each year thousands of unpaid hours of work are completed throughout the country as a result of this scheme, thereby benefitting many social, community and voluntary groups.

Community service is an alternative to a custodial sentence and will only be considered by the trial judge if a custodial sentence has first been considered by the court. In the first instance, the trial judge will request the probation service to complete an assessment as to whether or not the defendant is a suitable candidate to be considered for community service and whether there is work available in the community for the defendant to do. A probation officer will meet with the defendant in preparing the report and the defendant must agree to do the work assigned to him. The number of hours per week to be worked by the defendant is agreed with the probation officer and it is the defendant's responsibility to finish this work at the specified time. It is the responsibility of the probation officer to refer the defendant's case back to the court for any failure by the defendant to comply with the conditions of the order. The trial judge will specify the sentence to be served by the defendant for failure to comply with the conditions of the community service order.

Curfew and exclusion order

Judges sometimes use curfews and exclusion orders as a non-custodial sentencing option, which is essentially a condition of bail or of a suspended sentence. The trial court may make an order requiring the defendant to be at home at a particular address between certain hours of the day or night.

Likewise, the trial judge might impose a prohibition on the defendant from entering a certain street or premises, such as a social club or licensed premises. Section 3 of the Criminal Justice (Public Order) Act 2003 provides that, on conviction for certain offences under the Criminal Justice (Public Order) Act 1994 (s.4, intoxication in a public place; s.5, disorderly conduct; s.6, threatening, abusive, insulting behaviour; s.7, distribution or display of offensive material; s.8, failure to comply with a Garda direction; or s.9, wilful obstruction), the District Court, in addition to imposing any other sentence, may also prohibit that person by means of an exclusion order from entering or being in the vicinity of premises covered by the terms of the 2003 Act.

Probation order

The Probation of Offenders Act 1907 provides the courts with a way of dealing with first-time offenders, particularly those offenders who are unlikely to reoffend. The trial court effectively gives the offender an official warning devoid of imposing a sentence. A probation order will require the offender to be of good behaviour and may also contain other conditions such as payment of compensation, residing at a particular place, supervision, and any other conditions the court considers necessary to prevent a repeat of the offence, such as counselling.

Court poor box

The court poor box is an alternative method used by judges to deal with less serious criminal offences tried in the District Court. The defendant may be required, subject to his agreement, to pay a sum of money into the court poor box. This is offered as an alternative to having a conviction recorded. The option is only likely to be considered by District Court judges for first-time offenders who have committed relatively minor offences, such as littering or parking offences, or relatively minor public order offences. This option is only available where the defendant pleads guilty to the offence charged, or where there are special circumstances explaining the offender's behaviour. The Law Reform Commission's *Report on the Court Poor Box: Probation of Offenders* (LRC 75–2005) recommends that the court poor box should be incorporated into a reformed Probation Act, as the Probation of Offenders Act 1907 is in need of comprehensive reform as recommended by the *Final Report of the Expert Group on the Probation and Welfare Service* (Dublin: Stationery Office, 1999).

Binding over

In addition to the trial court's power to make a probation order, the court also has an inherent power to bind the defendant over, that is, to keep the peace and be of good behaviour for minor offences. This involves the defendant entering into a recognisance (monetary bond) for a specified period of time. If the defendant commits a criminal offence within the time stated in the order, he must pay that sum of money or alternatively be sentenced.

Orders for sex offenders

In addition to the general sentencing options available for all criminal offences, a trial judge can make a number of specific orders when dealing with defendants convicted of sexual offences. Under the provisions of the Sex Offenders Act 2001, the following are the orders which a judge can make where the defendant has been convicted of a sexual offence. A "notification order" obliges the defendant to notify the Gardaí of his name and address. A "certificate" states that the defendant has been convicted of the sexual offence, details the sentence imposed and specifies that there is a notification requirement. An "obligation to notify employers" is applicable where the defendant is applying for employment which involves unsupervised access to, or contact with, a child or mentally impaired person. The defendant is ordered to notify the employer, or potential employer, of the conviction for the particular sex offence. A "sex offender order" is imposed where the court considers it necessary to protect the public from the defendant because of the conviction for a sexual offence. The court can make such an order prohibiting the defendant from carrying out certain activities. The constitutionality of the registration requirements of the Sex Offenders Act 2001, which have retrospective effect, has been upheld by the High Court (*Enright v Ireland* [2003] 2 I.R. 321).

Restriction on movement order

Under s.101 of the Criminal Justice Act 2006, the trial court can impose a "restriction on movement order" on individuals. This may be imposed on defendants who are convicted of suitable offences, which typically include public order and assault offences, where the court has sentenced the defendant to imprisonment of three months or more. Section 102 of the 2006 Act also provides that compliance with such orders may be electronically monitored by an "electronic monitoring of restriction on movement order", often referred to as "electronic tagging". However, this provision under the 2006 Act has not yet been implemented.

The following offences under the Criminal Justice (Public Order) Act 1994 and the Non-Fatal Offences Against the Person Act 1997 can incur restriction on movement orders. Offences under the 1994 Act include: s.6, threatening, abusive or insulting behaviour in a public place; s.8, failure to comply with the direction of a Garda; s.11, entering a building with intent to commit an offence;

s.13, trespass on a building; s.16, affray; and s.19, assault or obstruction of a peace officer. Offences under the 1997 Act include: s.2, assault; s.3, assault causing harm; s.9, coercion; and s.10, harassment.

Forfeiture and confiscation of property

Trial courts are vested with the statutory authority to order property, which is connected with the offence that the defendant has been convicted of, to be forfeited or confiscated. For instance, s.10 of the Censorship of Publications Act 1929 provides that prohibited publications may be confiscated. The Proceeds of Crime Act 1996 provides for the forfeiture of property where the court is satisfied that it was obtained as a result of criminal activity. The provisions of the 1996 Act are enforced by the Criminal Assets Bureau that was established by the Criminal Assets Bureau Act 1996. A significant feature of the proceeds of crime legislation is that a conviction is not necessary to secure a forfeiture order and the constitutionality of this procedure has been upheld by the High Court (*Gilligan v Criminal Assets Bureau* [1998] 3 I.R. 185).

Compensation order

Section 6 of the Criminal Justice Act 1993 provides trial judges with the power to order a defendant convicted of certain offences to compensate the victim of crime. This may be in addition to, or instead of, any other punishment at the discretion of the trial judge. The amount of compensation which a court can order is limited to the amount it could award in damages in a civil case, that is, €6,350 in the District Court, and €38,100 in the Circuit Court.

CRIMINAL LAW JURISDICTION OF THE COURTS

Depending on the seriousness of the offence with which the defendant has been charged, a criminal trial may proceed in courts of local and limited jurisdiction without a jury, or alternatively, for more serious offences in the criminal calendar the trial may proceed in one of the higher criminal courts. The jurisdiction of the courts also reflects the severity of sentence that may be imposed on conviction as stipulated for by the legislative provision creating the offence. In criminal trials on indictment, with the exception of the Special Criminal Court, a jury is empanelled to determine issues of fact while the judge rules on points of law and ensures that the defendant receives a fair and impartial criminal trial in due course of law, in accordance with Art.38.1 of the Constitution. In this context, trial judges will also rule on the admissibility of evidence and procedural issues.

District Court

Article 34.3.4° of the Constitution provides that, "Courts of First Instance shall also include courts of local and limited jurisdiction with a right of appeal as determined by law." Article 38.2 provides that minor offences are tried summarily (without a jury), but the Constitution does not define what is meant by a minor offence. The District Court is a court of local and limited jurisdiction that deals with summary offences, that is, relatively minor offences which are tried without a jury. All minor criminal offences are tried summarily in the District Court without a jury. The maximum prison sentence this court can impose is one of 12 months' imprisonment and/or a maximum €5,000 fine, proportionate to the seriousness of the offence for which the defendant has been convicted. The court also has jurisdiction to hear certain indictable offences in circumstances where the defendant has waived their right to a trial by jury and the prosecution authorities agree to this arrangement. Indeed, many indictable offences under the Criminal Justice (Theft and Fraud Offences) Act 2001 are triable either way, and thus, may be tried in the District Court as with certain offences in the Schedule to the Criminal Justice Act 1951.

The District Court is the lowest court in the Irish court system. It is presided over by the President of the District Court and 54 District Court judges. The court is organised on a regional basis: there are 24 District Court Districts all over Ireland, including the Dublin Metropolitan District. Each District is divided into District Court areas.

Circuit Court

The Circuit Court consists of the President of the court and 33 ordinary judges. The Irish State is divided into eight circuits for the purposes of the Circuit Court, with one circuit judge assigned to each circuit, except in the cases of the Dublin and Cork Circuits. Ten judges can be assigned to the Dublin Circuit and three to the Cork Circuit. The President of the Circuit Court, who is also an *ex officio* judge of the High Court, has the duty of ensuring an equitable distribution of the work of the Circuit Court amongst the several judges and the prompt despatch of court business.

The Circuit Criminal Court deals with the more serious criminal offences in the criminal calendar. Most indictable offences are tried in this court, with the exception of particular offences which are only heard in the Central Criminal Court or the Special Criminal Court.

The Circuit Criminal Court is a court of local and limited jurisdiction and to this extent is restricted as to which cases it can decide in both civil and criminal matters. The court has the jurisdiction to hear all non-minor offences except: murder, rape, aggravated sexual assault, treason, piracy and related offences. In criminal matters, the Circuit Court judge sits with a jury of 12.

A verdict need not be unanimous in a case where there are not fewer than 11 jurors, if 10 of them agree on a verdict after considering the case for a reasonable time (not less than two hours).

HIGH COURT

When the High Court is dealing with criminal offences, it is referred to as the Central Criminal Court. The court tries the most serious criminal offences in the criminal calendar, including murder and rape. A jury is empanelled to determine issues of fact. A verdict need not be unanimous in a case where there are not fewer than 11 jurors, if 10 of them agree on a verdict after a reasonable time has passed (not less than two hours). Most trials involve one High Court judge and a jury of 12.

The following types of offences must be heard by the Central Criminal Court sitting with a judge and jury: treason; encouragement or concealing knowledge of treason; offences relating to the obstruction of Government and obstruction of the President; murder, attempted murder, conspiracy to murder; piracy; offences under the Genocide Act 1973; and rape, aggravated sexual assault and attempted aggravated sexual assault under the Criminal Law (Rape) (Amendment) Act 1990.

SPECIAL CRIMINAL COURT

Occasionally, the High Court will sit as the Special Criminal Court, first established in 1972 under the provisions of Pt V of the Offences against the State Act 1939. The Special Criminal Court is used when the ordinary criminal courts are deemed inadequate to try serious criminal offences, typically when there is a real risk of jury tampering or witness intimidation. The court hears cases involving terrorism and gangland crime, especially relating to key gangland figures.

The Special Criminal Court deals with criminal trials only and is established where the ordinary courts are inadequate to secure the effective administration of justice and the preservation of public peace and order. The present court is comprised of three judges of the ordinary courts, that is, one High Court judge, one Circuit Court judge and one District Court judge. There is no jury.

This Court has no civil jurisdiction and its jurisdiction is confined to criminal cases. Occasionally, criminal trials are transferred from the ordinary criminal courts to the Special Criminal Court if the offence charged is a "scheduled offence", which typically relates to subversive offences that are automatically transferred to the court. The current list of scheduled offences includes: any offence under the Criminal Damage Act 1991; an offence under Pt 7 of the Criminal Justice Act 2006 (excluding conspiracy); any offence under the

Explosive Substances Act 1883; any offence under the Firearms Acts 1925 to 2006; and any offence under the Offences against the State Act 1939. It has been held that any serious offence can be tried by the Special Criminal Court (*People (DPP) v Quilligan* [1986] I.R. 495).

If the criminal offence is not a "scheduled offence", the DPP can issue a certificate stating that in his opinion the ordinary courts are inadequate to secure the administration of justice and the preservation of public peace and order. Once a certificate is issued, the case must be transferred from the ordinary court for trial in the Special Criminal Court. It has been held that decisions by the DPP are not amenable to judicial review (*Savage and McOwen v DPP* [1982] I.L.R.M. 385). An appeal against conviction or sentence by the Special Criminal Court may be taken to the Court of Criminal Appeal.

COURT OF CRIMINAL APPEAL

The Court of Criminal Appeal was established in 1961, in accordance with Art.34 of the Constitution and is a superior court of record. The court is comprised of two judges of the High Court and a judge of the Supreme Court. It hears appeals, in certain circumstances, of defendants convicted on indictment in the Circuit Court, Central Criminal Court, or the Special Criminal Court. The Court of Criminal Appeal also has jurisdiction to hear appeals by the DPP against the leniency of sentences (Criminal Justice Act 1993, s.2).

In an appeal against conviction, the court has several options including: dismissing the appeal; quashing the conviction and releasing the defendant; quashing the conviction and ordering a re-trial; quashing the conviction; and if the person appealing their conviction or sentence is considered to be guilty of some other offence, substituting a verdict and imposing a sentence which is not more severe than the original one.

Appeals are based on transcripts from the trial court. The court will hear newly discovered evidence relating to an alleged miscarriage of justice and may issue a certificate to that effect (*People (DPP) v Wall*, unreported, Court of Criminal Appeal, December 16, 2005; *People (DPP) v Shortt (No. 2)* [2002] 2 I.R. 696; *People (DPP) v Pringle* [1997] 2 I.R. 225).

Section 4 ("vesting the powers of the Court of Criminal Appeal in the Supreme Court") of the Court and Court Officers Act 1995 apparently provides for the eventual abolition of the Court of Criminal Appeal, with all powers and functions to be transferred to the Supreme Court. The transfer of functions has not yet occurred, which means the Court of Criminal Appeal continues to function and presently hears appeals against conviction or sentence from the Circuit Criminal Court, the Central Criminal Court and the Special Criminal Court.

Supreme Court

Article 34.4.1° of the Constitution provides that, "[t]he Court of Final Appeal shall be called the Supreme Court". The Supreme Court consists of the Chief Justice and seven ordinary judges and is located in Dublin. The court hears appeals from the lower courts. Appeals are heard and determined by five Supreme Court judges, unless the Chief Justice directs that any appeal or other matter (apart from matters relating to the Constitution) should be heard and determined by three judges.

The Supreme Court decides civil and criminal matters. Appeals to the Supreme Court concern criminal matters only in exceptional circumstances. The jurisdiction of the Supreme Court in criminal matters will increase if and when the Court of Criminal Appeal is eventually abolished. This means that appeals against convictions and sentences from trials on indictment in the Circuit Criminal Court and the Central Criminal Court will go directly to the Supreme Court. Appeals from the Special Criminal Court would also go to the Supreme Court.

The Supreme Court has jurisdiction to hear an appeal from the Court of Criminal Appeal if the Court of Criminal Appeal or the Attorney General certifies that the decision involves a point of law of exceptional public importance and it is desirable in the public interest that an appeal should be taken to the Supreme Court (*People (DPP) v Pringle* [1997] 2 I.R. 225; *People (DPP) v Murray* [1977] I.R. 360).

The DPP may appeal a point of law from a trial on indictment to the Supreme Court (Criminal Procedure Act 1967, s.34, as amended by the Criminal Justice Act 2006, s.21). This is a "without prejudice" appeal, which means that the Supreme Court may not overturn an acquittal but rather appeal for a ruling to clarify an important point of law for future criminal law cases.

Working Group on the Jurisdiction of the Courts

In 2002, the Chief Justice (and Chairman of the Courts Service Board) set up a working group on the jurisdiction of the courts in Ireland. The terms of reference was to carry out a comprehensive review of the current structure of the courts system with a view to refor. This was the first such examination of the courts system in Ireland since the establishment of the courts by the Courts of Justice Act 1924 ("re-established" by the Courts (Establishment and Constitution) Act 1961). In 2003, the working group published a report on the Criminal Jurisdiction of the Courts, which found that the Central Criminal Court is unable, due to its case load, to eliminate the very serious delays experienced by that court. The report found that there is a high level of satisfaction with the District and Circuit Courts. The working group did not recommend any departure from the existing structure of the criminal courts. However, the report made significant recommendations regarding the trial and sentencing process.

COURTS OF JUSTICE COMPLEX

The Criminal Courts of Justice building opened in January 2010 and was designed to centralise and augment Dublin's existing courts services. The Criminal Courts of Justice complex houses the Court of Criminal Appeal, Special Criminal Court, Central Criminal Court, the Circuit Criminal Court, the District Court and associated facilities. The basement of the criminal court complex contains cell accommodation for approximately 100 detainees, which will eventually end the previous practice of defendants being brought to court handcuffed in public view. Approximately half of the courtrooms have electronic evidence display facilities and six have video conferencing and video link facilities. The criminal court complex also provides greatly improved facilities for jurors including a dining area, and jury retiring rooms within a segregated area.

A large office area has been rented to the Bar Council for the criminal bar and library. The criminal courts deal with approximately 400,000 criminal cases each year, more than half of which are heard in Dublin. Dublin's criminal courts, which were previously located across the city centre in the Four Courts complex, had struggled to contend with the ever-increasing case load, particularly in recent decades. The Courts Service of Ireland has indicated that the new Criminal Courts of Justice complex has the potential to deal with approximately 200,000 criminal cases each year. This new criminal court complex provides a centralised facility to cater for all criminal cases and related matters in the Dublin region.

PRINCIPLE OF LEGALITY

The common law principle of legality stipulates that conduct should not be punished as criminal unless it has been clearly and precisely prohibited by the terms of a pre-existing rule of law. The principle has two important elements: *nullum crimen sine lege* (no crime without law) and *nulla poena sine lege* (no punishment without law). In accordance with the principle of legality, it is imperative that criminal laws are clear, simple and accessible to everyone.

The reason that the principle of legality was formulated was that it was essentially the function of judges to determine the scope and extent of criminal law, which then led to considerable uncertainty as to what the boundaries of criminal law were and what conduct is contrary to criminal law. The courts invoked analogical reasoning when determining the extent of a criminal offence.

Non-retroactivity

This stipulates that a person should not be tried or convicted in respect of conduct that was not criminal at the time that it was engaged in. This is probably the least controversial element in the principle of legality and has generally been widely accepted. It is also a constitutional imperative (Art.15.5.1°).

Criminal offences should be clear and precise

The issue here is whether the scope of an existing rule is too uncertain to justify a prosecution and conviction. In *Shaw v DPP* [1962] A.C. 220, the defendant published a book called the "Ladies Directory", which advertised the names and addresses of prostitutes, indicating special services they might provide, together with accompanying photographs. The defendant was charged with, inter alia, a conspiracy to corrupt public morals and was convicted. This behaviour had not previously been held to come within the terms of the offence and it seems that the defendant had published the directory having received legal advice to that effect. The House of Lords, while acknowledging that they were entering into the legislative field, defended this position. Viscount Simonds opined:

> "When Lord Mansfield, speaking long after the Star Chamber had been abolished, said that the Court of King's Bench was the *custos morum* of the people and had the superintendency of offences *contra bonos mores*, he was asserting, as I now assert, that there is in that court a residual power, where no statute has yet intervened to supersede the common law, to superintend those offences which are prejudicial to the public welfare. Such occasions will be rare, for Parliament has not been slow to legislate when attention has been sufficiently aroused. But gaps remain and will always remain since no one can foresee every way in which the wickedness of man may disrupt the order of society." [1962] A.C. 220 at 268

This raises the issue as to whether the Superior Courts should be empowered to "legislate" where a lacuna exists in criminal law.

Criminal offences should be strictly construed

The issue here is whether the scope of an existing rule is too uncertain to justify punishing someone who has failed to perform to it. In *CW Shipping Co Ltd v Limerick Harbour Commissioners* [1989] I.L.R.M. 416, the issue for determination was whether a tug came within the licensing requirements of s.53(1) of the Harbours Act 1946. The High Court, per O'Hanlon J., held that it did not because:

> "... a penal provision in a statute must be construed strictly, and this rule is a further constraint on giving to the terminology of s. 53(1) of the Act of 1946 the wide interpretation necessary if the use of tugs is to be brought within its ambit." [1989] 1 I.L.R.M. 416 at 424

The adverse consequences of a conviction for a criminal offence for the defendant include the possible deprivation of personal liberty and adverse social stigma associated with a conviction. It is imperative that the courts strictly construe the statutory provision at issue and decide whether the defendant's conduct comes within the definition of the offence.

CONSTITUTIONAL CONSIDERATIONS IN CRIMINAL LAW

The Constitution is the fundamental and basic law of the Irish State and sets out the fundamental rights and obligations of individuals. All powers of central and local government must conform to these laws, both when interacting with each other, and when interacting with citizens. If legislation that is in violation of a constitutional principle is enacted, it will be declared unconstitutional and invalid. Unlike ordinary law, that is legislation and decisions of the Superior Courts, the Constitution cannot be amended by the Parliament, but only by the people by a constitutional referendum; hence the importance of constitutional considerations in criminal law.

NON-RETROACTIVE PENAL STATUTES

Parliament is constitutionally prohibited from enacting laws criminalising behaviour which was lawful at the time it was engaged in. Article 15.5.1° of the Constitution provides that, "[t]he Oireachtas shall not declare acts to be infringements of the law which were not so at the date of their commission." This prohibits the Oireachtas from creating new criminal offences with retrospective effect and effectively affords constitutional status to the common law principle of legality.

PRESUMPTION OF INNOCENCE

It is a fundamental principle of common law, and widely reflected in international human rights instruments, that every person charged with a criminal offence has a right to be presumed innocent until proven guilty. This is now an implied constitutional right in accordance with the provisions of Art.38.1 of the

Constitution (*O'Leary v Attorney General* [1993] 1 I.R. 102), and also impacts on the burden of proof in a criminal trial (*Hardy v Ireland* [1994] 2 I.R. 550).

PERSONAL LIBERTY

The presumption of personal liberty is a fundamental right in liberal democratic states. Article 40.4.1° of the Constitution provides that, "[n]o citizen shall be deprived of his personal liberty save in accordance with law." However, as with many constitutional provisions, this is a qualified right and a citizen's right to personal liberty may be suspended following lawful arrest and detention by the Gardaí, or imprisonment following a conviction. Until 1996, there existed a very strong presumption in favour of granting bail to a defendant. This stemmed from the Supreme Court decisions in *People (AG) v O'Callaghan* [1966] I.R. 502 and *Ryan v DPP* [1989] I.R. 399. However, in 1996 the electorate approved the Sixteenth Amendment of the Constitution Act 1996, inserting a new Art.40.4.6° to the Constitution:

> Provision may be made by law for the refusal of bail by a court to a person charged with a serious offence where it is reasonably considered necessary to prevent the commission of a serious offence by that person.

Such provision was duly made by s.2(1) of the Bail Act 1997, which authorises a court to refuse bail to a person charged with a serious offence, where the court is satisfied that such refusal is reasonably considered necessary to prevent the commission of a serious offence by that person.

RIGHT TO SILENCE

The constitutional right to silence has been interpreted as a corollary of the right to freedom of expression protected by Art.40.6 (*Heaney v Ireland* [1996] 1 I.R. 580 (SC); [1994] 3 I.R. 593 (HC)), and subsequently as a right protected by Art.38.1 (*People (DPP) v Finnerty* [1999] 4 I.R. 364; *Re National Irish Bank* [1999] 1 I.R. 145). Legislation has provided for adverse inferences to be drawn in circumstances where the defendant exercised the right to silence: Criminal Justice Act 2007; Criminal Justice (Drug Trafficking) Act 1996; Criminal Justice Act 1984; and Offences against the State Act 1939 (as amended). This could adversely impact on the defendant's right to a fair criminal trial in due course of law, in accordance with Art.38.1. However, a defendant cannot be convicted on the basis of adverse inferences alone. In *Murray v United Kingdom* (1996) 22 E.H.R.R. 29, the ECtHR held that it would be incompatible with the right to silence and the right to a fair and impartial trial under art.6(1) of the ECHR if a conviction was based solely on the suspect's failure or refusal to answer police questions.

VOID FOR VAGUENESS

In accordance with the rule of law, criminal offences must be defined in clear and unambiguous terms so that people will know in advance what conduct is prohibited by criminal law. This issue was addressed in *King v Attorney General* [1981] I.R. 233, where the High Court considered the legality of the offence of "loitering with intent". The case concerned s.4 of the Vagrancy Act 1824 which stated: "[e]very suspected person or reputed thief frequenting [named public places] with intent to commit felony ... shall be deemed to be a rogue and a vagabond ...". Henchy J. stated:

> "... that the offence [loitering with intent to commit a felony], both in its essential ingredients and in the mode of proof of its commission, violates the requirement in Article 38, s. 1, that no person shall be tried on any criminal charge save in due course of law; that it violates the guarantee in Article 40, s. 4, sub-s. 1, that no citizen shall be deprived of personal liberty save in accordance with law – which means without stooping to methods which ignore the fundamental norms of the legal order postulated by the Constitution; that, in its arbitrariness and its unjustifiable discrimination, it fails to hold (as is required by Article 40, s. 1) all citizens to be equal before the law: and that it ignores the guarantees in Article 40, s. 3, that the personal rights of citizens shall be respected and, as far as practicable, defended and vindicated, and that the State shall by its laws protect as best it may from unjust attack and, in the case of injustice done, vindicate the life, person, good name, and property rights of every citizen." [1981] I.R. 233 at 257

The court held that the offence was overly vague and, therefore, unconstitutional. Henchy J. opined:

> "... the ingredients of the offence and the mode by which its commission may be proved are so arbitrary, so vague, so difficult to rebut, so related to rumour or ill-repute or past conduct, so ambiguous in failing to distinguish between apparent and real behaviour of a criminal nature, so prone to make a man's lawful occasions become unlawful and criminal by the breadth and arbitrariness of the discretion that is vested in both the prosecutor and the judge, so indiscriminately contrived to mark as criminal conduct committed by one person in certain circumstances when the same conduct, when engaged in by another person in similar circumstances, would be free of the taint of criminality, so out of keeping with the basic concept inherent in our legal system that a man may walk abroad in the secure knowledge that

he will not be singled out from his fellow-citizens and branded and punished as a criminal unless it has been established beyond reasonable doubt that he has deviated from a clearly prescribed standard of conduct, and generally so singularly at variance with both the explicit and implicit characteristics and limitations of the criminal law as to the onus of proof and mode of proof, that it is not so much a question of ruling unconstitutional the type of offence we are now considering as identifying the particular constitutional provisions with which such an offence is at variance." [1981] I.R. 233 at 257

Criminal offences that are defined in equivocal terms not only violate the rule of law, but also the constitutional rights of the citizen in the criminal trial process.

Declaration of Unconstitutionality

A common law rule or statutory provision creating a criminal offence is susceptible to being challenged on grounds of unconstitutionality and, if struck down, is deemed void ab initio. In *Dillon v DPP* [2008] 1 I.R. 383, the defendant was charged with the offence of begging on a public street, contrary to s.3 of the Vagrancy (Ireland) Act 1847. This section constituted a prohibition against begging in any public place in all circumstances. The High Court per De Valera J. stated that s.3 of the 1847 Act which deals with begging infringes the constitutional right to freedom of expression and communication with others. Likewise, in *CC v Ireland* [2006] 4 I.R. 1, part of the law on statutory rape under s.1(1) of the Criminal Law (Amendment) Act 1935 Act was struck down as being unconstitutional due to the absence in any circumstances of a defence of honest mistake as to the age of the complainant.

McGee v Attorney General [1974] I.R. 284 concerned s.17 of the Criminal Law (Amendment) Act 1936, which essentially prohibited the use of contraceptives by forbidding their sale or importation, even for married people. The applicant claimed that this provision violated her right to marital privacy. While the right to marital privacy is not a specified right in the Constitution, the plaintiff's contention was that it was an unenumerated right. The Supreme Court recognised a right to marital privacy and held that s.17 of the 1936 Act interfered with this right. Henchy J. stated:

"... s. 17 of the Act of 1935 violates the guarantee in sub-s. 1 of s. 3 of Article 40 by the State to protect the plaintiff's personal rights by its laws; it does so not only by violating her personal right to privacy in regard to her marital relations but, in a wider way, by frustrating and making criminal any efforts by her to effectuate the decision of her husband and herself, made responsibly, conscientiously and on medical advice, to avail themselves of a particular contraceptive method so as to ensure her life and health as well as the integrity, security and well-being of her marriage and her family." [1974] I.R. 284 at 328

The impugned section was deemed unconstitutional.

In *Norris v Attorney General* [1984] I.R. 36, the plaintiff brought a case seeking a declaration that ss.61 and 62 of the Offences against the Person Act 1861 and s.11 of the Criminal Law Amendment Act 1885, which criminalised consensual homosexual behaviour between two men, but not women, infringed his constitutional rights. The majority of the Supreme Court held that the constitutional right to privacy did not prohibit a ban on homosexuality which the court viewed as being "unnatural". O'Higgins C.J. suggested that the historical Christian prejudice against homosexuality justified his conclusion that there was no constitutional right to engage in homosexual activity. A minority of the court was of the view that the ban on homosexuality contravened the natural rights of male homosexuals, as a person's sexuality was a natural characteristic of each individual. The case was appealed to the European Court of Human Rights who agreed with the applicant (*Norris v Ireland* (1991) 13 E.H.R.R. 186). Subsequently, the Criminal Law (Sexual Offences) Act 1993 was enacted to decriminalise sexual relations between consenting males.

DUE PROCESS RIGHTS

Article 38.1 of the Constitution mandates a trial "in due course of law". The Superior Courts have interpreted this provision to include multifarious fundamental rights of the defendant in the criminal justice process including: the presumption of innocence (*Hardy v Ireland* [1994] 2 I.R. 550; *O'Leary v Attorney General* [1993] 1 I.R. 102); the right to a speedy criminal trial (*B v DPP* [1997] 2 I.L.R.M. 18; *State (O'Connell) v Fawsitt* [1986] I.R. 362); the right to be present at one's criminal trial (*People (AG) v Kelly* [1982] I.L.R.M. 1; *People (AG) v Mesitt* [1972] I.R. 204); the ability to understand the nature of the criminal trial (*State (Buchan) v Coyne* (1936) 70 I.L.T.R. 185); the right to fair, independent and impartial trial (*Magee v O'Dea* [1994] 1 I.R. 500; *People (AG) v Singer* [1975] I.R. 408); the constitutional right to proportionate sentencing (*People (DPP) v M* [1994] 3 I.R. 306); and the principle of double jeopardy (*DS v Judges of the Cork Circuit and the DPP* [2008] 4 I.R. 379).

CLASSIFICATION OF CRIMINAL OFFENCES

The manner in which a criminal offence is investigated and prosecuted depends on the seriousness of the offence involved. Criminal offences are classified according to the mode of trial which depends on whether the offence charged is an indictable offence or a summary offence. An indictable offence is simply one that carries the right to trial by jury, although that right may not always be exercised by the defendant. A summary offence is triable only in a court of summary jurisdiction, that is, the District Court, which is a court of local and limited jurisdiction. Criminal offences may be defined in different ways, such as: summary offences, indictable offences, minor offences, serious offences, arrestable offences, and mode of trial.

SUMMARY AND INDICTABLE OFFENCES

There are two modes of trial in Irish criminal law: summarily and on indictment. In the District Court a defendant is tried before a judge without a jury. In the higher criminal courts, that is, the Circuit Criminal Court and Central Criminal Court, a defendant is tried before a judge and jury. Summary and indictable offences indicate the manner in which these offences are tried or dealt with in the courts. A summary offence is one which can only be dealt with by a judge sitting without a jury, that is, the District Court, while an indictable offence is one which may be or must be tried before a judge and jury.

Most common law offences are indictable offences as the common law did not differentiate between indictable and non-indictable offences. However, legislation does make a distinction between types of criminal offences, and therefore, differentiates on how offences will be dealt with by the courts.

When an offence is dealt with in by the District Court, the maximum prison sentence available to the trial judge is limited. Section 11 of the Criminal Justice Act 1984 provides that the maximum term of imprisonment that can be imposed by the District Court in respect of any number of offences for which sentence is passed at the same time cannot exceed two years. The District Court cannot exceed a maximum sentence of one year in respect of one offence.

As stated above, indictable offences are those offences that may or must be tried on indictment before a judge and jury, typically in the Circuit Court or the Central Criminal Court. However, not all indictable offences are tried before a jury. Indictable offences can be divided into a number of categories. There are specified offences which must be tried before a judge and jury and these include: murder, attempted murder, conspiracy to murder; piracy; rape; and aggravated sexual assault. There are numerous offences which do not include an option to be dealt with in the District Court and must be dealt with on indictment, for example, s.4 of the Non-Fatal Offences Against the Person

Act 1997 (causing serious harm) and s.14 of the Criminal Justice (Public Order) Act 1994 (riot).

OFFENCES WHICH ARE TRIABLE EITHER WAY

Some criminal offences may be tried summarily or by indictment at the request of the DPP, the trial judge or the defendant. Section 2 of the Criminal Justice Act 1951 provides that offences listed in the First Schedule to the 1951 Act can be dealt with in the District Court if three conditions are satisfied. First, the court must be of the opinion that the facts proved, or alleged, constitute a minor offence which the court deems suitable to be tried summarily. Secondly, the defendant, when told by the court of his right to be tried on indictment by a judge and jury, must not object to being tried summarily in the District Court. Thirdly, the DPP must consent to the defendant being tried summarily for such an "indictable" offence. Examples of some of the offences listed in the First Schedule to the 1951 Act include: perjury, offences under the Criminal Law Act 1997, offences under the Criminal Law (Rape) (Amendment) Act 1990, and offences under the Criminal Justice (Theft and Fraud Offences) Act 2001.

As a matter of practice, trial judges first consider what the DPP has directed and then question the prosecuting Garda for an outline of the facts of the case against the defendant. The trial judge will then decide whether or not to hear the case, or alternatively send the case forward to a higher court to be tried on indictment. If the trial judge decides to hear the case in the District Court, the defendant is given an opportunity to choose whether to be dealt with in the District Court or the Circuit Criminal Court. Typically, if a defendant is given this choice, he will elect to be tried in the District Court as the maximum sentence available to the District judge is substantially less than that available in the Circuit Court and the matter is dealt with expeditiously.

MINOR AND NON-MINOR OFFENCES

Article 38.2 of the Constitution provides that, "minor offences may be tried by courts of summary jurisdiction", that is, in the District Court. However, there is no definition of what constitutes a minor offence and the Constitution does not provide guidance. The distinction between the constitutional concepts of minor and non-minor offences equates more or less with the statutory distinction drawn between summary and indictable offences.

The Supreme Court has considered the issue of what constitutes a minor offence in *Melling v Ó Mathghamhna* [1962] I.R. 1, the court examined the criteria for determining whether an offence was minor and laid out the following guidelines: the severity or seriousness of the punishment; the moral guilt of the defendant; the law in 1937 when the Constitution was adopted;

and public opinion. Of these criteria, the most important is the severity or seriousness of the sentence which the court may impose on conviction.

All that can be said with certainty is that an offence is minor where the punishment is less than six months' imprisonment (*Conroy v Attorney General* [1965] I.R. 411), whereas an offence is non-minor where the punishment is two years or more (*Mallon v Minister for Agriculture, Food and Forestry* [1996] 1 I.R. 517). As a general rule, an offence with a maximum prison sentence of 12 months constitutes a minor offence and an offence that carries a penalty of more than 12 months' imprisonment is considered a non-minor offence.

SERIOUS AND NON-SERIOUS OFFENCES

The Bail Act 1997 created a new distinction between serious and non-serious offences. The 1997 Act allows the court to refuse bail in circumstances where a defendant is charged with a serious offence. The prosecution must establish to the satisfaction of the court that the defendant is likely to commit further serious offences, or intimidate potential witnesses if released on bail. The 1997 Act defines a serious offence as an offence for which the defendant, if convicted, could be sentenced to a minimum term of imprisonment of five years.

ARRESTABLE AND NON-ARRESTABLE OFFENCES

The Criminal Law Act 1997 abolished the common law distinction between a felony and misdemeanor and replaced this distinction with arrestable and non-arrestable offences. The 1997 Act defines an arrestable offence as one for which a defendant could be punished by a term of imprisonment of five years or more. This distinction is important in terms of Garda powers of arrest and detention. For example, s.4 of the Criminal Law Act 1997 allows a Garda to arrest without warrant any person whom he, with reasonable cause, believes to be guilty of committing or having committed an arrestable offence.

IRISH CRIME CLASSIFICATION SYSTEM (ICCS)

This new system for the classification of criminal offences was designed to replace the Headline/Non-Headline system that An Garda Síochána had been using since 2000. The ICCS was developed by the Central Statistics Office in association with An Garda Síochána, assisted by information and advice from the Advisory Group on Crime Statistics. A significant feature of the ICCS is that it is written in clear and unambiguous language, whereas the previous classification systems were legalistic in their language. Although the ICCS will initially be used by An Garda Síochána for recorded crimes, it is intended that the system will be adopted in other areas of the criminal justice system as well.

Elements of Criminal Offences

The Latin maxim *actus non facit reum nisi mens sit rea* is translated to mean that an act by itself is not, as a general rule, sufficient to constitute criminal liability, unless the defendant's mind is also guilty. The exception to this rule is the offence of absolute liability where criminal liability is imposed on the occurrence of the actus reus, notwithstanding the absence of mens rea. The maxim has provided criminal lawyers and legal scholars with the expressions actus reus and mens rea, which are conventionally used to identify the key elements of most criminal offences. The actus reus and mens rea are stipulated for in the statutory provision creating the criminal offence. Thus, the general basis for imposing criminal liability is that the defendant must be proven to have committed a guilty act at the same time as having a guilty state of mind. The physical elements of liability are collectively called the actus reus and the accompanied mental state or fault element is called the mens rea. The defendant's mental state must have some external manifestation or actus reus at the time of the commission of the criminal offence.

There is an exception to this general rule for offences of strict liability in that the prosecution authorities do not have to prove mens rea as to one or more elements of the actus reus. In fact, we must go one step further and say that, in addition to conduct and mental element having to be present, any available defence must be absent. For example, X might kill Y while intending to kill him or to cause him serious injury. This will generally be murder. However, if X intentionally killed Y in order to save his (X's) own life, that would not be murder, as people whose lives are put in danger by another are entitled to act in self-defence.

In technical terms, therefore, three elements must be present. First, the actus reus is the conduct constituting the offence. This will usually be an act such as aiming a gun at somebody and pulling the trigger. In a limited number of instances, failure to act will constitute the actus reus of an offence. Secondly, the mens rea is the so-called mental element. The precise nature of the mental element required to hold a person criminally liable varies from one offence to another. In the case of some offences, intention will be required (e.g. murder); in others, knowledge will be required; and in others, recklessness. Thirdly, certain defences are recognised by criminal law, for instance: self-defence or defence of others, provocation, insanity and diminished responsibility, automatism, mistake, duress, and necessity. Not all of them lead to a complete acquittal and not all are applicable to every offence, but one must always examine the circumstances in which an alleged offence was committed in order to identify if any defence was possibly present.

Taken together then, the study of the elements of criminal offences, that is actus reus and mens rea, as well as the study of defences, create what is often described as the general part of criminal law. This is the part which is concerned with the way in which criminal liability is constructed and will occupy the first part of most criminal law courses. The second part of a typical criminal law syllabus will deal with definitions of specific offences including: homicide, non-fatal offences, sex offences, theft offences, criminal damage, public order offences, and so forth.

FURTHER READING

Campbell, Kilcommins and O'Sullivan, *Criminal Law in Ireland: Cases and Commentary* (Dublin: Clarus Press, 2010), Chs 1 and 2.

Hamilton, "The Summary Trial of Indictable Offences" (2004) 4 (2) J.S.I.J. 154.

Hanly, *An Introduction to Irish Criminal Law*, 2nd edn (Dublin: Gill & Macmillan, 2006), Chs 1 and 2.

McAuley and McCutcheon, *Criminal Liability: A Grammar* (Dublin: Round Hall, 2000), Ch.1.

McCutcheon, "Morality and the Criminal Law: Reflections on Hart-Devlin" (2002) 47 Crim. L. Quart. 15.

Ní Raifeartaigh, "Reversing the Burden of Proof in a Criminal Trial: Canadian and Irish Perspectives on the Presumption of Innocence" (1995) 5(2) I.C.L.J. 135.

O'Malley, "Common Law Crimes and the Principle of Legality" (1989) 7 I.L.T. 243.

His Honour Judge Michael White, "The New Criminal Court Complex" (2007) 7 (1) J.S.I.J. 1.

Working Group on the Jurisdiction of the Courts, *The Criminal Jurisdiction of the Courts* (Dublin: Stationery Office, 2003).

2. Actus Reus

INTRODUCTION

The actus reus is sometimes referred to as the external, physical or action element of criminal offences. A defendant is deemed to have committed the actus reus of an offence if he has performed an act that is an example of the type of conduct prohibited by the offence in question. Thus, a person might perform an act which leads to somebody else's death, but that will not be murder unless, at the time of the act, the actor intended either to kill or cause serious injury to some person. As a general rule, a defendant cannot be convicted on the basis of conduct (whether act or omission) alone because there is also a mental element in most criminal offences (mens rea).

CATEGORIES OF CRIMINAL OFFENCES

The actus reus consists of more than just the conduct constituting the offence in that it also consists of whatever circumstances and consequences are required for the offence under consideration. In other words, the actus reus consists of all the elements of an offence other than the mental element. At the outset, it is important to differentiate between the different categories of offences for the purpose of the actus reus.

CONDUCT CRIMES

There are conduct crimes where the actus reus is the prohibited conduct itself rather than any consequence of that conduct, such as the offences of assault, perjury and rape. A conduct crime is one where the only external element of the offence is the prohibited conduct. Once the defendant has performed the prohibited conduct, he has committed a criminal offence regardless of any consequences.

RESULT CRIMES

The second types of offences are result crimes, where the actus reus of the offence requires proof that the defendant's conduct caused a prohibited result or consequence. These offences are committed when the defendant's conduct produces a proscribed consequence. Murder and criminal damage are result crimes because what is prohibited is the bringing about of a certain consequence, that is, the death of another person or damage to property. It is not so much the act done, but rather the result produced, for example shooting or poisoning the victim resulting in death.

CRIMES OF CIRCUMSTANCES

For crimes of circumstances the conduct by itself might not be unlawful, except if performed in particular circumstances. The conduct is not intrinsically illegal. An example of this element of the actus reus is the offence of rape in that it is an essential element of the actus reus that the complainant did not consent to the act of sexual intercourse. Similarly, while telling a lie is not a criminal offence by itself, such conduct would constitute the offence of perjury if the defendant deliberately and wilfully gave false, misleading, or incomplete testimony under oath or affirmation.

CONSTRUCTING THE ACTUS REUS

The actus reus is simply a convenient shorthand term to describe the conduct element of criminal offences. It does not always mean the performance of an illegal act, but might also include a failure to act in circumstances whereby the defendant was under a legal obligation to perform certain functions. The actus reus might also pertain to a certain state of affairs for which the defendant might be deemed criminally liable, despite the fact that his conduct may have been involuntary. Words alone will constitute the actus reus for some offences such as the inchoate offence of incitement.

A guilty state of mind independent of some external manifestation (such as an assault, speaking, writing or merely gesticulating) will not of itself suffice to constitute criminal liability. For some offences the conduct element will be minimal, for example, the inchoate offence of conspiracy, which is an agreement between two or more persons to commit an unlawful act and then take some action towards its completion. In determining whether the actus reus of an offence is present on the basis of the defendant's conduct, the following preliminary observations should be considered.

There is a certain category of offences, usually minor in nature, for which a person can be held criminally responsible once it is proved that he or she committed the actus reus. These are known as strict liability offences. However, all offences with serious consequences require proof of actus reus and mens rea. For instance, there are two umbrellas beside a door, one belongs to X and the other to Y. Suppose when X is leaving he takes Y's umbrella by accident, believing it is his (X's). Or suppose X *intends* to take Y's because it is more valuable, but *actually* takes his own (X's). In which of these situations, if either, should X be criminally liable? This issue was considered in *R v Deller* (1952) 36 Cr. App. R. 184, in which the defendant believed that a car was mortgaged to a finance company and then fraudulently induced an individual to purchase the car with assurances that it was free from any encumbrances. However, unbeknownst to the defendant, the mortgage document on the car was legally invalid. He was convicted of obtaining property by false pretences under the Larceny Act 1916 (repealed in Ireland by the Criminal Justice (Theft and Fraud) Offences Act 2001). The conviction was overturned on appeal on the basis that, while the defendant had the requisite mens rea, the actus reus necessary to prove the offence was absent as there was, in fact, no false pretence. The actus reus and mens rea must both be present.

Status Offences

One group of cases which cannot be discussed in terms of voluntary acts are often referred to as the "state of affairs" or "status" offences. These are defined not by the defendant performing a positive act, but, rather, by the defendant "being found", "being in possession" or "being in charge". In some cases, all the prosecution needs to prove is the existence of the factual circumstances which constitute the offence, i.e. the existence of the state of affairs.

The unlawful act constituting the actus reus must be voluntary; this is self-evident and seldom causes a problem in practice. However, suppose X is carrying a knife in lawful circumstances and somebody else comes along, grabs X's hand and plunges the knife into a third person and that third person dies as a result of the stab wound. In a sense, X stabbed the victim, but X did not do so as a result of a voluntary act. The real offender is the person who physically forced X to do what he did. Somewhat more difficult problems can occasionally arise in relation to voluntariness as the following two leading cases illustrate.

In *R v Larsonneur* (1933) 24 Cr. App. R. 74, the defendant, a French national, was given leave to enter the United Kingdom on the condition that she left by a certain date. She travelled to Ireland before that date but was then deported back to the United Kingdom. It was not the defendant's voluntary act but the act of the Irish authorities that brought about her return to the United Kingdom. She was convicted of being in England contrary to the Aliens Act 1920, which was a strict liability offence. The defendant's involuntary conduct resulted in the imposition of criminal liability, despite the fact that '"being found" was not accompanied by a voluntary act on the part of the defendant. The question on appeal was whether she was voluntarily in the United Kingdom. It was argued that she was brought back to the United Kingdom by a superior force over which she had no control, but the Court of Appeal upheld her conviction. The problematic issue with this decision is that there was no voluntary conduct on the part of the defendant as she did not choose to return to England. She could not have refrained from doing anything that would have altered the eventual outcome. The opposing view is that the defendant was the author of her own misfortune as she should have foreseen the train of events that would unfold and could, therefore, have avoided them.

A more extreme example of so-called "state of affairs" cases or "status offences" is *Winzar v Chief Constable of Kent, The Times*, March 28, 1983, in which the defendant was charged with being found intoxicated on a public highway, contrary to the provisions of the Licensing Act 1872. The police had been called to remove the defendant who was drunk from a hospital, which they did, and then having formed the opinion that he was drunk, put him in a patrol car that was on the public road. He was then convicted with being found drunk on a public highway. Policy considerations were instrumental in this case, and the Divisional Court justified its position by comparing the defendant to an intoxicated person who was asked to leave a restaurant and who had complied with that request. The court noted that an individual in these circumstances would be clearly capable of being found drunk in a public place having entered it voluntarily. If the defendant in *Winzar* was not found criminally liable, he would have effectively benefited from non-cooperation, while the person agreeing to a request to leave a restaurant would have been punished for cooperating. The court considered this unjust.

In these cases, criminal liability is imposed on the basis of a certain "state of affairs" constituting the actus reus. The prosecution only needs to prove the existence of the factual circumstances that constitutes the offence, that is, the existence of the state of affairs.

VOLUNTARY CONDUCT

The defendant's conduct must be "voluntary" or "freely willed" if he is to incur criminal liability. What is somewhat confusing about the difference between voluntary conduct and involuntary conduct is that the Superior Courts in common law jurisdictions have tended to focus on events that are, not as such, voluntary acts. The issue of voluntariness in the construction of criminal liability has been defined in terms of involuntary conduct. Therefore, the conduct element of the actus reus is defined in negative as opposed to positive terms, which tends to obscure the concept of voluntariness in criminal law.

Notwithstanding the policy considerations of the above-mentioned status offences, a more enlightened view of voluntary acts can perhaps be derived from the New Zealand case of *Kilbride v Lake* [1962] N.Z.L.R. 590, in which a driver was charged with operating a car without a warrant of fitness. It appeared that the warrant of fitness had been in the car, but had subsequently been removed from it. The Supreme Court of Auckland per Woodhouse J. held that the driver was not criminally liable and noted that the ability to choose a different course of events lies at the heart of the voluntary conduct:

> "... it is a cardinal principle that ... a person cannot be made criminally responsible for an act or omission unless it was done or omitted in circumstances where there was some other course open to him. If this condition is absent, any act or omission must be involuntary, or unconscious, or unrelated to the forbidden event in any causal sense regarded by the law as involving responsibility ... the condition that there must be freedom to take one course or another involves free and conscious exercise of will in the case of an act, or the opportunity to choose to behave differently in the case of omissions." [1962] N.Z.L.R. 590 at 593

As regards the difference between the voluntary act requirement and the mens rea, Woodhouse J. stated:

> "The [*mens rea*] is the intention or the knowledge behind or accompanying the exercise of will, while the former is simply the spark without which the *actus reus* cannot be produced at all. In the present case there was no opportunity at all to take a different course, and any inactivity on the part of the appellant after the warrant was removed was involuntary and unrelated to the offence. In these circumstances I do not think it can be said that the *actus reus* was in any sense the result of his conduct, whether intended or accidental. There was an act of the appellant which led up to the prohibited event (the *actus reus*), and that was to permit the car to be on the road. The second factual ingredient was not satisfied until the warrant disappeared during his absence. The resulting omission to carry the warrant was not within his conduct, knowledge, or control: on these facts the chain of causation was broken." [1962] N.Z.L.R. 590 at 593

This is clearly a pragmatic approach to such issues in the construction of criminal liability and should be adopted in this jurisdiction as a matter of logic.

PHYSICAL FORCE

The prohibited conduct may be involuntary because it is physically forced by someone else other than the defendant, in which case there will be no actus reus. In *Leicester v Pearson* [1952] 2 Q.B. 668, a car driver was prosecuted for failing to give precedence to a pedestrian on a zebra crossing, but was acquitted when it was established that his car had been pushed onto the crossing by another car hitting it from behind.

AUTOMATISM

Another issue that arises in relation to the voluntary act requirement in the construction of the actus reus is the issue of the defendant's consciousness. Automatism occurs where the defendant performs a physical act but is unaware of what he is doing, or is not in control of his actions, typically because of some external factor, such as a spasm or reflex action, which may negate the defendant's criminal liability. In *R v Quick* [1973] 1 Q.B. 910, the defendant, a diabetic nurse, was charged with assaulting a patient at a mental hospital. The assault occurred while the defendant was in a state of hypoglycaemia (low blood sugar level due to an excess of insulin). The Court of Appeal held that the defendant should have been acquitted on the ground of automatism. The defendant's unconscious state had been the result of external factors, that is, the taking of insulin.

Sometimes people respond to something with a spontaneous reflex action over which they have no control. Although slightly different, this is sometimes classed as a form of automatism. In *Hill v Baxter* [1958] 1 Q.B. 277, the defendant was charged with dangerous driving as he had gone through a stop sign and collided with another car. He argued that he was unconscious at the time of the collision and could not have been said to have engaged in voluntary conduct at the time of the act. The Court of Queen's Bench held that based on the evidence, including the fact that the defendant had navigated a complex route, he was not unconscious at the time of the accident. The court discussed the circumstances in which an individual's conduct would be deemed involuntary. Pearson J. stated:

> "(1) The man in the driving seat is having an epileptic fit, so that he is unconscious and there are merely spasmodic movements of his arms and legs. (2) By the onset of some disease he has been reduced to a state of coma and is completely unconscious. (3) He is stunned by a blow on the head from a stone which passing traffic has thrown up from the roadway. (4) He is attacked by a swarm of bees so that he is for the time being disabled and prevented from exercising any directional control over the vehicle, and any movements of his arms and legs are solely caused by the action of the bees. In each of these cases it can be said that at the material time he is not driving and, therefore, not driving dangerously." [1958] 1 Q.B. 277 at 286

Pearson J. stated that after the driver has fallen asleep he can no longer be said to be driving; however, it is at the point when the driver is in the process of falling asleep and does not stop driving that criminal liability for the offence of dangerous driving attaches:

> "Then suppose that the man in the driving seat falls asleep. After he has fallen asleep he is no longer driving, but there was an earlier time at which he was falling asleep and therefore failing to perform the driver's elementary and essential duty of keeping himself awake and therefore he was driving dangerously. Similarly, in the case of a man who knows that he is liable to have an epileptic fit but, nevertheless, drives a vehicle on the road, there is a question of fact whether driving in these circumstances can properly be considered reckless or dangerous. The answer might depend to some extent on the degree and frequency of the epilepsy and the degree of probability that an epileptic fit might come upon him." [1958] 1 Q.B. 277 at 286–287

The approach is neatly encapsulated in *HM Advocate v Ritchie* (1926) SC (J) 45, in which it was stated that a person is obliged to take account of the risk of falling asleep when driving, but if that condition arose through no fault of the driver from some cause which was beyond his control and which he could not foresee, then he could not be criminally liable. This would appear to be a logical approach to the actus reus of such criminal offences.

In *Jiminez v The Queen* [1992] 173 C.L.R. 572, the High Court of Australia suggested a solution to the aforementioned dilemma. The defendant was convicted of dangerous driving causing death. Evidence proved that the defendant had fallen asleep at the wheel and his car had veered off the road. Waking suddenly, he tried to regain control of the car but failed. The car then crashed into a tree and killed his passenger. The majority of the High Court held that dangerous driving must, in a practical sense, be the cause of the impact and the resulting death. The court held that actions during sleep are not voluntary:

> "... if a person's condition is such that his actions are unconscious or involuntary, it does not matter what the cause is: he cannot be found guilty of an offence, whether statutory or otherwise, unless the acts which constitute it have been done voluntarily. As we have said, a driver who drives when tired and drowsy may, depending upon all the circumstances, be guilty of driving in a manner dangerous to the public. But if he does fall asleep his actions during the period of sleep are neither conscious nor voluntary." [1992] 173 C.L.R. 572 at 581

Thus, it appears that the sleeping driver will be convicted if he continued to drive while drowsy, thereby causing the injury in a practical sense. The issue is one of causation. The key element here is that, at some stage, the defendant had acted voluntarily, at least in choosing to continue driving and responsibility for the relevant conduct or result can be attributed to him. The reasoning here is different to the "prior fault" reasoning in *Larsonneur*. If prior fault is absent here, conduct by the defendant is not voluntary, as no choice exercised by him resulted in the state of affairs emerging. Criminal liability is imposed because of the causal link between the drowsy driving and the illegal act that resulted.

Possession

The concept of possession as an element of the actus reus is important in two types of offending: first, for certain offences under the Criminal Justice (Theft and Fraud Offences) Act 2001; and secondly, there are several criminal offences that criminalise the mere possession of a certain item, such as illegal drugs, child pornography or unlicensed firearms. Possession is not a very clear concept, particularly in legal terminology, and can include a number of notions. In *Warner v Metropolitan Police Commissioner* [1969] 2 A.C. 256, the legal meaning of possession was explained by Lord Wilberforce in the following terms:

> "Ideally, a possessor of a thing has complete physical control over it; he has knowledge of its existence, its situation and its qualities: he has received it from a person who intends to confer possession of it and he has himself the intention to possess it exclusively of others. But these elements are seldom all present in situations with which the courts have to deal, and where one or more of them is lacking, or incompletely present, it has to be decided whether the given approximation is such that possession may be held sufficiently established to satisfy the relevant rule of law." [1969] 2 A.C. 256 at 309

While this is the ideal concept of possession in criminal law, it does not necessarily arise in all circumstances.

Constructive possession

Constructive possession pertains to a situation where a defendant is deemed to have control over property, without actually having physical control. In the construction of criminal liability a defendant with constructive possession stands in the same legal position as a person with actual possession. In *Sullivan v Earl of Caithness* [1976] Q.B. 966, the defendant was charged with an offence of possessing firearms without holding a firearms certificate. He lived in Oxfordshire and kept the firearms in his mother's house in Surrey. The defendant contended that he did not possess the firearm and therefore did not require a certificate. May J. stated:

> "... the owner of a firearm who does not at the relevant time have physical possession of it can nevertheless truly be said still to be in possession of it. In the present case the defendant was at all material times the owner of the firearms. He could no doubt obtain them from his mother's flat at any time when he wanted them. She had the barest of custody of them, not because she had any interest in them, but because her flat was safer than the defendant's home in Oxford." [1976] Q.B. 966 at 970

Although the defendant left firearms in his mother's house, he was nevertheless deemed to have had constructive possession of the items.

In *Minister for Posts and Telegraphs v Campbell* [1966] I.R. 69, judgment was given on a case stated from the District Court in respect of an unlicensed television set. The High Court held that the complainant had not discharged the onus of showing that the defendant, on the specified date, kept the television set or had it in his possession, actual or constructive. Davitt P. explained the elements of possession in the following terms:

> "In my opinion a person cannot, in the context of a criminal case, be properly said to keep or have possession of an article unless he has control of it either personally or by someone else. He cannot be said to have actual possession of it unless he personally can exercise physical control over it; and he cannot be said to have constructive possession of it unless it is in the actual possession of some other person over whom he has control so that it would be available to him if and when he wanted it. Normally speaking, a person can properly be said to be in possession of the contents of his own dwellinghouse, but only if he is aware of what it contains. He cannot properly be said to be in control or possession of something of whose existence and presence he has no knowledge. Assuming, for the sake only of the argument, that the evidence established that the cottage was the defendant's dwellinghouse, there is in this case no evidence as to how the television set came to be there, how long it was there, or whether the defendant was ever at any time aware of its presence or existence. There is therefore no evidence that it was ever actually in his control or possession. There is no evidence as to who was the woman who was present in the house on the occasion of [the inspectors] or as to what was her relation, if any, to the defendant. There is nothing to indicate that he

had any control over her actions. There are therefore no grounds for concluding that he had constructive possession of the television set. As far as the evidence goes, the set may have been placed in the cottage without his knowledge or consent." [1966] I.R. 69 at 73

It is an established rule of law that in order for an individual to have legal possession over an item, he must not only have control over the item, but also knowledge as to the existence of that item.

In *Williams v Douglas* [1949] 78 C.L.R. 521, the meaning of constructive possession was considered by the High Court of Australia. The defendant, Williams, while staying at a hotel, acknowledged that he owned certain gold bars which were found in a bathroom some distance from his bedroom. The bathroom was used by all lodgers who were on the same floor as Williams. The contraband gold bars were held to be in William's possession or control within the meaning of s.36 of the Gold Buyers Act 1921. Rich J. said:

"The phrase in the section we are called upon to interpret is 'possession or control'. Possession does not mean actual physical possession or manual detention. 'Suppose I request a bystander to hold anything for me, it still remains in my possession. So also possession may be required or retained over goods which are in the manual detention of a third person': *R. v. Sleep* (1861) Le. & Co. 44 ... *per* Willes J. And the phrase possession and control denotes the right and power to deal with the article in question. In the instant case the question resolves itself into one of fact. In any given case it is necessary to take into consideration all the circumstances and the nature of the thing the subject of the inquiry. In the circumstances of this case as the accused claimed the gold when it was 'discovered' I consider that the inferences which can be drawn are that the accused knew that the gold was concealed under the bath, that it was placed there by himself or an accomplice and to use the words of Dwyer C.J. that 'he could have got it when he wished'. He had it as effectually under his control or his *de facto* possession as if he had locked it in a box in the bathroom, a box of which he and he alone had the key, or if you like he and an accomplice alone had keys." [1949] 78 C.L.R. 521 at 527

Latham C.L. with whom Dixon J. and McTiernan J. agreed, stated:

"The result is much the same as if the word 'actual' had been written before the word 'possession'; but [*de facto*] possession is a conception which is itself much more extensive than that of physical custody. It is wide enough to include any case where the person alleged to be in possession has hidden the thing effectively so that he can take it into his physical custody when he wishes and where others are unlikely to discover it except by accident." (1949) 78 C.L.R. 521 at 526

This case is authority for the proposition that a person may be held in law to possess something which could be many miles away from his person.

CONTROL ELEMENT

The defendant must have actual or constructive control of an item to be legally in possession of that item. In *People (AG) v Kelly and Robinson* [1953] 1 Frewen 147, the defendants were found in a room in the presence of two others who appeared to be sorting through stolen goods. The two others pleaded guilty to stealing the goods, and the issue for determination was whether the two defendants were also in possession of the stolen goods. The jury were instructed that unless they were satisfied that the defendants had control over the goods, or that the goods were being held for them, they should acquit the defendants. One of the defendant's explanations for being in the room was that he was delivering eggs to the homeowner's sick child, but the jury clearly did not believe his explanation and convicted him. The issue on appeal was whether the jury had been properly instructed on the meaning of possession in law, and the Court of Appeal held that they were. However, if the jury had believed him, he would have been acquitted. Thus, on the facts of the case the question was whether the meeting was held for the purposes of dividing the stolen goods. The purpose of the applicant's presence was essential as to whether he had possessed the goods.

The question of momentary possession is important in the construction of criminal liability. This issue was considered in *R v Murphy, Lillis and Burns* [1971] N.I. 193 in which three men were found guilty on charges of being in possession of unlicensed firearms and ammunition. They appealed against the conviction on the ground that the jury had been misdirected on the legal meaning of "possession". The factual circumstances of the case were that three men had entered a premises consisting of a shop and dwelling-house at a time when shooting was taking place and a curfew had been imposed. When the premises were searched by army personnel, the men were found in rooms which contained two rifles and a quantity of ammunition. The Court of Criminal Appeal held that the concept of "possession" connotes voluntary possession by actual or potential physical control, with knowledge of the nature of what is kept or controlled, and held that there was sufficient evidence to substantiate the convictions. MacDermott L.C.J. considered the legal meaning of possession in the following terms:

"Possession is an ambiguous word and one which ... is always giving rise to trouble. Its precise meaning must depend on the context and policy of the statute using it and no comprehensive definition is therefore possible or desirable." [1971] N.I. 193 at 199

The court suggested that picking up a pistol with a view to throwing it into the river would amount to possession, while picking it up with the intention of handing it in to the police would not. Thus, according to the decision in *Murphy*, if the purpose of picking up the gun has a justifiable legal explanation, it does not amount to legal possession, while picking it up with the intention to abandon it does.

KNOWLEDGE ELEMENT

A key element in the concept of possession is that the defendant has knowledge of the item over which he has control. In *People v Nugent and Byrne* (1964) 98 I.L.T.R. 139, the defendants were convicted with receiving stolen money which was found in a car driven by the first defendant and in which the second defendant was a passenger. Their defence was that they did not know that the money was in the car. The Court of Appeal allowed the appeal, holding that the onus of proof was on the prosecution to prove knowledge on the part of the defendant that the money was in the car. This reasoning was applied in *Minister for Posts and Telegraphs v Campbell* [1966] I.R. 69, in which the defendant was charged with possession of an unlicensed television set in a house of which he was the occupier. The inspector was let into the house by a woman who was in the house at the time that he called. Davitt P. noted that there was no evidence as to how the TV came to be in the house, or as to whether the defendant had any knowledge of its presence, nor did he have any control over the woman who had let the inspector in. Davitt P. concluded that the evidence was consistent with the TV being put into the cottage without the knowledge or consent of the defendant. However, in certain circumstances, knowledge can be imputed (see also *R v Lewis* (1988) 87 Cr. App. R. 270).

Proximity can be an important issue pertaining to the knowledge element of possession constituting the actus reus. In *R v Whelan* [1972] N.I. 153, the defendants were found in a room occupied by 14 other people. A revolver and ammunition were found in the room on top of a cupboard and covered by clothes. They denied any knowledge of the guns. The Court of Criminal Appeal noted that while there was a strong case to be made that one of the men had knowledge, it was not possible to establish which one. The convictions were quashed. This case was distinguished in *People (DPP) v Foley* [1995] 1 I.R. 267, where the three defendants were found in a room with firearms and ammunition. The items were in reasonably plain view in the room. One of the defendants stated that he was there innocently, which the jury believed and he was acquitted. The other two were convicted. The essential point was that the firearms were out in the open. Foley was sitting on the bed beside a shotgun and a handgun was also clearly visible. The two defendants were convicted of possession by the Special Criminal Court, but a third defendant was acquitted on the basis of his explanation that he had called to the premises only on a casual visit. The Court of Criminal Appeal concluded that it was impossible, in the absence of any explanation, to find that the defendant was innocently sitting on the bed alongside the gun without being part of an enterprise that he, together with the occupier of the house (who was convicted but did not appeal), had possession of it as well as the handgun and amunition. Budd J. stated:

> "The crucial difference between the material facts of R. v. Whelan and the applicant's case is that the firearm was hidden under clothing in Whelan's case, whereas in the applicant's case the sawn-off shotgun was beside him clearly to be seen on the bed in the small bedsitter. In R. v. Whelan there was no evidence at all to suggest that any of the accused had any knowledge of the existence of the firearm nor was there any evidence from which an inference of intent to possess could be drawn. However, in the applicant's case, it was entirely open to the Special Criminal Court, on the evidence of the witnesses called by the prosecution, to draw the inference that all three occupants of the room were in joint possession of the firearms and ammunition." [1995] 1 I.R. 267 at 282–283

The court noted that the Special Criminal Court distinguished Whelan from the facts in the applicant's case. Where appropriate, the Superior Courts will draw reasonable inferences from the facts of the case, particularly where the defendants had clearly engaged upon a common enterprise. It then became considerably more difficult to infer common knowledge (cf. People (DPP) v O'Neill [1997] 1 I.R. 365).

There is a distinction in criminal law between knowledge of the existence of an item and knowledge of its characteristics and qualities. If the offence charged is one of strict liability, then the prosecution only needs to establish knowledge of the existence of the item. In Warner v Metropolitan Police Commissioner [1969] 2 A.C. 256, the appellant was charged with having drugs in his possession without being duly authorised, contrary to s.1(1) of the Drugs (Prevention of Misuse) Act 1964. His evidence was that he believed that a bottle in his possession contained scent while, in fact, it contained prohibited drugs. The House of Lords held that the prohibited conduct was a strict liability offence and, consequently, all the prosecution needed to establish was the defendant's knowledge of the existence of the item. The question then arises as to what characteristics of the item the defendant needs to know. Lord Pearce stated:

> "Though I reasonably believe the tablets which I possess to be aspirin, yet if they turn out to be heroin I am in possession of heroin tablets. This would be so I think even if I believed them to be sweets. It would be otherwise if I believed them to be something of a wholly different nature. At this point a question of degree arises as to when a difference in qualities amounts to a difference in kind. That is a matter for a jury who would probably decide it sensibly in favour of the genuinely innocent but against the guilty." [1969] 2 A.C. 256 at 305

The items in question must in every respect be physically distinct to exculpate the defendant of criminal liability (see also *R v McNamara* (1988) 87 Cr. App. R. 246). With regard to containers, the general rule of law is that a defendant will be held to have knowledge of anything in a container which is in his possession, as long as he thinks that there is something in the container. However, if the defendant thinks the container is empty, then knowledge will not be imputed. In *Warner*, it was held that knowledge will be imputed if the defendant had an opportunity to acquaint himself with knowledge of the contents of the container, but did not. It is a question for the jury to decide. Lord Pearce said:

> "The situation with regard to containers presents further problems. If a man is in possession of the contents of a package, *prima facie* his possession of the package leads to the strong inference that he is in possession of its contents. But can this be rebutted by evidence that he was mistaken as to its contents? As in the case of goods that have been 'planted' in his pocket without his knowledge, so I do not think that he is in possession of contents which are quite different in kind from what he believed. Thus the *prima facie* assumption is discharged if he proves (or raises a real doubt in the matter) either (a) that he was a servant or bailee who had no right to open it and no reason to suspect that its contents were illicit or were drugs or (b) that although he was the owner he had no knowledge of (including a genuine mistake as to) its actual contents or of their illicit nature and that he received them innocently and also that he had had no reasonable opportunity since receiving the package of acquainting himself with its actual contents. For a man takes over a package or suitcase at risk as to its contents being unlawful if he does not immediately examine it (if he is entitled to

do so). As soon as may be he should examine it and if he finds the contents suspicious reject possession by either throwing them away or by taking immediate sensible steps for their disposal." [1969] 2 A.C. 256 at 305–306

Essentially, an inference will be made that the defendant has knowledge of the contents and bears the onus of proving that in fact he did not have knowledge.

The concept of possession is continuous. In *R v Martindale* [1986] 1 W.L.R. 1042, a small amount of cannabis resin was found in the wallet of the defendant, who claimed to have forgotten about it. Notwithstanding that it was found two years after he had first come into possession of it, he was deemed to have possession. He was charged with unlawful possession, contrary to s.5(2) of the Misuse of Drugs Act 1971. The applicant sought a ruling on whether he had a valid defence on the assumption that he had been given the drug over two years previously in Canada, that he did not smoke cannabis, and had completely forgotten about it so that he could not be said to be in possession. The trial judge held that the assumed facts could not constitute a defence, which resulted in the defendant pleading guilty and he was thus convicted. He appealed against the conviction on the ground that possession did not exist in the absence of knowledge of the article's presence and nature, and that knowledge did not exist if the defendant had forgotten that he had the article in his possession. Lord Lane C.J. stated:

> "It is true that a man does not necessarily possess every article which he may have in his pocket. If for example some evil minded person secretly slips a portion of cannabis resin into the pocket of another without the other's knowledge, the other is not in law in possession of the cannabis ... Here the appellant himself put the cannabis in his wallet knowing what it was and put the wallet into his pocket. In our judgment, subject to the authorities, to which reference will have to be made in a moment, he remained in possession, even though his memory of the presence of the drug had faded or disappeared altogether. Possession does not depend upon the alleged possessor's powers of memory. Nor does possession come and go as memory revives or fails. If it were to do so, a man with a poor memory would be acquitted, he with the good memory would be convicted." [1986] 1 W.L.R. 1042 at 1044

On the facts of the case, the Court of Appeal upholding the conviction, held that although a person did not necessarily possess every article which he might have in his pockets, possession did not depend on the powers of memory of the defendant and did not come and go as memory revived and faded. Consequently, since the defendant had himself placed the drug in his wallet knowing it was cannabis, he was then in possession of it and he remained in possession, even though his memory of its presence had faded.

CRIMINAL LIABILITY FOR OMISSIONS

The general rule is that there can be no liability for failing to act, unless at the time of the failure to act the defendant was under a legal duty to take positive action. Unless a statute or common law specifically imposes a duty upon a person to act in a particular way towards another, a mere failure to act will not lead to criminal liability. The legal distinction between positive acts and omissions was highlighted in *Airedale N.H.S. Trust v Bland* [1993] 1 A.C. 789, in which the House of Lords held that euthanasia by means of positive steps to end a patient's life, such as administering a drug to bring about his death, is unlawful. However, withdrawing medical treatment, including artificial feeding, from an insensate patient with no hope of recovery when it is known that the result will be a hastening of the patient's demise is lawful if it is in the patient's best interests not to prolong his life.

If the defendant fails to perform a legal obligation, then criminal liability may be imposed on the basis that his failure to act has resulted in personal harm or damage to property. Most criminal offences are incapable of being committed by omission and require some act by the defendant, e.g. the offence of burglary. However, the offences of murder and manslaughter can be committed by omission, e.g. intentionally failing to feed a child or other person in your care may be classified as murder or manslaughter. The Superior Courts have been reluctant to extend this principle to other forms of harm against the person, most notably assault.

At common law there was a reluctance to impose criminal liability for omissions on the basis that criminal law serves to prevent individuals from causing harm by a positive act. Common law was not particularly concerned with promoting good acts as such, but was rather concerned with the legally culpable as opposed to individuals who are morally culpable. In order to be held criminally liable at common law based on omission liability, the defendant must have been under a positive duty to act. Many civil law jurisdictions have made it an offence for individuals to fail to take steps which one could take without the risk of personal injury, to save another from death or injury. However, unlike many European countries that have a "general rescue duty", there is no legal duty in common law jurisdictions on all persons to assist others whose lives or property are at risk, even if we are in a position to do so at no risk or inconvenience to ourselves. Thus, a stranger can watch a child drowning in a pond when he could easily rescue the child without being criminally liable, therefore avoiding a conviction for a criminal offence.

Common law gradually imposed criminal liability for failure to act when the defendant was under a legal duty to perform a positive duty. As a general rule, omission liability in criminal law is based on a duty to take action, and these legal duties can arise under contract, common law or statute.

CONTRACTUAL DUTY

Where a person is under a positive duty to act because of his obligations under a contract, his failure to perform the contractual duty can form the basis of criminal liability. This principle is illustrated in *R v Pittwood* (1902) 19 T.L.R. 37, in which the defendant, who was employed as a gatekeeper at a railway crossing, was responsible for ensuring that the gate was closed when a train was approaching. On the day of the incident, he opened the level-crossing gates so as to allow a cart to pass, but then went off to his lunch and forgot to close the gate (unlawful conduct within s.34 of the Offences against the Person Act 1861). A short time later, a hay-cart crossed the railway tracks and was struck by a train, with the result that a person was killed. The defendant was convicted of manslaughter and appealed against his conviction on the basis that he only owed a duty of care to his employers, that is, the railway company by whom he was contracted. The court held the fact that the victim was not a party to the contract was irrelevant. In finding him guilty of manslaughter, the court held that his omission was gross and criminally negligent as he was employed to keep the railway crossing gate shut so as to protect the public. In other words, his defence of privity of contract was rejected because the very nature of his contract of employment involved a duty of care to the public. This was not merely a case of nonfeasance (failing to act) but misfeasance (acting grossly negligent). The defendant breached his duty, not by opening the gate per se, but rather by neglecting to close it again. Wright J. was clearly of the opinion that the defendant's conduct amounted to gross and criminal negligence as he was paid to keep the gate shut and to protect the public against the dangers of passing trains.

DUTY ARISING FROM A RELATIONSHIP

Parents owe a duty of care to their children, and presumably, children over the age of responsibility and of full mental capacity owe a corresponding duty to their parents. Other close relationships, whether of a familial, domestic, or business nature, may also impose similar legal duties and failure to fulfil those duties will result in the imposition of criminal liability where harm is caused as a result of that failure.

Where there is a close personal relationship, there is a duty owed independent of any assumption of responsibility. In *R v Senior* [1899] 1 Q.B. 283, the defendant was a member of a religious organisation that believed that any form of medication was immoral as it constituted a lack of faith in God. His eight-month-old son contracted pneumonia and the defendant refused treatment. The child subsequently died following the failure by the defendant to call a doctor in circumstances where it was contrary to his religious beliefs to do so. The Court of Crown Cases Reserved held that there was evidence that the defendant had wilfully neglected the child in a manner likely to cause injury to the child's health. Therefore, having caused or accelerated the child's death, he was properly convicted of manslaughter.

VOLUNTARY ASSUMPTION OF CARE

A common law duty of care arises where there is a relationship of reliance between defendant and victim. If someone voluntarily assumes responsibility for another person, then they also assume the positive duty to act for the general welfare of that person, and may be liable for omissions which prove fatal. A positive duty to act may also arise from the defendant's voluntary assumption of responsibility for the helpless and infirm. In *R v Nicholls* (1874) 13 Cox C.C. 75, Brett J. directed the jury that:

> "... if a grownup person chooses to undertake the charge of a human creature, helpless either from infancy ... or other infirmity, he is bound to execute that charge without ... wicked negligence." (1874) 13 Cox C.C. 75 at 76

The principle was applied in *R v Instan* [1893] 1 Q.B. 450, in which a niece failed to provide medical or other assistance to her aunt who suffered from gangrene, with the result that she was unable to do anything for herself for the 10 days preceding her death. The Court of Crown Cases Reserved held that as there was a duty imposed upon the defendant, under the circumstances, to supply the deceased with the necessities of life and, as the death of the deceased had been accelerated by the neglect of such duty, the defendant was properly convicted of manslaughter.

In *R v Gibbins and Proctor* (1918) 13 Cr. App. R. 134, the wife of the first defendant had left him and he began living with the second defendant. They both had children, all of whom lived in the same house. Despite the fact that they were reasonably well off, one of the first defendant's daughters was starved to death while the others were well cared for. They were convicted of murder, and on appeal the first defendant argued that he had provided money to the second for the upkeep of the children. The Court of Appeal held that this was not sufficient, that he should have known that his daughter was starving, and that he should have come to her aid. The court held that the second defendant had taken charge of the child, and having taken on this responsibility, it was her duty to ensure that she was adequately cared for.

R v Stone and Dobinson [1977] Q.B. 354 involved a peculiar set of circumstances. The deceased was an old lady who lived with her brother and his housekeeper, who was his mistress. The brother was of low intelligence, with failing senses. The deceased paid for her lodging, but had a fear of putting on weight and refused to eat proper meals. She became bedridden, and the second defendant attempted to help her by cleaning her and calling a doctor, which was unsuccessful. She was found dead in her room in appalling conditions, and a doctor gave evidence that, had she received help two weeks before her death, she might have lived. The defendants argued that neither of them had accepted responsibility for her welfare and that she was a lodger who died through her own eccentricity. The Court of Appeal held that the deceased was a blood relative of the first defendant and that the second defendant had made attempts to help her. Accordingly, it was acceptable for a jury to conclude that they had accepted responsibility for her. Lane L.J. stated:

> "The duty which a defendant has undertaken is a duty of caring for the health and welfare of the infirm person. What the prosecution have to prove is a breach of that duty in such circumstances that the jury feel convinced that the defendant's conduct can properly be described as reckless, that is to say a reckless disregard of danger to the health and welfare of the infirm person. Mere inadvertence is not enough. The defendant must be proved to have been indifferent to an obvious risk of injury to health, or actually to have foreseen the risk but to have determined nevertheless to run it." [1977] Q.B. 354 at 363

In view of the fact that the defendants had accepted responsibility for the deceased, they were under a positive duty to act in her best interests and as a result of failing to do so, they were convicted of manslaughter. A conviction in this instance is justified because the defendants had acted recklessly and were criminally negligent. If they had acted intentionally, they would have been guilty of murder. *Stone and Dobinson* may be contrasted with *R v Lowe* [1973] Q.B. 702, in which the Court of Appeal quashed a conviction for manslaughter in respect of a father who was of low intelligence and had failed to summon a doctor for his sick child. Phillimore L.J. explained that:

> "... there is a clear distinction between an act of omission and an act of commission likely to cause harm. Whatever may be the position with regard to the latter it does not follow that the same is true of the former. In other words, if I strike a child in a manner likely to cause harm it is right that, if the child dies, I may be charged with manslaughter. If, however, I omit to do something with the result that it suffers injury to

health which results in its death, we think that a charge of manslaughter should not be an inevitable consequence, even if the omission is deliberate." [1973] Q.B. 702 at 709

Thus, it appears that omission liability would require a higher degree of mens rea. This decision is questionable.

While most cases deal with circumstances where there is a blood relationship, this is not always necessary to secure a conviction. If the prosecution relies on criminal negligence by omission, then the emphasis must be placed on the obligation to establish the existence of a legal duty and not simply a moral obligation. There must be a personal legal duty of such a nature that the natural and ordinary consequence of a breach of that duty is a real danger to life. In *R v Taktak* [1988] 14 N.S.W.L.R. 226, the defendant hired a prostitute to attend a party that he subsequently departed from, leaving the prostitute there. He subsequently returned and found her unconscious as a result of having taken heroin. He took her away, attempted to revive her and ultimately tried to call a doctor, but she was already dead. He was convicted on the basis that, by taking her away, and removing the possibility of help from others, the defendant had assumed responsibility for her and was therefore rightfully convicted of manslaughter. On appeal, the issue was whether the defendant had voluntarily assumed the care of the deceased and so secluded the helpless person as to prevent others from rendering aid. The New South Wales Court of Criminal Appeal said the defendant:

> "... may also incur liability for an offence which is defined in terms of the doing of a positive act, by virtue of an omission to act, where the common law or a statute expressed or by implication imposed upon the defendant a duty to act. Thus, although manslaughter is usually defined in terms of the doing of an act causing death, and indeed, it is usually committed by a person so acting, it can be committed by an omission to act." [1988] 14 N.S.W.L.R. 226 at 237

Carruthers J. said that omitting to obtain medical treatment for the deceased was conscious and voluntary. The defendant owed a duty of care as he placed the deceased in his exclusive custody and control, thus removing her from medical assistance and the aid of others. However, the question of time was also at issue in this case as it was not known if there had been enough time to assess the deceased's health. Yeldham J. stated that there may not have been enough time for medical assistance to come, and mere negligence or inadvertence would not be enough for the imposition of criminal liability; there must have been "wicked negligence". The decision in *Taktak* sets out the law pertaining to criminal negligence in circumstances where a person assumed the duty of care by removing all other avenues of assistance and then failed to provide the necessities of life.

DUTY ARISING FROM THE CREATION OF A PERILOUS SITUATION

If the defendant accidentally commits an act that causes harm and subsequently becomes aware of the danger that he has created, there arises a duty to act reasonably to avert that danger. If the defendant's conduct endangers a person, property, liberty or any other interest protected by criminal law and the defendant is aware that he has created that danger, then he is under a duty to take reasonable steps to prevent the potential resulting harm. While the conduct may have been performed in the absence of fault, if the defendant fails to intervene, his initial act will be deemed to have caused the resulting harm. In R v Miller [1983] 2 A.C. 161, the defendant was squatting in a house and on one particular night he went to sleep while holding a lit cigarette in his hand. The mattress upon which he was sleeping began to smoulder, thus waking up the defendant who then failed to extinguish the mattress, instead moving to another room to sleep. The house was destroyed by fire and the defendant was charged with arson. He was convicted by the trial court and his appeal against conviction was dismissed by both the Court of Criminal Appeal and the House of Lords. The House of Lords per Lord Diplock said that there was:

> "... no rational ground for excluding from conduct capable of giving rise to criminal liability, conduct which consists of failing to take measures that lie within one's power to counteract a danger that one has oneself created, if at the time of such conduct one's state of mind is such as constitutes a necessary ingredient of the offence." [1983] 2 A.C. 161 at 176

The defendant was convicted of arson for failing to take reasonable steps to extinguish the fire, which he had accidentally started. In other words, the defendant had created a dangerous situation and had failed to take reasonable steps to counteract that danger.

PUBLIC DUTY

The principle of omission liability in criminal law has been extended to individuals acting in an official capacity. In R v Dytham [1979] Q.B. 722, the defendant was a police officer on duty who saw the deceased being ejected from a nightclub and subsequently being kicked and beaten to death. He did not make any attempt to intervene and assist the deceased. The Court of

Appeal held that where a holder of a public office wilfully fails to perform any duty that common law or statute requires him to perform, he is guilty of that offence. Widgery L.J. stated:

> "In the present case it was not suggested that the appellant could not have summoned or sought assistance to help the victim or to arrest his assailants. The charge as framed left this answer open to him. Not surprisingly he did not seek to avail himself of it, for the facts spoke strongly against any such answer. The allegation made was not of mere non-feasance but of deliberate failure and wilful neglect. This involves an element of culpability which is not restricted to corruption or dishonesty but which must be of such a degree that the misconduct impugned is calculated to injure the public interest so as to call for condemnation and punishment. Whether such a situation is revealed by the evidence is a matter that a jury has to decide. It puts no heavier burden upon them than when in more familiar contexts they are called upon to consider whether driving is dangerous or a publication is obscene or a place of public resort is a disorderly house ...". [1979] Q.B. 722 at 727–728

The defendant had a common law duty to intervene to save the deceased's life because of the office which he held. This issue was considered by the Irish High Court in *People (DPP) v Bartley*, unreported, High Court, June 13, 1997, where the court dealt with a case involving the sexual abuse of a woman by her stepbrother. She had previously made a complaint to the Gardaí who had apparently responded appallingly. Because of this, she found herself in a cycle of abuse and depression. Carney J. explicitly endorsed the *Dytham* ruling in the following terms:

> "It is an indictable offence at common law for a public officer wilfully and without reasonable excuse or justification to neglect to perform a duty imposed on him either by common law or statute. That this is so was most recently confirmed in *R v Dytham* ...".

Thus, if a member of the Gardaí receives a credible complaint that a serious criminal offence has been committed, that member is under a common law duty to investigate it. Failure to perform a lawful duty with resulting harm will render the individual liable to prosecution (cf. *JR v Minister for Justice, Equality and Law Reform* [2007] 2 I.R. 748). This principle of criminal liability is equally applicable to associated public service employees for failing to perform statutory duties which might endanger the safety, health and welfare of individuals in precarious circumstances.

Failure to report the commission of an offence

Offences of which an omission to act is a constituent element are statutory offences because the common law did not recognise an omission to act as something which could lead to criminal liability, with one exception, misprision of felony, that is, failure to report the commission of serious criminal offences. However, s.3 of the Criminal Law Act 1997 abolished the distinction between felony and misdemeanour, and therefore the common law principle of misprision of felony was abolished by this provision. Consequently, the general common law duty to report the commission of serious criminal offences was abolished. This created a lacuna in criminal law pertaining to the general duty of citizens to report the commission of serious criminal offences. Section 9 of the Offences Against the State (Amendment) Act 1998 created a new offence of "withholding information", which might be of material assistance to the Gardaí in preventing the commission of a "serious offence", or securing the apprehension, prosecution or conviction of offenders. There is a defence in this provision in that a defendant might have a "reasonable excuse" for not disclosing pertinent information to a member of An Garda Síochána.

Failure to comply with statutory obligations

Criminal liability for failing to act will be imposed where the defendant can be shown to have been under a statutory duty to take positive action. In *R v Firth* (1990) 91 Cr. App. R. 217, a doctor was convicted of deceiving a hospital contrary to the English Theft Act 1968 by failing to inform it that certain patients were private patients. There are many statutory offences in Irish criminal law based on omission, for example, failure to provide a breath specimen when stopped on suspicion of drunken driving, or failure to make certain returns under companies and revenue legislation.

CAUSATION

When the definition of an actus reus requires the occurrence of certain consequences, the prosecution must prove that it was the defendant's conduct which caused those consequences to occur. Questions of causation frequently arise in relation to crimes of consequences, also referred to as result crimes.

This is a matter which seldom causes difficulty in practice. However, it can occasionally arise, especially in relation to homicide offences. For instance, *A* seriously assaults *B*, stabbing him with a knife. Consequently, *B* is brought to hospital where he is operated upon, but he dies after the operation. Later, evidence emerges that the surgeon who operated upon *B* was negligent and that if he had followed certain other procedures, there is a good chance that

B might have survived. The issue then is whether *A* should be held criminally liable for *B*'s death. Perhaps the surgeon's negligence was the immediate cause of death. On the other hand, had *A* not stabbed *B* in the first place, the problem would not have arisen. This is the kind of issue that can arise in relation to causation. The issue in such cases is who should be held responsible for *B*'s death: *A* or the medical personnel who treated him? The general principle is that causation is established if the result would not have occurred but for the defendant's conduct. The prosecution must prove that the defendant's behaviour caused the victim's death, although the defendant's conduct need not be the sole or the main cause of death. The victim may also have died while attempting to escape from the defendant.

Factual Causation

The general rule is that before a person can be held liable, the result would not have occurred "but for" that person's conduct. Another way of putting it is that the defendant's conduct must have been a sine qua non for bringing about the result. If the result, such as death, would have occurred in any event, the defendant will not be responsible. To establish causation in fact, the "but for" test established in *R v White* [1910] 2 K.B. 124 must be applied. The defendant put cyanide into his mother's drink with the intention of killing her. She drank the contents of the glass, but died of heart failure before the poison could take effect. Medical evidence showed that she died as a result of a heart attack and not as a result of the poison. He was acquitted of her murder because he had not caused the result (death). In other words, he did not commit the actus reus. He was, however, convicted of attempted murder, but he would have been convicted of that in any event, whether she lived or died, as an attempt is committed when somebody endeavours, successfully or otherwise, to bring about a prohibited result.

The criminal law recognises that there may be concurrent wrongdoers. As a general rule, if the result such as death would not have occurred "but for" the act of the defendant, even though a subsequent train of events occurred, the defendant's conduct must be a cause, and not just a minimal cause (de minimus). There may be many factors, or minimal causes, but, if the defendant's act was a cause, then he may be found guilty of the offence charged. A defendant can be convicted even though others have contributed to the result. This principle was recognised in one of the leading cases *R v Cato* [1976] 1 W.L.R. 110 at 116, where the defendant was convicted of manslaughter: he had supplied heroin to the deceased who subsequently overdosed. While both the defendant and the deceased had overdosed on the heroin, the defendant was saved. The Court of Criminal Appeal per Lord Widgery C.J said:

> "As a matter of law, it was sufficient if the prosecution could establish that it was a cause, provided it was a cause outside the [de minimis] range, and effectively bearing upon the acceleration of the moment of the victim's death."

Later in the judgment, the court referred to the requirement that the cause be substantial, that is, outside the de minimis range. The court held that a causal link had been established where the defendant injected the deceased who subsequently died from the overdose.

An issue that may occasionally arise in a medical context is whether a medical physician can be said to cause a person's death by shortening that person's life, despite the fact that the victim may already be facing death from natural causes. A doctor may administer palliative treatment, even if it may result in the shortening of life. The test is one of reasonableness in all the circumstances. In *R v Adams* [1957] Crim. L.R. 365, Devlin J. directed the jury that there is no special defence justifying a doctor in giving drugs which would shorten a person's life in the case of severe pain. Devlin J. explained that:

> "If life were cut short by weeks or months it was just as much murder as if it were cut short by years."

He continued:

> "But that does not mean that a doctor aiding the sick or dying has to calculate in minutes or hours, or perhaps in days or weeks, the effect on a patient's life of the medicine which he administers. If the first purpose of medicine – the restoration of health – can no longer be achieved, there is still much for the doctor to do, and he is entitled to do all that is proper and necessary to relieve pain and suffering even if measures he takes may incidentally shorten life." [1957] Crim. L.R. 365 at 375

The general rule of criminal liability is that it is as much an offence to shorten a person's life by days or weeks as it is to shorten it by months or years.

Factual causation is straightforward enough, but the situation gets more complicated when the victim is particularly vulnerable and when there is some intervening act, such as the negligent medical intervention mentioned in the example given above.

Legal causation

The issue here is whether the chain of causation was broken by intervening acts, that is, a novus actus interveniens. The courts have demonstrated a reluctance to shift blame away from the person who caused the initial wrongdoing, unless the negligence of a third party was of a very high level. The general rule is that a natural event occurring after the defendant's conduct may be treated as breaking the chain of causation, but not if the event was reasonably foreseeable. In *R v Smith* [1959] 2 Q.B. 35, the Courts-Martial Appeal Court held that the defendant's act would be regarded as the cause in law if it could be shown that it was the operating and substantial cause of the victim's death (see below).

Sometimes, after the defendant's conduct, there is an intervening act or event before the victim's death occurs which contributes to the death. Criminal law must therefore consider the legal effect of an intervening act and whether this can break the chain of causation. As a general rule, the defendant is not responsible for the death where the victim dies as a result of some subsequent act, unconnected with the defendant's conduct, which would have caused the death on its own, even if the defendant had not inflicted the original injury on the victim. However, not every intervening act will relieve the defendant from criminal liability for the subsequent death.

1. Voluntary intervening act of a third party

This will normally sever the chain of causation. However, the courts are often willing to find that an act was not voluntary because of a lack of capacity or because the third party acted out of necessity, duress or compulsion.

2. Incompetent medical treatment

Problems of causation arise pertaining to negligent medical treatment of the original injury in homicide cases. This becomes an issue in homicide cases when the victim of an assault dies as a result of negligent medical treatment. Consider the following two examples. In the first example, *A* assaults *B*, leaving *B* lying on the roadway. Consequently, *B* dies, though partly, it would seem, from exposure to the elements. In the second example, *A* assaults *B*. Consequently, *B* is brought to hospital on a stretcher, but those carrying him let him fall and he dies as a result. Should *A* be found guilty of murder or manslaughter in these circumstances? The basic principle is that a person will be found guilty of homicide if his conduct is the "operating cause and substantial cause" of the death, although some other cause may also be operating. Another way in which it is sometimes put is that the conduct of the defendant must have contributed significantly to the death of the victim, or other prohibited result.

In *R v Jordan* (1956) 40 Cr. App. R. 152, the defendant had stabbed the victim who was admitted to hospital and died eight days later. In the Court of Appeal, there was fresh evidence that the death had not been caused by the stab wound, which had healed at the time of death, but by the introduction, with a view to preventing infection, of a drug called terramycin after the deceased man had shown that he was intolerant to it, and by the intravenous introduction of large quantities of liquid, which filled his lungs causing pneumonia. This treatment, according to the evidence, was "palpably wrong". The court held that if the jury had heard this evidence they would have felt precluded from saying they were satisfied that the death was caused by the stab wound and quashed the murder conviction. The conviction was quashed, although the court was at pains to point out that this was an exceptional case and that death resulting from "normal treatment" would not relieve the person who inflicted the original injury of responsibility for the death.

It was the decision in *R v Smith* [1959] 2 Q.B. 35, that provided the leading test of "a substantial and operating cause", that is, not necessarily the sole cause but that which leads directly to the victim's death. In the course of a fight in an army barracks, Smith stabbed the victim with a bayonet. Others carried the victim to a medical station but dropped him twice on the way. As the medical personnel were busy with others injured in the fight, they did not give the victim the kind of attention that he needed and he died. They did not realise that one of the wounds had pierced a lung and caused a haemorrhage. Smith's conviction for murder was upheld on the basis of the "substantial and operating cause" principle. The medical personnel administered treatment to the victim, which in light of the information regarding the victim's condition available at the time of the trial, was "thoroughly bad and might well have affected his chances of recovery" ([1959] 2 Q.B. 35 at 52 per Lord Parker C.J.). The defendant's conviction for murder was upheld by the Court of Appeal. Lord Parker explained that:

> "... if at the time of death the original wound is still an operating cause and a substantial cause, then the death can properly be said to be the result of the wound, albeit that some other cause of death is also operating. Only if it can be said that the original wounding is merely the setting in which another cause operates can it be said that the death does not result from the wound. Putting it in another way, only if the second cause is so overwhelming as to make the original wound merely part of the history can it be said that the death does not flow from the wound." [1959] 2 Q.B. 35 at 43

The general rule of causation is that the defendant will be criminally liable if the unlawful conduct is a significant cause of death. *Jordan* was distinguished by the Court of Appeal in *Smith* as a "very particular case depending upon its exact facts".

R v Malcherek; R v Steel [1981] 1 W.L.R. 690, involved a doctor disconnecting a life support machine. The defendant had inflicted injuries upon the victim which resulted in a brain damage. She was put on a life support machine. A number of days later, after carrying out a series of tests, the doctors disconnected the life support machine and 30 minutes later she was pronounced dead. The trial judge withdrew the question of causation from the jury, ruling that there was no evidence on which they could decide that the defendant did not cause the victim's death. On appeal, it was argued that there was evidence on which the jury could have found that the doctors caused the death by switching off the life support machine. The Court of Appeal dismissed the defendant's appeal. There was no doubt that the injury inflicted by the defendant was an operating and substantial cause of death. Whether or not the doctors were also involved in the cause of death was immaterial. The *Smith* principle was applied.

R v Cheshire [1991] 1 W.L.R. 844 is one of the leading English authorities and is less tolerant of arguments based on intervening acts. Again, it was a case in which there appeared to have been some medical negligence in the manner in which the victim of a shooting was treated. The bullet wounds which the defendant had inflicted upon the victim had ceased to be a threat to life and there was evidence that the victim's death was caused by the tracheotomy, performed and negligently treated by the doctors, with the result that it had narrowed his windpipe and caused asphyxiation. The Court of Appeal held that the trial judge had misdirected the jury by instructing them that only recklessness on the part of the doctors would break the chain of causation, but upheld the conviction on the ground that, "rare complication ... was a direct consequence of the appellant's acts which remained a significant cause of his death" ([1991] 1 W.L.R. 844 at 852 per Bedlam L.J.). Bedlam L.J. opined:

> "It is sufficient for the judge to tell the jury that they must be satisfied that the [prosecution] have proved the acts of the accused caused the death of the deceased, adding that the accused's acts need not be the sole cause or even the main cause of death, it being sufficient that his acts contributed significantly to the result. Even though negligence in the treatment of the victim was the immediate cause of his death, the jury should not regard it as excluding the responsibility of the defendant unless the negligent treatment was so independent of his acts, and in itself so potent in causing death, that they regard the contribution made by his acts as insignificant." [1991] 1 W.L.R. 844 at 852

It will be rare for an intervening act to relieve the person who inflicted the original injury of liability. The test proposed by the court is not easy to apply. It is difficult to know what "so independent" and "so potent" mean. This appears to be the general approach adopted by the Irish courts as well. In

People (AG) v McGrath (1960) 1 Frewen 192, the intervention of persons who brought the victim of an assault to hospital did not relieve the defendant of responsibility for murder. The Court of Criminal Appeal per Maguire C.J. said:

> "Any such interference was admittedly a human and well-intentioned act, brought about by the wrongful act of the applicant; far from being a new act negativing causation or cutting the chain of causation between the blow struck and the death, it formed a normal link in the chain." (1960) Frewen 192 at 194

This authority has frequently been cited by the Irish courts in the meantime.

3. Natural consequences of the defendant's criminal act

A victim can die as a natural result of the defendant's conduct in circumstances where death is foreseeable and likely to occur in the normal course of events. In these circumstances, the defendant will still be criminally liable as having caused the death. For instance, if a person is attacked and left lying on the road, the assailant will be responsible for the death if the person dies from loss of blood, exposure, an infection of the wounds, or if he is run over by a vehicle. However, the defendant would not be liable if the person was struck by lightning, killed by another assailant or killed by a collapsing building during an earthquake, which are unforeseeable events. Human intervention, where it consists of a foreseeable act instinctively done for the purposes of self-preservation, or in the execution of a legal duty, does not break the chain of causation. Thus, in *R v Pagett* (1983) 76 Cr. App. R. 279, the defendant, in order to resist lawful arrest, held a girl in front of him as a shield and then shot at armed policemen. The police instinctively fired back and inadvertently killed the girl. The Court of Appeal held that the defendant's act had caused the death and that the reasonable actions of a third party (armed police) by way of self-defence could not be regarded as a novus actus interveniens. In other words, the defendant had caused the death, as the intervening act had been a foreseeable consequence of his criminal act which had not broken the chain of causation. The defendant was convicted of manslaughter.

4. Conduct or condition of the victim

If the intervening act is a characteristic of the victim, then it does not have to be foreseeable and will not break the chain of causation. The so-called "thin skull" which provides that a defendant must take his victim as he finds him, is applicable. Thus, if the defendant assaults the victim on the head with a degree of force that would usually cause nothing more than slight bruising, but because the victim has an unusually thin skull it causes the victim to suffer a fractured skull and brain damage, the defendant cannot rely on evidence of the victim's physical weakness to show the chain of causation has been broken.

With regard to the condition of the victim, the general rule in "eggshell skull" type cases is that you must take your victim as you find them. Suppose A hits B on the head. The blow is such that it would not cause any significant harm to an ordinary, healthy person, but in this case B dies because he suffers from a particular condition that makes him especially vulnerable to such injury. The issue then is whether A caused B's death. A will probably argue that he did not and that it was B's physical condition or disability which really caused B's death, as opposed to some more minor injury. Criminal law will not accept this argument. The so-called "thin-skull" principle applies in criminal law as it does in tort. One of the leading statements is that of Parke J. in *R v Martin* (1832) 5 C&P 123, where he stated:

> "It is said that the deceased was in a bad state of health; but that is perfectly immaterial, as, if the prisoner was so unfortunate as to accelerate her death, he must answer for it." (1832) 5 C&P 123 at 130

In *R v Hayward* (1908) 21 Cox C.C. 692, the defendant was charged with the manslaughter of his wife. Following a domestic argument, he had chased her out of the house and on to the road. She fell and he kicked her on the arm. She later died. Medical evidence showed that the injury to her arm had not been the cause of her death, but that she had suffered from a thyroid condition, which could cause a person to die from fright, strong emotion or physical exertion. Her husband was convicted of manslaughter. The trial judge said:

> "The abnormal state of the deceased's health did not affect the question of whether the prisoner knew or did not know of it if it were proved to the satisfaction of the jury that the death was accelerated by the prisoner's illegal act."

This principle applies not only to pre-existing medical conditions, but also to mental states, religious beliefs, or the conduct of the victim. It may be necessary, in some cases, for the trial judge to give a jury further instructions on the issue of causation, particularly in cases where it is possible that the victim's reaction was disproportionate to the circumstances of the defendant's threat. In *R v Roberts* (1971) 56 Cr. App. R. 95, the victim jumped out of a moving car so as to escape being indecently assaulted. The Court of Criminal

Appeal held that the chain of causation could only be broken if the victim's action was so unreasonable that no reasonable person could be expected to foresee it. Stephenson L.J. stated:

> "The test is: Was it the natural result of what the alleged assailant said and did, in the sense that it was something that could reasonably have been foreseen as the consequence of what he was saying or doing?" (1971) 56 Cr. App. R. 95 at 102

He continued:

> "As it was put in one of the old cases, it had got to be shown to be his act, and if of course the victim does something so 'daft,' in the words of the appellant in this case, or so unexpected, not that this particular assailant did not actually foresee it but that no reasonable man could be expected to foresee it, then it is only in a very remote and unreal sense a consequence of his assault, it is really occasioned by a voluntary act on the part of the victim which could not reasonably be foreseen and which breaks the chain of causation between the assault and the harm or injury."

It was held that the victim's conduct was a reasonably foreseeable response. Consequently, the chain of causation will only be broken if the victim's actions were unreasonable. In *R v Corbett* [1996] Crim. L.R. 594, the defendant had been out drinking with a friend, a 26-year-old man with low intelligence who suffered infrequently with mental illness. They had an argument and the defendant began to hit the victim. The victim ran away, fell into the gutter and was struck and killed by a passing car. At the defendant's trial for manslaughter, the trial judge directed the jury to consider whether the victim's actions were reasonably foreseeable and whether his conduct might be something expected of a person as intoxicated as he was. On appeal, the defendant contended that the trial judge should have directed the jury to consider whether the victim's death was the natural consequence of the defendant's conduct, and, if any other conclusion was possible, then the defendant should have been acquitted. Relying on *Roberts*, the Court of Appeal dismissed the appeal and held that the judge had properly directed the jury on the issue of foreseeability.

In *R v Blaue* [1975] 1 W.L.R. 1411, the defendant stabbed the victim, a young girl, and the stab wound penetrated her lung. She was brought to hospital where she was told that a blood transfusion and an operation could save her life. As she was a Jehova's Witness, she refused the blood transfusion and died. The defendant was convicted of manslaughter and appealed on the ground that the victim's refusal to have a blood transfusion, being unreasonable, had severed the chain of causation. The Court of Appeal held that the trial judge had correctly instructed the jury that the wound was a cause of death. Lawton L.J. opined:

> "It has long been the policy of the law that those who use violence on other people must take their victims as they find them. This in our judgment means the whole man, not just the physical man. It does not lie in the mouth of the assailant to say that his victim's religious beliefs which inhibited him from accepting certain kinds of treatment were unreasonable. The question for decision is what caused her death. The answer is the stab wound. The fact that the victim refused to stop this end coming about did not break the casual connection between the act and death." [1975] 1 W.L.R. 1411 at 1415

The conviction was upheld. The essential point here is that the victim's death was caused by the stab wound inflicted by the defendant. Some commentators have criticised this decision as being unduly harsh considering that the victim had unreasonably refused medical treatment.

This principle also applies to so-called "manslaughter by flight" cases where the victim died while trying to escape from an attack or threatened attack. In *R v Mackie* (1973) 57 Cr. App. R. 453, the defendant was looking after a three-year-old boy. It was alleged that the boy feared ill-treatment at the hands of the defendant and died as a result of falling down the stairs while running away from him. The conviction for manslaughter was upheld. Stephenson L.J. stated:

> "The attempt to escape must be the natural consequence of an unlawful act and that unlawful act must be such as all sober and reasonable people would inevitably recognise must subject the other person to, at least, the risk of some harm resulting therefrom, albeit not serious harm." (1973) 57 Cr. App. R. 453 at 460

Thus, in such "flight" cases, the English superior courts have adopted a reasonable foresight test, which was notably absent from *Blaue* (see also *DPP v Daley* [1979] 2 W.L.R. 239).

5. Drug abuse cases

As stated above, the general rule is that the victim's own conduct might break the chain of causation, but the defendant must take his victim as he finds him. However, a difficulty arises where a drug addict assists another who subsequently dies as a result of a drug overdose. In *R v Dias* (2002) 2 Cr.

App. R. 96, the defendant prepared a syringe filled with heroin and then gave it to the victim who injected himself and died as a result. The Court of Appeal quashed the defendant's conviction for manslaughter. Whereas possession of the heroin was an unlawful act, there was no direct causal link between possession and the death. Furthermore, the court held that, even if the victim's act of taking illegal drugs was a criminal offence, the defendant would not have been guilty of constructive manslaughter as "self-manslaughter" is not a criminal offence. The Court of Appeal then considered whether the defendant had caused the victim's death by the criminal act of supplying him with a dangerous and illegal drug. While the court quashed the defendant's conviction, as this issue had not been adequately considered by the trial court, the court nevertheless suggested that it might be possible in some cases to establish a chain of causation in such drug abuse cases. Keene L.J., stated:

> "Assistance and encouragement is not to be automatically equated with causation. Causation raises questions of fact and degree. The recipient does not have to inject the drug which he is encouraged and assisted to take. He has a choice. It may be that in some circumstances the causative chain will still remain. That is a matter for the jury to decide."
> (2002) 2 Cr. App. R. 96 at 103

It is a matter for the jury to decide whether they are satisfied that the chain of causation has been severed between the defendant's unlawful act and the resultant death (cf. *R v Rogers* [2003] 1 W.L.R. 1374). In *R v Kennedy (No. 2)* [2008] 1 A.C. 269, the House of Lords revisited the issue of unlawful act manslaughter and causation with drug dealers and suppliers of drugs where the victim subsequently died as a result of having taken unlawful and dangerous drugs. The defendant prepared a syringe for the victim who injected himself and died of an overdose. The defendant was convicted of unlawful act manslaughter; however, the court's reasoning ignored the problem of causation. As a general rule, where a third party acts in a free, voluntary and informed way and causes the result, this will break the chain of causation for the original defendant. In this case, the act of the victim in injecting himself with the drug was a free, voluntary and informed action. The defendant was not a secondary participant to an unlawful act of the victim, as injecting himself was not unlawful. The House of Lords stated the law on drug dealers and unlawful act manslaughter very clearly and ruled that where a drug dealer supplies drugs and the victim injects themselves and later dies, the drug dealer can never be guilty of unlawful act manslaughter, as the chain of causation is broken.

In *R v Evans (Gemma)* [2009] EWCA Crim. 650, which concerned gross negligence manslaughter and the duty of care owed by the supplier of drugs, the victim was a drug addict whose half-sister obtained drugs from a dealer and supplied them to the victim. The victim overdosed and died. The defendant (the deceased's half-sister) was charged and convicted of gross negligence manslaughter. The Court of Appeal held that the defendant owed a duty of care to the victim to seek help for her and the duty owed was to counteract the situation which the defendant had created by supplying the drugs. The defendant's appeal against conviction was dismissed. Thus, in English criminal law, where a person dies after taking drugs, the supplier will not be convicted of unlawful act manslaughter, but can, following *Evans*, be guilty of gross negligence manslaughter if they fail to "counteract the situation" which they have "created". It remains to be seen what approach the Irish superior courts will adopt.

> **FURTHER READING**
>
> Campbell, Kilcommins and O'Sullivan, *Criminal Law in Ireland: Cases and Commentary* (Dublin: Clarus Press, 2010), Ch.3.
>
> Charleton, "Causation in the Law of Homicide" (1991) 1 (1) I.C.L.J. 68.
>
> Hanly, *An Introduction to Irish Criminal Law,* 2nd edn (Dublin: Gill & Macmillan, 2006), Ch.3.
>
> McAuley, "The Action Component of *Actus Reus*" (1988) 23 Ir. Jur. (N.S.) 218.
>
> McAuley and McCutcheon, *Criminal Liability: A Grammar* (Dublin: Round Hall, 2000), Ch.2.
>
> McCutcheon, "Criminal Liability and the Duty to Remove Danger" (1984) 19 Ir. Jur. (N.S.) 91.
>
> McCutcheon, "Involuntary Conduct and the Case of the Unconscious 'Driver': Reflections on *Jiminez*" (1997) 21 Crim. L.J. 71.
>
> McCutcheon, "Involuntary Conduct and the Criminal Law: the Case of the Unconscious Driver" (1998) 21 (3) *International Journal of Law and Psychiatry* 305.
>
> McCutcheon, "Knowledge and the *Actus Reus* of Possession Offences" (1997) 32 Ir. Jur. (N.S.) 119.
>
> McCutcheon, "Omissions and Criminal Liability" (1993–1995) 28–30 Ir. Jur. (N.S.) 56.

3. Mens Rea

INTRODUCTION

The concept of mens rea incorporates a fault element of legal and moral culpability in the definition of criminal offences and the prosecution must prove that the defendant committed the actus reus with a requisite state of mind. If the defendant had no mens rea, then he will not be convicted unless the offence charged is one of absolute liability.

Mens rea inevitably varies in accordance with the seriousness of the defendant's conduct and the resulting injury to the person or damage to property. There are four principal states of mind which separately or together constitute the necessary mens rea for criminal offences: intention, recklessness, criminal negligence, and knowledge. The statutory definition of a criminal offence will stipulate which of these four mental states is required, but occasionally the superior court decisions explain the requirements of the definition more specifically. Intention and recklessness are the two fault elements that require a defined mental state by the defendant at the time the criminal offence is committed and have proven to be notoriously difficult concepts for the superior courts to grapple with.

MOTIVE AND MENS REA

The criminal law clearly distinguishes between motive and mens rea. The defendant's motive is the reason why he committed the offence and will usually assist the police in the investigation and apprehension of offenders. Mens rea is a core element in the construction of criminal liability, but the defendant's motive is irrelevant. The commission of criminal offences with apparently laudable motives will not excuse the defendant's criminal liability and will not negative the mens rea element of the offence charged. In *People (DPP) v Kelly*, Circuit Court, October 29, 2004; December 2, 2004, the defendant was charged with causing criminal damage without lawful excuse to a Unites States military plane at Shannon Airport. The defendant claimed that she did so to protect the lives of the Iraqi people and that it was an act of protest against what she believed was wrong. The Circuit Criminal Court held that while there was a defence of lawful excuse in criminal law, this did not apply to the case under consideration. She would have to accept the legal consequences of her actions no matter how laudable her aims. The defendant had committed more than civil disobedience and her actions constituted criminal damage. Judge Moran held, that although the defendant was a person of good character driven by ideological motives, this did not excuse her behaviour.

INTENTION

This is often expressed in statutory provisions to mean that the defendant performed the prohibited conduct "knowingly". In the prosecution of serious criminal offences, the factual circumstances may not be contentious and the issue for determination will typically pertain to whether or not the defendant committed the offence. In murder trials, the fundamental issue as to whether or not the defendant intended to kill the victim is key. While the meaning of intention in everyday language might appear straightforward, the jurisprudence of the superior courts in England, Wales, and Ireland, has been unclear in defining the concept.

DIRECT AND OBLIQUE INTENTION

Criminal law distinguishes between direct intent and indirect or oblique intent. Direct intent (also known as purpose intent) is where the defendant intended a specific consequence of the unlawful and voluntary act, that is, where the consequences of a defendant's actions are desired. Oblique intent (also known as foresight intent) pertains to situations where the consequence of the defendant's act is foreseen as virtually certain, although it is not necessarily desired. In other words, oblique intent is where the unlawful act has consequences that were not the defendant's primary purpose and, although the defendant might have foreseen them as a probable consequence of the criminal act, he maintains that he did not intend them.

In murder trials, indirect intention pertains to cases where the defendant engaged in objectively dangerous conduct but, nevertheless, asserts that his primary purpose was to achieve a goal other than the death of the victim. Consider the following scenarios: An aeroplane owner decides to make a fraudulent insurance claim on one of his planes. To that end, he plants a bomb on the plane knowing that, when it explodes, some passengers will undoubtedly be killed. In fact, he proceeds with his plan believing that the deaths of some passengers will make his fraudulent insurance claim more realistic. This is direct intention in that the consequences of the defendant's actions (i.e. the deaths of some passengers) are desired. On the other hand, if the aeroplane owner proceeds with his plan, knowing that some passengers will almost certainly die, but wishing that was not the case, this is oblique intention. It is oblique intention because the consequence (the deaths of the passengers) was not planned by the defendant, although he knew that this was a natural and probable consequence of his action in blowing up the plane. Criminal law requires proof of oblique intent (foresight intent) or direct intent. The requirement to prove that it was the defendant's purpose to bring about a particular consequence places a very heavy evidential burden on the prosecution.

English jurisprudence on oblique intention

The jurisprudence from the superior courts in England and Wales provides that foresight of consequences is evidence of intention *only* if the defendant knew that those consequences would certainly occur. It is not sufficient that the defendant merely foresaw a *possibility* of a particular occurrence. The nexus between foresight of consequences and the meaning of intention has been examined in a series of cases in England and Wales by the House of Lords and Court of Appeal.

DPP v Smith [1961] A.C. 290 was authority for the proposition that a person foresaw and intended the natural and probable consequences of his conduct. However, the ruling in *Smith* was widely criticised because it meant that a person intends the natural and probable consequences of his acts. This ruling was subsequently reversed by s.8 of the Criminal Justice Act 1967, which governs how intention or foresight must be proved:

> A court or jury in determining whether a person has committed an offence:
> (a) shall not be bound in law to infer that he intended or foresaw a result of his actions by reason only of its being a natural and probable consequence of those actions; but
> (b) shall decide whether he did intend or foresee that result by reference to all the evidence drawing such inferences from the evidence as appear proper in the circumstances.

If the prosecution endeavours to establish foresight of consequences, the defendant is not to be taken as intending the natural and probable consequences of his act simply because it was natural and probable, although a jury might infer this from the evidence. This is a subjective test and a jury must determine the defendant's intention from the evidence.

In *Hyam v DPP* [1975] A.C. 55, the defendant was romantically involved with a man. When the relationship ended, she became suspicious that the man had entered into a new relationship with another woman and sought to sabotage that relationship. She went to the house where her rival lived, poured petrol through the letter box of the front door and ignited it. She was aware that there were people sleeping in the house and, as a result of her actions, two children died in the fire. She claimed that she had merely intended to frighten her rival. The jury was informed that the necessary intention for murder was present if the defendant "foresaw" death or grievous bodily harm as a "highly probably" result of her conduct, and that it was not necessary to prove that she desired the consequences. The trial judge directed the jury that if they were satisfied that the defendant knew it was "highly probable" that her unlawful conduct would cause death or grievous bodily harm, the prosecution would have proved the necessary intent. The House of Lords agreed and upheld the defendant's conviction for murder. However, the majority differed as to whether the correct test for foresight of consequences was "highly probable", "probable", or merely a "serious risk." According to this decision, the defendant is deemed to have acted with intent if he had performed the prohibited conduct with foresight of consequences.

In *R v Moloney* [1985] A.C. 905, the deceased was killed by his stepson in the course of a contest involving loaded shotguns, to see which of them was quicker on the draw. It was apparent that there was a good relationship between the deceased and the defendant. Lord Bridge stated that foresight of the consequences as being probable or likely should not be equated with intention, although the jury could infer intention from such a state of mind based on the evidence. Lord Bridge also stated, that where the defendant had a purpose other than causing the prohibited harm, but where the result was a likely consequence, the jury should be directed to consider whether the result of the defendant's conduct was a natural consequence and whether the defendant foresaw it as such. If the defendant had foreseen that harm could be caused, then Lord Bridge propounded that it would be proper to infer that he had intended the consequence. The *Moloney* guidelines stipulate that where the jury require a direction from the trial judge, they should be instructed to consider first, whether death was a natural consequence of the defendant's conduct and secondly, whether the defendant foresaw that consequence. If so, then is it a proper inference for the jury to draw that the defendant intended the consequence of his actions?

R v Hancock and Shankland [1986] A.C. 455 concerned two striking miners who pushed a concrete block from a motorway bridge on top of a taxi in which a miner was travelling to work, so as to frighten him. The block hit the taxi's windscreen and killed the driver. The defendants claimed that, in order to frighten the miner, they had intended pushing the block from the bridge onto a different lane of the motorway to the one in which the taxi was travelling. The trial judge directed the jury by reference to Lord Bridge's guidelines in *Moloney*. The defendants were convicted. The Court of Appeal allowed their appeal stating that the trial judge ought to have explained that "natural consequence" meant highly likely. The House of Lords dismissed the prosecution's appeal and disapproved of Lord Bridge's guideline directions as potentially misleading. The direction in *Moloney* was criticised because it failed to refer to the issue of probability of the prohibited consequence occurring. Lord Scarman stated that the jury should have been told that the greater the probability of a consequence, the more likely it is that the consequence was foreseen, and that, if that consequence was foreseen, the greater the probability is that the consequence was intended. However, foresight of consequences should not be equated with intention and the highest degree of probability is only a factor to be considered by the jury taking into account all the evidence, in order to decide if the defendant acted with intent.

The facts of *R v Nedrick* [1986] 1 W.L.R. 1025 were almost identical to those in *Hyam*. The defendant harboured a grudge against a woman. One night, he poured paraffin through her letter box and ignited it. The house was destroyed by fire and one of the occupant's children was killed. The defendant claimed that he had not wanted to kill anyone, but had just wanted to frighten the woman. Lord Lane C.J. framed his direction to the jury in terms of the defendant's appreciation of a virtually certain result. If a defendant thought that the risk to which he was exposing the victim was only slight, then it was relatively easy for the jury to conclude that death or injury was not intended. However, if death or serious injury was a virtually certain consequence of his actions, the jury might find it easy to infer intent. If a defendant realised it was inevitable that his acts would result in death or serious injury, the inference that he intended the result might be overwhelming. Lord Lane framed his guideline direction to juries as a rule of evidence and not as a substantive rule of criminal law. The Court of Appeal accepted that, in most cases, a simple direction to the jury to consider whether or not the defendant had intended to kill or cause serious injury would be sufficient, but there are marginal cases where the defendant's primary motivation for his actions is not to kill but to achieve some other purpose. In these cases, the court held that the jury should be instructed to consider two issues: how probable the consequence that resulted from the defendant's actions was, and whether the defendant foresaw that consequence. The defendant must have foreseen the consequence as a virtual certainty if the inference of intent is to be made by the jury. Lord Lane C.J. stated:

> "Where the charge is murder and in the rare cases where the simple direction is not enough, the jury should be directed that they are not entitled to infer the necessary intention, unless they feel sure that death or serious bodily harm was a virtual certainty (barring some unforeseen intervention) as a result of the defendant's actions and that the defendant appreciated that such was the case." [1986] 1 W.L.R. 1025 at 1028

The Court of Appeal decision in *Nedrick* did not resolve the problematic issue as to the meaning of intention in criminal law and the use of the word "infer" in this context implied that foresight of virtual certainty was not equated with intention. However, the court did state that virtual certainty was the minimum degree of foresight of consequences required to substantiate an inference of intention.

In *R v Walker; R v Hayles* (1990) 90 Cr. App. R. 226, where the defendants threw the victim from a third floor balcony, the trial judge directed the jury that they could infer intention if there was a high degree of probability that the victim would be killed and if the defendants knew "quite well that in doing that there was a high degree of probability" of that happening. The defendants appealed on the ground that the trial judge was confusing foresight of death with an intention to kill and should have directed the jury in the *Nedrick* terms of "virtual certainty". The Court of Appeal did not accept that the reference to the "very high degree of probability" constituted a misdirection to the jury. However, Lloyd L.J. stated that in the rare cases where an expanded direction is required in terms of foresight of consequences, then trial judges should continue to use virtual certainty as the test rather than a test of high probability.

In *R v Wooliln* [1999] 1 A.C. 82, the House of Lords attempted to resolve the dilemma pertaining to the meaning of intention in criminal law. The defendant (father of the child), in a fit of temper, threw his three-month-old child on to a hard surface. The child died and the defendant was convicted of murder. The trial judge instructed the jury in accordance with the *Nedrick* direction. At the end of his summing up, however, the trial judge modified his direction to the jury in terms of appreciation of "a substantial risk". The Court of Appeal dismissed the defendant's appeal, but the House of Lords quashed the conviction. The prosecution had sought to uphold the conviction on the ground that the *Nedrick* guidelines of appreciation of a virtual certainty were an unnecessarily high threshold and prevented the jury from considering all the evidence in the case. However, the House of Lords approved Lord Lane's test subject to replacing the word "infer" with "find", which apparently was in the interests of clarity. Lord Steyn pointed out that the *Nedrick* guidelines had caused no practical difficulties, were simple and clear, and were similar to the threshold of being aware "that it will occur in the ordinary course of events", and then stated:

> "It may be appropriate to give a direction in accordance with *Nedrick* in any case in which the defendant may not have desired the result of his act. But I accept the trial judge is best placed to decide what direction is required by the circumstances of the case." [1991] 1 A.C. 82 at 95

Lord Hope emphasised the "great importance" of a direction to the jury that is both clear and simple and expressed in as few words as possible.

R v Matthews and Alleyn (2003) 2 Cr. App. R. 30, Rix L.J., in delivering the judgment of the Court of Appeal, stated that criminal law had not equated the definition of murder with a virtual certainty of the prohibited consequences occurring. Furthermore, the *Woollin* guidelines had not established a substantive rule of law but had merely changed one word in the *Nedrick* guidelines based on the pre-existing jurisprudence in the *Moloney, Hancock* and *Shankland* decisions.

The *Woollin* guidelines are applicable only where the facts of the case suggest an oblique intent by the defendant. In *R v D* [2004] EWCA Crim 1391, Hooper L.J. stated:

> "*Woollin* is designed to help the prosecution to fill a gap in the rare circumstances in which a defendant does an act which caused the death without the purpose of killing or causing serious injury, but in circumstances where death or serious bodily harm had been a virtual certainty (barring some unforeseen intervention) as a result of the defendant's actions and the defendant had appreciated that such was the case." [2004] EWCA Crim 1391 at para. 29

In all other cases, the jury should be instructed to consider the meaning of intention in the ordinary sense of the word, based on the facts tendered in evidence. Applying the *Woollin* guidelines in isolation would result in many people avoiding conviction for murder (and other offences that specify intention as the requisite mens rea), notwithstanding the fact that the purpose was to kill or cause serious injury to the victim. For instance, a defendant who shoots and kills could possibly avoid a conviction for murder if it was established that the consequence of their actions was not a virtual certainty because they had a bad aim when shooting.

It is important to note that foresight of consequences is not the same as intention but only evidence that the defendant intended the consequences of his actions. In *R v Scalley* [1995] Crim. L.R. 504, the defendant was alleged to have murdered a five-year-old boy by setting fire to a house in which the defendant had once lived. The defendant was convicted of murder following the trial judge's direction to the jury to the effect that they could convict if they were sure that the defendant intended death or grievous bodily harm, in the sense that he foresaw either consequence as virtually certain to result from his actions. The Court of Appeal quashed the murder conviction and substituted a conviction for manslaughter. The trial judge's direction to the jury did not make it clear that foresight of the virtual certainty of death or serious injury is not intention but, merely, evidence from which the jury are entitled to infer intention. The jury should have been instructed that if they were satisfied that the defendant did see either death or serious injury as virtually certain, they could infer intention, but they were not obliged to do so.

INTENTION IN IRISH CRIMINAL LAW

There is a dearth of Irish case law on the meaning of intention. Section 4 of the Criminal Justice Act 1964 provides:

(1) Where a person kills another unlawfully the killing shall not be murder unless the accused person intended to kill, or cause serious injury to, some person, whether the person actually killed or not.
(2) The accused person shall be presumed to have intended the natural and probable consequences of his conduct; but this presumption may be rebutted.

This provision was enacted in response to the controversial House of Lords decision in *DPP v Smith* [1961] A.C. 290 to exclude an objective test for intention from Irish criminal law, and stipulates that the meaning of intention in Irish criminal law must be judged subjectively. The question for the jury is whether the defendant actually foresaw the consequences of his unlawful act and whether the defendant foresaw objectively is the only evidence which the jury may consider in their deliberations. The presumption in s.4(2) introduced the issue of probability into Irish criminal law in cases where oblique intention is at issue. However, s.4 does not provide a statutory definition of intention in Irish criminal law, but rather stipulates for the manner in which the jury may consider the natural and probable consequences of the defendant's act. Thus, while the evidence may lead to the conclusion that the defendant should have foreseen that their conduct would result in the prohibited consequences occurring, the issue for determination is whether the defendant actually foresaw those consequences.

The meaning of intention in Irish criminal law is somewhat different to that which pertains in England and Wales. In *People (DPP) v Murray* [1977] I.R. 360, Walsh J. examined the concept of intention, and in so doing distinguished between intention and foresight of consequences. The defendants were charged with capital murder. The Supreme Court distinguished between intention and foresight of consequences and concluded that an intention to murder or cause serious injury is where the defendant had "a fixed purpose to reach that desired objective" (as per Walsh J. at 386). Consequently, the defendant must have foreseen the prohibited consequences. Walsh J. stated:

"To intend to murder, or to cause serious injury ... is to have in mind a fixed purpose to reach that desired objective. Therefore, the state of mind of the accused person must have been not only that he foresaw but also willed the possible consequences of his conduct. There cannot be intention unless there is also foresight, and it is this subjective element of foresight which constitutes the necessary *mens rea*. Therefore, where a fact is unknown to the accused it cannot enter into his foresight and his conduct cannot be taken to be intentional with regard to it. It is well established that before an act can be murder it must be 'aimed at someone' and must in addition be an act committed with the necessary statutory intention, the test of which is always subjective to the actual defendant." [1977] I.R. 360 at 386–387

He continued:

"... a person who does not intend to kill and does not intend to cause serious injury but nevertheless does an act which exposes others to the risk of death or serious injury would not be guilty of murder when the *mens rea* required is an intent to kill or an intent to cause serious injury. Even if the specified and specific intent can be established not only when the particular purpose is to cause the event but also when the defendant has no substantial doubt that the event will result from his conduct, or when he foresees that the event will probably result from his conduct, the test is still based on actual foresight. Even on that basis, foresight of probable consequences must be distinguished from recklessness which imports a disregard of possible consequences. The essential difference between intention and foresight on the one hand and recklessness on the other is the difference between advertence and inadvertence as to the probable result."

It appears that a defendant who deliberately took a risk by performing the prohibited act would not be convicted of murder under Irish criminal law, but would be convicted of the lesser included offence of manslaughter for which recklessness is the requisite mens rea. Conversely, in *Hyam* the House of Lords held that a deliberate risk-taker, who in effect had acted recklessly, could be convicted of murder.

In *People (DPP) v Douglas and Hayes* [1985] I.L.R.M. 25, the two defendants were convicted of shooting at another person with intent to kill. With regard to the presumption that a person intends the natural and probable consequences of their conduct, the Court of Criminal Appeal per McWilliam J. stated:

> "In the circumstances of any particular case evidence of the fact that a reasonable man would have foreseen that the natural and probable consequence of the acts of an accused was to cause death and evidence of the fact that the accused was reckless as to whether his acts would cause death or not is evidence from which an inference of intent to cause death may or should be drawn, but the court must consider whether either or both of these facts do establish beyond a reasonable doubt an actual intention to cause death." [1985] I.L.R.M. 25 at 28

Although foresight of death as a natural and probable consequence of the defendant's conduct is not equated with intention, this is evidence from which the jury may infer intention. In terms of oblique intention, the court held that it can and must draw inferences from the defendant's actions and the surrounding circumstances.

Irish criminal law on the meaning of intention appears to be as set out by the Court of Criminal Appeal in *Douglas and Hayes*, that is, foresight of natural and probable consequence of the defendant's conduct does not constitute intention per se, although it may be evidence from which intention can be inferred by the jury. However, the Court of Criminal Appeal decision was influenced by the House of Lords decision in *Hyam*, which has since been reformulated, thus rendering *Douglas and Hayes* questionable.

In *People (DPP) v McBride* [1996] 1 I.R. 312, the defendant was convicted of aggravated assault. With regard to the meaning of intention, the Court of Criminal Appeal per Blayney J. said:

> "The jury ought to have been told that while there was a presumption that the applicant intended the natural and probable consequences of his act, this was only a presumption and could be rebutted, one of the things that they had to consider was whether the State had satisfied them beyond reasonable doubt that the presumption had not been rebutted. And in considering that, they had to take into account what the applicant said in his statement. It was for them to decide if it affected their view as to whether he had the necessary intent." [1996] 1 I.R. 312 at 317

While there is a presumption that the defendant intended the natural and probable consequences of the prohibited act in accordance with s.4(2) of the 1964 Act, the jury must also consider whether or not that presumption was rebutted.

The meaning of intention in criminal law pertaining to trial judge's instructions to juries was considered by the Court of Criminal Appeal in *People (DPP) v Hull* unreported, Court of Criminal Appeal, July 8, 1996. The defendant had been convicted of murder having shot the victim through a closed door, and had appealed on the grounds that the trial judge's instruction to the jury contained legal and factual errors. The issue then centred on the mens rea for murder. The trial judge had instructed the jury to consider their verdict in two stages, based on the entirety of the evidence:

"The first step is to decide what were the natural and probable consequences. Then, if you believe that the natural and probable consequences were death or serious injury, that is the first hurdle, but you have to say have the State proved that he intended to cause death or serious injury. Even though there may be a presumption that he intended the natural and probable consequences of his act, nevertheless the State must show that the presumption has not been rebutted."

In determining whether the presumption was applicable, the jury had to consider whether or not the prosecution had established that when the defendant had discharged the gun, that his conduct was deliberate and not accidental. If the shooting was deemed accidental, this would rebut the presumption in s.4(2) of the 1964 Act.

In *Hull*, the trial judge's charge to the jury required, in the first instance, a consideration of whether the natural and probable consequence of firing at the closed door was to cause death or serious injury. The jury would then have to determine whether the defendant's conduct had been deliberate or accidental. The Court of Criminal Appeal was satisfied that this was a reasonable direction to the jury and if the jury determined that the natural and probable consequences of shooting through the door was to cause death or serious injury, then the (rebuttable) presumption arose that this was the defendant's intention. The trial judge was correct in directing the jury to acquit the defendant of murder if the act of shooting the victim was accidental, that is, the presumption to cause death or serious injury would have been rebutted. The Court of Criminal Appeal was satisfied that the trial judge's instruction to the jury was not legally or factually erroneous. The trial judge had dealt adequately with the jury's issue of the "natural and probable consequences" of the defendant's unlawful conduct. The trial judge's direction to the jury to acquit was correct if the jury determined that, when the defendant fired the gun, it was accidental, and consequently the presumption that he had intended to cause death or serious injury had been rebutted.

The decision in *Hull* illustrates the importance of taking into consideration the intent stipulated for in the statutory definition of the offence charged in the indictment. While the defendant may have intended to pull the trigger intentionally, he may not have had the intention to kill or cause serious bodily harm when he pulled the trigger. This depends on the essential issue as to whether the defendant pulled the trigger accidentally (inadvertence) or intentionally (advertence). From the limited case law on the meaning of intention in criminal law, it remains to be seen whether the English test of foresight of virtual certain consequences will be adopted into Irish criminal law. It seems that the concept of intention in Irish criminal law has a broader meaning than its English counterpart. In the absence of the formulation of a model direction for trial judges by the superior courts, the Law Reform Commission's *Report on Homicide: Murder and Involuntary Manslaughter* (LRC 87–2008, para.3.78) reviewed the mens rea for murder (intention) and recommended the following guidelines:

"(1) Where a person kills another unlawfully it shall be murder if:
   (a) the accused person intended to kill or cause serious injury to some other person, whether that other person is the person actually killed or not; or
   (b) the killing is committed recklessly under circumstances manifesting an extreme indifference to the value of human life.

(2) A person acts recklessly with respect to a killing when he disregards a substantial and unjustifiable risk that death will occur. The risk must be of such a nature and degree that, considering the circumstances known to him, its disregard involves a gross deviation from the standard of conduct that a law-abiding person would observe in the actor's situation.

(3) A result is intended if:
   (i) it is the defendant's conscious object or purpose to cause it; or
   (ii) he is aware that it is virtually certain that his conduct will cause it, or would be virtually certain to cause it if he were to succeed in his purpose of causing some other result.

(4) The accused person shall be presumed to have intended the natural and probable consequences of his conduct, but this presumption may be rebutted."

Recklessness suggests a lesser form of criminal responsibility and intention is not to be equated with recklessness. It is noteworthy that the Commission did not recommend that the fault element for murder be expanded to include recklessness as to serious injury. Expanding the mental element for murder to include subjective recklessness pertains to reckless killing by extreme indifference to human life. For instance, if the defendant claims not to have intended to kill or cause serious harm to the victim and that they did not foresee death as a probable consequence of their conduct, they may be found guilty of murder.

Since the meaning of intention is a matter for the jury to decide, a fundamental element of certain offences is undefined, which might infringe the defendant's right to a fair trial. The Law Reform Commission recommended that the *Woollin* formula be adopted in Irish criminal law, due to the fact that the distinction between murder and manslaughter is now unclear.

RECKLESSNESS

Recklessness as an element of mens rea involves the conscious taking of an unjustified risk and is a less culpable fault element or mental state than intention. In circumstances when the defendant is aware, or becomes aware, that there is a substantial risk that an element of the offence is present, but proceeds nonetheless, he is deemed to have acted recklessly. For instance, in the offence of rape where the assailant is aware that there is a substantial risk that a woman is not consenting to sexual intercourse, but proceeds regardless, he can then be convicted for the offence of rape. In English criminal law, there were traditionally two different tests, which were named after the cases in which they were established. As a result, recklessness had two different legal meanings applicable to different types of criminal offences. The first type is subjective or *Cunningham* recklessness, where the defendant knew of the risk but took it anyway. The second is objective or *Caldwell* recklessness, where the defendant did not know whether or not there was a risk. The English superior courts have reverted to the subjective test of recklessness.

SUBJECTIVE RECKLESSNESS

This is where the defendant is aware of the risk and takes it deliberately. The issue is whether there was an awareness of the risk in the defendant's mind at the time that the offence was committed. The subjective test was established in *R v Cunningham* [1957] 2 Q.B. 396, in which the defendant broke a gas meter with the intention of stealing money from it. However, as he had failed to switch off the gas supply before breaking the meter, gas escaped into the house next door and a neighbour was partially asphyxiated. The victim became ill and her life was endangered as a result of the defendant's conduct. He was charged under s.23 of the Offences against the Person Act 1861 with, "maliciously administering a noxious thing so as to endanger life". Allowing the defendant's appeal, the Court of Appeal held that for a defendant to have acted "maliciously" there had to be proof that he had intended to cause the harm in question, or had been reckless as to whether such harm would be caused. In this context, recklessness involved the defendant being aware of the risk that his conduct might cause the prohibited consequence. The court defined reckless behaviour as occurring when the defendant is aware of a risk but decides to act anyway, i.e. the subjective test of recklessness. According to the subjective test, the prosecution must establish that the defendant was aware of the existence of the unjustifiable risk.

OBJECTIVE RECKLESSNESS

The objective test stipulates that a risk must have been obvious to the reasonable person who had given any thought to the issue. A person is deemed to have been reckless if they perform a prohibited act that creates an obvious risk and, when performing the act, the defendant gives no thought to the possibility of such a risk arising, or having recognised that some risk might exist, proceeds to take the risk despite the probable consequences. The objective test was established in *Metropolitan Police Commissioner v Caldwell* [1982] A.C. 341, in which the defendant, having been dismissed from his employment at a hotel, consumed alcohol and returned at night to set a fire in the hotel. The fire was detected and extinguished before any serious damage was caused. The defendant was convicted of criminal damage, but pleaded not guilty to the more serious charge of criminal damage with intent to endanger life, or being reckless as to whether life would be endangered. He contended that as a result of having consumed alcohol, it had never occurred to him that his conduct would endanger anybody's life and that he had set fire to the hotel premises only because of the dispute with his former employer. The House of Lords reaffirmed the *Cunningham* subjective test of recklessness and also propounded an objective test of recklessness pertaining to the defendant's failure to advert to a risk that would have been obvious to the reasonable person. Lord Diplock held that a defendant was reckless as to whether he damaged property if he created a risk of damage which would have been obvious to the reasonable man, and either had not given any thought to the possibility of such a risk when he carried out the act in question (first limb), or had recognised that there was some risk involved and nonetheless continued with his actions (second limb). This represented a clear departure from the *Cunningham* test, as it was sufficient to convict a defendant in circumstances where the reasonable person would have recognised the risk even if the defendant did not, nor indeed even where the defendant could not recognise the risk because of some incapacity.

In *R v Lawrence* [1981] A.C. 510, the defendant, while riding a motorbike, collided with and killed a pedestrian. He was charged with causing death by reckless driving. The House of Lords held that the test of recklessness was the same for reckless driving as for criminal damage, but used the words, based on an "obvious and serious risk" (as opposed to an "obvious risk" in *Caldwell*). In *R v Seymour* [1983] 2 A.C. 493, the defendant had an argument with his common law wife and in an effort to move her car out of his way by pushing it with his truck, he jammed her body between his truck and her car. She sustained severe injuries and subsequently died. The defendant was convicted of manslaughter. The trial judge had directed the jury that they should convict if they were satisfied that the defendant had caused the death and had been reckless in so doing. In this context, recklessness had the meaning attributed to it by the House of Lords in Lawrence. The House of Lords upheld the conviction.

While the risk must have been obvious to the reasonably prudent person, it need not have been obvious to the defendant; this resulted in unjust convictions. For instance, in *Elliot v C (a minor)* [1983] 1 W.L.R. 939, the defendant was an underachieving 14-year-old schoolgirl. She entered a neighbour's garden shed, poured white spirit on the floor and ignited it. The defendant then fled as the shed burst into flames. The Magistrates' Court dismissed the charge of criminal damage on the basis that she had not given any thought to the risk of damage, and that, even if she had, she would not have been capable of appreciating it. The prosecution successfully appealed to the Divisional Court, which held that this issue was irrelevant to recklessness and when the court in *Caldwell* had referred to an "obvious" risk, this meant obvious to the reasonable person if they had thought about it, and not obvious to the particular defendant if she had thought about it. Thus, it was sufficient that the risk of fire would have been obvious to a reasonable adult. The court declined to adapt the test to take age and mental condition into account. In *R v R (Stephen Malcom)* (1984) Cr. App. R. 334, the Court of Criminal Appeal applied the objective test for recklessness but did not take into account the age and sex of the defendant. In *R v Coles* [1995] 1 Cr. App. R. 157, the defendant was aged 15 years at the time of the offence and was of lower than average mental capacity. He had been playing in a hay barn with other children and had tried to set fire to the hay while other children were in the barn. Those children escaped unhurt. The defendant was charged with arson and being reckless as to whether the lives of others would be endangered. The defence argued that the *Caldwell* direction should be amended so that the assessment of whether or not the defendant had, by his actions, created an obvious risk of harm, should be subjective. The trial judge rejected the defendant's submission, stating that the test was whether or not the risk would have been obvious to the reasonably prudent adult. The Court of Appeal dismissed the defendant's appeal and held that the first limb of the *Caldwell* direction was objective. The state of mind of the defendant was irrelevant to the issue as to whether or not he had, by his conduct, created an obvious risk of harm to persons or property. The defendant's appeal was based on the proposition that the second limb of the *Caldwell* test should have some regard to the defendant's capacity, or lack thereof, to foresee the risk. The Court of Appeal held that a similar argument had failed in *Elliot v C* and that decision had been confirmed by the Court of Appeal in *R v R (Stephen Malcolm)*. The court was clearly not predisposed to depart from its own previous decision.

If the defendant stops to consider his actions, he may still be criminally liable if he realises that there is some risk involved, but proceeds nonetheless. In *Chief Constable of Avon v Shimmen* (1987) 84 Cr. App. R 7, the defendant was a martial arts expert and was demonstrating his skill to friends by performing a move that he anticipated would bring his foot within inches of a shop window. However, he miscalculated the risk, broke the window, and was convicted of criminal damage. The defendant's argument that his conduct was not reckless because he had given thought to the risk, but mistakenly believed that he had minimised it, was rejected by the Divisional Court because he knew there was some risk.

What if the defendant considered whether a risk existed, but decided that there was none? A defendant in these circumstances would avoid a conviction and his conduct would not have been reckless within the terms of Lord Diplock's definition in *Caldwell*, because the defendant would have given considerable thought to the risk but determined, albeit mistakenly, that there was no risk. This situation is generally referred to as the lacuna or loophole in the *Caldwell* test of recklessness (see e.g. *R v Merrick* (1996) 1 Cr. App. R. 130).

RETURN TO SUBJECTIVE RECKLESSNESS

As a result of the unjustness inherent in the *Caldwell* test, the House of Lords ultimately departed from the objective test of recklessness and reverted to the subjective test. In *R v G* [2004] 1 A.C. 1034, the defendants, two boys aged 11 and 12 respectively, went camping and, in the early hours of the morning, entered the back yard of a shop where they found some bundles of newspapers. They set fire to some of the newspapers, threw them under a large plastic dustbin, and left the yard without putting out the burning papers. The dustbin caught fire and the fire spread to the shop and adjoining buildings, resulting in approximately one million pounds worth of damage. The defendants were charged with arson, in that they caused damage to property and were reckless as to whether such property would be destroyed or damaged. They argued that they had expected the burning newspapers to extinguish themselves on the concrete floor of the yard. It was accepted that neither of the defendants appreciated that there was any risk of the fire spreading. The trial judge ruled that he was bound by previous House of Lords authority to direct the jury that, in deciding whether the defendants had been reckless as to whether the property would be damaged or destroyed, the test to be applied was whether they had committed an act, which in fact created an obvious risk that property would be destroyed or damaged, and whether, when they committed that act, they had either not given any thought to the possibility of there being such a risk, or had recognised that there was some risk involved, and nevertheless continued to do it. He went on to say that the question of whether there was an obvious risk of property being destroyed or damaged, was to be assessed by reference to the reasonable man and not by reference to a person endowed with the defendants' characteristics. In accordance with that ruling, the judge directed the jury on the law by telling them that they could make no allowance for the defendants' youth, their lack of maturity or any inability they might have to assess the situation. The Court of Appeal dismissed the defendants, appeal against conviction. On further appeal, the House of Lords unanimously overruled *Caldwell*, and Lord Bingham referred to that decision as "neither just nor moral", while Lord Steyn described it as a "cynical strategy". However, Lord Bingham stated that his judgment was confined to a discussion of the Criminal Damage Act 1971. Notwithstanding the House of Lords' departure from *Caldwell*, the subjective test of recklessness is applicable to all offences of which recklessness in the requisite mens rea, otherwise there would be two tests for subjective recklessness, *Lawrence* and *G*, which could result in further confusion for juries and unjust judgments (cf. *R v G (Secretary of State for the Home Department)* [2009] 1 A.C. 92; *Attorney General's Reference (No. 3 of 2003)* [2005] Q.B. 73).

RECKLESSNESS IN IRISH CRIMINAL LAW

Irish criminal law has traditionally adopted a subjective test of recklessness. In *People (DPP) v Murray and Murray* [1977] I.R. 360, the defendants, a husband and wife, escaped in a car after a bank robbery and the driver of a private car who happened to be passing the bank at the time, pursued the defendant's car until it stopped and the defendants exited it and ran away. The pursuer followed them and eventually caught up with the husband. As he was about to seize the husband, the wife shot and killed the pursuer. As it happened, the pursuer was an off-duty Garda. The defendants were convicted of capital murder. On appeal to the Supreme Court, the key issue pertained to the defendant's assertion that they did not know that the deceased was a Garda. The court held that, for capital murder, the defendant must have known or been reckless as to whether the individual was a Garda. Walsh J. stated:

> "Recklessness may be found either by applying a subjective test as where there has been conscious taking of an unjustified risk of which the accused actually knew, which imports foresight, or by applying an

objective test as where there has been a conscious taking of an unjustified risk of which the accused did not actually know but of which he ought to have been aware." [1977] I.R. 360 at 386–387

He continued:

"The whole question of risk-taking has been the subject of much discussion and debate but it is, I think, accepted that a person who does not intend to kill and does not intend to cause serious injury but nevertheless does an act which exposes others to the risk of death or serious injury would not be guilty of murder when the [*mens rea*] required is an intent to kill or an intent to cause serious injury. Even if the specified and specific intent can be established not only when the particular purpose is to cause the event but also when the defendant has no substantial doubt that the event will result from his conduct, or when he foresees that the event will probably result from his conduct, the test is still based on actual foresight. Even on that basis, foresight of probable consequences must be distinguished from recklessness which imports a disregard of possible consequences. The essential difference between intention and foresight on the one hand and recklessness on the other is the difference between advertence and inadvertence as to the probable result. Some statutory offences are, by the terms of the statute, established by proving recklessness: but intention or specific intention can never be proved by recklessness, which is a lesser degree of criminal responsibility."

Henchy, Parke and Kenny JJ. favoured a subjective test, although Henchy J. confined his comments to capital murder, while Parke and Kenny JJ. did not specify whether or not their comments had general application. The subjective test was later adopted as the test for provocation by the Court of Criminal Appeal (*People (DPP) v MacEoin* [1978] I.R. 27). In *PSS v JAS,* unreported, High Court, May 22, 1995, Budd J. held that a defendant's conduct was reckless if he, "recognised that [interference with the due process of justice] was a possibility and deliberately took the risk that it might occur or if he was heedless of what was a perfectly obvious risk." However, in *People (DPP) v McGrath; People (DPP) v Cagney* [2008] 2 I.R. 111, the Supreme Court followed *Murray* and held that the required mens rea for the purposes of recklessness as to consequences was subjective and not objective. The subjective test for recklessness is preferable to the objective test for the reason that criminal liability should not be imposed on the basis of what a reasonable person would have known, intended or suspected in the circumstances of the case under consideration.

CRIMINAL NEGLIGENCE

Criminal negligence is a disregard for the life and safety of others. This applies only to the offence of manslaughter, but involves a degree of negligence beyond that which establishes civil liability. Negligence consists of falling below the standard of the ordinary reasonable person, i.e. it is a failure to exercise reasonable care in all the circumstances of the case. The test is objective, based on the hypothetical reasonable person, and involves the defendant either performing an act that the reasonable person would not perform, or failing to do something that the reasonable person would do. It does not matter that the defendant was unaware that something dangerous might happen if the reasonable person would have realised the risk, and taken steps to avoid it.

In *People (AG) v Dunleavy* [1948] I.R. 95, the Court of Criminal Appeal held that the degree of negligence required to justify a conviction is substantially higher than that which pertains in a civil law action based on negligence.

KNOWLEDGE AND BELIEF

Two aspects of the definitional part of the mens rea are the concepts of knowledge and belief. Knowledge and belief play an important role in determining the criminal liability of defendants for certain offences. A criminal offence may explicitly require proof of knowledge or may be interpreted by the superior courts to require such proof. Furthermore, knowledge may correspond with belief as an alternative form of criminal liability. Knowledge as a form of mens rea is simply true belief, i.e. a knowledge of things as they are. Belief, although necessary for knowledge, is not equated with the knowledge requirement but is more than mere suspicion by the defendant. In this context, although the meaning of "wilful blindness" has not been defined in criminal law, it implies that where a defendant becomes aware for the need to make sufficient enquiries but declines to do so, preferring to remain ignorant of certain facts, that this may suffice to attract criminal liability to the same degree as if they clearly and unambiguously have the relevant guilty knowledge. In *Halnon v Fleming* [1981] 1 I.R. 489, Henchy J. for the Supreme Court opined:

> "While knowledge and belief frequently coincide or overlap (for example, I both know and believe that this is the Supreme Court), there are many matters which one may believe to be correct without being able to say that one knows them to be correct. For example, I may believe that there is life in outer space, that evolution is the origin of species, that a

particular person did a particular act, but I may have to admit that I do not know, or do not know with any substantial degree of certainty, that such beliefs are well founded. Without entering into the intricate logical, metaphysical and philosophical problems involved in a comparison of knowledge with belief, and keeping the matter on the plane of ordinary usage (which is, presumably, how it would be dealt with by both judge and jury), I would point to the commonly used expression 'I believe it to be so, but I do not really know'." [1981] 1 I.R. 489 at 497

The definition of many criminal offences, including rape and possession in theft and fraud offences, specifies knowledge as the fault element.

TRANSFERRED MALICE

Under the doctrine of transferred malice, a defendant will be held criminally liable for an offence if he has the necessary mens rea and commits the actus reus, even if the victim differs from the one intended ("intent follows the bullet"). For instance, if X intends to kill Y, but mistakenly thinks that Z is Y, and kills Z instead, X did not have the intention to kill Z, but it would be clearly unjust to allow X to avoid criminal liability on the basis that he intended to kill Y instead of Z. In this scenario, X has caused the actus reus and did so with the requisite intention for murder. Consequently, X can be convicted for murder. The same applies if X shoots at Y but misses him and kills Z instead. In other words, the defendant's malice towards the intended victim is transferred to the actual victim and this justifies the imposition of criminal liability.

In *R v Latimer* (1886) 17 Q.B.D. 359, the defendant was involved in a pub brawl in which he used his belt, and in so doing aimed a blow at the man with whom he was fighting. However, the belt hit the landlord of the pub in the face instead. The defendant was convicted of assaulting the landlord, but appealed the conviction on the basis that he hit the landlord accidentally. The Court of Crown Cases Reserved upheld the conviction. Lord Coleridge stated:

> "... a man who has an unlawful and malicious intent against another, and, in attempting to carry it out, injures a third person, is guilty of what the law deems malice against the person injured, because the offender is doing an unlawful act, and has that which the judges call general malice, and that is enough." (1886) 17 Q.B.D. 359 at 361

This principle only applies when the actus reus and mens rea of the same offence coincide.

The doctrine is not applicable in circumstances where there is no coincidence of actus reus and mens rea. Thus, if the defendant has the mens rea for a different offence from that which he commits the intent is not transferred. In *R v Pembliton* (1874) L.R. 2 C.C.R. 119, the defendant had been fighting with persons in the street and had thrown a stone at them, which struck a window causing criminal damage. He threw the stone at the people he had been fighting with, intending to strike one or more of them, but not intending to break the window. He was convicted under the Malicious Damage Act 1861, s.51 for "unlawfully and maliciously" causing this damage. The Court of Crown Cases Reserved held that this negatived the existence of malice, either actual or constructive. The conviction was therefore quashed. Thus, as the defendant did not have the mens rea for the offence of causing criminal damage, his conviction was quashed.

In *Attorney General's Reference (No. 3 of 1994)* [1998] A.C. 245, the defendant (the father of the unborn child) stabbed the mother of the unborn child in the abdomen, knowing her to be pregnant. She received medical attention and her unborn child appeared not to have been harmed. Shortly thereafter, she went into early labour and gave birth to a grossly premature infant who survived for just 121 days. During the child's lifetime the defendant pleaded guilty to wounding the mother with intent and was sentenced to four years' imprisonment. On the death of the child, he was charged with the unborn child's murder. The trial judge directed that the defendant be acquitted. The Attorney General referred the question to the Court of Appeal as to whether the offences of murder or manslaughter could have been committed in these circumstances. The Court of Appeal held that, under the doctrine of transferred malice, an intention to injure the mother could be transferred to the unborn child, which could then be further transferred to the child when born. The House of Lords rejected this reasoning. Lord Mustill stated:

> "The effect of transferred malice, as I understand it, is that the intended victim and the actual victim are treated as if they were one, so that what was intended to happen to the first person (but did not happen) is added to what actually did happen to the second person (but was not intended to happen), with the result that what was intended and what happened are married to make a notionally intended and actually consummated crime. The cases are treated as if the actual victim had been the intended victim from the start. To make any sense of this process there must, as it seems to me, be some compatibility between the original intention and the actual occurrence, and this is, indeed, what one finds in the cases. There is no such compatibility here. The defendant intended to commit and did commit an immediate crime of violence to the mother. He committed no relevant violence to the foetus, which was not a person, either at the time or in the future, and intended no harm to the foetus or to the human person which it would

become. If fictions are useful, as they can be, they are only damaged by straining them beyond their limits. I would not overstrain the idea of transferred malice by trying to make it fit the present case."

The House of Lords held that the doctrine of transferred malice did not extend to imputing an intention to harm the human person which the foetus would become, so as to satisfy the requirements of the mens rea for murder. However, the defendant's conduct was more than merely unlawful and dangerous (sufficient for a manslaughter conviction), but was done with the mens rea for murder, as this caused the death of the child which might justify a murder conviction.

The doctrine of transferred malice is specifically provided for by s.4 of the Criminal Justice Act 1964, which stipulates that:

> Where a person kills another unlawfully the killing shall not be murder unless the accused person intended to kill, or cause serious injury to, some person, *whether the person actually killed or not*. (Emphasis added).

This places the principle of transferred malice pertaining to the offence of murder on a statutory basis. Likewise, s.6 of the Non-Fatal Offences Against the Person Act 1997 provides for the application of the doctrine of transferred intent pertaining to syringe offences.

PRINCIPLE OF DOUBLE EFFECT

The principle of double effect provides specific guidelines for determining when it is ethically permissible for someone to engage in conduct in pursuit of a good end, with full knowledge that the conduct will also bring about adverse consequences. The principle of double effect generally states that, in cases where a person contemplates conduct that has both good and bad outcomes, the course of conduct selected is ethically permissible only if it is not wrong in itself, and provided that it does not require that someone directly intends the bad result. The principle stipulates ethical criteria for evaluating the permissibility of acting when someone's otherwise legitimate act (such as relieving a terminally ill patient's pain) would also cause an effect which people would normally be obliged to avoid, for example, the patient's death when administering palliative care (cf. *R (Pretty) v DPP* [2002] 1 A.C. 800; *Airedale NHS Trust v Bland* [1993] A.C. 789).

FURTHER READING

Bacik, "If it Ain't Broke: A Critical View of the Law Reform Commission Consultation Paper on Homicide: The Mental Element in Murder" (2002) 12(1) I.C.L.J. 6.

Campbell, Kilcommins and O'Sullivan, *Criminal Law in Ireland: Cases and Commentary* (Dublin: Clarus Press, 2010), Ch.4.

Clarke, "Voting for Injustice" (2008) 26 I.L.T. 138.

Coffey, "Codifying the Meaning of 'Intention' in the Criminal Law" (2009) 73 J.C.L. 394.

Hanly, *An Introduction to Irish Criminal Law*, 2nd edn (Dublin: Gill & Macmillan, 2006), Ch.4.

Keane, "Murder: The Mental Element" (2002) 53 N.I.L.Q. 1.

Law Reform Commission, *Report on Homicide: Murder and Involuntary Manslaughter* (LRC 87–2008).

Law Reform Commission, *Consultation Paper on Homicide: The Mental Element of Murder* (LRC CP 17–2001).

McAleese, "Just What is Recklessness?" (1981) 4 D.U.L.J. 29.

McAuley, "*Mens Rea*: a Legal-Philosophical View" (1982) 17 Ir. Jur. (N.S.) 84.

McAuley, "Modelling Intentional Action" (1987) 22 Ir. Jur. (N.S.) 179.

McAuley and McCutcheon, *Criminal Liability: A Grammar* (Dublin: Round Hall, 2000), Ch.6.

Newman, "Reforming the Mental Element on Murder" (1995) 5(2) I.C.L.J. 194.

O'Higgins and Ó Braonáin, "Section 4 of the Criminal Justice Act 1964: A Constitutional Presumption?" (1992) 2(2) I.C.L.J. 179.

O'Higgins and Ó Braonáin, "Section 4 of the Criminal Justice Act 1964: The Redundant Presumption?" (1991) 1(2) I.C.L.J. 113.

Rogan, "The Mental Element in Murder: Tales from the Archives" (2008) 18(1) I.C.L.J. 19.

Stannard, "Murder, Intention and the Inference of Intention" (1999) 34 Ir. Jur. (N.S.) 202.

4. Coincidence of Actus Reus and Mens Rea

INTRODUCTION

The general rule of criminal liability is encapsulated by the Latin maxim *actus non facit reum nisi mens sit rea*, which is loosely translated as an act that does not make a person guilty of an offence, unless his or her mind is also guilty. This means that criminal liability not only requires proof of the prohibited conduct (actus reus), the fault element (mens rea) and the absence of a valid defence, but there must also be a coincidence or concurrence of mens rea with the act that constitutes the actus reus. Strict liability offences are an exception to this general rule. If the actus reus does not concur in point of time and law with the mens rea, then no offence has been committed. However, in some cases a literal interpretation of this rule would manifestly lead to injustice. The Superior Courts have developed methods of finding coincidence of actus reus and mens rea when the events take place over a period of time and where they constitute a course of events.

FAULT ELEMENT MUST COINCIDE WITH THE PROHIBITED CONDUCT

Criminal liability will not be imposed where the defendant forms mens rea once the actus reus has been completed. In *R v Hehir* [1895] 2 I.R. 709, the defendant was mistakenly given a £10 note by his employer. At the time the note was handed over, they both thought it was a £1 note. Having realised the employer's mistake, the defendant then decided to keep the £10 note. The issue as to whether he could be convicted of larceny (now the offence of theft) depended on when possession of the note took place. The actus reus of larceny constituted the taking and carrying away of property belonging to another, while the mens rea was to permanently deprive the owner of the property stolen. The Irish Court of Crown Cases Reserved held that the actus reus of larceny was completed before the defendant formed the mens rea of the offence. Therefore, the fault and conduct elements of the offence did not coincide. Under the Larceny Act 1861 (repealed by the Criminal Justice (Theft and Fraud) Offences Act 2001), there was a separate offence of "larceny by mistake" to deal with these situations.

COINCIDENCE IN LAW

The defendant must have the mens rea for the offence charged. In *R v Pembliton* (1874) L.R. 2 C.C.R. 119, the defendant was fighting with a group of people outside a public house. He picked up a stone and intentionally threw it at the group of people with whom he was fighting, but he missed and the stone broke a window of the pub. He was charged with "unlawfully and maliciously" (recklessness being the required mens rea) causing damage, contrary to the Criminal Damage Act 1851. The conviction was quashed as he did not have the mens rea for that offence at the time that he threw the stone. He did not intend to break the window, therefore, he should have been charged with attempting to injure the people that he had been fighting with. Lord Coleridge summarised the finding of the jury in the following terms:

> "... the prisoner threw the stone which broke the window, but that he threw it at the people he had been fighting with, intending to strike one or more of them with it, but not intending to break the window ..." (1874) L.R. 2 C.C.R. 119 at 20.

He went on to explain that if the defendant's conduct was reckless when he threw the stone, then he would have been convicted of "unlawfully and maliciously" breaking the window of the pub. Since he threw the stone with the intention of striking the people with whom he was fighting, the actus reus did not coincide with the required mens rea and he was, therefore, not guilty of the offence charged (cf. *R v Latimer* (1886) 17 Q.B.D. 359; *R v Mitchell* [1983] Q.B. 741).

COINCIDENCE IN TIME

The second means by which the courts have dealt with the issue of coincidence is to consider a chain of events, that is, a continuing series of acts constituting the actus reus. Several acts by the defendant, albeit separate in themselves, might nonetheless be deemed to form one continuing act. If the actus reus and mens rea are both present at some time during this chain of events, then the defendant is criminally liable. The defendant must have the necessary mens rea at the time of committing the act or omission or, indeed, causing the circumstances constituting the offence. The English Superior Courts have had to deal with some difficult cases where the prohibited conduct preceded the actus reus.

In *R v Jakeman* (1983) 76 Cr. App. R. 223, the defendant sent two cases containing cannabis by plane from Accra to Rome, and from there to London. The flight was diverted to Paris, but an official sent the cases on to London.

COINCIDENCE OF ACTUS REUS AND MENS REA

The defendant was charged with fraudulent evasion of the restriction on the importation of cannabis. She claimed that as soon as she had boarded the flight to Rome she repented and tore up the baggage slips. In effect, the defendant claimed that she did not have the mens rea at the time the bags had landed in London. Wood J. stated:

> "What matters is the state of mind at the time the relevant acts are done, i.e. at the time the defendant is concerned in bringing about the importation. This accords with the general principles of common law. To stab a victim in a rage with the necessary intent for murder or manslaughter leads to criminal responsibility for the resulting death regardless of any repentance between the act of stabbing and the time of death, which may be hours or days later. This is so even if, within seconds of the stabbing, the criminal comes to his senses and does everything possible to assist his victim. Only the victim's survival will save him from conviction for murder or manslaughter". (1983) 76 Cr.App.R. 223 at 228

The court upheld the defendant's conviction.

In *Thabo Meli v R* [1954] 1 W.L.R. 228, the defendants took the deceased to a hut and struck him over the head with the intention of killing him. The defendants, in accordance with their preconceived plan, rolled his unconscious body over a cliff to give the impression that it had been an accidental death. It later emerged that he had died, not from the assault, but as a result of exposure following the assault. The defendants argued that the two acts (striking the victim over the head with intent to kill, and rolling his body over a cliff so as to give the impression of accidental death) were separate acts and that, although they had mens rea for the first act, which was not the cause of death, they did not have mens rea for the second act, which was the cause of death. The Privy Council upheld the murder conviction. Lord Reid stated:

> "It appears ... impossible to divide up what was really one series of acts in this way. There is no doubt that the accused set out to do all these acts to achieve their plan, and as parts of their plan; and it is much too refined a ground of judgement to say that, because they were under a misapprehension at one stage and thought their guilty purpose was achieved before, in fact, it was achieved, therefore they are to escape the penalties of the law." [1954] 1 W.L.R. 228 at 230

The defendants had mens rea at all stages of the single criminal episode and were therefore convicted of murder.

In *R v Church* [1966] 1 Q.B. 59, during a fight, the defendant knocked the victim unconscious and, believing her to be dead, threw her body into a river to conceal his act, with the result that she drowned. The Court of Criminal Appeal was satisfied that the defendant's conduct constituted a series of acts which culminated in the victim's death and upheld the manslaughter conviction. The difference between this case and *Thabo Meli* is that there was no antecedent plan to kill the deceased and, therefore, the defendant was convicted of manslaughter, not murder.

In *R v Le Brun* [1992] 1 Q.B. 61, the defendant and his wife were arguing in the street as she did not want to go home. He struck her a blow on the chin, knocking her unconscious. He then dragged her from the street, presumably to get her home, and, while doing so, her head struck the pavement, thereby fracturing her skull, with the result that she died. The question was whether he should be convicted of manslaughter on the basis that he would have been guilty if his wife had died from the initial blow. The Court of Criminal Appeal upheld his conviction for manslaughter. Lane C.J. stated:

> "It seems to us that where the unlawful application of force and the eventual act causing death are parts of the same sequence of events, the same transaction, the fact that there is an appreciable interval of time between the two does not serve to exonerate the defendant from liability. That is certainly so where the appellant's subsequent actions which caused death, after the initial unlawful blow, are designed to conceal his commission of the original unlawful assault." [1992] 1 Q.B. 61 at 68

The defendant's conduct in moving the victim with the intention of evading detection did not break the chain of causation linking the initial blow with the victim's death. It was immaterial that there was no preconceived plan to kill, because the same principles of criminal liability which apply to manslaughter also apply to murder.

CONTINUING ACT

Where the actus reus is a continuing act, the mens rea can coincide during the continuance of the actus reus. The distinction between a failure to act, omission, and a positive action constituting the actus reus will not always be clear. It can be difficult to classify a certain type of behaviour as an omission rather than prohibited conduct.

Not all acts forming the basis of an actus reus are single, unconnected events, and the defendant's conduct must be placed in context. Provided that the requisite mens rea is formed before the sequence begins or during the sequence (and before it ends), the defendant will be criminally liable. In *Fagan v Metropolitan Police Commissioner* [1969] 1 Q.B. 439, the defendant had been directed by a police constable to park his car close to the kerb. While complying with the police constable's request, he accidentally drove his motor car so that one tyre went on to, and remained on, the constable's foot. It was only after the constable had told him several times to get off his foot that the defendant reversed his car. He was convicted by the Magistrates' Court of assaulting a police constable in the execution of his duty. On appeal to Quarter Sessions (periodic courts held in each county and county borough in England and Wales until 1972), it was held that, although there was doubt about whether the initial mounting of the wheel was intentional or accidental, the defendant had knowingly, provocatively and unnecessarily allowed the wheel to remain on the constable's foot after he had been told to drive off. The defendant's appeal against conviction for assault was dismissed by the Divisional Court. The defendant's act had not been completed at the moment when the car wheel came to rest on the constable's foot, but was a continuing act operating until the wheel was removed. Although the original mounting of the police officer's foot may have been accidental, there was thereafter sufficient actus reus that coincided with mens rea. It was on this basis that the appeal was dismissed. The defendant argued that his failure to remove his car from the police officer's foot was not an act, but a failure to act, and he should not, therefore, be convicted. While the Divisional Court agreed that an assault could not be committed by a failure to act, the court formulated the so-called "continuing act theory", that is, the actus reus began when the defendant drove over the police officer's foot and only ended when the wheel of the car was removed. Once the defendant formed the requisite mens rea during the continuance of the actus reus, the offence was complete in terms of coincidence in law and time. James J. stated:

> "It is not necessary that *mens rea* should be present at the inception of the [*actus reus*]; it can be superimposed on an existing act. On the other hand, the subsequent inception of *mens rea* cannot convert an act which has been completed without *mens rea* into an assault."
> [1969] 1 Q.B. 439 at 445

The defendant's argument that the act was complete before he had formed mens rea was rejected. The defendant's action was continuous in that it lasted from the point in time when he drove over the police constable's foot to the time when he removed it. The fault element coincided when he realised what had happened and decided not to remove the wheel of the car from the constable's foot. In such a case, where there is a continuing act, the mens rea coincides with the actus reus at any point in time during the continuance of the actus reus. Consider the following illustrations:

The above illustration represents a definite point in time when the actus reus and mens rea coincide in both law and time, such as shooting the victim with intent.

```
[                                              ]
A                                              B
```

In this scenario, at the inception of the actus reus, point A, the defendant might not have formed mens rea (as in *Fagan* when the defendant accidentally drove on the police constable's foot). Since the actus reus is a continuing act, if the defendant forms mens rea at any point during the continuance of the actus reus (up to point B when the actus reus is completed), then he will be guilty of the offence charged. This is often referred to as the "single transaction principle" in the construction of criminal liability.

In *Kaitamaki v R* [1985] A.C. 147, the defendant was convicted of rape. He argued that he believed the victim was consenting, but only realised after penetration that she was not. The Privy Council noted that the offence of rape was completed upon withdrawal, and the defendant's failure to withdraw constituted part of the continuing action. The defendant's conviction was upheld. Although sexual intercourse was complete upon penetration, it was a continuing act, only ending upon withdrawal. Rape is defined as having intercourse without consent, and a defendant would be guilty of rape if he continued intercourse after he realised that the woman was no longer consenting.

In both of these cases, the crucial element is that, while the offence pertained to an omission by the defendant, the courts nevertheless construed that omission as part of a continuing actus reus. The mens rea element of the offence could be superimposed on the actus reus at any time from its inception until completion. A different way of justifying the imposition of criminal liability in these types of situations would be to redefine the actus reus as an omission and to base the imposition of criminal liability on the failure to move the car or withdraw in the abovementioned case law.

FURTHER READING

Campbell, Kilcommins and O'Sullivan, *Criminal Law in Ireland: Cases and Commentary* (Dublin: Clarus Press, 2010), pp.158–161.

Hanly, *An Introduction to Irish Criminal Law*, 2nd edn (Dublin: Gill & Macmillan, 2006), Ch.5.

Stannard, "Stretching Out the *Actus Reus*" (1993–1995) 28–30 Ir. Jur. (N.S.) 200.

5. Strict Liability

INTRODUCTION

Offences of strict liability are those for which mens rea does not have to be proven with regard to one or more elements of the actus reus. Liability is said to be strict with regard to that element. Notwithstanding this general rule, the prosecution may have to prove intention, recklessness or knowledge in relation to other elements of the criminal offence. Criminal liability is strict. Individuals can be convicted even though they were unaware of one or more factors that made their acts or omissions criminal. A defendant will typically not even have been criminally negligent, which is the least blameworthy type of mens rea, and need not have intended or known about that circumstance or consequence.

Strict liability offences were created by legislation since the nineteenth century in order to improve working conditions and safety standards in factories. Prior to the creation of these offences, the prosecution had experienced great difficulties in proving the requisite mens rea on the part of factory owners and senior management. Conviction rates substantially increased with the enactment of such offences over the years.

CLASSIFICATION OF STRICT LIABILITY OFFENCES

In *Sherras v De Rutzen* [1895] 1 Q.B. 918 at 922, Wright J. stated that the principal types of strict liability can be reduced to three. The first is a class of acts which are not criminal in any real sense, but are acts which, in the public interest, are prohibited under a penalty, for example, the sale of adulterated food (*Roberts v Egerton* (1874) L.R. 9 Q.B. 494). The second class encompasses public nuisances as, for instance, in *R v Stephens* (1866) L.R. 1 Q.B. 702, in which an employer was held criminally liable for a nuisance caused by workmen without his knowledge and contrary to his orders. Thirdly, there may be cases in which, although the proceeding is criminal in form, it is really only a summary mode of enforcing a civil right as, for instance, in *Hargreaves v Diddams* (1875) L.R. 10 Q. B. 582, which related to a bona fide belief in a legally impossible right to fish.

STRICT AND ABSOLUTE LIABILITY

The terms "strict liability" and "absolute liability" are sometimes used interchangeably. Convictions on the basis of strict liability are subject to the defence of reasonable mistake, where the defendant acted without reasonable care to prevent the external element occurring. This may be contrasted with absolute liability, where the simple occurrence of the conduct element in certain circumstances makes the defendant criminally liable. If an offence requires no mens rea and the actus reus does not need to be voluntary, the offence is said to be one of absolute liability. Offences of absolute liability require no mens rea to be proved and are deemed complete once the actus reus has been performed. However, it is more common that mens rea is missing for one element of the actus reus and it is only in rare cases that no mens rea at all is required for criminal liability, thereby making the particular offence "absolute" (see *R v Larsonneur* (1933) 24 Cr. App. R. 74; *Winzar v Chief Constable of Kent, The Times*, March 28, 1983).

RATIONALE FOR STRICT LIABILITY OFFENCES

Strict liability is necessary in many so-called regulatory or quasi-criminal offences. If the prosecution were required to prove intent, recklessness, and criminal negligence in every case, convictions would be very difficult to secure.

In *Warner v Metropolitan Police Commissioner* [1969] 2 A.C. 256, the defendant, a floor-layer by occupation, also sold scent as a source of secondary income. He went to a café and asked if anything had been left for him and was given two boxes, one containing perfume and the other containing 20,000 tablets of drugs. He was charged with being in possession of a controlled drug, contrary to s.1 of the Drugs (Prevention of Misuse) Act 1964. He argued that he thought the boxes contained perfume. Lord Morris held that since the defendant was in physical control of the package and it's contents, either with his consent knowing that it had contents, or with knowledge that the package was in his control, his possession of the controlled drug was established for the purposes of s.1 of the 1964 Act, regardless of whether the defendant realised that he was in possession of a controlled drug. Lord Reid held that the inference that possession of a container by the defendant meant possession of its contents could be rebutted by reasonable doubt as to whether the defendant had a right to open the container and a reason to suspect that the contents of it were illegal.

The imposition of strict liability is justified in many types of cases pertaining to public safety and welfare. In *Alphacell Ltd v Woodward* [1972] A.C. 824, the defendants were charged with causing polluted matter to enter a river, contrary to s.2 of the Rivers (Prevention of Pollution) Act 1951. The river had, in fact, been polluted because a pipe connected to the defendant's factory had been blocked with leaves allowing the pollutants to escape, although the defendants had not been negligent. The House of Lords, nevertheless, held that the defendants were liable. Lord Salmon stated:

"If this appeal succeeded and it were held to be the law that no conviction could be obtained under the Act of 1951 unless the prosecution could discharge the often impossible onus of proving that the pollution was caused intentionally or negligently, a great deal of pollution would go unpunished and undeterred to the relief of many riparian factory owners. As a result many rivers which are now filthy would become filthier still and many rivers which are now clean would lose their cleanliness. The legislature no doubt recognised that as a matter of public policy this would be most unfortunate. Hence section 2(1)(a) which encourages riparian factory owners not only to take reasonable steps to prevent pollution but to do everything possible to ensure that they do not cause it." [1972] A.C. 824 at 848–849

Despite the fact that the defendants claimed that they had been unaware of the fact that the filtering mechanism was clogged up, the House of Lords held that the defendants had caused the pollution, whether or not there was any evidence of negligence and, accordingly, the conviction was upheld. The offence charged was one of strict liability because it was the defendants' responsibility to ensure that their manufacturing process did not cause pollution to enter the river. For that reason, the defendant should have regularly checked the filtering mechanisms so as to ensure that there were no blockages.

STRICT LIABILITY IN CONTEXT

Offences of strict liability are regulatory offences that enforce social behaviour where minimal stigma attaches to a defendant on conviction, or where society, through criminal law, is concerned with the prevention of harm and seeks to maximise the deterrent value of the offence. Examples of strict liability offences in contemporary society include: the selling of alcohol to underage persons, pollution, health and safety, and speeding offences.

In *R v Hibbert* (1869) L.R. 1 C.C.R. 184, the defendant met a girl on the street who was under 16 years of age. He persuaded her to accompany him to a considerably remote place where he seduced and detained her for several hours. He then took her back to where he had met her and she returned home to her father. The defendant was charged under s.55 of the Offences Against the Person Act 1861 (now s.20 of the Sexual Offences Act 1956). The Court of Crown Cases Reserved held that, in the absence of any evidence that the defendant knew, or had reason to know that the girl was under the care of her father at the time, a conviction could not be sustained. There was no finding of fact that the defendant knew, or had reason to believe, that the girl was under the care of either parent and the defendant was, therefore, not guilty of having unlawfully taken the girl out of the possession of her father, under s.55 of the 1861 Act. In *R v Prince* (1875) L.R. 2 C.C.R. 154, the defendant eloped with an underage girl and was charged with an offence of taking a girl under the age of 16 out of the possession of her parents, contrary to s.55 of the 1861 Act. The defendant knew that the girl was in the custody of her father but, he believed, on reasonable grounds, that the girl was aged 18. The Divisional Court held that knowledge that the girl was under the age of 16 was not required in order to establish the offence. It was sufficient to show that the defendant intended to take the girl out of the possession of her father.

The imposition of strict liability may operate very unfairly in individual cases. For instance, in *Pharmaceutical Society of Great Britain v Storkwain Ltd* [1986] 1 W.L.R. 903, the defendant pharmacist supplied drugs to a patient on the basis of a forged doctor's prescription. There was no finding that the defendant had acted dishonestly, improperly or even negligently, but the House of Lords upheld the conviction. The justification for the imposition of criminal liability in such cases, even though the defendant is morally blameless, is that the misuse of drugs is a grave social evil and pharmacists should be encouraged to take all necessary precautions to verify prescriptions before supplying drugs.

General Principles

Most strict liability offences are created by legislation, but many statutory provisions do not state explicitly that a particular offence is one of strict liability. If a statutory provision uses terms such as "knowingly" or "recklessly", then the offence being created is one that requires a fault element or mens rea. Alternatively, the statutory provision might specify that an offence of strict liability is being created. In many cases, it will be a matter for the Superior Courts to interpret the statute and decide whether or not mens rea is required for a conviction.

In *Cundy v Le Cocq* (1884) 13 Q.B.D. 207, the defendant was convicted of unlawfully selling alcohol to an intoxicated person, contrary to s.13 of the Licensing Act 1872, and argued that he had been unaware of the customer's drunkenness, and therefore should be acquitted. The Divisional Court interpreted s.13 of the 1872 Act as creating an offence of strict liability since the wording of the provision was silent as to mens rea, whereas other offences under the 1872 Act expressly required proof of knowledge on the part of the defendant. The court held that it was not necessary to consider whether the defendant knew, or had means of knowing, or could with ordinary care have detected that the person served was drunk. Stephen J. stated:

"... the object of this part of the Act is to prevent the sale of intoxicating liquor to drunken persons, and it is perfectly natural to carry that out by throwing on the publican the responsibility of determining whether the person supplied comes within that category." (1884) 13 Q.B.D. 207 at 210

If the defendant served alcohol to a person who was in fact drunk, then he was guilty on the basis of strict liability.

In *Sherras v De Rutzen* [1895] 1 Q.B. 918, the defendant was convicted of selling alcohol to a police officer while he was on duty, contrary to s.16(2) of the Licensing Act 1872. He argued that he had reasonably believed the constable to be off duty as he had removed his arm-band, which was the acknowledged method of signifying that a constable was off duty. The Divisional Court quashed the conviction, despite the absence from s.16(2) of any words requiring proof of mens rea as an element of the offence. Wright J. stated:

"It is plain that if guilty knowledge is not necessary, no care on the part of the publican could save him from a conviction under s. 16, sub-s. 2, since it would be as easy for the constable to deny that he was on duty when asked, or to produce a forged permission from his superior officer, as to remove his armlet before entering the public-house. I am, therefore, of opinion that this conviction ought to be quashed." [1895] 1 Q.B. 918 at 922–923

The court held that the presumption in favour of mens rea could only be displaced by the wording of the statute itself, or its subject matter at issue. In this case, the latter factor was significant because no amount of reasonable care by the defendant would have prevented the offence from being committed.

In *Lim Chin Aik v R* [1963] A.C. 160, the defendant was convicted of contravening an order prohibiting, in absolute terms, his entry into Singapore, despite his ignorance of the order's existence. In allowing the defendant's appeal against conviction, the Privy Council held that the imposition of strict liability could only really be justified where it would actually succeed in placing the onus to comply with the law on the defendant. Lord Evershed stated:

"... it is not enough in their Lordships' opinion merely to label the statute as one dealing with a grave social evil and from that to infer that strict liability was intended. It is pertinent also to inquire whether putting the defendant under strict liability will assist in the enforcement of the regulations. That means that there must be something he can do, directly or indirectly, by supervision or inspection, by improvement of his business methods or by exhorting those whom he may be expected to influence or control, which will promote the observance of the regulations. Unless this is so, there is no reason in penalising him, and it cannot be inferred that the legislature imposed strict liability merely in order to find a luckless victim." [1963] A.C. 160 at 174

Consequently, if the defendant is unaware that he has been made the subject of an order prohibiting him from entering a country, the imposition of strict liability, should he fail to comply with the provisions of the order, would not in any case promote its observance.

In *Sweet v Parsley* [1970] A.C. 132, the defendant was the landlady of a house let to tenants. She visited occasionally to collect the rent. While she was absent, the police searched the house and found cannabis. The defendant was convicted under s.5 of the Dangerous Drugs Act 1965 of, "being concerned in the management of premises used for the smoking of cannabis". She appealed against this conviction on the basis that she had no knowledge of the circumstances and could not be reasonably expected to have had such knowledge. The House of Lords quashed the conviction and held that the prosecution had to prove that the defendant had intended the house to be used for drug-taking, in view of the fact that the statutory provision created a serious or truly criminal offence. Consequently, a conviction for the offence would have grave consequences for the defendant. Lord Reid stated:

> "... a stigma still attaches to any person convicted of a truly criminal offence, and the more serious or more disgraceful the offence the greater the stigma ... And equally important is the fact that fortunately the Press in this country are vigilant to expose injustice and every manifestly unjust conviction made known to the public tends to injure the body politic by undermining public confidence in the justice of the law and of its administration." [1970] A.C. 132 at 149–150

It would be impractical to impose strict or absolute liability for an offence of this nature, as those who were responsible for letting properties could not reasonably be expected to know everything that their tenants were doing.

STRICT LIABILITY OFFENCES AT COMMON LAW

At common law, the general rule of criminal liability is that offences require proof of mens rea. Where liability arises under a statutory provision, there has been a considerable degree of inconsistency with different rules of construction in statutory interpretation, thereby producing varying assessments of the intent of the legislature. However, in *Sweet v Parsley* [1970] A.C. 132, Lord Reid postulated the following guidelines for all cases where the offence is criminal as opposed to quasi-criminal. First, wherever a statutory provision is silent as to mens rea, there is a presumption that in order to give effect to the will of Parliament, words importing mens rea must be read into the provision by the courts. Secondly, it is a universal principle that if a statutory provision creating a criminal offence is reasonably capable of two interpretations, that interpretation which is most favourable to the defendant must be adopted. Thirdly, the fact that other sections of the legislation expressly require mens rea is not by itself sufficient to justify a decision that another section that is silent as to mens rea creates an absolute or strict liability offence. Occasionally, it will be necessary for the courts to go outside the legislation and examine all relevant circumstances in order to establish the intention of the legislature. The canons of statutory interpretation currently invoked by the Irish Superior Courts are broadly divided into two categories: the literal approach, and the schematic or teleological approach. In cases where the literal approach clearly leads to an "absurdity", the courts may reject the literal approach and have recourse to the schematic or teleological approach. To that end, the scheme and purpose of the legislation at issue should be examined to determine if an offence of strict liability was intended by the legislature. The literal rule of statutory interpretation is qualified and there is a rebuttable presumption that the legislature intended a mens rea element to be a requirement in any provision that creates a criminal offence.

Legislation that is designed to deal with pollution offences and unlawful and dangerous drugs is generally interpreted as imposing strict liability. In *Gammon v Attorney General of Hong Kong* [1985] A.C. 1, Lord Scarman rebutted the presumption of mens rea because public safety was threatened by the defendant's conduct. In *Environment Agency v Empress Car Co (Abertillery) Ltd* [1997] 2 A.C. 22, the House of Lords gave examples of cases in which strict liability had been imposed for causing events that were the immediate consequences of the deliberate acts of third parties, but which the defendant had a duty to prevent or take reasonable care to prevent. If words such as "knowingly" or "wilfully" appear in the section, the inference is that the Parliament intended a mens rea requirement in that section. However, if words implying mens rea are present in some sections, but not others, this suggests that the Parliament deliberately excluded a fault element in those sections that are silent. In considering offences created in the Children Act 1960, Lord Hutton in *B (A Minor) v DPP* [2000] 2 A.C. 428 stated the current position in English criminal law:

"... the test is not whether it is a reasonable implication that the statute rules out [*mens rea*] as a constituent part of the crime—the test is whether it is a necessary implication." [2000] 2 A.C. 428 at 481

As to the meaning of "necessary implication", Lord Nicholls said:

"Necessary implication connotes an implication which is compellingly clear. Such an implication may be found in the language used, the nature of the offence, the mischief sought to be prevented and any other circumstances which may assist in determining what intention is properly to be attributed to Parliament when creating the offence."

Necessary implication may arise not only from the statutory provision under consideration, but also from the rules governing that provision; these rules can be deduced from other provisions of the legislation. The Superior Courts must examine the overall purpose of the statute. If the intention is to introduce quasi-criminal offences, then strict liability will be acceptable to facilitate prosecutions and to encourage future compliance as, for instance, in the case of fixed-penalty parking offences. However, if the policy issues involved are significant and the punishments are more severe, the test must be whether reading a mens rea requirement into the legislation will defeat the Parliament's intention in creating the offence at issue. For instance, if defendants could escape criminal liability too easily by pleading ignorance, this would not address the "mischief" that Parliament was attempting to remedy by creating such offences.

The common law offence of blasphemy is defined as a writing that is deemed to be blasphemous, in that it has a tendency to shock and outrage Christians. In *R v Lemon and Gay News Ltd* [1979] A.C. 617, the House of Lords held that it is unnecessary to prove that the defendant was aware of the tendency, but is sufficient that he intentionally used words which were in fact likely to shock and outrage. The majority rejected the contention that this was effectively imposing strict liability, but the minority disagreed. Arguably, the minority judgment was correct to regard this as the imposition of strict liability as the defendant could have been convicted and been completely unaware that his conduct had the quality which made it a criminal offence.

STATUTORY OFFENCES AND MENS REA

In contemporary criminal law, strict liability offences are created by legislation, including offences relating to the preparation of food, possessing unlawful weapons and drugs, and driving offences such as drink-driving and speeding. There are very few common law offences of strict liability; examples include public nuisance, blasphemous libel, outraging public decency and criminal defamatory libel.

The decision on whether or not the liability of an offence is strict is often also dependant on the severity of the penalty, that is, the larger the penalty, the less likely it is that the offence is one of strict liability. In *Toppin v Marcas* [1908] 2 I.R. 423, Palles C.B. opined:

> "... where an act, not in any real sense criminal, is in the public interest prohibited under a penalty, the innocent nature of the act is at least an element to assist the Court in determining whether or not mens rea is an essential ingredient." [1908] 2 I.R. 423 at 426

In *M'Adam v Dublin United Tramways Company Ltd* [1929] I.R. 327, the defendants were charged with overloading a tram, contrary to the by-laws under s.50 of the Dublin Carriage Act 1853 which provided that:

> No passenger shall be permitted to travel on the platform, or on any part of such stage carriage, except in or on the place or places set apart and specified in the licence for conveying passengers, and no stage carriage shall contain at any one time any greater number of inside or outside passengers than the number of same respectively specified in the licence.

Sullivan P., was of the opinion that these prohibitions were absolute, noting that the object of the regulation was to protect the public:

> "The acts in this case are not in any real sense criminal, but in the public interest they are prohibited under a penalty. Having regard to that fact, and to the terms of the regulation and the object it had in view, I am of opinion that [mens rea] is not an essential ingredient in the offences charged against the defendants." [1929] I.R. 327 at 334

Sullivan P. did note, however, that the issue of fault would mitigate the penalty on conviction. In that case, it was held that the prosecution did not have to prove mens rea in order to establish a breach of regulations as to the number of passengers carried on a tram. However, in *Duncan v Gleeson* [1969] I.R. 116, the use of the word "permit" in a statute was held to impute a requirement of mens rea in order to establish liability. Thus, it would appear that in order to find an offence to be one of strict liability, the courts will look both to the wording of the statute itself, and to the subject matter with which the offence deals.

R v K [2002] 1 A.C. 462 considered s.14 of the Sexual Offences Act 1956, which provided that neither a girl under 16 years of age nor a defective could give consent which would prevent an act being an assault for the purposes of the section. It was a defence for the person who had acted indecently towards the defective to prove that he did not know, and had no reason to suspect, that she was defective, but an honest belief she was not defective would not suffice. Subject to this statutory defence, the offence was one of strict liability. On the contrary, there was no statutory defence for the person who assaulted the consenting girl who was under the age of 16 years. The House of Lords held that it was for the prosecution to prove that the defendant did not have the honest belief that he asserted. Thus, offences of strict liability are vulnerable to challenge by the revitalised presumption of mens rea (cf. *R v Kumar* [2005] Crim. L.R. 470).

CRITERIA

In *Gammon v Attorney General for Hong Kong* [1985] 1 A.C. 1, the Privy Council considered the scope and role of strict liability offences in modern criminal law and their effect upon the presumption of mens rea. Lord Scarman laid down the following criteria upon which a court should decide whether or not it is appropriate to impose strict liability:

> "(1) there is a presumption of law that *mens rea* is required before a person can be held guilty of a criminal offence; (2) the presumption is particularly strong where the offence is 'truly criminal' in character; (3) the presumption applies to statutory offences, and can be displaced only if this is clearly or by necessary implication the effect of the statute; (4) the only situation in which the presumption can be displaced is where the statute is concerned with an issue of social concern, and public safety is such an issue; (5) even where a statute is concerned with such an issue, the presumption of *mens rea* stands unless it can also be shown that the creation of strict liability will be effective to promote the objects of the statute by encouraging greater vigilance to prevent the commission of the prohibited act." [1985] 1 A.C. 1 at 14

The Privy Council set out the relationship between the presumption of mens rea and the category of offences which justify its rebuttal.

Policy considerations governing strict liability offences typically relate to issues of social protection. In *Warner v Metropolitan Police Commissioner* [1969] 2 A.C. 256, the House of Lords held that the offence of possession was absolute and, once he was in possession, he was deemed to have committed the offence. His belief that both boxes contained only scent merely went to mitigation of sentence. In *R v Marriott* [1971] 1 W.L.R. 187, the defendant was convicted of being in possession of a small quantity of cannabis that was attached to a penknife. Although this was a strict liability offence, it was necessary for the prosecution to prove that something was stuck to the knife, but no further mens rea element was necessary to prove the offence.

The meaning of "truly criminal" offences was considered in *HSKAR v Paul Y-ITC Construction Ltd* [1998] 3 H.K.C. 189, in which the defendant was convicted of two offences: causing mechanical equipment to be used, and construction work to be carried out, without a construction noise permit. The Hong Kong Court of Appeal held that these offences were not "truly criminal" but rather based on the fact that such conduct was prohibited. The relevant legislation dealt with public wellbeing and pertained to public health issues. The court held that the legislative intent was that knowledge of the particular breaches of statutory provisions was necessary.

The propositions in *Gammon* have been accepted by the Irish Supreme Court in *Maguire v Shannon Regional Fisheries Board* [1994] 3 I.R. 581, but have been rejected in other jurisdictions, including Australia and New Zealand, because of their inherent vagueness. In *Millar v Ministry for Transport* [1986] 1 N.Z.L.R. 660, the New Zealand Court of Appeal per Cooke P. considered that the guidelines postulated in *Gammon* could give such wide scope to strict liability that the presumption would be displaced more often than not.

PRESUMPTION OF MENS REA

There is a rebuttable presumption in favour of mens rea for all statutory offences. In *Sherras v De Rutzen* [1895] 1 Q.B. 918, the defendant was convicted of selling alcohol to a police officer whilst the police officer was on duty, contrary to s.16(2) of the Licensing Act 1872. He had reasonably believed the constable to be off duty as the constable had removed his armband, which was the acknowledged method of signifying that he was off duty. The Divisional Court held that the conviction should be quashed, despite the absence from the relevant section of any words indicating that proof of mens rea is required as an element of the offence. The presumption in favour of mens rea would only be displaced by the wording of the statute itself, or its subject matter. In this case, the latter factor was significant, in that no amount of reasonable care by the defendant would have prevented the offence from being committed. Wright J. stated:

> "There is a presumption that *mens rea*, an evil intention, or a knowledge of the wrongfulness of the act, is an essential ingredient in every offence; but that presumption is liable to be displaced either by the words of the statute creating the offence or by the subject-matter with which it deals, and both must be considered ...". [1895] 1 Q.B. 918 at 921

As previously stated, there are three exceptions to this general rule. First, where the acts are not criminal in any real sense, but are in the public interest, prohibited by public policy, secondly, in cases of public nuisances, and thirdly, in the case of proceedings that are criminal in form, but are really just a summary means of enforcing a civil right.

The presumption that mens rea is usually required was affirmed in *Sweet v Parsley* [1970] A.C. 132, where Lord Reid stated:

> "... whenever a section is silent as to *mens rea* there is a presumption that, in order to give effect to the will of Parliament, we must read in words appropriate to require *mens rea* ... [I]t is a universal principle that if a penal provision is reasonably capable of two interpretations, that interpretation which is most favourable to the accused must be adopted." [1970] A.C. 132 at 148–149

In that case, the defendant was the subtenant of a farmhouse and had let rooms. Cannabis was smoked in the farmhouse but it was shown that she had no knowledge of this. She was convicted of being concerned in the management of a premises used for the purpose of smoking cannabis, as the lower court found that it was an offence of strict liability. However, the House of Lords quashed her conviction.

In *People (DPP) v Murray* [1977] I.R. 360, the Supreme Court agreed with the presumption of mens rea in statutory offences. Henchy J. referred to *Sweet v Parsley*, but went further than the House of Lords decision and stated that the presumption is that mens rea is required as to each element of the offence, which, in Murray, was the offence of capital murder.

Language

In determining whether the presumption in favour of mens rea is to be displaced, the courts are required to have reference to the whole statute in which the offence appears. The wording of the statutory provision creating the offence is indicative of whether the offence is one of strict liability. When interpreting the meaning of statutory provisions, the superior courts will generally look for key words and phrases in the legislation under consideration when determining whether or not the offence is one of strict liability. If the statutory provision contains words such as: "permitting", "allowing", "causing", "possession", "knowingly", "wilfully" and "maliciously", then the prosecution must prove mens rea and the offence is not one of strict liability. Indeed, the term "permitting" has been held to import a fault element (see *James & Son Ltd v Smee* [1955] 1 Q.B. 78). In the absence of words importing mens rea into the statutory provision, the Superior Courts have recourse to the other textual features of the legislation; for instance, if a fault element is required in other provisions creating offences but not in the offence at issue, this may be a determining factor. In *Alpacell Ltd v Woodward* [1972] A.C. 824, the interpretation of the Rivers (Prevention of Pollution) Act 1951 was at issue. The relevant provision stipulated for the punishment of a person who "causes or knowingly permits" pollutants to enter a river. The House of Lords held that the word "knowingly" modified the meaning of "permits", but not "causes." This decision was adopted by the Irish High Court in *Maguire v Shannon Regional Fisheries Board* [1994] 3 I.R. 581, where the appellant was convicted under s.171(1)(b) of the Fisheries (Consolidation) Act 1959 (the "1959 Act"), which provided that any person who "throws, empties, permits or causes to fall into any waters any deleterious matter" is guilty of an offence. The appellant was the proprietor of a piggery and a pipe had fractured, causing whey to flow into the river. The court held that the pollution of rivers was a strict liability offence and would therefore encourage greater vigilance by proprietors in that context. Lynch J. referred to the decision in Alphacell and the proposition that where there is no wrongful intention or indeed criminal negligence, that will serve to mitigate sentence, but the conviction will still stand. *Shannon Regional Fisheries Board v Cavan County Council* [1996] 3 I.R. 267 also concerned s.171(1)(b) of the 1959 Act. Owing to population increases, a sewage treatment works operated by the defendant had become inadequate, but as funding to upgrade it was controlled by the Department of the Environment, the treatment works was never upgraded. Eventually the river became polluted from the sewage outflow from the treatment works and the Supreme Court held that the issue of strict liability was not applicable as the defendants had the relevant intention. However, the court approved the position that the offence was in fact one of strict liability.

ENFORCEABILITY

The issue of enforceability has also been invoked by the Superior Courts when determining whether or not the statutory offence is one of strict liability. In *Lim Chin Aik v R* [1963] A.C. 160, the defendant was convicted of contravening an order prohibiting, in absolute terms, his entry into Singapore, despite the fact that he did not have knowledge of the order. In allowing the defendant's appeal against conviction, the Privy Council stated that the imposition of strict liability could only be justified where it would actually succeed in placing the onus on individuals to comply with legislative provisions. If the defendant is unaware that he has been made the subject of an order prohibiting him from entering a country, then the imposition of strict liability for failing to comply with that order would not in any way promote its observance. Lord Evershed stated:

"Where the subject matter of the statute is the regulation for the public welfare of a particular activity ... it can be and frequently has been inferred that the legislature intended that such activities be carried out under conditions of strict liability. The presumption is that the statute ... can be effectively enforced only if those in charged of the relevant activities are made responsible for seeing that they are complied with. When such a presumption is to be inferred, it displaces the ordinary presumption of [mens rea] ... But it is not enough in their Lordships' opinion merely to label the statute as one dealing with a grave social evil and from that to infer that strict liability was intended. It is pertinent also to inquire whether putting the defendant under strict liability will assist in the enforcement of the regulations. That means that there must be something he can do, directly or indirectly, by supervision or inspection, by improvement of his business methods or by exhorting those whom he may be expected to influence or control, which will promote the observance of the regulations. Unless this is so, there is no reason in penalising him, and it cannot be inferred that the legislature imposed strict liability merely in order to find a luckless victim."
[1963] A.C. 160 at 174

This issue was also referred to by the High Court in *Maguire v Shannon Regional Fisheries Board*. [1994] 3 I.R. 581

GRAVITY OF PUNISHMENT

As a general rule, the more serious the criminal offence created by statute, the less likely the courts are to view it as an offence of strict liability. The sanction stipulated for by the statutory provision creating the offence will be taken into account by the Superior Courts in determining whether or not an offence is one of strict liability. For instance, in *Sherras v de Rutzen* [1895] 1 Q.B. 918, the Divisional Court declined to impose strict liability on the basis that a direct consequence of a conviction would be endorsement of the defendant's licence. Likewise, in *The Queen v Strawbridge* [1970] N.Z.L.R. 909, the Court of Appeal for Wellington refused to accept the prosecution's arguments that parliament would have intended an offence carrying a maximum penalty of 14 years' imprisonment to be one that could be imposed in the absence of a fault element or mens rea. However, this issue is not determinative as, for instance, in *Gammon v Attorney General for Hong Kong* [1985] A.C. 1, the Privy Council upheld a conviction on the basis of strict liability, despite the fact that the offence was one that attracted a penalty of three years' imprisonment or a fine of HK$250,000.

Defence of Due Diligence

In *The Queen v Strawbridge* [1970] N.Z.L.R. 909, the New Zealand Court of Appeal outlined a three-fold classification of criminal offences. The first requires mens rea; the second consists of what the court described as absolute offences where no question of criminal liability without fault pertains; and the third is an intermediate division of offences, where an inference of mens rea can be drawn from proof of the prohibited conduct. However, if there was evidence that the defendant acted on an honest and reasonable belief in the facts that would make his conduct innocent, then he should be acquitted. Likewise, in *R v City of Sault Ste Marie* (1978) 85 D.L.R. (3d) 161, the Canadian Supreme Court established a three-fold classification of criminal offences and recognised a defence of due diligence to strict liability offences. First, there are offences, that require proof of full mens rea. Secondly, there are strict liability offences where proof of the defendant's prohibited conduct will prima facie be sufficient for the imposition of strict liability, but the defendant will avoid criminal liability if it can be established that he exercised all reasonable care. The burden of proof rests with the defendant to prove that he took reasonable care in the circumstances. Thirdly, there are offences of absolute liability for which there is no exculpatory defence available to the defendant. Truly criminal offences fall into the first category, while public welfare and other regulatory offences would fall into the second category, unless the wording of the statutory provision imported a fault element (mens rea). The third category is effectively residual and few criminal offences would be included in this category.

In *Millar v Ministry for Transport* [1986] 1 N.Z.L.R. 660, the Court of Appeal for Wellington noted that the inherent difficulty with the Strawbridge decision is that it involved reading a mixed objective and subjective mens rea formula into the statutory provision at issue. Cooke P. stated that the proper approach to be adopted when dealing with statutory offences was:

> "... a general approach to statutory offences when the words give no clear indication of legislative intent and there is no overriding judicial history, it will be right to begin by asking whether there is really anything weighty enough to displace the ordinary rule that a guilty mind is an essential ingredient of criminal liability. If there is, the next inquiry should be whether the statutory purpose and the interests of justice are on balance best served by allowing a defence of total absence of fault, with the onus on the defendant." [1986] 1 N.Z.L.R. 660 at 668

The court held that justice would be better served with an absence of fault formula, with the onus placed on the defendant.

In *Shannon Regional Fisheries Board v Cavan County Council* [1996] 3 I.R. 267, Keane J. endorsed the appropriateness of an indeterminate state between offences requiring full mens rea and strict liability, and cited *R v City of Sault Ste Marie*. Keane J. was, however, in the minority and his judgment is therefore obiter. However, this approach is logical and a reconsideration of the issue might influence the Superior Courts to endorse the trend that is evident in certain commonwealth jurisdictions.

Applying the defence of due diligence for strict liability offences, the prosecution would continue to be relieved of the requirement of proving the mens rea of the offence, but the defendant could plead a defence of due diligence. In the absence of a clear legislative intent to the contrary, all regulatory offences are presumed to impose strict liability.

IMPACT OF THE ECHR

Offences of absolute liability would conceivably violate art.6(2) of the European Convention on Human Rights (the "ECHR"), which guarantees the presumption of innocence in criminal proceedings. The reasoning is that, once the prohibited conduct is proved, the defendant is presumed to be criminally liable. Notwithstanding this proposition, the ECtHR has held that strict liability offences are compatible with the article, stating in *Salabiaku v France* (1991) 13 E.H.R.R. 379 that:

> "... in principle, the Contracting States may, under certain conditions, penalise a simple or objective fact as such, irrespective of whether it results from criminal intent or from negligence. Examples of such offences may be found in the laws of the Contracting States." (1991) 13 E.H.R.R. 379 at 387

The applicant was charged with unlawful importation of narcotics and customs offences of smuggling prohibited goods. He was acquitted on the first charge, but convicted on the second. The ECrtHR unanimously held that there was no violation of art.6(2) of the Convention, since the applicant was convicted not for the mere possession of unlawfully imported prohibited goods, but for smuggling such goods.

CONSTITUTIONALITY OF STRICT LIABILITY OFFENCES

The constitutionality of strict liability offences that provide severe penalties on conviction was considered by the Supreme Court in *CC v Ireland* [2006] 4 I.R. 1, pertaining to s.1(2) of the Criminal Law (Amendment) Act 1935, that was struck down as being unconstitutional because the offence created by this provision failed to provide for a defence of honest belief as to the age of the complainant. The maximum sentence on conviction for this offence was life imprisonment, but the section was silent as to mens rea, hence the offence was deemed to be one of strict liability. Thus, if the Oireachtas purports to impose strict liability for serious criminal offences, this will not survive a constitutional challenge, as the defendant has a right to a trial in due course of law, in accordance with Art.38.1.

FURTHER READING

Campbell, Kilcommins and O'Sullivan, *Criminal Law in Ireland: Cases and Commentary* (Dublin: Clarus Press, 2010), pp.164–183.

Coen, "Whither Strict Liability" (2007) 25 I.L.T. 77.

Hanly, *An Introduction to Irish Criminal Law,* 2nd edn (Dublin: Gill & Macmillan, 2006), pp.91–93.

McAuley and McCutcheon, *Criminal Liability: A Grammar* (Dublin: Round Hall, 2000), Ch.7.

6. Introduction to Defences

INTRODUCTION

For criminal law to be effective, it has to proceed on certain presumptions, such as self-restraint and the capacity of the individual to refrain from committing offences. Otherwise, it would be difficult for the law to create a sufficient degree of order in society. A great deal of crime occurs out of anger, greed, revenge and depravation, but if all defences prevailed in all circumstances, then no one would be found guilty.

The prosecution must prove beyond a reasonable doubt that the defendant committed the actus reus with the requisite mens rea for the offence charged in the indictment. In discharging this burden of proof, the prosecution must also disprove any defences raised by the defendant. A complete defence, such as duress, necessity or self-defence, may exculpate the defendant from liability, resulting in a complete acquittal. Conversely, a partial defence, such as provocation, reduces the defendant's level of criminal responsibility but will not result in a complete acquittal.

JUSTIFICATION AND EXCUSE

The criminal law distinguishes between a justification and an excuse. A justification denies the objective wrongness of the defendant's conduct, that is, conduct of which society approves (or at least does not condemn), such as self-defence. Necessity and duress may proceed either from justification or excuse.

This doctrinal conflict, though important in its own right, is part of a broader and more significant dispute about the nature of criminal defences and the balance between defences of justification and defences of excuse. A justification denies the objective wrongness of the defendant's conduct, that is, conduct of which society approves (or at least does not condemn), such as self-defence. A justification refers to something that the defendant was entitled to do, such as where he acted in self-defence. Most defences, however, are classified as excuses, whereby the defendant was not entitled to do what he did, but the law may nevertheless excuse (either wholly or partially) the offender. An excuse is where the conduct is wrong but the defendant is excused because of some condition that negates culpability on his part, such as where the defendant acted out of necessity. Acts are justified while actors might be excused.

Burden of Proof

The prosecution authorities must discharge the burden of proof pertaining to all facts that constitute a denial of the offence charged, or the defence put forward by the defendant. The burden of proof must be discharged by the prosecuting authorities disproving the evidence supporting the defendant's denial or defence. In *People (AG) v Quinn* [1965] I.R. 366, Walsh J. provided the following analysis of self-defence, and the same principles are applicable to defences in criminal law:

> "When the evidence in a case, whether it be the evidence offered by the prosecution or by the defence, discloses a possible defence of self-defence the onus remains throughout upon the prosecution to establish that the accused is guilty of the offence charged. The onus is never upon the accused to raise a doubt in the minds of the jury. In such case the burden rests on the prosecution to negative the possible defence of self-defence which has arisen and if, having considered the whole of the evidence, the jury is either convinced of the innocence of the prisoner or left in doubt whether or not he was acting in necessary self-defence they must acquit. Before the possible defence can be left to the jury as an issue there must be some evidence from which the jury would be entitled to find that issue in favour of the appellant. If the evidence for the prosecution does not disclose this possible defence then the necessary evidence will fall to be given by the defence. In such a case, however, where it falls to the defence to give the necessary evidence it must be made clear to the jury that there is a distinction, fine though it may appear, between adducing the evidence and the burden of proof and that there is no onus whatever upon the accused to establish any degree of doubt in their minds. In directing the jury on the question of the onus of proof it can only be misleading to a jury to refer to 'establishing' the defence 'in such a way as to raise a doubt.' No defence has to be 'established' in any case apart from insanity. In a case where there is evidence, whether it be disclosed in the prosecution case or in the defence case, which is sufficient to leave the issue of self-defence to the jury the only question the jury has to consider is whether they are satisfied beyond reasonable doubt that the accused killed the deceased (if it be a case of homicide) and whether the jury is satisfied beyond reasonable doubt that the prosecution has negatived the issue of self-defence. If the jury is not satisfied beyond reasonable doubt on both of these matters the accused must be acquitted." [1965] I.R. 366 at 382–383

The standard of proof is beyond reasonable doubt. The exception to this general rule is where the defence of insanity is pleaded by the defendant: he must discharge the burden of establishing this defence on the balance of probabilities.

Proposed Law Reform

The Law Reform Commission's *Report on Defences in Criminal Law* (LRC 95-2009) makes 46 specific recommendations for reform of the law governing defences and includes a draft Criminal Law (Defences) Bill 2009 to implement these proposed recommendations. The Report deals with: legitimate defence (self-defence); defence of the home; use of force in law enforcement; the defence of provocation; and the defences duress and necessity, which will be discussed in subsequent chapters.

FURTHER READING

Campbell, Kilcommins and O'Sullivan, *Criminal Law in Ireland: Cases and Commentary* (Dublin: Clarus Press, 2010), Ch.21.

Law Reform Commission, *Report on Defences in Criminal Law* (LRC 95–2009).

Robinson, "Criminal Law Defenses: A Systematic Analysis" (1982) 82 Colum. L. Rev. 199.

7. Infancy

Introduction

The criminal law assumes that young children do not sufficiently understand the difference between right and wrong in order for them to be responsible for their conduct. One of the most difficult areas of criminal justice policy pertains to the provision of appropriate legal mechanisms to reflect the transition from the age of childhood innocence through to maturity and full responsibility under the criminal law. The defence of infancy is an excuse in order that defendants are excluded from criminal liability for their actions, if, at the time of committing the offence, they had not reached an age of criminal responsibility.

Age of Criminal Responsibility

Section 52 of the Children Act 2001, as amended by s.129 of the Criminal Justice Act 2006, provides that the age of criminal responsibility is 12 years of age (doli capax):

(1) It shall be conclusively presumed that no child under the age of 12 years is capable of committing an offence.
(2) There is a rebuttable presumption that a child who is not less than 12 but under 14 years of age is incapable of committing an offence because the child did not have the capacity to know that the act or omission concerned was wrong.

As a general rule, children under 12 years of age cannot be charged with an offence and are considered incapable of committing an offence in law. There is an exception to this general rule in that children aged 10 or 11 years can be charged and prosecuted for murder, manslaughter, rape, rape under s.4 of the Criminal Law (Rape) (Amendment) Act 1990, or aggravated sexual assault. In other words, there is a rebuttable presumption that a child aged 10 or 11 years is incapable in law of committing an offence (doli incapax). Where a child under 14 years of age is charged with an offence, no proceedings can be taken without the consent of the DPP.

Duty of Gardaí in Relation to Under-Age Children

While the Children Act 2001 (the "2001 Act") generally exempts children under 12 years of age from criminal responsibility, provision is made for children to be dealt with in other ways. Section 53 of the 2001 Act, as amended by s.130 of the Criminal Justice Act 2006, places an onus on the Gardaí to bring a child under 12 years of age to his or her parents or guardian in circumstances where the Gardaí have reasonable grounds for believing that the child has committed a criminal offence.

Where this is not possible, as is frequently the case, the Gardaí will arrange for the child to be taken into the custody of the Health Service Executive (the "HSE") for the area in which the child normally resides. Although it is possible that children under 12 years of age who have performed an illegal act will be dealt with by the HSE and not the criminal justice system, the practical issue of the effectiveness of these procedures will depend on the resources available to HSE personnel. It is the general policy of criminal law that children should only be detained as a last resort and community based measures should be considered in the first instance.

FURTHER READING

Campbell, Kilcommins and O'Sullivan, *Criminal Law in Ireland: Cases and Commentary* (Dublin: Clarus Press, 2010), pp.986–993.

Hanly, *An Introduction to Irish Criminal Law*, 2nd edn (Dublin: Gill and MacMillan, 2006), Ch.12.

Hanly, "Child Offenders: The Changing Response of Irish Law" (1997) 19 D.U.L.J. 113.

Hanly, "The Defence of Infancy" (1996) 6(1) I.C.L.J. 72.

Kilkelly, "Reform of Youth Justice in Ireland: the 'New' Children Act 2001: Part 1" (2006) 16(4) I.C.L.J. 2.

Kilkelly, "Reform of Youth Justice in Ireland: the 'New' Children Act 2001: Part 2" (2007) 17(1) I.C.L.J. 2.

8. Insanity and Diminished Responsibility

Introduction

Criminal law stipulates that individuals suffering from a mental disorder need hospital treatment, as opposed to a term of imprisonment. Conviction and punishment is not likely to deter future antisocial conduct by mentally impaired individuals. A defendant may plead insanity, in that he did not have the capacity to form mens rea. Alternatively, a defendant might raise diminished responsibility as a partial defence to murder, where he knew what he was doing and that it was wrong but, due to an irresistible impulse, could not refrain from committing the illegal act. In the case of diminished responsibility, the defendant will have formed mens rea for murder and understood the nature and quality of his illegal conduct, but his responsibility is diminished due to an irresistible impulse. The law governing insanity and diminished responsibility is now provided for by the Criminal Law (Insanity) Act 2006 (the "2006 Act"), which clarified, modernised and reformed the law on criminal insanity and fitness to be tried.

An insanity defence is based on the theory that most people can make rational choices and obey the law, but some individuals cannot be held criminally liable because of a mental disorder which deprives the individual of the ability to make a rational and voluntary choice. In other words, some defendants would not have the capacity to form mens rea. A mental disorder is defined by s.1 of the 2006 Act as including: "mental illness, mental disability, dementia or any disease of the mind but does not include intoxication."

The mental state of a defendant charged with a criminal offence may be raised at two different stages in the criminal process: at the commencement of the criminal trial and, subsequently, during the decision on the guilt or innocence of the defendant. Individuals who are deemed to be, or have been, suffering from a mental disorder might be unfit to be tried and, in these circumstances, the trial will be stayed until such time as the defendant is deemed fit to be tried. If a criminal trial proceeds and the evidence establishes that the defendant committed the offence but was suffering from a mental disorder when the offence was committed, then the jury may return a verdict of not guilty by reason of insanity.

The 2006 Act brought Irish law into line with the jurisprudence of the European Convention on Human Rights pertaining to the review of continued detention of persons found not guilty by reason of insanity.

Fitness to be Tried

Section 4 of the 2006 Act sets out the procedures that apply if a defendant is deemed to be unfit to stand trial. The decision on whether or not a defendant is fit to be tried is made by the trial judge and, if there is a reasonable doubt that the defendant committed the offence, the defendant may be acquitted. If the defendant cannot understand the nature of the criminal charge or is unable to instruct his legal advisors, make a proper defence, challenge jurors or follow the evidence, then he will be deemed unfit to be tried (cf. *State (Coughlan) v Minister for Justice* [1968] I.L.T.R. 177). While this finding is not a decision as to guilt or innocence, if the defendant is found to be unfit to be tried, the trial is stayed until such time as the defendant is deemed fit to be tried. The trial judge decides how the individual should be dealt with in the interim; this usually involves committal to a designated centre, such as the Central Mental Hospital, or other suitable psychiatric hospital or unit, particularly if the individual is suffering from a mental disorder and is, therefore, in need of in-patient treatment, under the provisions of the Mental Health Act 2001. An individual will be committed to a designated centre if he remains a danger to himself and other members of society. Alternatively, the individual may be ordered to undergo out-patient psychiatric assessment although, in the first instance, he would be committed to a psychiatric hospital or unit for 14 days in order to determine his suitability for out-patient treatment. The person may appeal against a committal order. Similarly, the DPP may appeal against a decision that a person is unfit to be tried.

Verdict and Disposition

If the defendant was suffering from a mental disorder at the time that the offence was committed, the jury may return a verdict of not guilty by reason of insanity. The trial judge will then order that the person is detained in a psychiatric hospital or unit.

Appeals

Section 8(1) of the 2006 Act provides that a defendant tried in the District Court and found not guilty by reason of insanity may appeal against the finding to the Circuit Court. Section 8(6) provides that a person tried on indictment in the Circuit Court, the Central Criminal Court or the Special

Criminal Court and found not guilty by reason of insanity, may appeal against the finding to the Court of Criminal Appeal.

DIMINISHED RESPONSIBILITY

Section 6 of the Criminal Law (Insanity) Act 2006 introduced a statutory partial defence of diminished responsibility, which is applicable only to a murder charge. It is a partial defence to murder, in that a verdict of manslaughter is returned, not an acquittal. A conviction for murder carries a mandatory life sentence (Criminal Justice Act 1990, s.2), but for most other offences, including manslaughter, trial judges are vested with a wide measure of discretion in relation to sentencing. The defendant can plead an "irresistible impulse" only under the defence of diminished responsibility, not the defence of insanity (cf. *Doyle v Wicklow County Council* [1974] I.R. 55).

MENTAL HEALTH (CRIMINAL LAW) REVIEW BOARD

The Mental Health (Criminal Law) Review Board (the "Board") was established under s.11 of the 2006 Act and is the independent body responsible for reviewing the detention of patients at the Central Mental Hospital. The Board is permanent and replaces the pre-existing ad hoc Advisory Committee. The main function of the Board is to review the continued detention of detainees found not guilty by reason of insanity or unfit to be tried, who have been detained in a designated centre by order of a court. The Board also has responsibility for defendants who have been convicted and who suffer from a mental disorder while serving their sentences.

The Review Board is independent in the exercise of its functions and must have regard to the welfare and safety of the person whose detention it reviews, and also to the interests of the general public (s.11(2) of the 2006 Act). The Board may assign a legal representative to the detainee, unless one has already been assigned or retained on behalf of the detainee.

The Board is composed of a legal chairperson with at least 10 years' experience as a practising barrister or solicitor, and a number of other people as determined by the Minister for Health and Children, at least one of whom must be a consultant psychiatrist (Sch.1 of the 2006 Act). The Board is legally obliged to review each detention at least once every six months (s.13(2) of the 2006 Act).

REVIEW OF DETENTION

Section 13 of the 2006 Act provides for the various ways in which the detention of persons in a designated centre may be reviewed. This applies to persons found not guilty by reason of insanity or unfit to be tried, including persons detained under military law. A review of continued detention in a psychiatric hospital will be the responsibility of the clinical director of the centre where the patient is detained. Otherwise, the Board is responsible for ensuring that the continued detention of persons is reviewed at six-monthly intervals, or at such lesser intervals as the Board considers appropriate.

Where a person is deemed no longer unfit to be tried, the court of committal must be so informed and shall order that the person be brought before that court to be dealt with as the court considers proper. Where a person has been detained under military law, the appropriate authority has to be similarly informed so that the court-martial shall be reconvened.

Temporary Release and Transfer of Prisoners

Section 13 of the 2006 Act provides that the Review Board is legally obliged to review the continued detention of patients in designated centres and is empowered to grant a conditional, or unconditional, discharge if it considers that the person's detention is no longer required. However, this provision does not provide that the conditions attached to an order for conditional discharge can be enforced and this lacuna has resulted in difficulties for the Board in considering whether or not to grant such orders.

Section 14 provides for the temporary release, transfer and other matters pertaining to detained persons under the provisions of the 2006 Act. The purpose of this provision is to permit the arrangement for temporary release, transfer and related matters, without the need to apply to the Board on every occasion. The consent of the Minister for Justice and Law Reform must be obtained in order to ensure that the public interest is safeguarded. The Minister for Health and Children might also have an interest, particularly with regard to transfers to another designated centre and that is also provided for in s.14.

Criminal Law (Insanity) Bill 2010

The main purpose of the Criminal Law (Insanity) Bill 2010 (the "2010 Bill") is to provide greater power to the Mental Health (Criminal Law) Review Board pertaining to the conditional discharge of patients who are detained in a designated centre, having been found unfit to be tried or not guilty by reason of insanity. Under the 2006 Act, the Review Board can approve a conditional discharge where it is satisfied that the patient is suitable for discharge, but no power exists to recall the patient if the conditions of the discharge are breached. The 2010 Bill will amend the 2006 Act so as to provide that a patient can be returned to the centre if he or she is in material breach of the conditional discharge order. This is imperative in order to strike a fair and proportionate balance between safeguarding the rights of the person and the need to protect the community. If enacted, the Bill will provide that the conditional discharge provisions in the 2006 Act will enable patients who are no longer in need of detention in the Central Mental Hospital to be released, while ensuring that the safety and welfare of patients and the public interest are fully protected.

The 2010 Bill proposes to improve the operation of the 2006 Act dealing with the issue of fitness to be tried. Current procedures under the 2006 Act provide that, where an issue of a defendant's fitness to be tried arises, that person can be referred to the designated centre for assessment. To remove any doubt about compliance with art.5 of the European Convention on Human Rights, the 2010 Bill provides that a court must first hear evidence from a consultant psychiatrist before requiring a full assessment of the defendant. The 2010 Bill also provides that the court can order the assessment to be carried out on an in-patient or out-patient basis.

FURTHER READING

Boland, "Diminished Responsibility as a Defence in Irish Law" (1995) 5(2) I.C.L.J. 173.

Boland, "Diminished Responsibility as a Defence in Irish Law: Past English Mistakes and Future Irish Directions" (1996) 6(1) I.C.L.J. 19.

Campbell, Kilcommins and O'Sullivan, *Criminal Law in Ireland: Cases and Commentary* (Dublin: Clarus Press, 2010), pp.993–1006 and 1081–1086.

Conway, "Fitness to Plead in Light of the Criminal Law (Insanity) Bill 2002" (2003) 13(4) I.C.L.J. 2.

Hanly, *An Introduction to Irish Criminal Law*, 2nd edn (Dublin: Gill & Macmillan, 2006), Ch.8.

McAuley, *Insanity, Psychiatry and Criminal Responsibility* (Dublin: Round Hall, 1993).

McGillicuddy, "The Criminal Law (Insanity) Act 2006" (2006) 11(3) B.R. 95.

Mills, "Criminal Law (Insanity) Bill 2002: Putting the Sanity back into Insanity" (2003) 8(3) B.R. 101.

Yeo, "Rethinking the Incapacities of Insanity" (2001) 36 Ir. Jur. (N.S.) 275.

9. Automatism

Introduction

As a general rule, criminal liability will not be imposed on an individual for their conduct if they had no control over their actions. Automatism is an involuntary act, such as sleepwalking, which is performed while the individual is in a state of unconsciousness. The defendant cannot be said to have acted voluntarily because they were not fully aware of their actions while in a state of automatism. Automatism may be a defence in circumstances where the defendant lacked the requisite mental state (fault element) for the commission of a criminal offence. A defence based on automatism asserts that there was no offence committed in the legal sense because at the time of the commission of the prohibited act, the defendant had no psychic awareness or volition. Conversely, the defence of insanity asserts that the defendant possessed a degree of psychic awareness or volition, but at the time of performing the prohibited conduct the defendant had suffered from a mental disorder that had caused them to perform the prohibited conduct or had prevented them from understanding the wrongfulness of that conduct. It is the involuntary nature of the defendant's actions that justifies the defence of automatism in the appropriate circumstances.

Definition

The concepts of consciousness and involuntariness are linked in the definition of automatism, proposed by the Court of Appeal of Ontario in *R v K* (1970) 3 C.C.C. (2d) 84, where Lacourciére J. stated:

> "Automatism is a term used to describe unconscious, involuntary behaviour, the state of a person who, though capable of action is not conscious of what he is doing. It means an unconscious involuntary act where the mind does not go with what is being done."

The defendant's conduct must be voluntary for the imposition of criminal liability.

The relationship between voluntariness and consciousness was also addressed in *R v Falconer* (1990) 50 A. Crim. R. 244, where the High Court of Australia per Mason C.J. stated:

> "Although the prosecution bears the onus of proving beyond a reasonable doubt that an act which is an element of an offence charged was a willed act or, at common law, was done voluntarily ... the prosecution may rely on the inference that an act done by an apparently conscious actor is willed or voluntary to discharge that onus unless there are grounds for believing that the accused was unable to control that act." (1990) 50 A.Crim.R. 244 at 250

The jury may infer voluntariness from consciousness, although evidence of a lack of consciousness may support the defendant's plea of automatism. In *Rabey v R* [1980] 2 S.C.R. 513, Dickson J. opined:

> "Automatism may be subsumed in the defence of insanity in cases in which the unconscious action of an accused can be traced to, or rooted in, a disease of the mind. Where that is so, the defence of insanity prevails." [1980] 2 S.C.R. 518 at 524

Unless a state of automatism can be attributed to some cause external to the mind of the defendant, the proper plea is one of insanity.

Automatism and lack of voluntariness were succinctly described in *Bratty v Attorney General for Northern Ireland* [1963] A.C. 386, where Viscount Kilmuir L.C. Lord adopted the Court of Appeal's definition:

> "... as connoting the state of a person who, though capable of action, is not conscious of what he is doing ... It means unconscious involuntary action, and it is a defence because the mind does not go with what is being done." [1968] A.C. 386 at 401

In *Bratty*, the appellant suffered from psychomotor epilepsy. He claimed that a "sort of blackness" came over him during which he strangled and killed a woman. The trial judge instructed the jury to consider the defence of insanity, but not automatism. On appeal against his conviction, the appellant asserted that automatism should have been available to the jury in their deliberations as an alternative defence on the basis that the appellant's conduct was not directed by his mind. This was rejected by the House of Lords, who held that the only cause of the automatism alleged was a defect of reason from a disease of the mind. Lord Denning stated:

> "The requirement that it should be a voluntary act is essential, not only in a murder case, but also in every criminal case. No act is punishable if it is done involuntarily: and an involuntary act in this context—some people nowadays prefer to speak of it as 'automatism'—means an act

which is done by the muscles without any control by the mind, such as a spasm, a reflex action or a convulsion; or an act done by a person who is not conscious of what he is doing, such as an act done whilst suffering from concussion or whilst sleep-walking ... The term 'involuntary act' is, however, capable of wider connotations: and to prevent confusion it is to be observed that in the criminal law an act is not to be regarded as an involuntary act simply because the doer does not remember it ... Nor is an act to be regarded as an involuntary act simply because the doer could not control his impulse to do it ... Nor is an act to be regarded as an involuntary act simply because it is unintentional or its consequences are unforeseen." [1963] A.C. 386 at 409

Lord Denning drew a distinction between insanity and automatism in the following terms.

"... if the involuntary act proceeds from a disease of the mind, it gives rise to a defence of insanity, but not to a defence of automatism. Suppose a crime is committed by a man in a state of automatism or clouded consciousness due to a recurrent disease of the mind. Such an act is no doubt involuntary, but it does not give rise to an unqualified acquittal, for that would mean that he would be let at large to do it again. The only proper verdict is one which ensures that the person who suffers from the disease is kept secure in a hospital so as not to be a danger to himself or others. That is, a verdict of guilty but insane." [1963] A.C. 386 at 410

There are two key elements of automatism that require further elaboration, namely the degree of consciousness necessary to render conduct involuntary, and the relationship between insanity and automatism.

INTERNAL AND EXTERNAL FACTORS

If the automatic state is caused by an internal factor, physical or mental, then it is deemed a disease of the mind and, thus, a form of insanity. It is referred to as insane automatism and dealt with under the law of insanity. External factors, such as a blow to the head, will result in an acquittal because the defendant is deemed to have had no control over his actions and it is unlikely to recur, unlike insane automatism, which is likely to recur. A dilemma arises where an external factor causes an internal factor. In *R v T* [1990] Crim. L.R. 256, the defendant was raped and suffered post-traumatic stress disorder. She subsequently participated in a robbery and was prosecuted for that offence. Southan J. (Snaresbrook Crown Court) held that the issue of non-insane automatism should have been considered by the jury on the basis that the internal factor, post-traumatic stress disorder, had in effect been caused by the external factor, which in this case was the prior rape of the defendant. The jury nevertheless convicted her.

DEGREE OF CONSCIOUSNESS

In *Bratty*, Lord Denning indicated that something less than complete unconsciousness might constitute automatism; however, the authorities in England and Wales seem to suggest that complete unconsciousness is required. In *Attorney General's Reference (No. 2 of 1992)* [1994] Q.B. 91, the defendant was a lorry driver who crashed into a broken-down vehicle on the hard shoulder of a motorway, resulting in the deaths of two people. The defence of automatism was left to the jury and the defendant was acquitted of causing death by reckless driving on the grounds of automatism. The expert evidence suggested that the defendant had been lulled into a trance-like state by the monotonous nature of the journey and, because of this, was suffering from reduced awareness. The Court of Appeal held that, as his awareness was only reduced, the defence of automatism should not have been left to the jury. In other words, the defence of automatism required a total destruction of voluntary control by the defendant, and reduced or partial control was insufficient to form a defence.

The meaning of automatism was considered by the Irish High Court in *O'Brien v Parker* [1997] 2 I.L.R.M. 170. This was a civil case in which the defendant had been involved in a road traffic accident. He contended that, at the time of the accident, he suffered an epileptic fit that had come on without any forewarning, but he did concede that he retained some degree of awareness and could make certain decisions. The High Court noted the existence of the defence of automatism in Irish law and stated that it must be established that the defendant had no control at all over his actions. As he had retained a degree of control, the defence of automatism would not be available. Applying the objective test, a driver who had crashed into another vehicle after suffering from an epileptic fit would have been negligent if they had been aware of the symptoms beforehand and had failed to react.

This strict approach was not followed in *Ryan v The Queen* [1967] 121 C.L.R. 205, in which the High Court of Australia held that the key issue was whether an exercise of will by the defendant was absent. A less strict approach was also adopted in *R v Tait* [1976] V.R. 151, in which there was sufficient evidence that the defendant was in a state of clouded consciousness for the jury to consider the defence of automatism. The less strict approach to automatism seems logical as it focuses on the essence of automatism, that is, whether the defendant acted voluntarily and not whether he was conscious or aware of what was happening to him at the pertinent time.

AUTOMATISM AND INSANITY

The defence of automatism is effectively an intermediate position between criminal responsibility and legal insanity. Distinguishing between automatism and insanity gives rise to a dilemma in criminal law. As a consequence of the close relationship between the two legal concepts, criminal law distinguishes between insane automatism and non-insane automatism.

The law governing insanity deals with insane automatism, which means that the burden of proof is on the defendant and the verdict is "not guilty on grounds of insanity". As a consequence of being found "not guilty on the grounds of insanity", individuals will be detained in a designated centre. This verdict is appropriate when the state of mind of the defendant arises from a disease of the mind. The law relating to the definition of "a disease of the mind" in this context is complex, with certain medical conditions including hyperglycaemia and epilepsy causing particular problems. Two approaches have been established. The first depends on whether the defendant's mental condition is the product of an external factor, such as a blow to the head or suchlike, or alternatively, an internal factor resulting from a defect of reason from a disease of the mind. The second approach is whether the medical condition is one which is likely to recur, in which case it is deemed to be a disease of the mind. For instance, in *R v Sullivan* [1984] A.C. 156, the House of Lords held that epilepsy is a disease of the mind, which is an internal factor and likely to recur, and will therefore be classified as insane automatism.

In *R v Burgess* [1991] 2 Q.B. 92, in which the issue of somnambulism was considered, the defendant had committed a violent attack on the victim and was charged with wounding with intent. While asleep, he hit the victim on the head with a bottle and a video recorder and then held her by the throat. The victim awoke to find the defendant holding the video above her head and she managed to wake him up. He claimed that he had no memory of the event and woke up dazed and confused. The prosecution argued that he was sleep-walking, and a defence of non-insane automatism was raised. The trial judge held that an insanity verdict was appropriate as the defendant was not aware of what he was doing at the time that he had committed the assault. The Court of Appeal upheld the trial judge's decision, stating that, if the defendant laboured under a disorder which was due to an internal factor, and, therefore, was likely to recur, then insane automatism was the correct defence. This case can be contrasted with *R v Parks* [1992] 95 D.L.R. (4th) 27, in which the defendant was charged with murder. He claimed to have been asleep when he drove his car some 23 kilometres at night to the house of his wife's parents, where he then proceeded to stab and beat both his mother-in-law and his father-in-law. His mother-in-law died as a result and his father-in-law sustained serious injuries. A number of defence witnesses, including experts in sleep disorders, gave evidence to the effect that sleep walking is not regarded as a disease of the mind, mental illness or mental disorder, and the trial judge directed the jury that, if the defendant was in a state of somnambulism at the time of the killing, then he was entitled to be acquitted on the basis of non-insane automatism. The defendant was acquitted of the murder of his mother-in-law and subsequently acquitted of the attempted murder of his father-in-law. The prosecution appealed, and the Supreme Court of Canada upheld the reasoning of the trial judge for two reasons. First, as regards the evidence put before the court, there was no way for the court to hold that sleep-walking was a disease of the mind. The second reason is policy based, and La Forest stated:

> "One could argue that the particular amalgam of stress, excessive exercise, sleep deprivation and sudden noises in the night that causes an incident of somnambulism is, for the sleeping person, analogous to the effect of a concussion upon a waking person, which is generally accepted as an external cause of non-insane automatism ... In the end, the dichotomy between internal and external causes becomes blurred in this context, and is not helpful in resolving the inquiry." [1992] 95 D.L.R. (4th) 27 at 28

The possibility of recurrence was one of several factors to be considered, and its absence would not necessarily preclude a finding of insanity. However, it is questionable whether any purpose is served by classifying somnambulism as a disease of the mind. The courts might be justified in treating somnambulism as a defence of non-insane automatism. In this context, the decision in *Parks* is preferable to *Burgess*.

SELF-INDUCED AUTOMATISM

Automatism is deemed to have been self-induced if the automatic state was brought about by the defendant having consumed alcohol or drugs. Where the defendant commits an offence in these circumstances, the issue of the defendant's criminal liability is usually dealt with under the law of intoxication (see *People (DPP) v Reilly* [2005] 3 I.R. 111).

PSYCHOLOGICAL BLOW AUTOMATISM

A physical blow that results in a concussion might provide the defendant with a defence of non-insane automatism. Where the defendant loses his self-control, to an extent that amounts to automatism as a result of an emotionally traumatic event, the issue is whether the state of automatism is classified as insane or non-insane automatism. In *Rabey v R* [1980] 2 S.C.R. 513, the defendant was infatuated with the complainant and, when he realised that his feelings were not reciprocated, he attacked her. Evidence suggested that he was in a complete dissociative state in which he was capable of performing physical actions without apparent consciousness. The defendant's psychiatrist contended that it was not a disease of the mind, but the prosecution's psychiatrist stated that the defendant was either in a state of extreme rage or suffered from hysterical neurosis. The trial judge favoured the evidence of the defendant's psychiatrist and he was acquitted on the basis of non-insane automatism. The Court of Appeal overturned the decision on the grounds that the question was one of insane automatism, which was confirmed by the Canadian Supreme Court applying the internal factor test. The Court of Appeal per Martin J.A. stated:

> "In general, the distinction to be drawn is between a malfunction of the mind arising from some cause that is primarily internal to the accused, having its source in his psychological and emotional make-up, or in some organic pathology, as opposed to a malfunction of the mind which is transient in effect produced by specific external factor such as, for example, concussion. Any malfunctioning of the mind, or mental disorder, having its source primarily in some subjective condition or weakness internal to the accused (whether fully understood or not) may be a 'disease of the mind' if it prevents the accused from knowing what he is doing, but transient disturbances of consciousness due to certain specific external factors do not fall within the concept of disease of the mind." [1980] 2 S.C.R. 513 at 519.

The defendant's reaction was held to have its source in his internal, emotional disposition and was, therefore, a disease of the mind. However, there was a strong dissenting judgment by Dickson J., who, in an analogy to the eggshell-skull rule, stated:

> "The fact that other people would not have reacted as he did should not obscure the reality that the external psychological blow did cause a loss of consciousness. A person's subjective reaction, in the absence of any other medical or factual evidence supportive of insanity, should not put him into the category of persons legally insane." [1980] 2 S.C.R. 513 at 549

In *R v Radford* (1985) 42 S.A.S.R. 266, the accused was charged with murder. Medical evidence was tendered in evidence that the accused had acted in a state of depersonalisation or dissociation, brought on by stress as a consequence of his belief that his wife and the deceased had been involved in a lesbian relationship. The trial judge refused to leave the defence of automatism to the jury, stating that the medical evidence could be regarded only as raising a defence of insanity. The accused was convicted of murder and appealed to the Supreme Court of South Australia, which upheld the appeal and ordered a re-trial. King C.J. stated the distinction between insane automatism and non-insane automatism in the following terms:

> "The expression 'disease of the mind' is synonymous, in my opinion, with 'mental illness' ... In one sense automatism must always involve some disorder or disturbance of the mental faculties, but I do not think that a temporary disorder or disturbance of an otherwise healthy mind caused by external factors can properly be regarded as disease of the mind as that expression is used in the M'Naghten rules ... The essential notion appears to be that in order to constitute insanity in the eyes of the law, the malfunction of the mental faculties called 'defect of reason' in the M'Naghten rules, must result from an underlying pathological infirmity of the mind, be it of long or short duration and be it permanent or temporary, which can be properly termed mental illness, as distinct from the reaction of a healthy mind to extraordinary external stimuli." (1985) 42 S.A.S.R. 266 at 274

The court held that a psychological blow can support a defence of non-insane automatism. This was endorsed in *R v Falconer* (1990) 171 C.L.R. 30, in which the defendant was convicted of the murder of her husband. She had been the victim of spousal sexual abuse and had separated from her husband after discovering that he had sexually abused her daughters. On the day of the fatal incident, he arrived at her home and physically and sexually assaulted her. She testified that, from that point onwards, she remembered nothing until she awoke with a gun beside her and the deceased dead on the floor. The trial judge rejected psychiatric evidence that she did not act voluntarily. On appeal, this evidence was admitted, and the distinction was made between an underlying mental infirmity and a "transient non-recurrent mental malfunction" caused by external forces. Citing the minority view in *Rabey*, Mason C.J. stated:

> "... [t]here seems to be no reason in principle why psychological trauma which produces a transient non-recurrent malfunction of an otherwise sound mind should be distinguished from a physical trauma which produces a like effect." [1990] 171 C.L.R. 30 at 54

However, the court stated that a degree of physical fortitude is expected of a person who is subjected to a psychological blow. Thus, an offence committed during a state of automatism resulting from psychological trauma may grand a successful plea of automatism, subject to the evidence tendered at trial.

FURTHER READING

Campbell, Kilcommins and O'Sullivan, *Criminal Law in Ireland: Cases and Commentary* (Dublin: Clarus Press, 2010), pp.959–973.

Dillon, "Intoxicated Automatism is no Defence: *Majewski* is Law in Ireland" (2004) 14(3) I.C.L.J. 7.

Hanly, *An Introduction to Irish Criminal Law*, 2nd edn (Dublin: Gill & Macmillan, 2006), pp.61–63.

10. Intoxication

INTRODUCTION

Intoxication is not a defence as such in criminal law, but the defendant may rely on it as evidence that he did not have the capacity to form mens rea. The impact of intoxication on criminal liability arises where the defendant was deemed to have been so intoxicated, due to the ingestion of alcohol or drugs, that he was unable to form the necessary mens rea for the offence charged in the indictment. At sentencing, the court may take the issue of intoxication into consideration as an aggravating factor.

OFFENCES OF SPECIFIC AND BASIC INTENT

Throughout the development of the common law, the general rule was that intoxication could not be raised as a defence to a criminal charge. However, by the nineteenth century, the courts accepted that the plea of intoxication would be available to all criminal offences of specific intent, which are those offences where the mens rea goes beyond the actus reus. These are distinguished from offences of basic intent in which the conduct and fault elements coincide. The offences of murder, wounding or causing grievous bodily harm with intent, theft, robbery, burglary, handling stolen goods and obtaining by false pretences are crimes of specific intent, while manslaughter, rape, and assault are offences of basic intent. In *DPP v Beard* [1920] A.C. 479, the defendant raped a girl and then suffocated her to death. He argued that intoxication was a defence and the Court of Appeal agreed. The House of Lords held that there is a distinction between *intoxication* that could be a defence if the defendant was so incapable of forming the specific intent required to constitute the offence, and mere drunkenness, which is never a defence as the defendant knows what he is doing.

In *DPP v Majewski* [1977] A.C. 443, the House of Lords unanimously held that the plea of intoxication is available to all offences of specific intent, but it is not a defence to offences of basic intent. The defendant had consumed large quantities of alcohol and drugs and claimed not to have had the capacity to form mens rea on a charge of occasioning bodily harm. The basic common law rule that intoxication is never a defence still applies, but it is no longer absolute. Where an offence requires proof of specific intent, intoxication could operate as a defence if it negatived that specific intent. Lord Simon justified this distinction on the basis that:

> "... much anti-social conduct is still criminal notwithstanding the intoxication – murder is reduced, not to innocent homicide, but to manslaughter; intoxication may reduce the offences of causing grievous bodily harm with intent, or wounding with intent to do grievous bodily harm, to unlawful wounding, but gives no entitlement to an acquittal of all crime; similarly, assault with intent may be reduced to common assault, and stealing a motor car to taking and driving it away without the owner's consent." [1977] A.C. 443 at 477

There are three justifications for the decision: first, individuals should not be allowed to rely by way of defence of an automatistic state brought about by one's own voluntary actions; secondly, for the protection of the community; and thirdly the deterrent effect against intoxication being a complete defence to all offences. Furthermore, offences of basic intent are excluded on the basis that such offences can be committed recklessly, and indeed the defendant could be deemed to have been reckless in the first instance in becoming intoxicated.

In *R v O'Connor* [1980] 29 A.L.R. 449, the High Court of Australia criticised the English approach on the basis that it leaves open the possibility of a person being indicted for an offence notwithstanding the fact that he did not intend to perform the prohibited conduct, or the consequences thereof, and that his conduct did not include the pertinent elements of criminal liability. Barwick C.J. stated:

> "In my opinion, evidence of the state of the body and mind of an accused tendered to assist in raising a doubt as to the voluntary character of the physical act involved in the crime charged is admissible on the trial of an accused for any criminal offence, whether an offence at common law or statute. Further, in my opinion, such evidence tendered to raise a doubt as to the actual intention with which the physical act involved in the crime charged, if done, was done, is admissible on the trial of an accused for any offence, whether at common law or by statute, with the exception of such statutory offences as to not require the existence of an actual intent, the so-called absolute offences." [1980] 29 A.L.R. 449 at 466.

The court considered that the classification into offences of specific and basic intent was arbitrary, and the deterrence argument was also rejected. Stephen J. stated:

> "[By] the very nature of the case, concerned as it is with the grossly intoxicated, deterrence, if it operates at all, will only do so at the time of

the offence, but at the earlier time when the drugs or alcohol are taken in excess. It would, in my view, require convincing evidence before one might conclude that, as a matter of human behaviour, the person who both becomes grossly intoxicated and also commits a crime while in that condition will be in any way discouraged from his initial act of become intoxicated by the knowledge that the fact of his intoxication will not be available for use in evidence at his trial to deny the presence of any mental element involved in his crime." [1980] 29 A.L.R. 449 at 477.

The distinction between offences of specific and basic intent has been upheld in England and Wales, but it has not been accepted in other jurisdictions. While the *Majewski* decision was subject to much criticism as being illogical in terms of the specific/basic intent dichotomy, the House of Lords defended the decision on public policy grounds. The decision favoured protecting members of society against harm caused by persons who have consumed alcohol and drugs.

In *People (DPP) v Reilly* [2005] 3 I.R. 111, the Court of Criminal Appeal followed *DPP v Majewski* [1977] A.C. 443 (which was also followed by the Canadian Supreme Court in *Leary v The Queen* [1978] 1 S.C.R. 29 and *R v Bernard* [1988] 2 S.C.R. 833), consequently, the specific/basic intent dichotomy has been accepted in Irish criminal law.

VOLUNTARY INTOXICATION

This is where the defendant consumes alcohol or drugs of his own volition. In *R v Lipman* [1970] 1 Q.B. 152, the defendant had taken LSD and subsequently killed his girlfriend in the belief that he was defending himself against being attacked by snakes. The Court of Appeal upheld his conviction for manslaughter on the basis that he committed an unlawful and dangerous act that resulted in death. Manslaughter is not an offence of specific intent; therefore, intoxication would not operate as a defence.

INVOLUNTARY INTOXICATION

As a general rule, involuntary intoxication can be pleaded as a defence to a criminal charge. A person can become intoxicated innocently if their drink is spiked or as a result of unexpected or unknown side effects of a lawfully prescribed drug. In *R v Hardie* [1985] 1 W.L.R. 64, the issue was whether a defendant could rely on an involuntary intoxication defence when he took prescribed drugs and subsequently committed an offence. In this case, the defendant, having just broken up with his girlfriend, took some valium tablets in order to calm him down. However, instead of becoming calm after taking the valium tablets, he became agitated and set fire to his girlfriend's apartment. The Court of Appeal held that the defendant could not have known that the tablets would cause aggression and he was not, therefore, voluntarily intoxicated. The court stated that, if he had known that the drug would cause aggressive behaviour, the defence of intoxication would not have been available to him. Likewise, the defence is not available in circumstances where the defendant knows that a substance has an intoxicating effect but is unaware of its potency (*R v Allen* [1988] Crim. L.R. 698).

A dilemma arises where the defendant intends or foresees his conduct or the result of his conduct despite being involuntarily intoxicated. For instance, in *R v Kingston* [1995] 2 A.C. 355, the defendant was a man with paedophiliac inclinations. K's co-defendant, who also had paedophiliac tendencies, planned to blackmail him and, to that end, lured a 15-year-old boy to his flat, spiked the defendant's drink, and then invited the defendant to abuse the boy. The defendant argued that his conduct was brought about by the fact that his drink had been spiked, and that, on that basis, he should not be convicted. The trial judge directed the jury that the defendant should only be acquitted if the intoxication had in fact negatived mens rea. The defendant was convicted and his conviction was overturned by the Court of Appeal, but subsequently reinstated by the House of Lords. While their Lordships accepted that the defendant had surrendered to his paedophiliac tendencies due to his drink having been spiked, they were of the opinion that he had, despite his intoxication, known what he was doing. Thus, a drugged intent was nonetheless an intention to commit an offence. However, their Lordships held that where involuntary intoxication resulted in a complete inability on the part of the defendant to form mens rea, there would be a complete defence.

INTOXICATION AND DUTCH COURAGE

The issue of intoxication in the construction of criminal liability is based on the absence of the defendant's capacity to form mens rea at the time of committing the criminal offence. If a defendant had formed an intention to commit an offence and then purposefully became intoxicated in order to give himself the necessary courage to perform the illegal act constituting the offence, could he then plead intoxication as a defence on the basis that the mental element did not exist when the offence was committed? This issue was considered in *Attorney General for Northern Ireland v Gallagher* [1963] A.C. 349, in which the defendant suffered from a mental illness which had manifested itself in periodic explosive outbursts that were more likely to occur when he consumed alcohol. On the day of his release from a mental hospital, the defendant purchased a knife and a bottle of whiskey. Shortly thereafter, he arrived at a neighbour's house and said he had killed his wife. He was convicted of murder. Lord Denning stated:

"If a man, whilst sane and sober, forms an intention to kill and makes preparation for it, knowing it is a wrong thing to do, and then gets himself drunk so as to give himself Dutch courage to do the killing, and whilst drunk carries out his intention, he cannot rely on this self-induced drunkenness as a defence to a charge of murder, nor even as reducing it to manslaughter. He cannot say that he got himself into such a stupid state that he was incapable of an intent to kill. So also when he is a psychopath, he cannot by drinking rely on his self-induced defect of reason as a defence of insanity. The wickedness of his mind before he got drunk is enough to condemn him, coupled with the act which he intended to do and did do." [1963] A.C. 349 at 382

The mental element of criminal responsibility must coincide with the external element.

PROPOSED LAW REFORM

The Law Reform Commission's Consultation Paper on *Intoxication as a Defence to a Criminal Offence* (February, 1995) propounded two approaches with regard to the issue of intoxication in criminal law. Self-induced intoxication should not afford the defendant a defence to any criminal charge per se, but evidence of intoxication could afford a defence to offences of specific intent if the defendant lacked the capacity to form mens rea. In its *Report on Intoxication* (LRC 51–1995), the Commission advocated the first approach, that is, self-induced or voluntary intoxication should never afford a defence to a criminal charge. With regard to involuntary intoxication, the Commission recommended that it should be a defence to any charge where the level of intoxication was such that the defendant could not have formed the necessary mens rea. This would be available where the intoxication caused the offence, rather than merely facilitated it, as occurred in *Kingston*.

FURTHER READING

Campbell, Kilcommins and O'Sullivan, *Criminal Law in Ireland: Cases and Commentary* (Dublin: Clarus Press, 2010), pp.1015–1041.
Dillon, "Intoxicated Automatism is no Defence: *Majewski* is Law in Ireland" (2004) 14(3) I.C.L.J. 7.
Hanly, *An Introduction to Irish Criminal Law*, 2nd edn (Dublin: Gill and MacMillan, 2006), Ch.9.
Law Reform Commission, *Report on Intoxication* (LRC 51–1995).

Law Reform Commission, *Consultation Paper on Intoxication as a Defence to a Criminal Offence* (February, 1995).

O'Leary, "Post-Mortem on the Special Position of the Innocently Intoxicated Person" (1996) 6(1) I.C.L.J. 55.

O'Malley, "Intoxication and Criminal Responsibility" (1991) 1(1) I.C.L.J. 86.

McAuley, "The Intoxication Defence in Criminal Law" (1997) 32 Ir. Jur. (N.S.) 243.

McCutcheon, "Criminal Law and the Defence of Intoxication" in Kilcommins and O'Donnell (eds), *Alcohol, Society and the Law* (Chichester, Barry Rose, 2003), pp.212–254.

Spencer, "The Intoxication 'Defence' in Ireland" (2005) 15(1) I.C.L.J. 2.

11. Duress and Necessity

INTRODUCTION

The defences of duress and necessity may provide a defence to a defendant who is constrained or coerced into committing a criminal offence because of serious threats (duress) or dire circumstances (necessity). While most of the case law dealing with these offences pertains to homicide, these defences are equally applicable to other offences, including receiving stolen property or unlawful possession of firearms.

While the defences of duress and necessity can be treated as separate defences, there is a considerable degree of overlap between them. The defence of duress *per minas* applies when a person's choice is constrained by threats to do an act that would otherwise be a criminal offence. Necessity pertains to a situation where a person's choice is constrained due to the circumstances. As with the defence of duress, the person performed the prohibited acts because he was compelled to do so, not by threats from a person, but rather by threats arising from the circumstances in which the defendant found himself.

DURESS

Duress or coercion can be raised as a defence on the basis that the defendant should not be held criminally liable if his unlawful conduct was performed out of an immediate fear of personal injury to himself or another. The defendant bears the burden of introducing evidence of duress and it is then up to the prosecution to prove that the defendant was not acting under duress when the offence was committed. If duress is established, the defendant will usually be acquitted. There are two types of duress: duress by threats (*per minas*) and duress of circumstances.

DURESS BY THREATS

The fundamental nature of the defence of duress is that the defendant was forced by someone else to commit an offence under an immediate threat of serious harm befalling the defendant or someone else. The defendant would not have committed the offence but for the threat. In *AG v Whelan* [1934] I.R. 518, the defendant was charged with receiving stolen goods and his defence of duress was successful. The Court of Criminal Appeal held that the threat of immediate death or serious personal harm must be so great as to overbear ordinary human resistance to be accepted as a justification. Murnaghan J. stated:

> "... threats of immediate death or serious personal violence so great as to overbear the ordinary power of human resistance should be accepted as a justification for acts which would otherwise be criminal. The application of this general rule must however be subject to certain limitations." [1934] I.R. 518 at 526

This is an objective test. The Court of Criminal Appeal set out the following limitations to the defence: the will of the defendant must be overborne by the threats; the defence does not apply to murder; the duress must be have been in operation when the offence was committed; and, if there were a reasonable opportunity for the defendant's will to reassert itself, then there is no justification based on antecedent threats.

1. Nature of the threat

The defence is based on threats to kill or do serious bodily harm to the defendant if he does not perform the unlawful conduct. If the threat is less serious, the defence of duress is not established, but these threats might serve to mitigate the sentence imposed. It is generally accepted that threats of violence to the defendant's family or others within a close relationship would also suffice. In *R v Hurley* [1967] V.R. 526, the Supreme Court of Victoria allowed the defence when the threats had been made towards the defendant's girlfriend with whom he was living at the time.

The threats must be directed at the commission of a particular offence. In *R v Coles* [1995] 1 Cr. App. R. 157, the defendant was charged with committing several robberies. He sought to adduce evidence that he had committed these offences under duress. The basis for the defence was that he owed money to moneylenders who had threatened him, his girlfriend, and their child with violence if the money was not repaid. The trial judge held that the facts did not give rise to the defence as the threats had not been directed at the commission of a particular offence, but rather to the repayment of the debt. The defendant's appeal against conviction was dismissed. The Court of Appeal held that the defence of duress by threats was only made out where the person who made the threats specified the offence to be committed by the defendant. In *Coles*, the moneylender indicated that he wanted the defendant to repay the debt that would not typically involve the commission of a criminal offence.

2. Test for duress

In *R v Graham* [1982] 1 W.L.R. 294, the Court of Appeal propounded a two-stage test for duress. The defendant lived in a flat with his wife and his homosexual lover, *K*. The defendant was taking drugs for anxiety, which made him more susceptible to bullying. *K* was a violent man and was jealous of the defendant's wife. One night after the defendant and *K* had been drinking heavily, *K* put a flex around the defendant's wife's neck, pulled it tight and then instructed the defendant to take hold of the other end of the flex and pull on it. The defendant did so for about a minute, with the result that the wife died. Both were charged with murder. The defendant pleaded not guilty and said that he had complied with *K*'s demand to pull on the flex only because of his fear of *K*. The trial judge directed the jury on the defence of duress, but the defendant was convicted. The Court of Appeal, in confirming the conviction, laid down the model direction to be given to a jury where the defence of duress was raised. The jury should consider the following two issues.

- Whether or not the defendant was compelled to act as he did because, on the basis of the circumstances as he honestly believed them to be, he thought his life was in immediate danger (subjective test).
- Would a sober person of reasonable firmness sharing the defendant's characteristics have responded in the same way to the threats? (objective test).

The jury should be instructed to disregard any evidence of the defendant's intoxicated state when assessing whether he had acted under duress, although the defendant may be permitted to raise intoxication as a separate defence in its own right.

This issue as to whether the test is objective or subjective arose for consideration in *R v Howe* [1987] A.C. 417, in which the House of Lords held that there must be some objective criteria involved. In comparison with the law on provocation, Lord Mackay stated:

> "In provocation the words or actions of one person break the self-control of another. In duress the words or actions of one person break the will of another. The law requires a defendant to have the self-control reasonably to be expected of the ordinary citizen in his situation. It should likewise require him to have the steadfastness reasonably to be expected of the ordinary citizen ... ". [1987] A.C. 417 at 458

The objective test fails to take into consideration a weak-willed person who is not able to resist threats and demands unreasonable standards from such a person, thereby undermining the purpose of the defence. In *People (DPP) v MacEoin* [1978] I.R. 27, the Court of Criminal Appeal reverted to a purely subjective approach for the defence of provocation, so it remains to be seen how the Irish courts will approach duress in light of this.

3. Relevant characteristics

The reasonable person is one of average fortitude, with strength and firmness of mind. In *R v Hegarty* [1994] Crim. L.R. 353 and *R v Horne* [1994] Crim. L.R. 584, the defendants sought to introduce psychiatric evidence that he was especially vulnerable to threats. The aim was to argue that this characteristic of vulnerability should be attributed to the reasonable man when the objective test was applied. The Court of Appeal refused to admit the evidence in both cases because it rejected the argument that the reasonable person should be endowed with this characteristic. The rationale of the objective test was to require reasonable firmness to be displayed and it would completely undermine the operation of that test if evidence were admissible to convert the reasonable person into a person of little firmness.

What are the relevant characteristics of the defendant to which the jury should have regard in considering the objective test? In *R v Bowen* [1996] Crim. L.R. 577, the Court of Appeal held that a low IQ, short of mental impairment or mental defectiveness, was not a relevant characteristic, since it did not make individuals less courageous or less able to withstand threats and pressure compared to an ordinary person. Stuart-Smith L.J. stated that age and sex were, and physical health might be, relevant characteristics.

4. Immediacy

The threat must be "immediate" or "imminent" in the sense that it is operating upon the defendant at the time that the crime was committed. If a person under duress is able to resort to the protection of the law, he must do so. When the threat has been withdrawn or becomes ineffective, the person must desist from committing the crime as soon as he reasonably can. In *DPP for Northern Ireland v Lynch* [1975] A.C. 653, Lord Morris stated:

> "Where duress is in issue many questions may arise such as whether threats are serious and compelling or whether ... a person the subject of duress could reasonably have extricated himself or could have sought protection or had what has been called a 'safe avenue of escape'." [1975] A.C. 653 at 668

In circumstances where the defendant had an opportunity to seek police protection but fears that such protection will be ineffective, the defence might still be available. In *R v Hudson and Taylor* [1971] 2 Q.B. 202, two teenage girls aged 17 and 19 committed perjury when giving evidence at a criminal trial because of the threats of injury made against them before the trial and the presence in the court during the trial of those who had uttered the threats. They claimed that members of the criminal gang had threatened them with bodily harm if they told the truth and that one of those gang members was sitting in the public gallery during the trial. The defendants were convicted of perjury following the trial judge's direction to the jury that the defence of duress was not available because the threat was not sufficiently immediate. The Court of Appeal held that the defence of duress should be available in circumstances where the defendant "had no opportunity for delaying tactics but had to make up his mind whether or not to commit the criminal act", and the threats were "no less compelling because they could not have been given effect to in the courtroom." Widgery L.J. stated:

> "It is essential to the defence of duress that the threat shall be effective at the moment when the crime is committed. The threat must be a 'present' threat in the sense that it is effective to neutralise the will of the accused at that time. Hence an accused who joins a rebellion under the compulsion of threats cannot plead duress if he remains with the rebels after the threats have lost their effect and his own will has had a chance to re-assert itself ... Similarly a threat of future violence may be so remote as to be insufficient to overpower the will at that moment when the offence was committed, or the accused may have elected to commit the offence in order to rid himself of a threat hanging over him and not because he was driven to act by immediate and unavoidable pressure. In none of these cases is the defence of duress available because a person cannot justify the commission of a crime merely to secure his own peace of mind. When, however, there is no opportunity for delaying tactics, and the person threatened must make up his mind whether he is to commit the criminal act or not, the existence at that moment of threats sufficient to destroy his will ought to provide him with a defence even though the threatened injury may not follow instantly, but after an interval." [1971] 2 Q.B. 202 at 206–207

Allowing the appeals, Lord Widgery C.J. identified the following salient points. The threat was no less compelling because it could not be carried out there, as it could still be carried out in the streets of the town that same night. The matter should have been left to the jury with a direction that, while it was always open to the prosecution to establish that the defendants had not availed themselves of some opportunity to neutralise the threats and that this opportunity might negate the immediacy of the threat, regard had to be had to the age and circumstances of the defendant.

5. Violent associations voluntarily joined

The defence of duress is not available to persons who commit crimes as a consequence of threats from members of violent gangs which they have voluntarily joined. A defendant who joins a criminal association that could force him to commit crimes can be blamed for his actions. In joining such an organisation, fault can be laid at his door and his subsequent actions described as blameworthy. In *R v Sharp* [1987] 1 Q.B. 853, the defendant was a party to a conspiracy to commit robberies, who said that he wanted to pull out when he saw his companions equipped with guns, whereupon one of the robbers threatened to shoot the defendant if he did not carry out the plan. In the course of the robbery, one of the other robbers killed a person. The defendant was convicted of manslaughter and appealed. In dismissing the appeal, the Court of Appeal held that a man must not voluntarily put himself in a position where he is likely to be subjected to such compulsion. Lord Lane C.J. stated:

> "... where a person has voluntarily, and with knowledge of its nature, joined a criminal organisation or gang which he knew might bring pressure on him to commit an offence and was an active member when he was put under such pressure, he cannot avail himself of the defence of duress." [1987] 1 Q.B. 853 at 861

The defence is not inevitably barred merely because the duress comes from a criminal organisation which the defendant has joined. It depends on the nature of the organisation and the defendant's knowledge of it. If the defendant was unaware of any propensity to violence, then duress may be available. In *R v Shepherd* (1987) 86 Cr. App. R. 47, the defendant joined a group of thieves. They would enter retail premises and, while one of them distracted the shopkeeper, others would carry away boxes of goods, usually cigarettes. The defendant claimed that he no longer wanted to take part after the first burglary, but was threatened with violence to himself and his family if he did not carry on with the thefts. He was convicted of burglary and appealed against conviction. In allowing the appeal, the Court of Appeal held that it should have been left to the jury to decide if the defendant could be said to have taken on the risk of violence from a member of the gang, simply by joining its activities.

In *R v Fitzpatrick* [1977] N.I. 20, the defendant, who had voluntarily joined the IRA, tried to raise the defence of duress to a charge of robbery. He claimed that he had committed the offence following threats that had been made to him by other IRA members if he did not take part. The Court of Criminal Appeal for Northern Ireland held that the trial judge had been correct in withdrawing the defence of duress from the jury. On public policy grounds, duress should not be made available as a defence to those who voluntarily joined violent criminal associations and then found themselves forced to commit offences by their fellow criminals. Otherwise, the availability of the defence in these circumstances would positively encourage terrorist acts, because the actual perpetrators could escape criminal liability on the ground of duress. Furthermore, the availability of the defence in these circumstances would result in a situation where, the more violent and terrifying the criminal gang was that the defendant chose to join, the more compelling would be his evidence of the duress under which he had committed the offences charged. *Fitzpatrick* was endorsed by the Court of Appeal in *R v Sharp*, therefore the principle was limited to cases involving terrorist organisations.

The principle established in *Sharp* was extended by the Court of Appeal in *R v Ali* [1995] Crim. L.R. 303. The defendant was a heroin addict who also sold drugs. He had fallen into debt to his supplier. From the outset, he knew that the supplier was a violent man and had been threatened by him with serious personal injury if he did not repay the debt. The supplier gave him a gun and told the defendant that he wanted the money by the following day and then instructed the defendant to get the money from a bank or building society. The defendant alleged that he was scared that the supplier would "get him" if he went to the police and so he committed a robbery at a building society. He was convicted despite his defence of duress and the Court of Appeal dismissed his appeal. The court held that the defence was not available in circumstances where the defendant knew of a violent disposition in the person involved with him in the criminal activity, which he voluntarily joined. Thus, if the defendant voluntarily participated in a criminal offence with an individual whom he knew to be of a violent disposition and likely to perform other criminal acts, he could not rely on duress if that individual did prove to be violent (cf. *R v Z* [2005] 2 A.C. 467).

LIMITS ON THE DEFENCE

Although duress is considered to be a general defence in criminal law, there are a number of offences in relation to which duress cannot be raised as a defence.

Murder

The defence of duress does not extend to murder. In *Attorney-General v Whelan* [1934] I.R. 518, Murnaghan J. opined:

> "The commission of murder is a crime so heinous that murder should not be committed even for the price of life and in such a case the strongest duress would not be any justification." [1934] I.R. 518 at 526

In *R v Steane* [1947] 1 K.B. 997, Lord Goddard stated, obiter, that murder should be excluded from the scope of duress. However, in *DPP for Northern Ireland v Lynch* [1975] A.C. 653, the House of Lords held that duress would be available to an accomplice to murder. Furthermore, in *Abbott v R* [1977] 1 A.C. 755, the following statement of the Appellate Division in South Africa in *S v Goliath* (1972) (3) S.A. 1 was approved by the minority judgment delivered by Lord Wilberforce and Lord Edmund-Davies. Rumpff J. stated:

> "It is generally accepted ... that for the ordinary person in general his life is more valuable than that of another. Only they who possess the quality of heroism will intentionally offer their lives for another. Should the criminal law then state that compulsion could never be a defence to a charge of murder, it would demand that a person who killed another under duress, whatever the circumstances, would have to comply with a higher standard than that demanded of the average person. I do not think that such an exception to the general rule which applies in criminal law is justified." (1972) (3) S.A. 1 at 25

However, the minority opinion expressed by Lord Wilberforce and Lord Edmund-Davies was rejected by the majority decision in *Abbott*, who held that the principal in the first degree to murder could not rely on duress.

In *R v Gotts* [1992] 2 A.C. 412, the House of Lords held that duress is not a defence to attempted murder. Their Lordships held that, since attempted murder requires proof of an intention to kill, whereas murder demands no more than an intention to do grievous bodily harm, there could be no logical reason for distinguishing between them with respect to the scope of duress. The availability of the defence to murder is now governed by the House of Lords' decision in *R v Howe* [1987] A.C. 417, in which it was held that duress would not be available to a defendant who committed murder, either as principal or accomplice. Two appellants, Howe and Bannister, participated with others in torturing a man who was then strangled to death by one of the others. These events were repeated on a second occasion, but this time it was Howe and Bannister themselves who strangled the victim to death. They claimed that they had acted under duress, at the orders of, and through fear of, Murray, who, through acts of actual violence or threats of violence, had gained control of each of the defendants. Lord Hailsham opined:

"... I do not at all accept in relation to the defence of murder it is either good morals, good policy or good law to suggest, as did the majority in Lynch and the minority in *Abbott* that the ordinary man of reasonable fortitude is not to be supposed to be capable of heroism if he is asked to take an innocent life rather than sacrifice his own. Doubtless in actual practice many will succumb to temptation, as they did in *Dudley and Stephens*. But many will not, and I do not believe that as a 'concession to human frailty' the former should be exempt from liability to criminal sanctions if they do. I have known in my own lifetime of too many acts of heroism by ordinary human beings of no more than ordinary fortitude to regard a law as either 'just or humane' which withdraws the protection of the criminal law from the innocent victim and casts the cloak of its protection upon the coward and the poltroon in the name of a 'concession to human frailty'." [1987] A.C. 417 at 432

The House of Lords dismissed their appeals against conviction.

Attempted murder

Duress is not available as a defence to attempted murder. In *R v Gotts* [1992] 2 A.C. 412, the defendant, aged 16, seriously injured his mother with a knife. In his defence to a charge of attempted murder, he claimed that his father had threatened to shoot him unless he killed his mother. The trial judge ruled that such evidence was inadmissible as duress was not a defence to such a charge. The defendant pleaded guilty and then appealed. Lord Jauncy stated:

"The reason why duress has for so long been stated not to be available as a defence to a murder charge is that the law regards the sanctity of human life and the protection thereof as of paramount importance. Does that reason apply to attempted murder as well as to murder? As Lord Griffiths pointed out in [Howe] ... an intent to kill must be proved in the case of attempted murder but not necessarily in the case of murder. Is there logic in affording the defence to one who intends to kill but fails and denying it to one who mistakenly kills intending only to injure? ... It is of course true that withholding the defence in any circumstances will create some anomalies but ... nothing should be done to undermine in any way the highest duty of the law to protect the freedom and lives of those that live under it. I can therefore see no justification in logic, morality or law in affording to an attempted murderer the defence which is withheld from a murderer. The intent required of an attempted murderer is more evil than that required of a murderer and the line which divides the two offences is seldom, if ever, of the deliberate making of the criminal. A man shooting to kill but missing a vital organ by a hair's breadth can justify his action no more than can the man who hits that organ. It is pure chance that the attempted murderer is not a murderer ...". [1992] 2 A.C. 412 at 425–426

The House of Lords held that the defence of duress could not be raised where the charge was one of attempted murder.

Duress of circumstances

The requirements of the defence of duress of circumstances were explained by the Court of Appeal in *R v Coles* [1995] 1 Cr. App. R. 157. During the defendant's trial for robbing two building societies, he claimed that he had been driven to commit the robberies because of his inability to repay money lenders who had threatened him, his girlfriend and child. The trial judge ruled that no defence of duress was open to the defendant. Dismissing the defendant's appeal against conviction, the Court of Appeal held that the defence of duress by threats was not open to the defendant because the persons who had threatened him did not specify the offences which he had committed. In order to rely on the defence of duress of circumstances, there would have to be a greater degree of directness and immediacy between the danger to the defendant or others and the offence charged. Criminal law required evidence that the commission of the offence had been a spontaneous reaction to the prospect of death or serious injury.

NECESSITY

Necessity arises where a defendant is forced by circumstances beyond his control to transgress criminal law, but the defence is not, as a general rule, available where the defendant himself brought about the circumstances that created the necessity. The defence arises if the defendant was faced with a choice of either committing an offence or allowing a greater evil to occur. In the case of necessity, the will of the defendant is overborne by *circumstances*, as opposed to in the case of duress, when the will of the defendant is overborne by the *threats of a third party*. For instance, it might be justifiable to pull a house down in order to prevent a fire from spreading, or for a prisoner to leave a burning jail, or for a crew to throw cargo from a ship in danger. Necessity is sometimes called duress by circumstances, while duress is referred to as duress by threats (*per minas*). Indeed, it has been suggested that necessity and duress by circumstances are the same thing.

In *Brown v Dyerson* [1969] 1 Q.B. 45, the Divisional Court held that a medical emergency does not justify driving while under the influence of alcohol. Likewise, in *Buckoke v Greater London Council* [1971] 1 Ch. 655, Lord Denning M.R. opined:

> "A driver of a fire engine with ladders approaches the traffic lights. He sees 200 yards down the road a blazing house with a man at an upstairs window in extreme peril. The road is clear in all directions. At that moment the lights turn red. Is the driver to wait for 60 seconds, or more, for the lights to turn green? If the driver waits for that time, the man's life will be lost. I suggested to both counsel that the driver might be excused in crossing the lights to save the man. He might have the defence of necessity. Both counsel denied it. They would not allow him any defence in law. The circumstances went to mitigation, they said, and did not take away his guilt. If counsel are correct – and I accept that they are – nevertheless such a man should not be prosecuted. He should be congratulated." [1971] 1 Ch. 655 at 688

The Court of Appeal held that an instruction to firemen to ignore red traffic lights is unlawful, although this finding was not made without reservation.

While criminal law was originally reluctant to allow a defence of necessity, from the 1980s on, a trend towards the application of a defence of necessity was evident. The courts began to show a willingness to allow the defence of necessity in cases where a fear of death or serious bodily injury existed. In *R v Willer* (1986) 83 Cr. App. R. 225, the defendant had driven recklessly to escape from a crowd of youths who appeared intent upon causing physical harm to the passengers in his car. The Court of Appeal held that the defendant should have been permitted to put the defence of necessity before the jury in view of the apparent threat of death or bodily harm created by the circumstances. In *R v Conway* [1989] Q.B. 290, the Court of Appeal upheld a plea of necessity when the defendant, who had been charged with reckless driving, claimed successfully that he reasonably believed that two men who had approached his car would endanger the life of his passenger. In *R v Martin* (1989) 88 Cr. App. R. 343, the Court of Appeal held that the jury should consider, first, whether the defendant was impelled to act because he had good reason to believe death or serious injury would result, and, secondly, whether a sober person of reasonable firmness sharing the defendant's characteristics would have responded in the same manner.

In *Coles*, the connection between the threat and the offences was not as close and immediate as in *Willer*, *Conway* and *Martin* in which the offences had been virtually a spontaneous reaction to the physical threat arising.

LIMITS ON THE DEFENCE

Necessity, or duress of circumstances, will not excuse the commission of an offence when the threat has ceased. In *R v Pommel* (1995) 2 Cr. App. R. 607, police officers discovered the defendant in possession of an unlicensed firearm. The defendant sought to raise the defence of necessity on the basis that he had previously been visited by a friend who intended to kill another person. The defendant had taken the gun in order to prevent the killing and had intended handing over the gun to the police the following day. The trial judge ruled that the defendant's failure to go to the police immediately deprived him of the opportunity to plead the defence. The defendant was convicted and the Court of Appeal allowed the appeal and ordered a retrial. It was held that the continued availability of the defence of necessity depended on the defendant desisting from the commission of the criminal offence as soon as he reasonably could. Whether or not the defendant had done so is a question for the jury, unless the trial judge determines there was no evidence (indicating that the defendant had acted as soon as he reasonably could) upon which a jury could act. Thus, the trial judge had erred in ruling that the defendant's failure to hand over the gun to the police at the earliest opportunity effectively denied him the right to have the matter left to the jury. The court held that the jury must be satisfied that the defendant acted from a reasonable belief of necessity and also that a sober person of reasonable firmness, sharing the characteristics of the defendant, would have acted in the same way. The test requires a degree of objective justification in the circumstances.

Thus, a defendant has a right to protect himself, another person or property from immediate harm or threats of harm. However, the defendant's conduct must also be reasonable according to his view of the circumstances, and this must stand up to objective scrutiny.

Necessity as a defence to murder

Necessity is never available as a defence to murder. In *R v Dudley and Stevens* (1884) 14 Q.B.D. 273, three defendants and a cabin boy were cast adrift on a boat following a shipwreck. The defendants agreed that, as the cabin boy was already weak and looked likely to die soon, they would kill him and feed and drink from his body for as long as they could in the expectation that they would be rescued before they themselves died of starvation. A few days after killing the cabin boy, they were rescued and subsequently charged with murder. The Queen's Bench Division held that the defendants were guilty of murder in killing the cabin boy and that their necessity was not a defence to murder. The defendants were sentenced to death, but this was commuted to six months' imprisonment. Lord Coleridge C.J. doubted that the defence of necessity could ever be extended to a defendant who killed another to save his own life. After referring to the Christian aspect of actually giving up one's own life to save others, rather than taking another's life to save one's own, he referred to the impossibility of choosing between the value of one person's life and another's:

> "Who is to be the judge of this sort of necessity? By what measure is the comparative value of lives to be measured? Is it to be strength, or intellect, or what? It is plain that the principle leaves to him who is to profit by it to determine the necessity which will justify him in deliberately taking another's life to save his own. In this case the weakest, the youngest, the most unresisting, was chosen. Was it more necessary to kill him than one of the grown men? The answer must be 'No'." (1884) 14 Q.B.D. 273 at 287–288

Lord Coleridge rejected the defence of necessity on the basis that "temptation to act" does not equate to necessity as a defence, as defined by criminal law (cf. *United States v Holmes* (1842) 26 Fed. Cas. 360). *Dudley and Stephens* was affirmed by the House of Lords in *R v Howe* [1987] A.C. 417. Thus, necessity is never a defence to a charge of murder.

In *R v Bourne* [1939] 1 K.B. 687, the defendant gynaecologist performed an abortion on a young girl who had been raped, having formed the opinion that she could die if permitted to give birth. The procedure was performed in a public hospital with the consent of her parents. The defendant was found not guilty of "unlawfully procuring a miscarriage" following a direction from the trial judge to the jury that a defendant did not act "unlawfully" for the purposes of s.58 of the Offences against the Person Act 1861, where he acted in good faith, in the exercise of his clinical judgment. The Court of Criminal Appeal held that an abortion performed to save the life and health of a pregnant woman was not a criminal offence as the act was not unlawful. Likewise, in *Attorney General v X* [1992] 1 I.R. 1, the Supreme Court held that abortion is permissible where the life, as opposed to the health of the mother, is at risk.

In *Re A (Children) (conjoined twins)* [2001] 2 W.L.R. 480, the case involved two conjoined twins: Mary and Jodie. At the time of the court hearing, it was clear that Jodie was the stronger of the two babies. She was found to have normal brain development and she appeared relatively healthy. It was also shown that Mary was drawing nutrition from Jodie and growing at her expense. Mary had a very poorly developed brain and there was no blood flow into her heart. The evidence showed that if the twins were left unaided, Jodie would be liable to progressive high-output heart failure, as her heart was essentially doing the work for the two of them. If they were separated by way of elective surgery, then, in all probability, Jodie could lead a reasonably normal, healthy life, but this surgery would definitely result in Mary's death. The Court of Appeal held that the operation should go ahead, and Brooke L.J. was of the opinion that the operation could be lawfully carried out. The reasoning for the decision was that killing Mary was the lesser of two evils (the death of one twin rather than both).

Proposed Law Reform

The Law Reform Commission's *Report on Defences in Criminal Law* (LRC 95–2009) recommended that the defence of duress, which applies where threats of death or serious injury are made, should continue to apply as a defence to most offences except treason, murder and attempted murder, and should also include threatening situations, or what is otherwise known as duress of circumstances.

The defence of necessity, which applies in very limited situations (such as where damage to property is committed to save a life, or in cases of medical necessity, such as the case of operating on conjoined twins), should continue to develop on a case-by-case basis.

FURTHER READING

Bennum, "Necessity: Yet another Analysis" (1986) 21 Ir. Jur. (N.S.) 186.

Campbell, Kilcommins and O'Sullivan, *Criminal Law in Ireland: Cases and Commentary* (Dublin: Clarus Press, 2010), pp.917–959.

Hanly, *An Introduction to Irish Criminal Law*, 2nd edn (Dublin: Gill & Macmillan, 2006), Chs 10 and 11.

Law Reform Commission, *Consultation Paper on Duress and Necessity* (LRC CP 39–2006).

McAuley and McCutcheon, *Criminal Liability: A Grammar* (Dublin: Round Hall, 2000), Ch.17.

McAuley, "Necessity and Duress in Criminal Law: The Confluence of two great Tributaries" (1998) 33 Ir. Jur. (N.S.) 120.

Spain, "Duress and Necessity in Ireland: Reform on the Horizon (2008) 18(3) I.C.L.J. 70.

12. Self-Defence and Defence of Others

INTRODUCTION

The common law permitted people to use reasonable force to defend: themselves, another, one's property or the property of another, or prevent the commission of an offence. While there is no requirement of a close relationship in Irish criminal law (*People (AG) v Keatley* [1954] I.R. 12), this requirement is necessary in England (*Devlin v Armstrong* [1971] N.I. 17). The force used must have been objectively reasonable in the circumstances; there are two elements to this: the force must be immediately necessary, and the force used must be proportionate to the threat. The common law position has now been put on statutory footing through ss.18 to 20 of the Non-Fatal Offences against the Person Act 1997 (the "1997 Act"). Section 18 provides that the use of reasonable force is justifiable, and can be used as a defence. Section 20(4) provides:

> The fact that a person had an opportunity to retreat before using force shall be taken into account, in conjunction with other relevant evidence, in determining whether the use of force was reasonable.

The impact of the 1997 Act on the law governing the use of lethal force is dependent on whether the defence provisions contained in the 1997 Act apply to homicide offences. This pertains to whether the Act creates general defences or whether it merely codifies the law in relation to non-fatal offences. There are compelling arguments in support of both schools of thought. On the one hand, both the Short and Long Titles of the 1997 Act suggest that it is confined to "non-fatal offences". Furthermore, the Law Reform Commission's *Report on Non-Fatal Offences Against the Person* (LRC 45–1994), upon which the 1997 Act was substantially based, expressly restricted its ambit to non-fatal offences. Conversely, the provisions of the 1997 Act do not expressly draw any distinction between fatal and non-fatal uses of defensive force. However, it should be noted that the 1997 Act contains no express provision stating that the defence and general principles apply to all offences.

IMMINENCE

The use of reasonable force can only be used by the defendant in circumstances where there is a reasonable apprehension of imminent danger. In *Devlin v Armstrong* [1971] N.I. 13, the Court of Appeal per Lord MacDermott L.C.J. held:

> "The police were then in the throes of containing a riot in the course of their duty, and her interventions at that juncture were far too aggressive and premature to rank as justifiable efforts to prevent the prospective danger of the police getting out of hand and acting unlawfully ...". [1971] N.I. 13 at 33.

The court held that:

> "The plea of self-defence may afford a defence where the party raising it uses force, not merely to counter an actual attack, but to ward off or prevent an attack which he has honestly and reasonably anticipated. In that case, however, the anticipated attack must be imminent ...". [1971] N.I. 13 at 33.

What constitutes an imminent attack may not always be clear.

PREPARATION

In *R v Fegan* [1972] N.I. 80, the Court of Appeal of Northern Ireland per Lord MacDermott L.C.J. stated:

> "Possession of a firearm for the purpose of protecting the possessor or his wife or family from acts of violence, may be possession for a lawful object. But the lawfulness of such a purpose cannot be founded on a mere fancy, or on some aggressive motive. The threatened danger must be reasonably and genuinely anticipated, must appear reasonably imminent, and must be of a nature which could not reasonably be met by more pacific means." [1972] N.I. 80 at 88

A firearm in lawful possession could be possessed for an unlawful object and vice versa. Lord MacDermott opined:

> "The threatened danger must be reasonably and genuinely anticipated, must appear reasonably imminent, and must be of a nature which could not reasonably be met by more pacific means. A lawful object in this particular field therefore falls within a strictly limited category and

cannot be such as to justify going beyond what the law may allow in meeting the situation of danger which the possessor of the firearm reasonably and genuinely apprehends. One does not, for example, possess a firearm for a lawful object if the true purpose is merely to stop threats or insults or the like." [1972] N.I. 80 at 88

Fegan was followed in *Attorney-General's Reference (No. 2 of 1983)* [1984] Q.B. 456, in which the defendant made petrol bombs in anticipation of a future attack. Lord Lane C.J. stated:

"He may still arm himself for his own protection, if the exigency arises, although in so doing he may commit other offences. That he may be guilty of other offences will avoid the risk of anarchy contemplated by the reference. It is also to be noted that although a person may 'make' a petrol bomb with a lawful object, nevertheless if he remains in possession of it after the threat has passed which made his object lawful, it may cease to be so. It will only be very rarely that circumstances will exist where the manufacture or possession of petrol bombs can be for a lawful object." [1984] Q.B. 456 at 471

The Court of Appeal held that the defendant had possession of the bombs for a lawful object, providing that he intended to use them solely for the purpose of repelling an attack on his premises (cf. *R v Clinton* [2001] N.I. 207). In *DPP v Kelso* [1984] I.L.R.M. 329, the Special Criminal Court considered whether armed RUC Officers, who ventured across the border into the Irish State for recreational purposes, had possession of their firearms for an unlawful purpose. The officers claimed that they carried their guns intending to use them to protect their lives should the necessity arise. The court held that unlawful possession of a firearm may be for a lawful purpose. Although the circumstances gave rise to a reasonable inference that the defendants had carried the loaded guns for an unlawful purpose, it would be a good defence if they could prove, on the balance of probabilities, that they had an honest and reasonable belief that their lives might be in danger and that protection of their lives required them to carry their guns. On the facts of the case, the court was satisfied that the defendants had discharged this onus.

REQUIREMENT TO RETREAT

Common law originally took the view that a failure to retreat would defeat a claim of self-defence, but this rule no longer exists. In *R v McInnes* [1971] 1 W.L.R. 1600, the defendant killed another during a fight. The Court of Appeal held that the defendant's failure to retreat was not conclusive evidence that he had not acted in self-defence, but a failure to retreat could be taken into consideration by the jury in determining whether the force used by the defendant was reasonable in the circumstances (cf. *People (AG) v Dwyer* [1972] I.R. 416).

Mistake

Self-defence may only be invoked by the defendant in circumstances where there is a real threat. A problematic issue arises, though, if the defendant genuinely, but mistakenly, believes that a threat exists. In R v Williams (1984) 78 Cr. App. R. 276, a man saw a youth rob a woman in the street. He caught the youth and held him but the youth broke from the man's grasp. The man caught the youth again and knocked him to the ground. The defendant (Williams), who had only seen the later stages of the incident, was told by the man that he (the man) was arresting the youth for mugging a woman. The man told the defendant that he was a police officer, which was untrue, so when asked by the defendant for his warrant card, he could not produce one. A struggle followed and the defendant assaulted the man by punching him in the face and was charged with assault occasioning actual bodily harm, contrary to s.47 of the Offences against the Person Act 1861. His defence was that he honestly believed that the youth was being unlawfully assaulted by the man. The jury were directed that, on the assumption that the man was acting lawfully, the defendant's state of mind on the issue of defence of another was to be determined by whether the appellant had an honest belief based on reasonable grounds that reasonable force was necessary to prevent the commission of a crime. The defendant was convicted and appealed on the ground that the trial judge had misdirected the jury. The Court of Appeal held that the jury should have been directed to the effect that the prosecution had the burden of proving the unlawfulness of the defendant's actions, and secondly if the defendant might have been labouring under a mistake as to the facts he should be judged according to his mistaken view of the facts, whether or not that mistake was, on an objective view, reasonable or not. The reasonableness or unreasonableness of the defendant's belief was material to the question as to whether the belief was held by him at all. If the belief was held, its unreasonableness, so far as guilt or innocence was concerned, was irrelevant. The court quashed the conviction. This reasoning was followed in *Beckford v R* [1988] A.C. 130, where the Privy Council held that the defendant is entitled to be judged on his perception of the facts, whether that belief was reasonable or not. This position is placed on a statutory footing in s.18 of the 1997 Act.

SUBJECTIVE OR OBJECTIVE TEST?

In *People (DPP) v McGinty*, unreported, Court of Criminal Appeal, April 3, 2006, the court had to consider the test put by the trial judge to the jury:

> "Did Mr McGinty have reasonable grounds to believe that a needle or syringe was held by Jason?"

Keane C.J. stated:

> "What the section requires the jury or the trier of fact to do is to have regard to the presence or absence of reasonable grounds in concluding whether the person honestly believed that the methods he was using were reasonable in the circumstances, that he had an honest belief that this was reasonable to protect himself from an apprehended injury. It is admittedly a somewhat confusing test but it is the one the legislature has provided for. The test is whether the applicant honestly believed (that is the essence of the defence) that the complainant had a needle or syringe and in coming to that conclusion, the jury are entitled to have regard to the presence or absence of reasonable grounds for the belief. That clearly leaves open the possibility that there may be no reasonable objective grounds for the belief that the jury can see, because it may simply depend, of course, on their view of the defendant's evidence. If that evidence is such as to leave them under a reasonable doubt as to whether the prosecution have excluded the possibility of a defence of honest belief that an assault as going to take place and that he amount of force used was reasonable, then the defendant is entitled to an acquittal."

This was quoted with approval by McCracken J. in *People (DPP) v O'Reilly*, unreported, Court of Criminal Appeal, July 30, 2004.

USE OF EXCESSIVE FORCE

In *People (AG) v Dwyer* [1972] I.R. 416, three young men, including the deceased, had sought out the defendant to exact revenge after the appellant had insulted the mother of one of their group earlier that evening. They located the defendant at a café and called him out onto the street. When the defendant and his companion emerged, a fight ensued. The defendant was engaged with two of the opposing group and claimed that he was caught from behind and hit on the head with some instrument. Fearing that he would be killed, the defendant brandished a knife he was carrying and stabbed the deceased. The question for the Supreme Court was:

> "Where a person, subjected to a violent and felonious attack, endeavors, by way of self-defence, to prevent the consummation of that attack by force, but, in doing so, exercises more force than is necessary but no more than he honestly believes to be necessary in the circumstances, whether such person is guilty of manslaughter and not murder."

The court was unanimous in answering the certified question in the affirmative and recognising the plea of excessive defence. The two separate judgments of the court were delivered by Walsh and Butler JJ., both of whom agreed that a defendant who believes that he or she is using necessary force, but who in fact uses force that is objectively unnecessary, is guilty of manslaughter and not murder. Both placed reliance on s.4 of the Criminal Justice Act 1964, which sets out the mental element required for murder. Walsh J. stated:

> "Our statutory provision makes it clear that the intention is personal and that it is not to be measured solely by objective standards." [1972] I.R. 416 at 424

Butler J. stated:

> "... the Act of 1964 rather pointed the way to this development by its insistence on the intention to kill or cause serious bodily injury as an essential ingredient in the crime of murder, and by providing that the presumption that an accused person intended the natural and probable consequences of his act may be rebutted." [1972] I.R. 416 at 432

However, although their ultimate conclusion was the same, there were subtle differences between the reasoning of the two judgments. Walsh J. framed the question in the following terms:

> "If an accused person [who acts with an intention to kill or cause serious injury] only does what he honestly believes to be necessary in the circumstances, even though that involves the use of a degree of force greater than a reasonable man would have considered necessary in those circumstances, the accused has been guilty of an error of judgment in a difficult situation which was not caused by himself. Should he then be convicted of murder?" [1972] I.R. 416 at 423

Answering the question in the negative, Walsh J., at 424, held that the necessary malice for murder would be lacking if a defender "honestly believed that the force he did use was necessary". On the contrary, Butler J. held that a defendant who used objectively unnecessary force, but whose, "intention ... was primarily to defend himself ... should not be held to have the necessary intention to kill or cause serious injury" ([1972] I.R. 416 at 429). Although Walsh J. took the view that such a defendant would lack the necessary malice for murder (allowing the plea to operate where it was accepted that the defendant intended to kill), Butler J. held that a defensive motive would negate any intention to kill or cause serious harm. However, Walsh and Butler JJ. agreed that a manslaughter verdict should be returned on the grounds that the objective test of legitimate defence is not satisfied. Walsh J. opined:

> "If [the prosecution] does establish that the force used was more than was reasonably necessary it has established that the killing was unlawful as being without justification and not having been by misadventure. In those circumstances the accused in such a case would be guilty of manslaughter." [1972] I.R. 416 at 424

The clearest endorsement of *Dwyer* was in the Court of Criminal Appeal's judgment in *People (DPP) v Clarke* [1994] 3 I.R. 289. The court quoted at length from Walsh J.'s judgment in *Dwyer* and O'Flaherty J. summarised the law of excessive defence in the following terms:

> "... where self-defence fails as a ground for acquittal because the force used by the accused went beyond that which was reasonable in the light of the circumstances but was no more than the accused honestly believed to be necessary in the circumstances, he is guilty of manslaughter and not of murder." [1994] 3 I.R. 289 at 299

In overturning the defendant's murder conviction on other grounds, the court described as "impeccable" the portion of the trial judge's direction to the jury which "dealt fully with what might be termed [the] ... *Dwyer* ... manslaughter option" (per O'Flaherty J. at 300).

SELF-DEFENCE IN THE HOME

Irish criminal law provides that a householder is entitled to defend his home. However, the use of force by a householder against a burglar must be proportionate and householders cannot lawfully kill a person merely on the basis that he is a burglar.

In *People (DPP) v Nally* [2007] 4 I.R. 145, the defendant lived in fear of being the victim of a burglary and, when the deceased ventured onto his property, the defendant shot him twice in the back and beat him around the head with a piece of wood. Carney J. directed the jury to return a verdict of murder or manslaughter as he considered that the force used by the defendant was so excessive that it could not be held to be reasonable. Carney J. held that the defendant did not have a duty to retreat while he had been initially protecting the inviolability of his dwelling, but that once he became the "aggressor", his legal obligations towards the burglar changed. Consequently, the defendant was not permitted to avail of the full defence of self-defence by the jury instruction of murder or manslaughter. The defendant's conviction for manslaughter was quashed by the Court of Criminal Appeal and a re-trial was ordered on the grounds that Carney J. had only allowed the jury to consider a partial defence. At the retrial, the defendant was acquitted of manslaughter by a jury. Thus, the defendant's plea of full self-defence was accepted by the jury. It is arguable whether this was a case of jury nullification, i.e. where the jury acquits against the evidence.

The lawful use of lethal force by an intruder was considered by the Court of Criminal Appeal in *People (DPP) v Barnes* [2007] 3 I.R. 130, in which the defendant was a burglar who stabbed and killed a householder who had disturbed him while committing a burglary at the victim's home. The defendant raised a defence of self defence. In delivering the judgment of the court, Hardiman J. stated that under Art.40.3.1 and Art.40.3.2 of the Constitution, "a person cannot lawfully lose his life simply because he trespasses in the dwelling house of another with intent to steal." The court stated that, although there may be many situations in which householders might be well advised to flee from an intruder, one can never be under a legal obligation to do so. However, with regard to the use of lethal force, Hardiman J. indicated that it would be unjust to provide for an entirely subjective standard:

> "... a person cannot lawfully lose his life simply because he trespasses in the dwelling house of another with intent to steal. In as much as the State itself will not exact the forfeiture of his life for doing so, it is ridiculous to suggest that a private citizen, however outraged, may deliberately kill him simply for being a burglar." [2007] 3 I.R. 130 at 146–147

Consequently, neither an entirely subjective nor objective test is justified in this kind of circumstance.

Proposed Law reform

The Law Reform Commission's *Report on Defences in Criminal Law* (LRC 95–2009) recommended that self-defence be re-named "legitimate defence" to highlight the fact that a person is justified in using reasonable force against an unlawful attack in certain situations. The defence should be applicable not only to protect the person themselves but also other people, including their family, and also to protect their home. Legitimate defence should be divided into four key elements: a threshold requirement (only certain types of unlawful attack can justify use of defensive force, especially lethal defensive force); the attack must be immediate; the use of defensive force must be necessary (a person should usually retreat if possible); and the defensive force must be proportionate to the unlawful attack. The test of whether the use of force was necessary and proportionate in the circumstances of the case under consideration is based on an objective standard of a reasonable person (if the person attacked used lethal force, and subjectively believed it was necessary and proportionate but objectively it was not, the person should be found guilty of manslaughter, not murder: this is usually referred to as excessive or disproportionate force).

With regard to self-defence in the dwelling, the general requirements for legitimate defence should apply to defence of the dwelling and its vicinity (curtilage). The general rule that a person should retreat where possible should not apply where the attack is in the home. If all the requirements of the defence are met, use of lethal force would be a complete defence to murder and would lead to an acquittal.

The use of lethal force in law enforcement (to assist in arresting a person, to deal with serious public disorder, such as a riot, or to prevent prison escapes) should be limited to members of An Garda Síochána and prison officers, and the use of force, including lethal force, is permitted only when it is necessary and proportionate in the circumstances.

CRIMINAL LAW (DEFENCE AND THE DWELLING) BILL 2010

The purpose of the Bill is to clarify and update the law pertaining to the application of justifiable force in self-defence for occupiers of a dwelling so as to defend themselves or their property against attack from an intruder entering the dwelling with the intention of committing a criminal offence. The provisions of the Bill are an acknowledgment that the home should be a place of safety for those who live in it, and that the application of self-defence in the context of an attack in the home is different from a situation that obtains in other circumstances. The Bill provides that a tenant, home-owner or visitor may use "reasonable force" against intruders to defend themselves, others or their property and to stand their ground when attacked in a home, i.e. there will be no requirement for a person to retreat. The Bill is a clarification of the existing law and states that the justifiable use of reasonable force could, in some circumstances, result in the death of an intruder. Each case would be decided by a court or a jury so as to determine whether the force used was justifiable, but the court or jury will have regard to the circumstances as the person using the force believed them to be at the time. It will be immaterial whether such a belief is justified or not as long as it is honestly held. Once the Bill is enacted, people will be allowed to use "reasonable force" against intruders to defend themselves or their home. The Bill defines "justifiable use of force" to include: the protection of the occupant's property or the property of another from appropriation, destruction or damage caused, and allows for such force to be used by the occupier or another lawful occupant to defend themselves, others or the property. The burglar will not be permitted to sue the occupier for damages if injured by the occupier legitimately defending themselves or their property.

FURTHER READING

Campbell, Kilcommins and O'Sullivan, *Criminal Law in Ireland: Cases and Commentary* (Dublin: Clarus Press, 2010), pp.889–917.

Dwyer, "Homicide and the Plea of Self-Defence" (1992) 2(2) I.C.L.J. 73.

Hanly, *An Introduction to Irish Criminal Law*, 2nd edn (Dublin: Gill & Macmillan, 2006), Ch.7.

Law Reform Commission, *Consultation Paper on Legitimate Defence* (LRC CP 41–2006).

O'Sullivan, "The Burglar and the Burglarised: Self-Defence, Home-Defence and Barnes" (2007) 17(4) I.C.L.J. 10.

Spencer, "Self Defence and Defence of the Home" (2007) 17(2) I.C.L.J. 17.

13. Provocation

INTRODUCTION

The defence of provocation might be applicable where the defendant is induced to kill by the provocative words or conduct of the deceased. This defence is only available to a murder charge and a successful plea of provocation leads not to an acquittal, but to a verdict of manslaughter. It is a partial defence. The advantage of this for the defendant is that the trial judge has a wide measure of discretion when sentencing for manslaughter, which carries a maximum life sentence, whereas a murder conviction carries a mandatory life sentence (Criminal Justice Act 1990, s.2). For other offences, provocation might be relevant as a mitigating factor at sentencing.

The defence of provocation is consistent with the presence of those external and mental elements constituting the offence of murder in that the defendant will have mens rea (caused by the provocation) in the sense of intention to kill or cause serious bodily injury, but criminal law grants a partial excuse. Furthermore, if the defendant, having been genuinely provoked by *A*, hit out at *A*, but accidentally killed *B* instead, he would be convicted of the manslaughter of *B* on the basis of the doctrine of transferred malice.

MEANING OF PROVOCATION

The leading common law definition of provocation is that of Devlin J. in his summing-up to the jury in *R v Duffy* [1949] 1 All E.R. 932:

> "Provocation is some act, or series of acts, done by the dead man to the accused which would cause in any reasonable person, and actually causes in the accused, a sudden and temporary loss of self-control, rendering the accused so subject to passion as to make him or her for the moment not the master of his mind." [1949] 1 All E.R. 932 at 932–933

As with most common law jurisdictions, the test for provocation in English criminal law is objective.

If the defendant had time to reflect or killed in a fit of passion, revenge or anger, this would not suffice to constitute a defence of provocation. The further removed the provocation was from the killing the less likely it is that the defence would be available to the defendant. Provocative conduct or words, such as a taunt or insult, may lead to a loss of self-control. The defence of provocation is justified as a "concession to human frailty" (*R v Howard* (1833) 172 E.R. 1188) or "the infirmity of man's nature" (*R v Selton* (1871) 11 Cox C.C. 674). However, if the defendant was prone to losing his self-control easily, then this may indicate a defect of reason from a disease of the mind, for which the defence of insanity or diminished responsibility might be a more appropriate defence under the provisions of the Criminal Law (Insanity) Act 2006.

PROVOCATIVE WORDS OR CONDUCT

The provocative words or conduct required to substantiate a defence of provocation do not have to be criminal offences. In *R v Doughty* (1986) 83 Cr. App. R. 319, the defendant was convicted of the murder of his 17-day-old son. He claimed that the baby's constant crying and restlessness had provoked him. The trial judge refused to advise the jury as to the defence of provocation. The Court of Appeal held that the trial judge had erred in law and should, as a matter of law, have instructed the jury as to the possibility that the defendant had been provoked. The murder conviction was quashed and the court substituted a verdict of manslaughter.

PROVOCATION IN IRISH CRIMINAL LAW

The defence of provocation in Irish criminal law is governed by common law principles, although there have been recommendations for reform.

An important aspect of the definition in *Duffy*, the reference to the reasonable person, does not apply to Irish law. The test for provocation in Irish criminal law is subjective, taking into consideration the defendant's character, temperament and the circumstances of the case that caused the defendant to temporarily lose self-control to the extent that he was not the "master of his own mind" at the time of killing. Whether the issue of reasonableness (i.e. that the defendant used no more force than was reasonable in light of the effect of the provocation) is pertinent to the defence of provocation is questionable. In *People (DPP) v Davis* [2001] 1 I.R. 146, the Court of Criminal Appeal per Hardiman J. suggested that the defence of provocation should be reformed:

> "We think that it may, perhaps, require restatement. First that the defence is in the nature of a concession. Second, that concession is based on policy considerations which may change from time to time. These considerations may dictate that the defence should be

circumscribed or even denied in cases where it would allow to promote moral outrage." [2001] 1 I.R. 146 at 159

Ireland is the only country in the common law world using the subjective test. Is the subjective test too generous? Is it a licence to murder?

It is the function of the jury to decide whether or not the defendant was provoked. In *People (DPP) v MacEoin* [1978] I.R. 27, the Court of Criminal Appeal pointedly stated that the question of whether provocation should or should not be left to the jury is to be dealt with at the close of all the evidence. While the burden of proof rests with the prosecution to prove beyond a reasonable doubt that the defendant did not kill the victim as a result of provocation, the defendant must also account for his conduct. The defence of provocation will not be available to the defendant in every case and the trial judge may exercise a discretion based on the evidence as to whether or not the issue of provocation should be considered by the jury. In *People (DPP) v Kelly* [2000] 2 I.R. 1, the Court of Criminal Appeal indicated that there should be evidence of certain matters for the jury's consideration before the issue of provocation is left to them. There must be evidence of: "a sudden and temporary loss of self-control, rendering the defendant so subject to passion as to make him or her for the moment not master of his mind" and there must be some evidence that the loss of self-control was "total" and that the reaction came "suddenly and before there is time for the passion to cool." However, this burden is not discharged merely by pointing to evidence that, "the defendant lost his temper or merely that he was easily provoked or merely that he was drunk though all of these may be factors in the situation." In *People (DPP) v McDonagh* [2001] 3 I.R. 201, the Court of Criminal Appeal held that, when considering whether the defence of provocation should go to the jury, the question was whether the state of the evidence was such that it would be open to a jury to conclude that it was reasonably possible that the defendant had been the subject of provocation which triggered a total loss of self-control having regard to the particular defendant, given his state of mind, his personality and all the circumstances. Some evidence from which provocation leading to total loss of control could be inferred was required.

EVIDENCE OF PROVOCATION

The defendant must have been provoked at the time of the unlawful killing. In *R v Cocker* [1989] Crim. L.R. 740, the defence of provocation was not available to the defendant who had yielded to the entreaties of his incurably ill wife. One morning, having deliberately kept the defendant awake most of the night, she woke him and demanded that he kill her, which he did with a pillow. In evidence, he said that her final request and her entreaties had become too much for him. There was no evidence that he had lost his self-control. He was not provoked, and there was no evidence of provocation. The defendant had not lost his self-control at the time of the killing, but had acceded to his wife's entreaties to end her life. The Court of Appeal dismissed the defendant's appeal against conviction.

It is immaterial if the defendant regained his self-control immediately afterwards. The fundamental issue pertaining to the defence is whether he had, or had not, lost self-control at the time of the fatal act. In *R v Clarke* [1991] Crim. L.R. 383, the defendant, in response to being provoked, head-butted the victim and strangled her. He then panicked and put live wires from a lamp in her mouth, electrocuting her so as to give the appearance of accidental electrical shock. He may have regained self-control by the time he did the latter act. The important question was therefore, which act had caused her death? If it was the strangulation, he was entitled to rely on the defence of provocation. If it was the electrocution, he was not, assuming that he had regained self-control at the pertinent time. If, however, the defendant's conduct causing the death was part of one continuing assault on the victim, then the jury should consider everything which the defendant had done. The same rule would apply if a person acting under provocation had seriously injured another and then failed to do anything to revive or assist that other on regaining self-control, as a result of which the other died. In these circumstances, the defendant, having been under a common law duty to act, would be guilty of murder.

THIRD-PARTY PROVOCATION

The provocation could have been directed at a person other than the defendant and the person killed might have been someone other than the provoker. In *R v Pearson* [1992] Crim. L.R. 193, two brothers were charged with killing their violent and tyrannical father. They had armed themselves with a sledgehammer and, in turn, hit their father over the head. One brother, *M*, had suffered violent treatment from the father over a period of eight years while the other, *W*, had been away from home. It was held that the father's behaviour was also relevant to *W*'s defence, especially as he had returned home to protect *M* from further violence. However, the ruling that there was evidence of a "sudden and temporary" loss of self-control appears to be generous, since the defendants had armed themselves in advance. In *R v Gardner* (1993) 14 Cr. App. R. (S) 364, the defendant entered the bedroom of his former lover who taunted him about his lack of sexual prowess and indicated that she had just had sex with another man who was sleeping in an adjacent room. The defendant went into that room where the man was asleep and naked, killed him with a statue and then returned to his former lover's room and killed her. The Court of Appeal held that, in view of the proximity of the provocation, the defence was open to the defendant.

SELF-INDUCED PROVOCATION

Self-induced provocation can give rise to problems. Under English law, where the jury must take everything into account, it has been held that behaviour by the defendant which caused the deceased to act provocatively towards him does not necessarily preclude the defendant from raising the defence of provocation. In *R v Johnson* (1989) 89 Cr. App. R. 148, the defendant's behaviour in a nightclub resulted in provocative behaviour towards him, but this did not automatically preclude the defence of provocation. In other words, the defence of provocation might be considered by the jury even when the provocation was self-induced, but this will depend on the factual circumstances of the case. *Johnson* may be contrasted with *Edwards v R* [1973] A.C. 648, in which the appellant followed the deceased from Hong Kong to Australia with the intention of blackmailing him. He went to the deceased's bedroom and pressed him for payment of the money that he was demanding. The deceased then swore at him and attacked him with a knife, inflicting several wounds on the appellant. The appellant then grabbed the knife from the deceased and stabbed him in a fit of "white hot" passion. The Privy Council allowed the appeal against murder conviction and substituted a verdict of manslaughter.

SUBJECTIVE TEST

The major point of difference between the law governing provocation in Ireland and in other common law jurisdictions is that, in this jurisdiction, the test is subjective. Prior to the decision of the Court of Criminal Appeal in *People (DPP) v MacEoin* [1978] I.R. 27, the question of whether a defence of provocation had been established in a murder trial was determined by "the objective test." In *MacEoin*, the court rejected the objective test and substituted a subjective test. The defendant and the deceased, both of whom consumed large quantities of alcohol, shared a flat. On the night in question, the deceased came towards the defendant with a hammer and hit him on the head. In the struggle that followed, the defendant hit the deceased with the hammer. The defendant said: "I simmered over and completely lost control of myself." The essential point before the Court of Criminal Appeal was whether the trial judge was correct in instructing the jury that the defence of provocation was not open to a defendant who formed the necessary intention for murder. This was stated by the Court of Criminal Appeal to have been erroneous; the court went on, however, to state that the test for provocation was, in Ireland, a subjective test. Kenny J. explained that:

> "The objective test is profoundly illogical: we assume that the reasonable man whom it propounds as the criterion is not the accused. If he were, the question would not be whether the reasonable man would be provoked but whether the accused was provoked. But what are the characteristics of this reasonable man? Is he to be endowed with the knowledge and temperament of the accused? Words which would have no effect on the abstract reasonable man may be profoundly provocative to one having knowledge of what people say about him. A hot-tempered man may react violently to an insult which a phlegmatic one would ignore. These are difficulties which those who support the objective test have never attempted to answer." [1978] I.R. 27 at 32

The trial judge must decide whether to leave the defence of provocation to the jury. The jury must then decide (based on the evidence) if the defendant was provoked and whether the provocation bore a reasonable relationship to the amount of force used. In *People (DPP) v Noonan* [1998] 2 I.R. 439, Geoghan J., giving the judgment of the Court of Criminal Appeal, emphasised that the test laid down in *MacEoin and People (DPP) v Mullane*, unreported, Court of Criminal Appeal, March 11, 1997, was a subjective test, but, again, referred to the issue of credibility in the following terms:

> "The test laid down in *MacEoin* rejects the concept of the reasonable man and concentrates on the accused himself [subjective]. This does not, of course, mean that a jury is totally precluded from considering how a reasonable man might react. It may well be reasonable to consider how a reasonable man might react in taking into account the overall credibility of the accused, but that is quite a different concept of the reasonable man." [1998] 2 I.R. 439 at 444

In *People (DPP) v Kelly* [2000] 2 I.R. 1, the Court of Criminal Appeal was asked to clarify the apparent conflict between the subjective and objective elements of *MacEoin*. The court said that it was quite clear that Irish criminal law has adopted a subjective test in relation to provocation; in this respect Ireland is unique among common law jurisdictions. Barrington J. explained that:

> "The question the jury have to decide is not whether a normal or reasonable man would have been so provoked by the matters complained of as totally to lose his self-control but whether this particular accused with his particular history and personality was so provoked. At the same time, they are entitled to rely upon their common

sense and experience of life in deciding this as in deciding other matters. If the reaction of the accused in totally losing his self control in response to the provocation appears to them to have been strange, odd, or disproportionate that is a matter which they are entitled to take into consideration in deciding whether the evidence on which the plea of provocation rests is credible ... The loss of self control must be total and the reaction must come suddenly and before there has been time for passion to cool ... But in the final analysis, the trial judge will tell the jury, it is their job to decide not whether a normal man or a reasonable man would have lost his self control in these circumstances but whether this particular accused in his situation with his particular history and personality was provoked, or may have been provoked, to such an extent as totally to lose his self control."

How would ordinary individuals have acted in the totality of the circumstances? The jury may use the objective test in this regard, but must use the subjective test in determining whether the accused was provoked.

CUMULATIVE PROVOCATION

The requirement of suddenness caused problems for cumulative provocation or "slow burn cases." One distinction which must be made is that the provocative act need not be sudden; it is the fatal reaction that must, apparently, have the sudden quality. The question of cumulative provocation is of tremendous importance in the context of battered spouses or partners. The typical scenario is that the defendant will have endured abuse from the deceased over a long period and eventually attacks and kills him. Should a defendant be entitled to the defence of provocation in these circumstances? The suddenness requirement then takes on a new importance. If there is a delay, problems arise. There must be a sudden and temporary loss of self-control, but it does not have to occur immediately after the provoking act. However, the longer the delay, the less likely the courts are to accept that there was a sudden and temporary loss of self-control. There may be a permitted time lag.

In *R v Thornton* (1993) 96 Cr. App. R. 12, which considered the effect of "battered woman syndrome", the defendant had been abused by her husband over a long period of time. On the day of the fatal act, the husband had verbally abused the defendant and had told her that he was going to kill her. She went to the kitchen, picked up a carving knife, sharpened it, and then went back to the room where her husband was lying on the couch. He informed her that he was going to kill her when she was asleep; the defendant then told him that she would kill him first. The husband sarcastically suggested that she should kill him, so she stabbed him in the stomach, and then called for an ambulance and the police. The Court of Appeal rejected the argument that the words "sudden and temporary" were no longer appropriate; in other words, the court rejected the idea of cumulative provocation. There had been a "cooling-off" period, which was inconsistent with provocation.

In *R v Ahluwalia* (1993) 96 Cr. App. R. 133, the defendant was convicted of murder but was granted leave to appeal. Her conviction was set aside and a plea of manslaughter was accepted, for which she received 40 months' imprisonment: the time she had already served. As in *Thornton*, the Court of Criminal Appeal refused to abandon the "suddenness" requirement. Taylor C.J. stated:

> "We accept that the subjective element in the defence of provocation would not as a matter of law be negatived simply because of the delayed reaction in such cases, provided that there was at the time of the killing a 'sudden and temporary loss of self-control' caused by the alleged provocation. However, the longer the delay and the stronger the evidence of deliberation on the part of the defendant, the more likely it will be that the prosecution will negative provocation." (1993) 96 Cr. App. R. 133 at 139

This seemed to remove delay as a legal bar to provocation—a sudden and temporary loss of self-control does not have to be immediate. It becomes evidence as to whether self control was actually lost.

Eventually, the Court of Appeal gave an important ruling in the case of *R v Humphreys* [1996] Crim. L.R. 431, which made it clear that cumulative provocation could be taken into account in deciding if a reasonable person (the objective test pertains in English criminal law) would have acted as the defendant did. Hirst L.J. stated, in relation to the facts of the case that:

> "This tempestuous relationship was a complex story with several distinct and cumulative strands of potentially provocative conduct building up until the final encounter."

In *R v Thornton (No. 2)* [1996] 1 W.L.R. 1174, following the introduction of fresh evidence, a retrial was ordered by the Court of Appeal to consider the effect of battered woman syndrome and the defendant was subsequently convicted of manslaughter on the grounds of diminished responsibility.

Proposed Law Reform

The Law Reform Commission's *Report on Defences in Criminal Law* (LRC 95–2009) recommended that the defence of provocation in homicide cases should continue to operate as a partial defence, reducing what would otherwise be murder to a manslaughter conviction. The defence should be based primarily on whether the provocative words or conduct were such that it was reasonable for the defendant, based on the standard of an ordinary person, to have temporarily lost self-control. However, the fact that the killing did not immediately follow the provocation does not per se mean that the defence cannot be raised. The presence or absence of an immediate response to the provocative acts or words should be considered by the jury together with all the evidence, in determining whether or not the defendant had lost self-control at the time of the killing. This would incorporate cumulative provocation.

> **FURTHER READING**
>
> Campbell, Kilcommins and O'Sullivan, *Criminal Law in Ireland: Cases and Commentary* (Dublin: Clarus Press, 2010), pp.1044–1069.
> Donnelly, "Battered Women who Kill and the Criminal Law Defences" (1993) 3(2) I.C.L.J. 161.
> Hanly, *An Introduction to Irish Criminal Law*, 2nd edn (Dublin: Gill and MacMillan, 2006), pp.216–232.
> Law Reform Commission, *Consultation Paper on Homicide: The Plea of Provocation* (LRC CP 27–2003).
> McAlese, "The Reasonable Man Provoked?" (1978) D.U.L.J. 53.
> McAuley, "Anticipating the Past: the Defence of Provocation in Irish Law" (1987) 50 M.L.R. 133.
> Mac Giollabhuí, "Back to the Future: Provocation in Ireland" (2005) 15(3) I.C.L.J. 2.
> Stannard, "Making Sense of *MacEoin*" (1998) 8(1) I.C.L.J. 20.

14. Secondary Participation

Introduction

Criminal liability is not confined to the actual perpetrator whose conduct is the immediate or direct cause of the actus reus. The conduct of other individuals may have facilitated the commission of the criminal offence. In this context, criminal liability may be imposed on individuals who provide assistance to the perpetrator before, during or after the commission of the principal offence.

Accessories

The law of complicity is applicable where individuals promote the commission of a criminal offence by means of encouraging or assisting through supplying some physical means at the time of its commission. Section 7(1) of the Criminal Law Act 1997 (the "1997 Act") provides:

> Any person who aids, abets, counsels or procures the commission of an indictable offence shall be liable to be indicted, tried and punished as a principal offender.

Section 22 of the Petty Sessions (Ireland) Act 1851 provides for secondary participation in relation to summary offences.

Principal offence

Criminal liability for complicity is derived from the principal offence having been committed by the principal offender; this must be proved by the prosecution authorities to the satisfaction of the jury before the secondary participant can be convicted (cf. *People (DPP) v Ward*, unreported, Special Criminal Court, November 27, 1998). The danger of convicting a defendant on uncorroborated testimony lies in the possibility of fabricated and exaggerated evidence; in the danger of witness evidence being "coached" in consideration of any inducements by the State; and in the possibility that uncorroborated evidence may undermine the standard of proof in criminal trials, particularly the trial of offences by the non-jury Special Criminal Court (see *People (DPP) v Ward*, unreported, Court of Criminal Appeal, March 22, 2002; *People (DPP) v Meehan*, unreported, Special Criminal Court, July 29, 1999; *People (DPP) v Gilligan*, unreported, Special Criminal Court, March 15, 2001).

An accessory can be convicted of a more serious offence than the offence for which the principal offender is convicted. In *R v Howe* [1987] A.C. 417, the House of Lords per Lord Mackay stated:

> "... where a person has been killed and that result is the result intended by another participant, the mere fact that the actual killer may be convicted only of the reduced charge of manslaughter for some reason special to himself does not, in my opinion in any way, result in a compulsory reduction for the other participant." [1987] A.C. 417 at 458

For instance, if the principal offender, in response to serious provocation, attacks the victim with the intent to kill, the verdict will usually be manslaughter, not murder. If a secondary participant arrives on the scene during the attack and, being unaware of the provocative words or conduct by the victim, and perhaps, because of a grudge against the victim, encourages the principal offender to continue the attack, he can be convicted of a more serious offence. If the victim is eventually killed, the secondary participant is liable to be convicted of murder, notwithstanding the fact that the principal offender is convicted of the lesser offence of manslaughter by reason of his partial defence of provocation. In other circumstances, a secondary participant can be charged with a lesser offence than that with which the principal offender has been charged. For instance, if the principal offender kills with the mental element for murder, while the secondary participant intends only to assist or encourage an offence which he thinks is likely to cause harm, but not serious injury, then the person who actually kills will be convicted of murder, while the accessory would only be convicted of manslaughter on the basis that he did not have the intent to kill or cause serious injury.

CONDUCT ELEMENT

Under s.7(1) of the 1997 Act, an accessory will be criminally liable on the grounds that they "aid, abet, counsel or procure" the commission of the principal (indictable) offence. In *Attorney General's Reference (No. 1 of 1975)* [1975] Q.B. 773, the Court of Appeal considered the interpretation of the equivalent English legislation (Accessories and Abettors Act 1861, s.8), and held that, since the four words were used in the statutory provision, they should each have a different legal meaning. The principal offence must have been committed before one can be convicted on the basis of secondary participation under the provisions of the 1997 Act.

1. Aiding and abetting

Although the courts have tended to use the terms "aiding" and "abetting" interchangeably, in *R v Taylor* (1875) 13 Cox C.C. 68, two persons about to fight one another with their fists, deposited £1 each with the defendant, as stake-holder, who consented to hold it until after the fight and then to pay the £2 to the winner. The defendant did not in any way, other than by holding the money, promote or encourage the fight. The fight took place, and, from injuries then received, one of the men subsequently died. The defendant was not at the fight, but afterwards paid the £2 to the winner of the fight. The Court of Criminal Appeal held that the defendant was not an accessory before the fact to the manslaughter. The court said that abetting meant giving some active assistance to the commission of the criminal offence (cf. *R v Buck and Buck* (1960) 44 Cr. App. R. 213). As a general rule, aiding and abetting the commission of the principal offence can be established by proving that the defendant's conduct assisted or encouraged the principal offender. In *Gillick v West Norfolk and Wisbech Area Health Authority* [1986] 1 A.C. 112, the issue for consideration was whether a doctor who prescribed contraceptives for an underage girl without the consent of her parents had committed an offence. The House of Lords held that an offence could be committed depending on the doctor's intention, and that a doctor could be held criminally liable for aiding and abetting unlawful sexual intercourse with a girl under the age of consent.

It is not necessary for the secondary participant to be present when the offence is committed. In *People (DPP) v O'Reilly* [1991] 1 I.R. 77, the High Court held that the provision of a vehicle to assist the commission of a burglary could justify a conviction for aiding and abetting that offence, notwithstanding the fact that the defendant had not actually participated in the burglary. The defendant had knowingly and wilfully aided and abetted the commission of the offence.

2. Counselling

The meaning of "counselling" was considered in *R v Calhaem* [1985] 1 Q.B. 808 at 813, in which the defendant hired an assassin to kill the deceased. The Court of Appeal held that "to counsel" should be given its ordinary meaning, that is, to "advise, solicit, or something of that sort". While it is not necessary to establish the existence of a causal relationship between the encouragement or advice by the secondary participant and the commission of the offence by the principal offender, it is necessary to establish that the principal offence was committed in consequence of the counselling. In *R v Gianetto* (1997) 1 Cr. App. R. 1, the trial judge had instructed the jury in the following terms:

"Supposing somebody came up to [the defendant] and said, 'I am going to kill your wife', if he played any part, either in encouragement, as little as patting him on the back, nodding, saying, 'Oh goody', that would be sufficient to involve him in the murder, to make him guilty, because he is encouraging the murder." (1997) 1 Cr. App. R. 1 at 13

The Court of Appeal per Kennedy L.J., in affirming the trial judge's direction, held that any involvement, from mere encouragement upwards, would suffice for secondary participation. However, if the evidence proves that the principal offender would have committed the offence anyway, the conduct of the secondary participant might not be held to have had an effect on the principal offender and, therefore, might not constitute secondary liability.

3. Procuring

This is the only form of secondary participation for which the prosecution must establish causation. It is not necessary that the principal offender was aware that he was the subject of the procurement. The prosecution does not have to establish a meeting of minds between the principal offender and the secondary participant, which may be contrasted with aiding, abetting and counselling, for which a meeting of minds is required to establish secondary criminal liability.

In *Attorney General's Reference (No. 1 of 1975)* [1975] Q.B. 773, the defendant spiked a friend's non-alcoholic drink with alcohol, knowing that he would shortly thereafter drive home. The friend was convicted of driving under the influence of alcohol and the defendant was charged as an accomplice to this offence, but was acquitted. The trial judge found that there had to be sufficient evidence of some agreement between the accomplice and the principal offender. The Court of Appeal held that, since the lacing of the principal offender's drink was surreptitiously done so that he was unaware of what had happened, and there was a causal link between the defendant's conduct and the offence committed by the principal offender, who would not otherwise have committed the offence, the defendant had procured the commission of the principal offence. The court held that the trial judge should have directed the jury that an offence was committed if the defendant knew that his friend was going to drive and also knew that the ordinary and natural result of the alcohol would be to bring his friend above the prescribed blood/alcohol limit. The Court of Appeal held that the principal offence had been procured by the secondary participant because, unbeknownst to the driver and without his collaboration, he had been put in a position in which he had committed an offence that he, otherwise, would never have committed. Lord Widgery C.J. opined:

> "To procure means to produce by endeavour. You procure a thing by setting out to see that it happens and taking the appropriate steps to produce that happening. We think that there are plenty of instances in which a person may be said to procure the commission of a crime by another even though there is no sort of conspiracy between the two, even though there is no attempt at agreement or discussion as to the form which the offence should take." [1975] Q.B. 773 at 779

Thus, a person could not be said to have procured an offence if there was no causal link between his conduct and the commission of the principal offence.

EXTENT OF PARTICIPATION

The actus reus of secondary participation requires that some assistance was provided to the principal offender, although the level of assistance provided can be minimal (see *R v Gianetto* (1997) 1 Cr. App. R. 1). Mere presence will not, of itself, suffice to constitute secondary liability. In *R v Coney* (1882) 8 Q.B.D. 534, the defendants were present as spectators at an illegally organised bare-fist prize-fight between two men. It did not appear that the defendants took any active part in the management of the event, nor did they do anything to encourage the illegal prize-fight. Cave J. stated:

> "... it is a general rule in the case of principals in the second degree that there must be participation in the act, and that, although a man is present whilst a felony is being committed, if he takes no part in it, and does not act in concert with those who commit it, he will not be a principal in the second degree merely because he does not endeavour to prevent the felony, or apprehend the felon." (1882) 8 Q.B.D. 534 at 539

It was a misdirection for the trial judge to instruct the jury that their mere presence at an illegal prize-fight was sufficient to sustain a conviction for abetting the illegal fight. Their presence at the event was simply one factor for the jury to take into consideration. In order to be convicted on the basis of secondary liability, the defendant must have done something more than be present at the time that the principal offence was committed. However, if it is the defendant's intention to encourage the principal by his presence, this may suffice to constitute secondary liability. Likewise, secondary liability might be imposed in circumstances where the defendant was under a duty to intervene, but failed in their duty (cf. *R v Dytham* [1979] Q.B. 722).

While mere presence at the scene of a crime will not of itself suffice to constitute criminal liability, non-accidental presence is evidence from which the jury are entitled to draw the inference that the defendant had the requisite intent. In *Wilcox v Jeffery* [1951] 1 All E.R. 464, the defendant attended a concert in circumstances where the performer had been permitted to enter the United Kingdom on the condition that he did not engage in employment. The defendant reported on the concert in his magazine and was subsequently charged with being an accessory to the unlawful performance. There was no evidence that the defendant had encouraged the performance by way of applause, but the Court of King's Bench was satisfied that his presence encouraged the performance. Lord Goodard C.J. stated:

> "There was not accidental presence in this case. The appellant paid to go to the concert and he went there because he wanted to report it. He must, therefore, be held to have been present, taking part, concurring, or encouraging, whichever word you like to use for expressing this conception. It was an illegal act on the part of Hawkins to play the saxophone or any other instrument at this concert. The appellant clearly knew that it was an unlawful act for him to play. He had gone there to hear him, and his presence and his payment to go there was an encouragement. He went there to make use of the performance, because he went there, as the magistrate finds and was justified in finding, to get 'copy' for his newspaper." [1951] 1 All E.R. 464 at 466

The court was clearly influenced by the commercial element of this case. The defendant was convicted of unlawfully aiding a jazz musician in obtaining employment in the United Kingdom on the basis that he attended the concert and paid for a ticket. Thus, when someone acts to encourage another in the commission of an illegal act, they are deemed to have satisfied the actus reus of accomplice liability. Where presence is unequivocally accidental, it is not evidence of aiding and abetting, but where the presence is prima facie not accidental, then this is evidence from which the jury may infer the defendant's intention to aid and abet the commission of a criminal offence. The difficulty with this decision is that it is unclear as to whether the actus reus of the offence was established, that is, whether the performer in fact had been encouraged by the appellant's attendance. This decision is best confined to its own facts.

In *R v Clarkson* [1971] 1 W.L.R. 1402, two soldiers entered a room where they found other soldiers raping a woman and remained on the scene to watch what was happening, although they did not actively participate in, or verbally encourage, the commission of the offence. They were convicted of abetting the rape and successfully appealed on the basis that their mere presence alone could not have been sufficient for liability. Their conviction was overturned by the English Courts-Martial Appeal Court. It was held that the jury should have been directed that there could only be a conviction if the defendants' presence at the scene actually encouraged the commission of the offence, and if it could be proven that the defendants had intended their presence to offer such encouragement. Mere presence of itself is insufficient to constitute the offence of "abetting": the defendants' presence must, in fact, have encouraged the principal offender(s). There must be an *intention* to encourage, in addition to actual encouragement of the principal offender, before criminal liability on the basis of secondary participation will be imposed. In *R v Bland* [1988] Crim. L.R. 41, the defendant lived with her co-accused in one room of a shared house. The co-accused was convicted of possession of drugs and the defendant was also charged with possession because she was living with the co-accused. The Court of Appeal quashed her conviction and held that there was no evidence of active or passive assistance. The fact that she and the co-accused lived together in the same room was not sufficient evidence from which the jury could draw such an inference. Assistance, albeit passive, required more than mere knowledge and required evidence of encouragement or some element of control that was absent in this case.

FAILURE TO EXERCISE CONTROL

In circumstances where a defendant failed to exercise that control so as to prevent the commission of the principal offence, this might suffice to constitute secondary liability. In *R v Lomas* (1914) 9 Cr. App. R. 220, the Court of Criminal Appeal held that the defendant who returned a jemmy (small crowbar) to a known burglar was not an accessory to burglaries that were subsequently carried out using the jemmy. Thus, mere knowledge that the principal intends to commit an offence does not by itself suffice to constitute an accessory before the fact because there must be some particular offence in contemplation (cf. *R v Bullock* [1955] 1 W.L.R. 1). In *Tuck v Robson* [1970] 1 W.L.R. 741, the licensee of a public house had failed to ensure that some of his customers had finished their drinks within the permitted time. He had called time and, while he was in another part of the pub clearing glasses, the customers continued to drink. When the police arrived, they discovered several customers still consuming alcoholic drinks in the bar. Despite the fact that none of the customers were prosecuted, the licensee was charged with aiding and abetting the commission of the offence. He was convicted of aiding and abetting the illegal act of consuming intoxicating liquor after the permitted hours. The defendant had knowledge that the offence was being committed and failed to eject the customers or even to withdraw their permission to be on the premises. It was held that the prosecution must establish knowledge on the part of the licensee, coupled with some form of voluntary assistance in the commission of the offence. The Court of Queen's Bench concluded that it was possible to draw the inference that the licensee acquiesced in the presence of the customers by failing to eject them or failing to revoke their licence to remain on the premises. In dismissing the defendant's appeal against conviction, the court held that the licensee was in control of the premises and had full knowledge that intoxicating liquor was being consumed after hours. The magistrate was entitled to draw the inference that there was passive assistance by the licensee in the sense of presence, with no steps having been taken by him to enforce his proprietary right either to eject the customers or to revoke their licence to be upon the premises. It was not unreasonable for the court to conclude that the failure by the licensee to exercise control in circumstances where it might otherwise be expected to be exercised would have encouraged, or aided and abetted, the commission of the principal offence.

MENS REA

The mens rea to secure a conviction for secondary liability is intention on the part of the accessory, notwithstanding the fact that the fault element for the principal offence might be recklessness. To secure a conviction for a secondary participant, the prosecution must establish that the accessory intended to assist or encourage the principal offender.

There are two approaches to the question of what constitutes intention for secondary participation. First, an accessory is deemed to have intended to assist or encourage if he acts with the knowledge that the principal offender intends to commit the criminal offence. This approach was taken in *National Coal Board v Gamble* [1959] 1 Q.B. 11, in which a weighbridge operator knew that a truck driver was carrying excess weight, but was indifferent as to the commission of the principal offence. The Divisional Court held that, as the accessory had knowledge of the circumstances that constituted the principal offence, he acted intentionally and was, therefore, criminally liable as a secondary participant. The natural and probable result of the defendant's actions are significant in that, if he performs an act, the natural and probable consequence of which is to assist the principal offender, the jury may infer that he intended to assist the principal offender. However, such a presumption can be rebutted by evidence to the contrary. The second approach pertains to situations in which the defendant is deemed to have intended to assist or encourage the principal offender only when he acts with that specific purpose in mind. In *Gillick v West Norfolk and Wisbech Area Health Authority* [1986] 1 A.C. 112, the House of Lords held that a doctor who supplied an underage girl with contraceptives would not necessarily be convicted of aiding and abetting the offence of unlawful carnal knowledge. A doctor in these circumstances might be convicted if he acts in order to facilitate the girl having intercourse, although intention is negated when the doctor is deemed to have acted in what he honestly believed to be the best interests of the underage girl. In *Attorney-General v Able* [1984] Q.B. 795, the Court of Queen's Bench held that, while the supplier of a suicide booklet might know that the reader would be assisted or encouraged to commit suicide, the supplier would only have the requisite intent where it was shown that he had acted with that objective. Without proof of the necessary intent, it could not be said in advance that any particular supply of the booklet would constitute an offence, and it was for a jury to decide in each case whether the necessary facts had been proved.

The issue then arises as to whether recklessness should be sufficient to constitute the mens rea of secondary liability. In *Blakely and Sutton v DPP* [1991] Crim. L.R. 763, the two defendants laced their companion's drink in the expectation that he would spend the night with one of them. However, before they could inform him what they had done, he left and was convicted of driving while intoxicated. The defendants were convicted of procuring the offence after the magistrates determined that their conduct had been reckless, but the Divisional Court quashed the convictions and held that objective recklessness was insufficient for secondary liability. The court noted obiter that occasionally advertent recklessness might be sufficient for secondary liability, but it would be necessary to show that the defendant contemplated that his conduct would, or might, bring about the commission of the principal offence. In *Giorgianni v R* (1985) 58 A.L.R. 641, recklessness as the fault element for accessories was rejected by the High Court of Australia, which held that intention was the required state of mind to establish secondary liability. The appellant was convicted as an accessory to culpable driving causing death. The prosecution argued that he was reckless as to the dangerous condition of the vehicle which his employee drove and that was the cause of the deaths of the victims. The High Court of Australia held that the prosecution must establish that, with knowledge of the essential facts that constitute the offence, the defendant intended to aid, abet, counsel or procure the principal offender in the commission of the substantive offence. A defendant could be criminally liable in circumstances where he was "wilfully blind" to the facts, but recklessness, per se, would not be sufficient. Gibbs C.J. stated:

> "It can never be right to direct a jury that recklessness is enough to constitute a person an aider, abettor, counsellor or procurer. Indeed in many, if not most, cases it will be unnecessary to introduce the subject of wilful blindness into a summing up and it would only be confusing to direct a jury on that subject if the facts of the case did not require it. My view of the law may be summed up very shortly. No one may be convicted of aiding, abetting, counselling or procuring the commission of an offence unless, knowing all the essential facts which made what

was done a crime, he intentionally aided, abetted, counselled or procured the acts of the principal offender. Wilful blindness, in the sense that I have described, is treated as equivalent to knowledge but neither negligence nor recklessness is sufficient." (1985) 58 A.L.R. 641 at 651

In view of the wide range of liability that might result from advertent recklessness, the statement of the law in *Giorgianni* is preferable to *Blakely*.

KNOWLEDGE OF SECONDARY PARTICIPANTS

It is not necessary to prove knowledge of the precise details of the principal offence on the part of accessories before the fact. In *R v Bainbridge* [1960] 1 Q.B. 129, the defendant purchased oxygen cutting equipment that was used to break into a bank. He suspected that the equipment might be used to perform an illegal act, but he did not know the precise details. The Court of Criminal Appeal upheld his conviction on the basis that it was not necessary for the prosecution to establish knowledge of the precise details, but rather that the accessory knew the principal offender intended to commit a "crime of the type" that was in fact committed. Lord Parker suggested that a belief by the accessory that the equipment would be used to dispose of stolen property would not be sufficient where the principal offence was burglary.

In *R v Maxwell* [1978] N.I. 42, the defendant was a member of an unlawful organisation that used firearms and bombs to carry out attacks against individuals and their property. He was instructed by a member of the organisation to drive his car to a public house so as to act as a guide to a second car containing four men. One of the men in the car following the defendant placed a bomb in the hallway of the public house. Soon after, the defendant learned that what he described as a "job" for the organisation was in fact an attempt to detonate a bomb in the public house. He was convicted of unlawfully and maliciously performing an act with intent to cause an explosion likely to endanger life and also with possession of the bomb. His appeal was dismissed by the Court of Appeal of Northern Ireland and subsequently by the House of Lords. Viscount Dilhorne stated:

> "... a person can be convicted of aiding and abetting the commission of an offence without his having knowledge of the actual crime intended ... [The defendant] knew that a 'military' operation was to take place. With his knowledge of the U.V.F.'s activities, he must have known that it would involve the use of a bomb or shooting or the use of incendiary devices. Knowing that he led them there and so he aided and abetted whichever of these forms the attack took. It took the form of placing a bomb." [1978] N.I. 42 at 65

It was sufficient to prove that the defendant knew that one of a series of offences was intended by the principal offender. While the defendant did not know which offence was intended, the trial court was satisfied that he was aware that the attack would involve violence in which lives would be endangered or property damaged. His conviction was upheld. The Court of Appeal per Lord Lowry, whose judgment was approved by the House of Lords, emphasised that the offence must have been contemplated by the accessory and it would rarely be concluded that the accessory gave a principal offender a carte blanche for all possible offences. In murder trials, the decision by the House of Lords in *R v Rahman (Islamur)* [2009] 1 A.C. 129, demonstrates that it is not necessary for the defendant to have foreseen that the principal would kill, just that they might commit serious harm.

In *People (DPP) v Madden* [1977] I.R. 336, the defendant was convicted of aiding and abetting the principal offender in a murder case as he had provided a vehicle in the knowledge that it would be used in the commission of a violent crime. The Court of Criminal Appeal per O'Higgins C.J. stated:

> "The kernel of the matter is the establishing of an activity on the part of the accused from which his intentions may be inferred and the effect of which is to assist the principal in the commission of the crime proved to have been committed by the principal, or the commission of a crime of a similar nature known to the accused to be the intention of the principal when assisting him." [1977] I.R. 336 at 341

To sustain a conviction of an accessory before the fact, it must be established that the defendant engaged in activity from which his intentions could be inferred. Further, it must be shown that the purpose and effect of the defendant's conduct was to assist the principal offender in the commission of the substantive criminal offence, or an offence of a similar nature that was known by the accessory to have been the intention of the principal offender at the time such assistance was given.

In *People (DPP) v Egan* [1989] I.R. 681, the defendant admitted that he had agreed to allow a van to be stored on his premises. He denied knowledge of a robbery, but admitted that he thought "a small stroke" was intended. The Court of Criminal Appeal concluded that he knew that theft was involved and, with that knowledge, assisted in the commission of the principal offence. Costello J. stated:

> "When goods are stolen it is not, in the opinion of this court, necessary for the prosecution to establish that a person who has aided the principal offender before the crime was committed knew either the means which were to be employed by the principal offender, or the place from which the goods were to be stolen or the time at which the

theft was to take place or the nature of the goods to be stolen. It will suffice if the prosecution is able to show that the accused who gave assistance to a principal offender before the crime was committed knew the nature of the crime intended, namely the theft of goods." [1989] I.R. 681 at 690

This decision presents a dilemma in that the offences of theft and robbery are legally and factually distinguishable and, therefore, are not of a similar type.

ACQUITTAL OF THE PRINCIPAL OFFENDER

It is not necessary for the principal offender to have been tried before secondary liability can be imposed on accessories. Indeed, the principal offender may have been acquitted of the substantive offence. In *R v Bourne* (1952) 36 Cr. App. R. 125, the defendant terrorised his wife into committing the offence of buggery with a dog and was convicted of aiding and abetting his wife to commit that offence. The Court of Appeal stated that, although the principal offender might have availed of the defence of duress to excuse his conduct, the secondary participant might nevertheless be convicted, and Lord Goddard C.J. stated that if the wife had been charged with committing the offence, she could have pleaded duress. However, once the act of buggery is completed, the offence is committed. The evidence showed that the defendant had caused his wife to have connection with a dog and he was, accordingly, convicted as an accessory. In *R v Cogan and Leak* [1976] Q.B. 217, Leak persuaded Cogan to have sexual intercourse with his (Leak's) wife, telling him that she liked being forced to have sexual relations against her will, and that, if she resisted, it was merely an indication of her enjoyment. Cogan was convicted of rape, but successfully appealed against his conviction on the basis that he had honestly thought Leak's wife had consented to sexual intercourse. Leak appealed against his conviction for aiding and abetting the rape on the basis that, if the principal offender had been acquitted, there was no offence to which he could have been an accomplice. The Court of Appeal held that the actus reus of rape had been committed by Cogan, in that Leak's wife had been forced to submit to sexual intercourse without her consent. Leak had known that she was not consenting and, therefore, had the necessary mens rea to be convicted as an accomplice. Thus, if an innocent agent is used to commit an offence, the accomplice can nonetheless be charged (cf. *Thornton v Mitchell* [1940] 1 All E.R. 339).

ACCESSORIES AFTER THE FACT

To aid, abet, counsel or procure the commission of the principal offence necessitates active assistance or advice given to the principal offender by the secondary participant before the substantive offence is committed. Offenders who provide assistance after the principal offence has been committed will also be criminally liable on the basis of secondary participation. Section 7(2) of the Criminal Law Act 1997 provides:

> Where a person has committed an arrestable offence, any other person who, knowing or believing him or her to be guilty of the offence *or of some other arrestable offence*, does without reasonable excuse any act with intent to impede his or her apprehension or prosecution shall be guilty of an offence. (emphasis added)

This provision of the 1997 Act does not limit secondary liability to the offence actually committed. For instance, if a principal offender who murdered his wife had sought assistance from his mistress in evading detection by the police by telling her that he had committed fraud, if she then provides assistance believing his version of events, she will be criminally liable under s.7(2).

DOCTRINE OF COMMON DESIGN

The common law principle of joint enterprise or common design is applicable where two or more offenders act together in furtherance of a common criminal purpose. In *R v Anderson and Morris* [1966] 2 Q.B. 110, Lord Parker C.J. approved of the principle of law:

> "... where two persons embark on a joint enterprise each is liable for the acts done in pursuance of that joint enterprise and that includes liability for unusual consequences if they arise from the execution of the joint enterprise but (and this is the crux of the matter) that, if one of the adventurers goes beyond what has been tacitly agreed as part of the common enterprise his co-adventurer is not liable for the consequence of that unauthorised act." [1996] 2 Q.B. 110 at 118

The doctrine stipulates that each participant is deemed to share criminal responsibility for the unlawful acts committed by others in the furtherance of their common agreement. All parties to the agreement are criminally liable, unless one or more of the parties to the agreement commits an offence that was not foreseeable to the remaining participants. Under the doctrine of common design, each participant is effectively a principal offender. Conversely, secondary participants are complicit in the substantive offence committed by the principal offender, although secondary participants are liable to conviction and punishment as the principal offender.

In *People (DPP) v Murray and Murray* [1977] I.R. 360, the Supreme Court considered whether the common design of armed bank robbers extended to the offence of capital murder. The two defendants, husband and wife, had committed an armed robbery and made their getaway in a car that was pursued by another car being driven by a man who was passing the bank at the time of their escape. When the defendant's car eventually stopped, they got out and made off, being pursued by the man in the car following them. He caught up with the husband, who was unarmed, and the wife shot the pursuer as he was about to seize her husband. He subsequently died, and it transpired that the pursuer was an off-duty Garda. The court held that there was no evidence, express or implied, of an agreement to kill a member of An Garda Síochána. The fact that murder, but not capital murder, was deemed to have been an element of the common design might be explained by the fact that the defendants were charged with an offence that carried the death penalty. A less strict approach was taken by the Court of Criminal Appeal in *People (DPP) v Pringle, McCann and O'Shea* [1981] 2 Frewen 57, which also involved a bank robbery. In the ensuing chase, two Gardaí were shot dead. The court was prepared to draw the inference from the evidence that a common intent to kill or seriously injure anyone who stood in their way existed among the defendants and that intent to kill included members of An Garda Síochána. The court adopted a similar approach in *People (DPP) v Eccles, McPhillips and McShane* (1986) 3 Frewen 36. The decisions in *Murray*, and *Pringle, McCann and O'Shea*, might be explained by the fact that, in the latter cases, there was evidence of an intention to use whatever force was necessary against the Gardaí so as to assist their escape, whereas in *Murray* there was no such evidence.

Proving common design

It is often the case that one or more of the participants in the agreement to commit a serious offence will assert that events took an undesired course and that the ultimate death of a third party, as frequently occurs in these cases, was not part of the common design. This will not necessarily absolve the parties from criminal liability, since these so-called undesired acts might be deemed by the court to fall within the common design.

The courts have adopted two approaches. The first is to establish that the participant's agreement pertaining to the common design, whether express or implied, included the particular offence that one or more of the parties to the agreement contend was not what they had agreed to. In *People (Attorney General) v Ryan* (1966) 1 Frewen 304, a tacit agreement to injure the intended victim was inferred from evidence that the defendant had known of the presence of a weapon and had contemplated its use. The second approach is a broader principle of common design, in that an offence is deemed to have been part of the agreement if it is within the contemplation of the defendant. In *Chan Wing-Siu v The Queen* [1985] A.C. 168, the Privy Council considered the issue of foresight. Sir Robin Cooke explained that:

> "... a secondary party is criminally liable for acts by the primary offender of a type which the former foresees but does not necessarily intend. That there is such a principle is not in doubt. It turns on contemplation or, putting the same idea in other words, authorisation, which may be express but is more usually implied. It meets the case of a crime foreseen as a possible incident of the common unlawful enterprise. The criminal culpability lies in participating in the venture with that foresight." [1985] A.C. 168 at 175

This alternative approach to the doctrine of common design or joint enterprise is a broader concept than secondary participation under the relevant provisions of the Criminal Law Act 1997.

In the joint appeals of *R v Powell; R v English* [1999] 1 A.C. 1, the House of Lords held that it was sufficient to have found a conviction for murder on the fact that the secondary party realised the possibility that, in the course of the joint enterprise, the principal might shoot with intent to kill or cause grievous bodily harm. Lord Hutton stated:

> "... the secondary party is subject to criminal liability if he contemplated the act causing the death as a possible incident of the joint venture, unless the risk was so remote that the jury take the view that the secondary party genuinely dismissed it as altogether negligible." [1999] 1 A.C. 1 at 30–31

Therefore, a party to a common design might be held criminally liable on either of two justifications. First, the participant's express or tacit agreement included the commission of the offence, if necessary, to facilitate the commission of the target offence. Secondly, the defendant actually contemplated the possibility that the secondary offence would be committed by one or other of the participants in the common design.

In *People (DPP) v Doohan* [2002] 4 I.R. 463, the defendant hired a man to carry out a punishment beating on another, but instructed him not to shoot the victim. The victim died from shotgun wounds to his leg and the defendant contended that the agreement to impose the punishment beating did not include the use of a shotgun. The defendant and his co-accused were convicted of murder. They argued that the death of the deceased and the use of the gun went beyond the contemplation of the defendant and that it was not reasonably foreseeable. The Court of Criminal Appeal held that, where two or more people embarked on a joint enterprise, each was liable for the acts done in pursuance of that joint enterprise, including liability for unusual consequences if they arose from the agreed joint enterprise. However, if one of the adventurers went beyond what had been tacitly agreed as part of the common enterprise, the other participants were not liable for the consequences of the unauthorised act. It was for the trial court to determine whether what had been done was part of the joint enterprise. The murder conviction was upheld.

WITHDRAWAL FROM COMPLICITY

If an accessory decides not to proceed with the commission of the offence, he will not be criminally liable for offences subsequent to such withdrawal. To constitute an effective withdrawal from complicity in a joint enterprise to commit a criminal offence, the defendant's withdrawal must be clear and unequivocal, timely, and communicated either to the other parties, to the joint enterprise, or alternatively, to the police. However, the closer to the completion of the substantive offence the withdrawal is, the less likely it is to negative the defendant's criminal liability. In *R v Whitehouse* (1941) 1 W.W.R. 112, three men agreed to rob a local merchant. One of the men approached the merchant with an iron pipe which was covered with a piece of hose, and as he got near him the other two men ran away. The merchant died some time later and the pipe was found with human blood on it. The trial judge instructed the jury that they must consider only two elements in order to find abandonment: first, a change of mental intention, and secondly, quitting the scene before the criminal offence was finally consummated. The British Columbia Court of Appeal per Sloan J.A. stated:

> "After a crime has been committed and before a prior abandonment of the common enterprise may be found by a jury there must be, in my view, in the absence of exceptional circumstances, something more than a mere mental change of intention and physical change of place by those associates who wish to disassociate themselves from the consequences attendant upon their willing assistance up to the moment of the actual commission of that crime. I would not attempt to define too closely what must be done in criminal matters involving participation in a common unlawful purpose to break the chain of causation and responsibility. That must depend upon the circumstances of each case but it seems to me that one essential element ought to be established in a case of this kind: where practicable and reasonable there must be timely communication of the intention to

abandon the common purpose from those who wish to dissociate themselves from the contemplated crime to those who desire to continue in it. What is 'timely communication' must be determined by the facts of each case but where practicable and reasonable it ought to be such communication, verbal or otherwise, that will serve unequivocal notice upon the other party to the common unlawful cause that if he proceeds upon it he does so without the further aid and assistance of those who withdraw. The unlawful purpose of him who continues alone is then his own and not one in common with those who are no longer parties to it nor liable to its full and final consequences." (1941) 1 W.W.R. 112 at 115–116

Sloan J.A. held that the trial judge had erred in law for these reasons. Whitehouse was followed by the Canadian Supreme Court in *Miller v The Queen* [1977] 2 S.C.R. 680, which involved the murder of a police officer. The two defendants had consumed large quantities of alcohol and were discussing their animosity towards the police, including the possibility of shooting a police officer. They then proceeded to drive around in an erratic manner so as to attract the attention of the police. Miller was at the wheel and Cockriell threw a beer bottle at the local court house to draw the attention of the police. They were subsequently stopped by the police and, as the police officer approached the car, Cockriell pulled the trigger on the rifle which had been sitting in Miller's lap. Ritchie J. followed the judgment of Sloan J.A. in *Whitehouse* and held that there was no clear evidence that the intention to abandon the common purpose had been communicated. The court found that there was no evidence to support a defence of abandonment.

In *R v Becerra; R v Cooper* (1976) 62 Cr. App. R. 212, the defendants agreed to burgle a house. Becerra had given Cooper a knife to use in case they were confronted by the occupants. When they were disturbed by one of the tenants, Becerra jumped out of the window and ran off, shouting "[t]here's a bloke coming, let's go." However, Cooper remained on the premises and murdered the tenant. Becerra was convicted as an accomplice to the murder, despite his contention that he had withdrawn from the joint enterprise. In dismissing Becerra's appeal against conviction, Roskill L.J. held that the actions which Becerra claimed amounted to a withdrawal from the common design were not capable of amounting to such withdrawal, and Becerra remained criminally liable for everything that Cooper had done, and continued to do, after Becerra's disappearance through the window as much as if he had done it himself. The knife had been contemplated for use when it was handed over by Becerra to Cooper, and consequently, if Becerra had wanted to withdraw at that stage, he should have repented in some manner vastly different and more effective than merely shouting to Cooper "come on, let's go" and leaving through the window. The Court of Appeal held that the appellant's sudden departure from the scene of the crime with the words "come on let's go" was an insufficient communication of withdrawal, and the appellant's conviction as a secondary party to the murder was upheld. In *R v Grundy* [1977] Crim. L.R. 543, the defendant had supplied a burglar with information about the premises and the habits of the owner. However, for two weeks before the burglary, the defendant had been trying to prevent him from committing the offence. The Court of Appeal, following *Becerra*, held that the issue of withdrawal should have been left to the jury for consideration. *Grundy* demonstrates that words alone might be sufficient to constitute withdrawal from a joint enterprise if they are spoken before the offence is actually committed (cf. *R v Perman* (1996) 1 Cr. App. R. 24). However, while the general rule is that withdrawal must be communicated, in *R v Mitchell; R v King* [1999] Crim. L.R. 497 there is a special exception to this in that a participant might successfully withdraw from a joint enterprise simply by leaving when "spontaneous" violence has occurred (see also *R v O'Flaherty, Ryan and Toussaint* (2004) 2 Cr App. R. 20).

In *R v Whitefield* (1984) 79 Cr. App. R. 36, two individuals burgled a flat while the occupier was absent. The defendant, who lived next door, admitted telling the principal offender that the flat would be empty and also admitted that he had initially agreed to participate in the burglary with the principal, but that he had later changed his mind. The defendant was present in his flat on the night that the burglary was committed and had heard the flat being broken into, but did not intervene to prevent the commission of the offence. At the defendant's trial for burglary, he asserted that he had withdrawn from the joint enterprise to burgle the adjoining flat. To that end, he contended that he had informed the principal that he did not wish to take part in the burglary and refused to allow him access to his flat and balcony for the purpose of effecting entry into his neighbour's flat. This contention was rejected by the trial court and the defendant was convicted, but the Court of Appeal quashed the conviction. Dunn L.J. opined:

> "If a person has counselled another to commit a crime, he may escape liability by withdrawal before the crime is committed, but it is not sufficient that he should merely repent or change his mind. If his participation is confined to advice or encouragement, he must at least communicate his change of mind to the other, and the communication must be such as 'will serve unequivocal notice upon the other party to the common unlawful cause that if he proceeds upon it he does so without the aid and assistance of those who withdraw'." (1984) 79 Cr.App.R. 36 at 39–40

There was evidence that the defendant had served unequivocal notice of his withdrawal from the joint enterprise on the principal offender and had informed him that if he proceeded with the burglary they had planned together, he would do so without the defendant's aid or assistance. Accordingly, the jury should have been instructed that if they accepted the defendant's evidence, that was a valid defence that the defendant had withdrawn from the joint enterprise.

In *R v Rook* [1993] 1 W.L.R. 1005, three men, including the defendant, were offered £20,000 by a husband if they would kill his wife. The three men met with the husband on the evening before the killing and agreed that, the next day, the husband would collect the three men and drive them to a lake and that he would later bring his wife to the lake in the car. However, of the three men commissioned to carry out the murder, only two showed up the next day. The defendant backed out and the murder was committed by the other two men. All four men were charged and the defendant claimed that he had never intended to kill the woman, but that he had just wanted to get his share of the money and disappear. He said he had deliberately absented himself that day because he had thought that, if he were not there, the other two participants would not commit the offence. The trial judge said that mere inactivity was insufficient; the defendant was convicted of murder. The Court of Appeal per Lloyd L.J. stated:

> "In the present case the appellant never told the others that he was not going ahead with the crime. His absence on the day could not possibly amount to 'unequivocal communication' of his withdrawal. In his evidence ... he said that he made it quite clear to himself that he did not want to be there on the day. But he did not make it clear to the others. So the minimum necessary for withdrawal from the crime was not established on the facts. In these circumstances, as in the *Becerra* case, it is unnecessary for us to consider whether communication of his withdrawal would have been enough, or whether he would have had to take steps to 'neutralise' the assistance he had already given." [1993] 1 W.L.R. 1005 at 1012

The defendant's conviction for murder was upheld. An accessory who provides assistance or encouragement before the commission of a criminal offence, but is not present at the scene of the crime, is in the same position as if he had been present in pursuance of a joint enterprise. It is not necessary to prove that an accessory intended the victim to be killed or injured, provided it is proved that the defendant contemplated or had foreseen the event as a real or substantial risk. An effective withdrawal can only be achieved by means of an unequivocal communication to the other participants in the joint enterprise.

DUTY TO REPORT CRIMINAL ACTIVITY

To constitute an effective withdrawal from complicity, such withdrawal must be communicated to the other participants, or some positive step must have been taken, such as notifying the police. At common law, there was an offence called misprision of a felony, that is, failure to report the commission of a serious offence. However, the Criminal Law Act 1997 abolished the common law principle of misprision of felony and thereby effectively abolished a general duty on citizens to report the commission of serious criminal offences. Section 9(1) of the Offences against the State (Amendment) Act 1998 provides that a person is guilty of a criminal offence if, without reasonable excuse, he fails to disclose information which he knows or believes might be of material assistance in preventing the commission of a serious offence or securing the apprehension, prosecution, or conviction of the perpetrators of a serious offence.

> **FURTHER READING**
>
> Campbell, Kilcommins and O'Sullivan, *Criminal Law in Ireland: Cases and Commentary* (Dublin: Clarus Press, 2010), Ch.8.
> Charleton, "The Scope of the Doctrine of Common Design" (1985) 3 I.L.T. 199.
> Finneran, "The Doctrine of Common Design: Beyond the Plain Vanilla Version" (2010) 28 I.L.T. 63.
> Hanly, *An Introduction to Irish Criminal Law*, 2nd edn (Dublin: Gill & Macmillan, 2006), Ch.6.
> McAuley and McCutcheon, *Criminal Liability: A Grammar* (Dublin: Round Hall, 2000), Ch.10.
> Ní Raifeartaigh, "The Mental Element for Accessories to Murder" (1994) 4(1) I.C.L.J. 31.

15. Inchoate Offences

Introduction

Inchoate offences relate to the offence for which the defendant would have been convicted if the substantive offence had actually been committed. These offences cannot exist in the abstract, in that a defendant cannot be convicted of "attempt", "conspiracy" or "incitement" alone, but must be charged in relation to a substantive offence, for example, attempted murder, conspiracy to defraud, or incitement to hatred. Although inchoate offences are sometimes referred to as "incomplete" offences, this term is misleading, as a defendant can be charged and convicted for an inchoate offence of its own accord. The legal policy underpinning inchoate offences is that certain types of preparatory behaviour are sufficiently harmful and dangerous to justify a conviction and the imposition of a criminal sanction. People who endeavour to commit a criminal offence are no less blameworthy just because they fail to succeed in committing that offence. Inchoate offences also serve to prevent the commission of serious criminal offences because they facilitate the prosecution of defendants who have been detected by the police working towards the commission of a substantive offence.

Attempt

Once the defendant has taken sufficient steps towards the commission of a criminal offence, but the substantive offence has not actually been committed, perhaps due to the intervention of a third party or the incompetence of the individual themselves, then he will not escape criminal liability. For instance, a person who tries to shoot someone dead should not avoid conviction and punishment simply because they are a bad shot. Criminal liability will be imposed in these circumstances on the basis that the defendant has done much more than merely prepare for the commission of the offence and has taken a further step beyond the preparatory stages. A defendant convicted of attempt may be punished as though he had in fact succeeded in committing the substantive offence.

The Criminal Law Act 1997 abolished the common law distinction between felonies and misdemeanours, replacing them with arrestable and non-arrestable offences. Section 2 of the 1997 Act defines an arrestable offence as one for which the punishment on conviction is a term of five years' or more imprisonment, or an attempt to commit such an offence.

WHAT IS AN ATTEMPT?

A criminal attempt is conventionally defined as an intention to perform the prohibited act, or to bring about a result that would constitute an offence, together with substantial steps taken by the defendant in furtherance of that intent. In *R v Eagleton* (1855) 6 Cox C.C. 559, Parke B. stated:

> "Acts remotely leading towards the commission of the offence are not to be considered as attempts to commit it, but acts immediately connected with are ..." (1855) 6 Cox C.C. 559 at 571

Likewise, in *R v Mohan* [1976] 1 Q.B. 1, James L.J. stated:

> "An attempt to commit crime is itself an offence. Often it is a grave offence. Often it is as morally culpable as the completed offence which is attempted but not in fact committed. Nevertheless it falls within the class of conduct which is preparatory to the commission of a crime and is one step removed from the offence which is attempted. The court must not strain to bring within the offence of attempt conduct which does not fall within the well-established bounds of the offence. On the contrary, the court must safeguard against extension of those bounds save by the authority of Parliament. The bounds are presently set requiring proof of specific intent, a decision to bring about, in so far as it lies within the accused's power, the commission of the offence which it is alleged the accused attempted to commit, no matter whether the accused desired that consequence of his act or not." [1976] 1 Q.B. 1 at 11

Preliminary activities that are merely preparatory are not sufficient, even when accompanied by the requisite intent. Criminal liability for attempt is imposed only when the defendant goes beyond mere preparation and begins to carry out the planned offence. In *R v Miskell* [1954] 1 Q.B.D. 137, Hilbery J. said that the issue was if, on the facts of the case, the defendant's conduct was sufficiently proximate to constitute an attempt. It is for the trial judge to determine as a matter of law if the impugned conduct is capable of constituting an attempt. Whether the defendant as a matter of fact performed the acts with intention are matters for the jury.

In *People (AG) v England* (1947) 1 Frewen 81, the defendant was convicted of attempted gross indecency as a result of a conversation which he had with a young man, *K*, to whom he described a flat in Dublin in which homosexual practices were apparently taking place. He told *K* the address and the best time to go, but did not make any appointment with him or offer any introduction. The Court of Criminal Appeal quashed the conviction on the basis that the conversation about the flat was not sufficiently proximate to the actual criminal procurement of *K* to constitute an attempt in law. In other words, the act did not directly approximate to the commission of an offence but was, instead, preparation towards the commission of the substantive offence. In *People (AG) v Thornton* [1952] I.R. 54, the Court of Criminal Appeal quashed a conviction for attempt to procure a miscarriage that was based solely on an enquiry made by the defendant to a doctor about the availability of a drug for that purpose. It was stressed that a mere desire to commit an offence, or a desire followed by an intention, was not sufficient to constitute an attempt. The defendant must have gone beyond the preparatory stages and attempted the commission of a criminal offence.

ACTUS REUS

The actus reus of the inchoate offence of attempt is conduct by the defendant that is deemed sufficiently proximate to the intended offence. One of the earliest definitions was provided in *R v Eagleton* (1854) Dears. C.C. 515 per Parke B. when he said:

> "The mere intention to commit a misdemeanour is not criminal. Some act is required, and we do not think that all acts towards committing a misdemeanour are indictable. Acts remotely leading towards the commission of the offence are not to be considered as attempts to commit it, but acts immediately connected with it are ..." (1854) Dears. C.C. 515 at 538

Various common law formulations of the conduct element of attempt have been offered in the case law. In *Davey v Lee* [1968] 1 Q.B. 366, Lord Parker C.J. opined:

> "What amounts to an attempt has been described variously in the authorities, and for my part I prefer to adopt the definition given in Stephen's *Digest of Criminal Law*, 5th ed. (1894), art. 50, where it says that: 'An attempt to commit a crime is an act done with intent to commit that crime, and forming part of a series of acts which would constitute its actual commission if it were not interrupted.' As a general statement that seems to me to be right, although it does not help to define the point of time at which the series of acts begins. That, as Stephen said, depends upon the facts of each case ..." [1968] 1 Q.B. 366 at 370

In *People (AG) v Thornton* [1952] I.R. 91, the Court of Criminal Appeal held that an enquiry made of a doctor about whether "there was some drug named ergot?" was insufficient to amount to an attempt to obtain poison or other noxious things to procure a miscarriage. Haugh J. stated:

> "... an attempt consists of an act done by the accused with a specific intent to commit a particular crime; that it must go beyond mere preparation, and must be a direct movement towards the commission after the preparations have been made; that some such act is required, and if it only remotely leads to the commission of the offence and is not immediately connected therewith, it cannot be considered as an attempt to commit an offence." [1952] I.R. 91 at 93

Therefore, it is not enough merely to have the intent to commit the substantive offence; there must also be some act, or series of acts, performed by the defendant in furtherance of the commission of the substantive offence. For example, if X plans to kill Y and X purchases a gun, learns how to shoot and plans his escape route, these are all preparatory stages for the intended commission of the substantive offence. It is only when the defendant can be said to have gone beyond the preparatory stages and actually attempted to commit the offence, i.e. in this scenario, if X actually aimed the gun at Y and pulled the trigger, but either missed or merely grazed Y, that X can be charged with attempted murder. The essential point is that X, having taken sufficient steps towards the commission of the substantive offence, then moved beyond the preparatory stages and attempted the offence. In *R v Campbell* [1991] Crim. L.R. 268, the defendant was observed "lurking around" outside a post office, and was found to have in his possession an imitation firearm. He was apprehended by the police outside the post office and was convicted of attempted robbery. However, this conviction was overturned on appeal on the basis that, although he had prepared for the commission of the substantive offence (in this case robbery), he had not yet reached the stage in the preparations that would qualify as an attempt (especially as the defendant had not even entered the building). This case illustrates the difficulties in deciding at what point preparations to commit an offence convert into an attempt.

The dilemma for the courts is to distinguish preparatory acts from an attempt, and this will depend on the facts of the case under consideration. An example of this dilemma would arise if a defendant expressed his desire to destroy the office of a former employer, purchased a box of matches, old newspaper, and a container of petrol, obtained dynamite with a long fuse, placed the dynamite and other incendiary materials in the building, and then lit the fuse. At what point in this sequence of events has the defendant attempted to commit an offence of criminal damage and arson? The jurisprudence of the Superior Courts dealing with such issues has traditionally invoked several analytic devices with broadly divergent results. The most important approaches are those requiring either commission of the last necessary act, or an act proximate to the result, or an act that unequivocally confirms the defendant's intent.

1. Last act theory

In determining how proximate the defendant's conduct must have been to the commission of the substantive offence, some commentators have postulated the "last act theory", that is, whether the defendant performed the final act before the completion of the substantive offence. This approach was suggested in *R v Eagleton* (1855) 6 Cox C.C. 559. Where the defendant has committed the last act, this will take the defendant's conduct out of the preparatory stage and convert it into an attempt. The last act must have been more than mere preparation for the commission of the substantive offence. In *R v Robinson* [1915] 2 K.B. 342, the defendant was charged with attempting to obtain money by false pretences in that he had staged a robbery and proposed to claim on the insurance, i.e. he intended making a false claim. The scam was uncovered before the defendant could submit a claim on the insurance policy. The Court of Criminal Appeal held that the defendant was still in the preparatory stages of the commission of the substantive offence because he had not communicated his intention to claim on the (staged) robbery to the insurance company. In other words, the last act was not completed. In *R v Ilyas* (1983) 78 Cr. App. R. 17, the defendant had reported to the police that his car had been stolen (whereas in fact it had not been stolen) and had also informed his insurers that he would be making an insurance claim and requested a claim form. However, as he did not fill in the claim form or submit it to the insurance company for processing, the Court of Criminal Appeal held that his conduct fell within the preparatory stages of the commission of the substantive offence.

Applying the last act theory, the disgruntled employee in the abovementioned scenario would be criminally liable of attempt only after lighting the fuse. Although the attempt might be unsuccessful, the defendant would have done everything necessary to carry it through to completion. The "last act test" is designed not only to ensure that the defendant intended to commit the offence, but also to provide an incentive for defendants to desist and avoid criminal liability right up to the last possible moment.

At exactly what point the preparatory acts are converted to an attempt was considered by Lord Diplock in *DPP v Stonehouse* [1978] A.C. 55, in which the defendant faked his death so that his wife could claim on five insurance policies. His wife, being unaware of this ruse, claimed on the insurance policies and the defendant was discovered a number of weeks later living in Australia. He was convicted of "attempting by deception to enable another to obtain property" and this conviction was upheld on appeal to the House of Lords, on the basis that he had, "done all the acts within his power to commit the offence and that all that was left for him to do was not to be discovered." Lord Diplock explained that:

> "Acts that are merely preparatory to the commission of the offence, such as, in the instant case, the taking out of the insurance policies, are not sufficiently proximate to constitute an attempt. They do not indicate a fixed irrevocable intention to go on to commit the complete offence unless involuntarily prevented from doing so ... In other words the offender must have crossed the Rubicon and burnt his boats." [1978] A.C. 55 at 68

The defendant must have been at the point of committing the substantive offence to constitute an attempt in law. The general principle emerging from the leading cases on attempt is that there is a grey area between the preparatory stages and the actual attempt to commit the substantive criminal offence.

2. Proximity test

To avoid the practical difficulties of the "last act test", the Superior Courts invoked the proximity test, requiring only that a defendant's preparatory actions came reasonably close to completion of the substantive offence. The issue for determination is how close is close enough? Some decisions have attempted to adapt the proximity test to the purposes of attempt law by focusing on whether the defendant's acts involved a close proximity to the substantive offence or whether the defendant was unlikely to desist.

There must be sufficient proximity between the act committed (the attempt) and the substantive/complete offence that was intended. For example, if *X* purchases a can of petrol and a lighter with the intention of burning down a hayshed, has he attempted (in law) the substantive offence of arson or criminal damage? It is doubtful that *X* would be convicted in these circumstances, as buying the petrol and lighter would not be proximate (too far removed) to the commission of the substantive offence.

The test adopted by the courts is proximity in the sense of being immediately, and not merely remotely, connected to the completed act. In other words, the act must be sufficiently close to the actual commission of the substantive offence to be classified as an attempt. This formulation was approved by the House of Lords in the leading case of *Haughton v Smith* [1975] A.C. 476.

The language of proximity makes it difficult to specify the nature of the act required for a conviction. The following two cases illustrate the fine distinction between remoteness and proximity. In *R v Cope* (1921) 16 Cr. App. R. 77, the defendant sent a letter to another man, proposing a meeting at a specific time and place. It did not refer expressly to an incident, but it could be interpreted as having had that objective. In dismissing his appeal against conviction, the Court of Criminal Appeal held that an invitation in writing, although prima facie innocent, might be shown by evidence to be an attempt to procure an act of gross indecency. On the other hand, in *R v Woods* (1931) 22 Cr. App. R. 41, the defendant sent letters purporting to be written by a woman to another man inviting him to engage in immoral acts, but this was deemed too remote to be construed as an attempt. On the basis of these and other cases, one might venture the proposition that a direct and specific invitation issued, or appointment made, with the intention of committing an act of gross indecency is likely to be construed as an attempt. The Irish Superior Courts have adopted a similar approach. In *People (AG) v England* (1947) 1 Frewen 81, the Court of Criminal Appeal held that a mere description in the course of a conversation of a house in Dublin in which homosexual practices took place was not sufficiently proximate to amount to an attempt to procure an act of gross indecency. Gavan Duffy P. opined:

> "The extreme difficulty of attaining precision in the conception of an attempt at crime has baffled many a court and this is one of the rare offences that has defied scientific definition in exact language." (1947) 1 Frewen 81 at 83

Thus, words alone will not constitute an attempt in the absence of some positive action having been taken by the defendant towards the completion of the substantive offence.

Another leading Irish case on attempt is *People (AG) v Sullivan* [1964] I.R. 169, which dealt with an attempt to obtain money by false pretences. The Supreme Court held that an act is sufficiently proximate if it is the first of a series of similar acts intended to result cumulatively in the commission of a crime. The defendant, a midwife, was paid a basic salary for up to, and including, 25 cases and, for every extra case, she was entitled to an additional allowance. She claimed for cases which she had not actually dealt with so as to reach the 25 case limit specified and, thereafter, to claim the extra allowance. The court reiterated the point of law that an act must be sufficiently proximate to the commission of the substantive offence to qualify as an attempt to commit the substantive offence. Walsh J. stated that, where an act is "the first of a series of similar acts intended to result cumulatively in the crime", then such an act will be sufficiently proximate to justify a conviction for an attempt to commit the substantive offence. Accordingly, each and every fictitious claim could, in law, constitute a separate attempt to defraud. The defendant argued that her actions merely amounted to preparations for the substantive offence that would be committed as soon as she claimed for patient 26 and all patients thereafter. The court, in rejecting this argument, held that, in applying the proximity test, each individual false claim by the defendant was, as a matter of law, sufficiently proximate to constitute an attempt (in this case to obtain by false pretences).

The difficulty with the proximity test is determining exactly at what point in the preparations that the defendant can be said to have attempted the commission of the substantive offence. In *R v Jones* [1990] 1 W.L.R. 1057, the defendant forced his way into the victim's car and pointed a sawn-off shotgun at the driver. The driver managed to wrestle the gun from the defendant and threw it out of the car window. The defendant was convicted of attempted murder, but appealed on the ground that his finger was not even on the trigger and the safety catch was on. His conviction for attempted murder was upheld on the basis that the acts done by the defendant constituted more than mere preparatory acts and, when the defendant had aimed the gun at the driver of the car, he had, at this point, attempted to murder the driver. Acts prior to getting into the victim's car, such as acquiring the gun, sawing off the butt, loading it, and so on, would constitute preparatory acts towards the commission of the substantive offence.

3. Equivocality approach

Sometimes the defendant's behaviour, while apparently in preparation to commit an offence, might be equivocal. For instance, if a person is seen attempting to open the door of a car, is he trying to forcibly open the door because he has misplaced his keys? Is he trying to steal the car, steal something from it or sleep in it for the night? Should criminal law automatically assume that an individual is attempting to commit an offence? In such cases, the act in itself may not be sufficiently proximate to lead automatically to one inference rather than another. In *Jones v Brooks and Brooks* (1968) 52 Cr. App. R. 614, the Divisional Court held that, where the act alleged to constitute an attempt is equivocal, then evidence of the defendant's intention is relevant to establish the object towards which the act was directed. Once the defendant's intention is established, the prosecution must prove that the act was sufficiently proximate.

Reluctance to convict on the basis of mere preparatory acts is based on the policy consideration that preliminary acts may not confirm the defendant's plans to carry into action his intention to commit an offence. In *R v Baker* [1924] N.Z.L.R. 865, the New Zealand Court of Appeal, per Salmond J., suggested that to justify a conviction, a preliminary act must be:

"An act done with intent to commit a crime is not a criminal attempt unless it is of such a nature as to be in itself sufficient evidence of the criminal intent with which it is done. A criminal attempt is an act which shows criminal intent on the face of it. The case must be one in which [*res ipsa loquitur*]." [1924] N.Z.L.R. 865 at 874

If applied literally, the equivocality approach might often prove even stricter than the last act test. For instance, if a defendant approached a haystack, filled his pipe, lit a match, lit the pipe, and, perhaps, even tossed the match on the haystack, these acts are not per se entirely unequivocal.

MENS REA

The inchoate offence of attempt is conventionally defined as an intention to perform an act or to bring about a result that would constitute a substantive offence, in conjunction with substantial steps taken in furtherance of that intent. Thus, it is apparent from this common law definition that the fault element required is the actual intent or purpose to achieve the proscribed result. Therefore, recklessness or criminal negligence will not suffice to constitute the mens rea of the offence. In *R v Whybrow* (1951) 35 Cr. App. R. 141 at 147, where a person is charged with an attempt, Lord Goddard said "the intent becomes the principal ingredient of the crime." The mens rea of attempt is clearly of crucial importance since the gravamen of the offence consists largely in the mental state of the defendant. It is generally accepted that the mens rea for all attempts is *intention*, even if recklessness, knowledge or negligence is sufficient for the substantive offence. The essential point here is that the defendant must have acted with intent to commit the substantive offence.

It is important to distinguish between intention as to results or consequences, and intention as to circumstances. For instance, the offence of "burning a premises while being reckless as to whether life might be in danger" necessitates that the defendant must have mens rea as to the result (the burning of the building) and the circumstances (whether life might be in danger). Likewise, the offence of rape stipulates that there must be an intention by the defendant to have sexual intercourse, but it also stipulates that there must be knowledge or recklessness on the part of the defendant as to the circumstances of the woman's lack of consent. In these cases, mens rea as to consequences requires intention, whereas *mens rea* as to circumstances may either be intention or recklessness.

Criminal law is stringent in criminalising and punishing attempts in the first place and stipulates that nothing less than intention as to the missing element of the completed result will suffice. But it is not clear, in English criminal law at least, that recklessness as to the circumstances will suffice, whereas it would suffice in respect of the completed offence. The first of these points may be illustrated by attempted murder. For cases involving a specific intent, it is necessary to establish an intention to bring about that specific result. Murder is an offence of specific intent; therefore, it is sufficient to establish that the defendant intended to cause death or serious injury. In the case of attempted murder, the prosecution must prove an intention to kill. In *People (DPP) v Douglas and Hayes* [1985] I.L.R.M. 25, the defendants were convicted of shooting with the intent to commit murder. The mens rea for murder is the intention to kill or to cause serious bodily harm to the victim; however, only an intention to commit murder will be sufficient for the conviction of attempted murder. Thus, an intention to cause serious bodily harm is insufficient to prove attempted murder, the mens rea for attempts being the intention to commit the substantive offence.

In *Attorney General's Reference (No. 3 of 1992)* [1994] 1 W.L.R. 409, the defendants threw petrol bombs at a stationary car, but missed, hitting a wall instead. They were convicted of attempted arson with intent to endanger life or being reckless as to whether or not life was actually endangered. In order for the prosecution to prove attempt, it was necessary for them to prove that the defendants had *intended* to commit the substantive offence, even though proving recklessness would have sufficed if they had committed the substantive offence. Recklessness would suffice, "as far as circumstances are concerned." In order to sustain a conviction for an *attempt* to commit an offence, the defendant must have *intended* the commission of the substantive offence, even if the mens rea for the substantive offence is less than intention, such as recklessness or criminal negligence.

ATTEMPTING THE IMPOSSIBLE

Attempting the impossible is another issue which has given rise to a great deal of legal difficulty. A person may attempt to do something which he believes to be a criminal offence, which, in fact, is not an offence. Alternatively, a person may attempt to commit an offence, which cannot be committed because of the circumstances. The issue, therefore, is whether an individual can be convicted of attempting the commission of a substantive offence, even when it is impossible for the substantive offence to be committed.

For instance, A attempts to commit adultery, believing it to be an offence, but it is not an offence in this jurisdiction, therefore no matter how he tries, he is not guilty of attempt (in law at least). This point is illustrated by the rather unusual case of *R v Taaffe* [1984] A.C. 539, in which the defendant imported a package into England believing that it contained foreign currency and that this was an offence under English law. Neither belief was true, so he could not, in law, be convicted of an attempt. In fact, unbeknownst to him, the package contained cannabis resin, which meant that he had committed the actus reus of a crime, but not the mens rea, and therefore he could not be convicted of importing drugs either. The actus reus and mens rea of a crime must coincide in both time and law.

B opens a safe with intent to steal the money it contains, but finds it empty. Is he guilty of an attempt to steal? This is the more difficult question. Consider the following three situations:

- X attempts to steal from somebody's pocket, but unbeknownst to him, the pocket is empty—physical impossibility.
- X attempts to force open a safe using an implement, such as a penknife, which is entirely inadequate for that purpose—attempt using inadequate means.
- X attempts to kill Y, who is lying on the ground, by kicking him on the head, not realising that Y is already dead; another example would be where X attempts to receive stolen goods which are not in fact stolen—legal impossibility.

One of the leading common law authorities is *Haughton v Smith* [1975] A.C. 476, in which it was held that impossibility is a general defence to a charge of attempt, save in cases where the failure results from inadequacy of means. The police had intercepted stolen goods, but had allowed the goods to proceed to the intended recipient as a ruse. When the defendant took possession of the stolen goods, he was charged with receiving stolen goods. However, the House of Lords held that, at the time that the defendant took possession, the goods were in fact in the control of the police, which effectively meant that the goods had returned to lawful custody. In other words, when the goods were received by the defendant, they were no longer stolen. Accordingly, the House of Lords quashed the defendant's conviction for attempting to handle stolen goods.

1. Physical impossibility

This is the most troublesome class of case. This class of case arises, for example, where the defendant attempts to steal from a person by putting his hand in their pocket, only to find it empty, or where the defendant attempts to murder a victim who is, in fact, already dead. In *Partington v Williams* (1975) 62 Cr. App. R. 220, the Divisional Court held that there could be no liability in such a case as the substantive offence could not be committed, i.e. there was nothing to steal or it was not possible to kill an already dead person. This appears to be the reasoning in *Haughton v Smith* by which the court in *Partington* felt itself bound.

In *DPP v Nock* [1978] A.C. 979, the House of Lords endeavoured to limit the effect of this rule by holding that the outcome could depend on the wording of the indictment. If it alleged an attempt to steal a specific item of property or property from a particular place, it would be impossible to prove an attempt to steal if that item of property was not there, or if there was no property in the particular place, as the case may be. However, if the indictment was drawn so as to allege an attempt to steal from the person generally, the "empty pocket" might lead to a conviction. This reasoning, merely obiter, has been justly criticised as paying scant attention to the proximity doctrine.

2. Impossibility through inadequate means

A person may attempt to commit a crime, but fail because he uses inadequate means, for example, if a defendant uses a nail file in an attempt to open a safe. Impossibility through inadequate means is not a defence where the objective, if achieved, would have been a criminal offence, but the defendant failed to achieve that objective because the means used were inadequate in the circumstances. In *R v White* [1910] 2 K.B. 124, the defendant attempted to murder his mother using poison, but failed because he did not use enough poison. His conviction for attempted murder was upheld. The reasoning in such cases is that the act attempted was not of itself impossible; it was merely the inadequacy of the means that led to the failure. Cases falling under this heading will lead to a conviction.

3. Legal impossibility

This is where the defendant performs all the necessary acts with the intention of committing a criminal offence, but, unbeknownst to him, the completed act is not an offence for one reason or another. A common example is where D takes an umbrella believing it to be somebody else's though it is in fact his own. The completed act is not an offence; therefore, he has attempted what is legally impossible and has not committed an offence. In *R v Taaffe* [1984] A.C. 539, the defendant believed that smuggling foreign currency into England was an offence, but it was not. In fact, the package he believed to contain currency contained drugs, and he was charged with unlawfully importing those. He was acquitted on all charges. He could not be convicted of attempting to smuggle currency because that was legally impossible and not, therefore, an offence. He could not be convicted on a drugs charge because he did not have the mens rea for that offence. In *Haughton v Smith* [1975] A.C. 476, the appellant's conviction for attempting to handle stolen goods was quashed because, at the time that the appellant handled the goods, they had ceased to be stolen for the technical reason that they had been returned to police custody. The principles set out here may be held to represent the current law in Ireland. The defendant's motive will not criminalise behaviour that does not infringe criminal law.

ABANDONMENT

Abandonment does not appear to be a defence for the reason that, once the proximate act has been completed, abandonment will not absolve the defendant from criminal liability. On the other hand, if the defendant abandoned his criminal enterprise before proximity was reached, then he would not be criminally liable as he would not have performed the last act constituting the inchoate offence. For instance, where a defendant has stolen property he cannot avoid criminal liability by making restitution because, once the defendant's attempt is sufficient to justify a conviction, an offence has been committed and subsequent actions by the defendant cannot change that fact, although they may have a bearing on the sentence imposed.

In *Haughton v Smith*, the House of Lords suggested that the crucial point is when the abandonment actually occurred and, if it occurred prior to the proximate act, then the defendant may not be criminally liable, whereas if it occurs after the proximate act, then he will be criminally liable. This decision clearly indicates that abandonment is not a defence where the proximate act has been performed by the defendant and, where the proximate act has not yet been committed, criminal liability cannot be imposed in any event. This principle has been applied by the Supreme Court in *People (AG) v Sullivan* [1964] 1 I.R. 169, where Walsh J. stated:

> "... even if there were evidence that [the defendant] had in fact changed her mind it would not amount to a defence because the offence charged is that of having the intent at the time the act constituting the attempt is carried out. That cannot be answered by evidence of a subsequent abandonment of the intent." [1964] 1 I.R. 169 at 196

In other words, where the defendant failed in his endeavours to commit the substantive criminal offence, he cannot then assert that he abandoned any further "attempts" for he will be criminally liable for the attempt by him to commit the offence. The only consequence of the defendant changing his mind is that he will not be convicted of the substantive offence.

CONSPIRACY

In criminal law, a conspiracy exists when two or more people agree to commit an unlawful act, or to do a lawful act by unlawful means and then take some action toward its completion (*R v Mulcahy* (1868) L.R. 3 H.L. 306). It will be noted from this formulation that the act contemplated need not be a criminal offence, but it must indicate that the co-conspirators knew of the plan and intended to commit an offence. It could be a tort as in *R v Kamara* [1974] A.C. 104, or indeed it could be a more open-ended form of behaviour like "corrupting public morals" or "creating a public mischief." Conspiracy is effectively an agreement about future conduct. The purpose of criminalizing a conspiracy is to distinguish those who coincidentally work towards the commission of an offence in the absence of a conspiracy. It is not necessary for a formal agreement or, indeed, a contract for a conspiracy to come into existence.

In *R v Parnell* (1881) 14 Cox C.C. 508, Charles Stewart Parnell was charged with soliciting tenants not to pay rent by using the unlawful means of "boycotting" those who did not participate. It was held that, although the planned action was a *civil* wrong, it still amounted to a conspiracy. The High Court of Justice in Ireland, Queen's Bench Division, held that this was justified because a wrong, even a civil wrong, against an individual becomes considerably more aggravated if it is conspired by several people, as opposed to one individual. Barry J. stated:

> "It is upon this principle that the law of conspiracy, by which the violation of private right, which if done by one, would only be the subject of a civil remedy, when done by several is constituted a crime, can be vindicated as necessary and just." (1881) 14 Cox C.C. 508 at 520.

Fitzgerald J. explained that:

> "Conspiracy has been aptly described as divisible under three heads – where the end to be attained is in itself a crime; where the object is lawful, but the means to be resorted to are unlawful; and where the object is to do injury to a third party or to a class, though if the wrong were effected by a single individual it would be a wrong but not a crime." (1881) 14 Cox C.C. 508 at 512.

Once the agreement has been concluded between the parties, the conspiracy is complete. It is not necessary that the co-conspirators commit the offence agreed between them. Thus, the essence of conspiracy is the agreement, not the commission, of the criminal offence. Furthermore, the prosecution does not have to establish proximity between the conspiracy and the offence committed.

The offence of conspiracy is punishable per se. For example, Dan, Timmy and Jimmy plan a bank robbery. They visit the bank first to assess security, pool their money, buy a gun together, and write a demand letter. All three co-

conspirators can be charged with conspiracy to commit robbery, regardless of whether the robbery itself is actually attempted or completed; the agreement being the inchoate offence. The justification for criminalizing conspiracies is that a person might be able to defend his interests against an individual, but it would be considerably more difficult against a group, thus requiring the intervention of the State for public policy reasons. Conspiracies are distinguished from attempts on the basis that conspiracies do not require any act towards the commission of a criminal offence. The agreement between two or more people is sufficient to constitute a conspiracy.

The punishment for conspiracy is at the discretion of the court, but must not be more than the substantive offence permits.

Types of conspiracies

The offence of conspiracy includes agreements to commit civil, as well as criminal, wrongs, including conspiracies to commit a crime; to defraud: to pervert the course of justice; to effect a public mischief; to corrupt public morals (*Knuller v DPP* [1973] A.C. 435; *Shaw v DPP* [1962] A.C. 221; *Attorney General (SPUC) v Open Door Counselling Ltd* [1988] I.R. 593); and to outrage public decency (*Knuller v DPP* [1973] A.C. 435; *R v Gibson* [1990] 2 Q.B. 619).

Actus reus

The actus reus is the agreement concluded between the co-conspirators. The essence of a criminal conspiracy is the agreement between two or more persons and the agreement may be either express or implied. The conspiracy is complete as soon as the co-conspirators agree, even if the agreement has not been put into effect. This may cause some confusion, as an agreement is essentially a mental exercise, i.e. something we usually associate with the mens rea of an offence. There will be some outward act to indicate the agreement, but the offence is complete as soon as the agreement has been reached, though this will be difficult to prove in practice in the absence of a confession or some other extrinsic evidence. In *R v Griffiths* [1966] 1 Q.B. 589, the Court of Criminal Appeal per Paull J. stated:

> "… in law all must join in the one agreement, each with the others, in order to constitute one conspiracy. They may join in at various times, each attaching himself to that agreement; any one of them may not know all the other parties but only that there are other parties; any one of them may not know the full extent of the scheme to which he attaches himself. But what each must know is that there is coming into existence, or is in existence, a scheme which goes beyond the illegal act or acts which he agrees to do." [1966] 1 Q.B. 589 at 597

The actus reus of conspiracy is complete on the making of an agreement between co-conspirators to carry out an offence. The inchoate offence of conspiracy is complete even if the parties do not carry out their agreement, that is, even if the substantive offence is not thereafter committed by any of the conspirators or by anyone else.

The agreement must have been *concluded* between the parties. Mere discussions pertaining to the commission of a criminal offence will not be sufficient for the purposes of a criminal conspiracy. In *R v Mills* [1963] 2 W.L.R. 137, the defendant was charged with conspiring with a woman to procure an abortion. The woman (co-conspirator) had telephoned the defendant seeking an abortion and he invited her to attend his premises with payment for the procedure. When she arrived at his premises, a discussion took place regarding the proposed abortion, including a discussion of the risks involved. During the course of the discussions, the police entered the premises and charged both with conspiring to procure an abortion. The Court of Criminal Appeal rejected their contention that there had been no concluded agreement, ruling that the agreement had been concluded following the telephone conversation. The court explained that the agreement was concluded although it was subject to conditions, but this did not necessarily vitiate the agreement. Furthermore, the court stated that almost all agreements are subject to conditions, whether express or implied.

Conspiracy is an ongoing offence, so it is possible for a person to join a conspiracy after the initial agreement has been reached, for instance, C joins a conspiracy already in existence between A and B. The conspiracy will continue until such time as it is put into effect or abandoned or becomes frustrated.

Criminal law is not concerned with the identity of the parties so long as there are two or more of them and that there is an agreement between them to commit an unlawful act or to commit a lawful act by unlawful means. There is an exception where the parties are married because there cannot in law be a conspiracy between a husband and wife. This point was averted in *Mawji v R* [1957] A.C. 126, where the Privy Council held that spouses could not enter a conspiracy with each other, on the basis that a husband and wife were in law regarded as being one, and the essence of a conspiracy is an agreement between "two or more persons." Irish law is unclear on this issue as a result of the decision in *People (DPP) v Murray* [1977] I.R. 360, in which the doctrine of common design was applied, i.e. each spouse was treated independently and as independent persons they formed a common design to kill, if necessary, in the course of a robbery. English statute law has specifically provided for the preservation of the legal principle that a husband and wife are regarded by law as being one person (Criminal Law Act 1977 s.2). It is widely believed that Irish law will follow these principles based on public policy considerations, namely, the preservation of the institution of marriage as mandated by the Constitution (Art.41). However, a husband and wife can be convicted of a conspiracy if a third party is involved or, indeed, where they had entered the conspiracy prior to their marriage.

The essence of a conspiracy is that two or more people agree to commit an offence, but this must be distinguished from independent actions by two or more persons acting towards the same unlawful objective. In other words, if two or more people act independently in the commission of the same criminal offence, there has been no agreement and, accordingly, no conspiracy. The conspiracy does not have to be a secret. In *R v Parnell*, Fitzgerald J. stated that secrecy is not an essential element of the offence.

There must be an agreement to commit a criminal offence, and the issue as to whether or not an agreement has in fact been concluded among the parties will be a matter for the jury to determine. Unless one or more of the co-conspirators actually confesses, it will be necessary for the prosecution to establish that the co-conspirators' criminal acts were concerted, leading to an inference that the actions must have been co-ordinated beforehand. In *R v Porter* [1980] N.I. 18, there was sufficient evidence from which it could be inferred that the defendant had in fact joined the criminal conspiracy.

The basis for a criminal conspiracy is not the concerted acts, but the prior agreement which the court will infer from the acts. In *R v Bolton* [1991] Crim. L.R. 57, it was stressed that, "it is what was agreed to be done and not what was in fact done which is all important."

MENS REA

There is little authority on this, but at the same time, there are seldom difficulties in proving it by virtue of the agreement. It seems, though, that each defendant must have knowledge of the relevant circumstances and that he must intend to commit the offence. The mens rea of conspiracies is the intention to engage in a course of conduct that pertains to the commission of a substantive offence by one or more of the co-conspirators. The conspirators must intend to perform the act constituting the substantive offence, such as murder, fraud, etc. The conspirators' state of mind must also satisfy the fault element of the substantive offence; for instance, if one of the ingredients of the offence is that the prohibited act is performed with a specific intent (such as in the case of murder), then the conspirators must intend to perform the prohibited act with intent.

CO-CONSPIRATORS

Where two or more persons conspire towards the commission of a criminal offence, it appears that it is not necessary that each co-conspirator is aware of the existence of the other co-conspirator, provided that each co-conspirator is a participant in the same conspiracy. Each co-conspirator must know the objectives of the agreement, but it is not essential that each knows the exact details. Furthermore, each co-conspirator must also know that they are part of the agreement, but it is not necessary that each has knowledge of the exact method of execution, nor indeed that each knows how many co-conspirators are involved.

All of the co-conspirators must have the intention to commit the offence charged, and for the co-conspirator to have intended the commission of the substantive offence implies that he had knowledge of the conspiracy's objective. In *Porter (op. cit.)*, the Court of Criminal Appeal for Northern Ireland stated that co-conspirators will not always have absolute knowledge of what the other co-conspirators have done and, furthermore, this knowledge is not necessary to convict each co-conspirator (cf. *R v Orton* [1922] V.L.R. 469).

It is not necessary that co-conspirators know all of the other conspirators. In *AG v Oldridge* [2000] 4 I.R. 593, the Supreme Court held that, if a conspiracy was already formed, and a person joined it afterwards, he was equally guilty.

The issue is whether, in order to convict a co-conspirator, it is also necessary to convict the other co-conspirators. In *DPP v Shannon* [1975] A.C. 717, the House of Lords held that where co-conspirators are tried separately, if one is acquitted, this will not prejudice the conviction of the remaining co-conspirators. However, a minority stated that, in circumstances where co-conspirators are tried together, all must either be convicted or acquitted. In *R v Coughlan* (1976) 64 Cr. App. R. 11, the defendant and another had been jointly tried for conspiracy to cause explosions. The trial judge directed the jury that both defendants must be acquitted or convicted. The defendant appealed his conviction on the basis that the evidence against his co-conspirator was substantially stronger than the evidence against him, and that, as a result of the judge's direction, his chances of an acquittal had been severely diminished. He relied on the *Shannon* judgment in support of his argument. His argument was rejected by the Court of Criminal Appeal; however, the court did say that, where the evidence against one of the co-conspirators is conclusive as to his guilt, then the remaining co-conspirators may request separate trials. An application for separate trials will be decided by the trial judge based on the weight of the evidence presented against each co-conspirator.

IMPOSSIBILITY

If two or more people conspire to do something, but it transpires that it is impossible to do this act, are they criminally liable on the basis of a conspiracy? This will depend on the nature of the agreement made between them. If the agreement was to perform a particular act or pursue a specific course of conduct which subsequently transpires to be impossible to complete, then they will not be criminally liable based on a conspiracy. In *DPP v Nock* [1978] 1 A.C. 979, the agreement (conspiracy) was to produce cocaine. The defendants were in possession of powder that they believed to be cocaine and they proceeded to separate the cocaine from the other constituents of the powder. However, since the powder did not contain cocaine, it was impossible for them to produce cocaine. On appeal, the House of Lords held that, since the agreement was for the specific purpose of producing cocaine, which proved to be impossible to achieve, the defendants should be acquitted. If, however, the agreement had been of a more general purpose that would not necessarily have been defeated by impossibility, then it is more likely that the defendants would have been convicted.

ABANDONMENT

If the defendant abandons the conspiracy, will he have a complete defence or will this abandonment merely amount to a mitigating factor? Since a conspiracy is completed once two or more people agree to commit an offence, a subsequent abandonment will not constitute a defence, but might be a mitigating factor at sentencing. The Criminal Justice (Surveillance) Act 2009 (the "2009 Act") provides that State agencies, An Garda Síochána, Defence Forces, and Revenue Commissioners, can, subject to an authorisation order issued by the District Court, engage in covert surveillance of suspected criminals and use the product of that surveillance in criminal proceedings. This legislation will facilitate investigation and conviction of conspiracy where there is evidence of an agreement to commit an offence. Consequently, it will serve to prevent the commission of heinous criminal offences, as the police will have sufficient information to intervene and prevent the commission of those offences. The 2009 Act serves to enhance intelligence-led policing.

INCITEMENT

An incitement to commit an offence arises when someone tries to influence another person to commit a criminal offence. It is not necessary that the person incited actually commits the offence. If the person incited commits a further offence, the defendant will not be criminally liable for that additional offence. It might also be the case that a person is induced to commit an offence because of duress exerted on them by the inciter. In the South African case of *Nkosiyana* (1966) (4) S.A. 655, Holmes J.A. explained that an inciter is:

> "... one who reaches and seeks to influence the mind of another to the commission of a crime. The machinations of criminal ingenuity being

legion, the approach to the other's mind may take various forms, such as suggestion, proposal, request, exhortation, gesture, argument, persuasion, inducement, goading or the arousal of cupidity." 1966 (4) S.A. 655 at 688

This passage omits the use of the word "encourages." Encouragement involves words or actions amounting to a positive step or steps aimed at inciting another to commit a criminal offence. It is not necessary to a charge of incitement to prove that the offence incited was actually carried out. However, whatever the intention of the inciter, if what is incited would, if done, not be an offence, then the inchoate offence of incitement has not been committed.

If, while persuading or attempting to persuade someone else to commit a crime, the other person then actually carries out the criminal act, the inciter becomes a participator in the crime and is guilty of aiding and abetting it. If the other person does not carry out the crime, the person who attempted to persuade him to do so may, nonetheless, be guilty of the crime of incitement. Incitement may be committed by means of suggestion, persuasion, threats, or pressure, by words or by implication, e.g. advertising for sale an article to be used to commit an offence may constitute incitement to commit that offence. Something must be said or done by the inciter and the incitement can involve persuasion, encouragement, influence, threats or promises that a benefit will accrue to the person who commits the substantive offence. It is most often effected by persuading another to commit the offence, although in appropriate circumstances, the defendant may have the defence of duress available to him. Unlike the inchoate offence of attempt, the incitement does not have to be proximate to the completed offence.

The Prohibition of Incitement to Hatred Act 1989 makes it an offence to, "publish, distribute or broadcast any threatening, abusive or insulting material that it intended or is likely to incite hatred", and the Gardaí have significant powers of search and seizure in relation to material which is likely to incite hatred.

The punishment on conviction for incitement depends on whether or not the substantive offence was committed. Punishment on summary conviction for incitement is governed by s.22 of the Petty Sessions (Ireland) Act 1851, whereas conviction on indictment is governed by s.7(1) of the Criminal Law Act 1997. If the substantive offence was not actually committed, then the sentence imposed is at the discretion of the trial court.

ACTUS REUS

The actus reus of incitement is the persuasion of another, by whatever means, to commit an offence. In *R v Fitzmaurice* [1983] Q.B. 1083 at 1089, the Court of Appeal per Neill J. said that this could be effected by evidence of a "suggestion, proposal or request coupled with an implied promise of a reward." Incitement involves more than a "mere desire" that the person incited to commit an offence, but, rather, that the defendant has taken some positive step towards recruiting some other person to commit the offence charged. However, the incitement may be effected by threats as well as by persuasion. In *Race Relation Board v Applin* [1973] Q.B. 815, Lord Denning said that incitement could be effected by the use of threats or pressure placed on the person "incited" to commit the offence, which might also provide the basis for a defence of duress. Encouraging includes threatening or putting pressure on another person to commit the offence. The criminal liability of the person who incites another to commit the offence is limited to the offence incited. So, for example, if *X* incites *Y* to commit a burglary, and *Y* decides to burn down the building, then *X*'s criminal liability will only extend to the burglary.

Incitement involves soliciting some other person to commit the offence charged, but not all solicitations will amount to incitements. In the leading Irish case on incitement, *People (AG) v Capaldi* (1949) 1 Frewen 95, the defendant brought to a doctor a girl who was pregnant and asked the doctor "to do something for her." When the doctor enquired if what he had in mind was an abortion, the defendant replied "yes". The doctor, in the words of the court, "showed him the door". The defendant was charged with incitement to the crime of bringing about an abortion. He was convicted by the Circuit Criminal Court. The defendant argued that he had merely expressed a desire and had not intended to incite the commission of an offence. The Court of Criminal Appeal dismissed the defendant's appeal against conviction. Black J. stated:

> "... the Court is of opinion that a person may truly incite another to commit a crime by the action of stirring up enmity in his mind against another, or by offering him some pecuniary or other inducement. Such action would be an incitement if, but for it, it would not have occurred to the party incited to commit the crime, whether he had any particular reluctance to commit it or not." (1949) 1 Frewen 95 at 97

The specificity of the request, in addition to the financial incentive offered, was more than a mere desire, and the actions of the defendant amounted to an incitement.

The defendant must have communicated the words to those being incited. Can a person be convicted of incitement where the solicitation is addressed to "all and sundry"? In *R v Most* (1881) 14 Cox C.C. 583, an article published in a newspaper urging revolutionaries worldwide to "assassinate their Heads of State" was deemed sufficient communication for incitement to commit murder. Likewise, in *Invicta Plastics Ltd v Clare* [1976] Crim. L.R. 131, the Divisional Court held that a company which advertised a device that could detect police radar traps was properly convicted of inciting the readers of the advertisement to use unlicensed apparatus for wireless telegraphy, contrary to s.1(1) of the Wireless Telegraphy Act 1949. It appears from the decision in *Re Chlemsford Justices*, ex parte *Amos* [1973] Crim. L.R. 437 that, if the communication had failed to reach those being incited, or indeed, if the communication had been intercepted by the police, the defendant may nevertheless be charged with "attempted incitement."

One important aspect of the offence is that the act in question must be an offence if committed by the person indicted. In the case of murder, it would seem obvious that, if a person incites a person to kill another, he will be guilty of incitement to murder and this requirement would be easily satisfied. However, if the person incited is under the age of criminal responsibility, the inciter will not be responsible as no offence would be committed. The implications of this rule are to be seen most clearly in the case of *R v Whitehouse* [1977] Q.B. 868, in which the defendant was charged with the offence of inciting his 15-year-old daughter to commit incest with him. Under the relevant English law, a girl under the age of 16 would not be guilty of incest. Consequently, the charge amounted to one of inciting the girl to commit an offence that she was not, in law, capable of committing. The Court of Criminal Appeal quashed the conviction. The prosecution argued that the defendant could be convicted of inciting the girl to aid and abet the man to commit the crime of incest against her. However, in *R v Tyrell*, [1894] 1 Q.B. 710, it had been decided that the relevant legislation governing sexual relations with minors had been enacted for the protection of underage girls and not to criminalise them and, consequently, this argument was rejected. The anomaly created by this was rectified in England by the Criminal Law Act 1977, which makes it a statutory offence for a man to incite a girl under the age of 16 to have incestuous relations with him.

MENS REA

The mens rea for all inchoate offences is intention. The defendant must have intended the person incited to commit the substantive offence charged. As to the mens rea of incitement, there must be an intention to bring about a criminal result. It must also be proved that the defendant had knowledge of all the circumstances of the act incited.

IMPOSSIBILITY

Impossibility may be a defence to a charge of incitement if the persuasion related to a specific type of offence, but impossibility will not negate criminal liability in the case of incitement to commit a general offence that is not specified. In *R v Fitzmaurice* [1983] 1 Q.B. 1083, a father asked his son to recruit a number of others for the commission of a robbery, which he did. However, the father had no plan to commit the robbery, but was, instead, going to inform the police and claim a reward for preventing the robbery. The Court of Appeal endorsed *DPP v Nock*, and the approach taken would also appear to be applicable to incitement, that is, liability will depend on the nature of the incitement. In other words, if the offence incited is of a general nature, impossibility is not a defence; whereas if the offence incited is specific, and the specific objective is impossible, then impossibility may be a defence. The offence in *Fitzmaurice* was incitement to commit a robbery and was of a general nature and therefore it was not impossible to commit such an offence.

Proposed Law Reform

The Law Reform Commission's *Consultation Paper on Inchoate Offences* (LRC CP 48–2008) reviewed the current state of the law, identified uncertainty in the scope of inchoate offences and made provisional recommendations for reform. This contains the Commission's provisional recommendations for reforming the law on conspiracy, attempts and incitement, including the codification of such offences. The Commission is due to publish a Report on inchoate offences in 2010.

Attempt

The Commission provisionally recommends that the physical aspect of attempt should be defined as an act that is close to the completion of the substantive offence, which ensures that the defendant can justly be considered to have been attempting to commit a substantive offence. With regard to the fault element, the Commission recommends that the mens rea of attempt should be defined as intention that an act constituting a substantive criminal offence be completed. This will also serve to make sure that the defendant was endeavouring to commit the substantive offence.

Conspiracy

The Commission provisionally recommends that only agreements to commit a substantive criminal offence should be criminal conspiracies and the abolition of conspiracy to corrupt public morals. This would constitute a significant reform of current law on conspiracy, which includes agreements to commit civil as well as criminal wrongs.

Incitement

The Commission provisionally recommends that the offence of incitement should be codified and that the offence is committed by encouraging, commanding or requesting the carrying out of a criminal act with the intention that the act is carried out. This purpose of this proposal is to include in the definition of incitement people who are trying to get another person to commit an offence.

IMPOSSIBILITY

The Commission provisionally recommends that impossibility should not be a defence for all three inchoate offences. For instance, someone who pickpockets an empty pocket could still be convicted of attempted theft, even though the pocked might have been empty. Likewise, hiring someone to kill a person who is already dead would constitute an incitement to commit murder. This proposal reflects the commonsense view that the blameworthiness of someone who tries to bring about the commission of an offence is the same, regardless of whether or not the substantive offence was committed.

FURTHER READING

Campbell, Kilcommins and O'Sullivan, *Criminal Law in Ireland: Cases and Commentary* (Dublin: Clarus Press, 2010), Chs 5, 6 and 7.

Daly, "Reform of the Prohibition of Incitement to Hatred Act 1989: Part I" (2007) 17(3) I.C.L.J. 16.

Daly, "Reform of the Prohibition of Incitement to Hatred Act 1989: Part II" (2007) 17(4) I.C.L.J. 16.

Hanly, *An Introduction to Irish Criminal Law*, 2nd edn (Dublin: Gill & Mcmillan, 2006), Chs 15, 16 and 17.

Hocking, "Conspiracy as a Very Enduring Practice: Part I" (1998) 8(1) I.C.L.J. 1.

Hocking, "Conspiracy as a Very enduring Practice: Part II" (1998) 8(2) I.C.L.J. 121.

Keogh, "The Prohibition of Incitement to Hatred Act 1989: A Paper Tiger?" (2000) 6(3) B.R. 178.

Law Reform Commission, *Consultation Paper on Inchoate Offences* (LRC CP 48–2008).

McAuley, "Relational Liability in Criminal Law" (1999) 34 Ir. Jur. (N.S.) 100.

Prendergast, "Codifying Inchoate Offences" (2008) 26 I.L.T. 134.

16. Homicide

INTRODUCTION

Homicide is the generic term that describes all forms of unlawful killings including: murder, manslaughter, infanticide, dangerous driving causing death (penalty on conviction for dangerous driving causing death is the same as for manslaughter), and assisted suicide. It involves the unlawful killing of a human being by another human being. Lawful killings might include death through misadventure, including surgery and certain sports, or where a state is authorised to impose the death penalty as a mode of punishment on conviction for heinous criminal offences, which has been abolished in Irish criminal law (Criminal Justice Act 1990, s.1; see also Art.15.5.2° of the Constitution that was inserted by amendment in 2002).

MURDER

There is no full statutory definition of murder in Ireland or England. Since murder is a common law offence, its definition is to be gathered from the decisions of the courts. The classic definition of murder is considered to be that given by Lord Chief Justice Coke (*Institutes of the Laws of England* (1797)), defining murder as occurring when:

> "... a man of sound memory, and of the age of discretion, unlawfully killeth ... any reasonable creature [*in rerum natura*] ... with malice aforethought, either expressed by the party or implied by law, so that the party wounded die of the wound or hurt within a year and a day after the same".

This is the most widely accepted definition of murder.

Previously, there was a common law rule that the victim died within a "year and a day", which stipulated that for the purposes of offences involving unlawful killings, the defendant's conduct was conclusively presumed not to have caused the deceased's death if more than a year and a day had elapsed before death (see *R v Dyson* [1908] 2 K.B. 454). This rule has now been repealed in Ireland by s.38 of the Criminal Justice Act 1999, and in England by s.1 of the Law Reform (Year and a Day Rule) Act 1996.

The defendant must have been of sound memory. If at the time of committing the offence, the defendant was legally insane, then he would not have had the capacity to form the mens rea for that offence. The defendant must also have attained the legal age at which one becomes criminally responsible for one's criminal acts or omissions, which is currently set at 12 years of age.

ACTUS REUS

Murder is the unlawful killing of a human being. Certain activities, such as self-defence and death through misadventure, might render the killing "lawful". The unlawful killing must have been of a living human being. The person killed must have been alive, and a newborn child must have had an independent existence from its mother for it to be capable of being murdered (cf. *R v Poulton* (1832) 5 C. & P. 329; *R v Reeves* (1839) 9 C. & P. 25). The unlawful killing need not be by direct violence, for instance, abandoning a child so that the child dies may be sufficient (omission liability), provided that the defendant has the required mens rea.

MENS REA

Murder occurs if a person intended to kill, or cause serious injury to, another person who dies as a result. The mens rea for murder does not require proof of malice, spite or ill will, nor indeed does it require premeditation. The fault element is simply an intention to kill or to cause grievous bodily harm, as stipulated by s.4(1) of the Criminal Justice Act 1964:

(1) Where a person kills another unlawfully, the killing shall not be murder unless the accused intended to kill, or cause serious injury to, some person, whether the person actually killed or not.
(2) The accused person shall be presumed to have intended the natural and probable consequences of his conduct; but this presumption may be rebutted.

This definition provides for subjective intention and the doctrine of transferred malice. The Law Reform Commission's *Report on Homicide: Murder and Involuntary Manslaughter* (LRC 87–2008), at para.3.40), recommends that the fault element for murder be broadened to embrace reckless killing manifesting an extreme indifference to human life.

In *R v Vickers* [1957] 2 Q.B. 664, the English Court of Criminal Appeal held that an intention to cause grievous bodily harm was evidence of a willingness to accept a substantial risk that the victim might actually die. In *R v Cunningham* [1982] A.C. 566, the defendant had repeatedly struck the victim over the head with a chair, with the result that the victim died. Although there had not been an intention to kill, there certainly had been an intention to cause serious bodily harm. The defendant was convicted of murder and his appeal to the House of Lords against conviction was rejected, stating that there had been an intention to cause "really serious injury" and this was sufficient mens rea for a murder conviction.

The defendant is presumed to have intended the natural and probable consequences of his conduct, but this presumption may be rebutted by evidence to the contrary. In *People (DPP) v Cullen,* unreported, Central Criminal Court, November 17, 1982, the defendant was convicted of murder after he had thrown a fire bomb through the window of a house, in which three occupants died in the resulting blaze. The defendant was a pimp who claimed that he merely wanted to frighten the deceased, who had previously worked as a prostitute for him. The defendant was convicted of murder and malicious damage based largely on the uncorroborated evidence of his accomplice, another prostitute, who had watched the defendant throw a fire bomb.

Murder is an offence of specific intent and intention, and in this context, can be either direct or oblique. Direct intention is where the defendant actually desired the result, whereas oblique intention is where the defendant had foreseen death as a virtually certain result, although this may not have been desired for its own sake (see Ch.3 Mens Rea).

ATTEMPTED MURDER

This is an inchoate offence. One of the leading Irish cases on attempted murder is *People (DPP) v Douglas and Hayes* [1985] I.L.R.M. 25, which dealt with "shooting with attempt to commit murder", contrary to s.14 of the Offences against the Person Act 1861. The Court of Criminal Appeal held, that for the purposes of this offence, it was necessary to prove the actus reus together with an intention to kill and not just an intention to cause serious injury. If the defendant's intention was to cause serious injury, this would be insufficient to justify a conviction for attempted murder.

SENTENCE FOR MURDER

Murder also carries a mandatory life sentence (Criminal Justice Act 1990 s.2). A life sentence means a life sentence. However, the Constitution and statutory provisions stipulate for the commutation and remission of sentences in limited circumstances. Article 13.6 of the Constitution provides that:

> The right of pardon and the power to commute or remit punishment imposed by any court exercising criminal jurisdiction are hereby vested in the President, but such power of commutation or remission may, except in capital cases, also be conferred by law on other authorities.

Section 23 of the Criminal Justice Act 1951 provides that:

(1) Except in capital cases, the Government may commute or remit, in whole or in part, any punishment imposed by a Court exercising criminal jurisdiction, subject to such conditions as they may think proper.
(2) The Government may remit, in whole or in part, any forfeiture or disqualification imposed by a Court exercising criminal jurisdiction and restore or revive, in whole or in part, the subject of the forfeiture.
(3) The Government may delegate to the Minister for Justice any power conferred by this section and may revoke any such delegation
(4) This section shall not affect any power conferred by law on other authorities.

In the case of a murder conviction, the defendant can be released on licence after a significant term of imprisonment has been served. The life sentence still stands and the defendant who has been released on licence will be subject to certain conditions, any violation of which will result in the licence being revoked.

Aggravated Murder

Originally this offence was termed capital murder and carried a death sentence. However, with the abolition of the death penalty in Ireland by s.1 of the Criminal Justice Act 1990, a new offence of aggravated murder was created under s.3 which applies to the murder of a Garda or prison officer acting in the course of their duty; a murder done in the course or furtherance of specified offences created by the Offences against the State Act 1939 as amended; or murder committed within the State for a political motive of the head of a foreign state or of a member of its government or of its diplomatic officer. These are the aggravating circumstances (the identity of the victim) that distinguish the offence of aggravated murder from ordinary murder.

It must be proved that the defendant knew of the existence of each ingredient of the offence or was reckless as to whether or not that ingredient existed, for example, in relation to the killing of a Garda, by establishing that the defendant knew the deceased was a Garda acting in the course of his duty, or was reckless as to whether he was a Garda so acting.

There is a minimum period of imprisonment specified for aggravated murder, 40 years, and attempted aggravated murder, 20 years (Criminal Justice Act 1990, s.4). There are also restrictions on the power to commute or remit or to grant temporary release in the case of aggravated murder. Where the evidence does not warrant a conviction for aggravated murder, the defendant may be convicted of murder or manslaughter.

Causation

Since murder is a result offence, the prosecution must establish that the defendant's conduct constituted both a factual and a legal cause of the death of the victim. Thus, if the chain of causation between the defendant's conduct and the victim's death is broken by a novus actus interveniens then, as a general rule, the defendant will not be criminally liable for the defendant's death. Issues of causation (discussed in Ch.2 dealing with the actus reus) are directly applicable to homicide offences in that the defendant's conduct must have caused the victims death.

Alternative Verdict

Where the evidence does not justify a conviction for murder, the defendant may be convicted of any of the following offences based on the entirety of the evidence: attempted murder; manslaughter; causing serious harm; aiding or abetting suicide (Criminal Law Act 1997, s.9(2)).

Manslaughter

Manslaughter is any unlawful killing that is not murder and currently consists of two broad categories: voluntary manslaughter and involuntary manslaughter. At common law, all unlawful killings other than murder are classified as manslaughter. There will be many cases in which a person brings about the death of another by causing harm to that other, typically by an assault, but not intending to cause serious harm, let alone death. In such a case, the assailant will be guilty of manslaughter. Manslaughter is a common law offence and carries a maximum life sentence. It is classified as a lesser form of homicide in the sense that the mens rea for manslaughter falls short of the mens rea required for murder.

Voluntary manslaughter

Voluntary manslaughter pertains to unlawful killings that would otherwise be murder, but due to the presence of some excusing circumstance, such as the partial-defences of provocation or excessive self-defence, the defendant is likely to be convicted of voluntary manslaughter, not murder. In these circumstances, the defendant intentionally kills the victim with the mens rea for murder but successfully pleads the partial defence. Alternatively, the defendant kills the victim, again with the mens rea for murder, and honestly believes he is acting in self-defence, but the force used is excessively disproportionate in the circumstances. These two categories involve the intentional killing of the victim under extenuating circumstances. Provocation and excessive self-defence are partial defences only available to a murder charge. An acquittal would be unjustifiable because the defendant performed the actus reus of murder with the mens rea for that offence, but the conviction is for the lesser-included offence of manslaughter principally because the defendant killed due to the actions of the deceased, The main advantage for the defendant convicted of manslaughter as opposed to murder is that the trial judge has a wide measure of discretion and may impose a proportionate sentence up to and including the maximum sentence for manslaughter which is life imprisonment.

INVOLUNTARY MANSLAUGHTER

The defendant may be convicted of involuntary manslaughter where he does not have the mens rea for murder but his acts or omissions cause the death of the victim. The defendant will have the mens rea for manslaughter by virtue of the fact that his conduct was reckless or criminally negligent. This arises where a person brings about the death of another by acting in some unlawful manner, but without the intention of killing or doing an act likely to kill. The defendant's state of mind is less culpable than that required for a murder charge. Involuntary manslaughter may arise by the person doing an act which is intrinsically unlawful, or doing some lawful act but doing it recklessly, or culpably leaving unperformed some act which he had a legal duty to perform.

1. Manslaughter as a result of a criminal and dangerous act

The first sub-category of involuntary manslaughter is where the defendant caused the deceased's death by an unlawful and dangerous act. In these circumstances, the unlawful killing involves an act constituting a criminal offence, carrying with it the risk of bodily harm to the person killed. For instance, in *People (DPP) v O'Donoghue* [2007] 2 I.R. 336, which involved an assault of a youth resulting in death, the defendant was convicted for unlawful and dangerous act manslaughter.

Where the defendant killed the victim by an unlawful act that was objectively dangerous, a manslaughter conviction is justified. The only mens rea required is the intention to do the act and any requisite fault element. It is not necessary that the defendant should have been aware of either the unlawfulness or the dangerousness of the act or of the circumstances that made it dangerous. In *DPP v Newbury and Jones* [1977] A.C. 500, Lord Salmon said:

> "The test is still the objective test. In judging whether the act was dangerous the test is not did the accused recognise that it was dangerous but would all sober and reasonable people recognise its danger." [1977] A.C. 500 at 507

The test is whether the defendant's conduct was objectively dangerous.

At one time, it was thought than any unlawful act that resulted in the death of another would be sufficient to sustain a verdict of manslaughter, even a tort would suffice. But now it is reasonably settled that the defendant's conduct must be a criminal offence. The two leading English cases are *R v Lamb* [1967] 2 Q.B. 981, and *R v Scarlett* (1993) 98 Cr. App. R. 290. In *Lamb*, the defendant aimed a revolver in jest at a friend believing it to be empty and pulled the trigger, killing the friend. Sachs L.J. stated:

> "When the gravamen of a charge is criminal negligence – often referred to as recklessness – of an accused, the jury have to consider among other matters the state of his mind, and that includes the question of whether or not he thought that that which he was doing was safe. In the present case it would, of course, have been fully open to a jury, if properly directed, to find the defendant guilty because they considered his view as to there being no danger was formed in a criminally negligent way. But he was entitled to a direction that the jury should take into account the fact that he had undisputedly formed that view and that there was expert evidence as to this being an understandable view. Strong though the evidence of criminal negligence was, the defendant was entitled as of right to have his defence considered, but he was not accorded this right and the jury was left without a direction on an essential matter." [1967] 2 Q.B. 981 at 990

The appeal was allowed and the conviction was quashed. In *Scarlett*, the defendant was the landlord of a public house and requested the deceased to leave. The deceased refused to leave voluntarily and therefore the landlord took hold of his arms and escorted him from the bar. The deceased fell down a flight of five steps into the street hitting his head and sustained injuries from which he subsequently died. Bedlam L.J. stated:

> "[The jury] should be directed that the accused is not to be found guilty merely because he intentionally or recklessly used force which they consider to have been excessive. They ought not to convict him unless they are satisfied that the degree of force used was plainly more than was called for by the circumstances as he believed them to be, and, provided he believed the circumstances called for the degree of force used, he is not to be convicted even if his belief was unreasonable." (1993) 98 Cr.App.R. 290 at 296

The conviction for manslaughter was quashed because the trial judge's directions to the jury were inadequate to support a verdict of manslaughter.

Furthermore, the defendant had given clear evidence that he only intended to use sufficient force to remove the deceased from the bar, which he was lawfully entitled to do. It was not contended that he acted recklessly.

If the defendant commits an act with the intention of causing the victim physical harm, and the victim dies, he will be charged with manslaughter. However, if the intention was to cause serious physical harm then the proper charge will be murder. Accordingly, it appears that a minor injury will suffice for a manslaughter conviction. In *R v Wild* (1837) 2 Lew 214, the victim was a guest in the defendant's house who had overstayed his welcome, so the defendant kicked him as an encouragement to leave. The victim died and the defendant's conviction for manslaughter was upheld because, although he did not intend any real harm to the victim, his behaviour in kicking him was unjustifiable.

The defendant's conduct must have been both dangerous and unlawful. In *R v Larkin* (1942) 29 Cr. App. R.18, the defendant brandished an open razor so as to intimidate the lover of his mistress, however, his mistress who was drunk, fell against the razor with the result that her throat was cut. The defendant's actions were both unlawful (assault) and dangerous, and therefore his conviction for manslaughter was upheld. In *People (AG) v Crosbie and Meehan* [1966] I.R. 490, the victim died from a stab wound. The defendant claimed that he carried a knife for self-defence. How the stab wound was inflicted was not conclusive, although the defendant claimed that he had brandished the knife so as to scare off the aggressors and that he had accidentally stabbed the victim. Therefore, as he had not intended to stab the victim (or so he claimed) he could not be convicted of manslaughter by assault. The Court of Criminal Appeal held that the defendant could be convicted of manslaughter by committing a criminal and dangerous act in view of the fact that he had brandished the knife not in self-defence but to scare of the aggressors. Kenny J. stated:

> "A person who produces a knife with the intention of intimidating or frightening another and not for self-defence commits an assault and the act done is therefore unlawful. When a killing resulted from an unlawful act ... the act causing death must be unlawful and dangerous to constitute the offence of manslaughter. The dangerous quality of the act must however be judged by objective standards and it is irrelevant that the accused person did not think that the act was dangerous."
> [1966] I.R. 490 at 495

The defendant's conduct that caused the victim's death had to be unlawful and dangerous. Whether or not the act in question was dangerous is an issue for the jury to decide, applying the objective test. The court approved *Larkin*.

In *R v Pagett* (1983) 76 Cr. App. R. 279, the defendant had used a girl as a human shield and then fired at the police who instinctively returned fire, killing the girl. The defendant was convicted of manslaughter, since he had committed not one but two unlawful and dangerous acts: he had used the girl as a human shield and fired at the police.

The unlawful and dangerous act need not be directed at the victim. In *R v Mitchell* [1983] 1 Q.B. 741, the defendant while standing in a queue in a post office decided to skip the queue. However, another man in the queue objected to the defendant's behaviour, resulting in the defendant punching him, but the man fell against an old lady with the result that she suffered a broken leg. She was hospitalised and while recovering from surgery she suffered a blood clot in her leg from which she died. This was sufficient to convict the defendant of manslaughter.

2. Manslaughter by criminal negligence

This sub-category of manslaughter pertains to cases where the death arises from a negligent act or omission by the defendant that constitutes a high risk of substantial personal injury. The defendant must have purposively acted in a certain manner that is deemed to have been criminally negligent. The defendant's inadvertence must have been such that any reasonable person in the circumstances of the defendant would have realised, if he had given any thought to it, that what he was doing involved a high degree of risk of causing substantial personal injury to others.

Criminal negligence is higher than the standard of negligence in tort and the civil standard of negligence will not be sufficient. The defendant must have been reckless as to the consequences of his behaviour. The question to be considered by the jury is whether the defendant was guilty of the degree of negligence that is appropriate to sustain a charge of manslaughter. In *R v Adomako* [1995] 1 A.C. 171, during the course of a medical operation the defendant anaesthetist failed to notice that a tube had become disconnected. The House of Lords specified three criteria to be satisfied for gross negligence: the defendant was in breach of a duty of care under the ordinary principles of negligence; the negligence must have caused death; and if causation has been established, is the jury satisfied that the defendant's negligence amounted to gross negligence? The jury must be satisfied that the defendant's negligence was of a very high degree before returning a conviction for manslaughter.

In *Adomako*, the House of Lords held that the appropriate test for criminal negligence was that laid down in *R v Batemen*, (1925) 19 Cr. App. R. 8, and *Andrews v DPP* [1937] A.C. 576. In *Bateman* a doctor was charged with the manslaughter of a woman who had died during childbirth. Hewart C.J. said that the jury should be directed that:

"To support an indictment for manslaughter the prosecution must prove the matters necessary to establish civil liability (except pecuniary loss), and, in addition, must satisfy the jury that the negligence or incompetence of the accused went beyond a mere matter of compensation and showed such disregard for the life and safety of others as to amount to a crime against the State and conduct deserving punishment." (1925) 19 Cr.App.R. 8 at 13

In *Andrews*, Lord Atkin stated:

"Simple lack of care such as will constitute civil liability is not enough: for purposes of the criminal law there are degrees of negligence: and a very high degree of negligence is required to be proved before the felony is established." [1937] A.C. 576 at 583

The defendant's conduct was such that it constituted a substantially higher degree of negligence than that for negligence in civil law.

One of the leading Irish cases is *People (AG) v Dunleavy* [1948] I.R. 95, where the defendant, a taxi driver, drove his unlit car on the wrong side of the road and killed a cyclist. The Court of Criminal Appeal held that in cases where criminal negligence is at issue, the jury should be directed on the various degrees of negligence, and informed that a very high degree of negligence is required for a manslaughter conviction. The degree of criminal negligence is much higher than the civil law standard. In other words, the negligence involved needs to be of a very high degree of risk of serious personal injuries. Davitt J. stated:

"... simple negligence is not enough [and] for the purposes of the criminal law, there are different degrees of negligence and that a very high degree of negligence must be proved before the felony of manslaughter is established ...". [1948] I.R. 95 at 101

Davitt J. continued:

"If the negligence proved is of a very high degree and of such a character that any reasonable driver, endowed with ordinary road sense and in full possession of his faculties, would realise, if he thought at all, that by driving in the manner which occasioned the fatality he was, without lawful excuse, incurring, in a high degree, the risk of causing substantial personal injury to others, the crime of manslaughter appears clearly to be established." [1948] I.R. 95 at 102

In quashing the manslaughter conviction, the Court of Criminal Appeal held that a conviction for manslaughter by gross criminal negligence will not be justified unless the prosecution establishes that the negligence was of a very high degree and involved a high degree of risk or likelihood of substantial personal injury to others. However, convictions for this type of manslaughter are extremely rare.

The standard of criminal negligence laid down in *Dunleavy* is a very high standard and the test applied is objective. In *People (DPP) v Cullagh,* unreported, Court of Criminal Appeal, March 15, 1999, the defendant owned and operated a fairground, and the victim was killed when a chairoplane became detached. Murphy J. described the standard of criminal negligence as:

> "... gross negligence—it had to be gross negligence and not the ordinary standard of civil negligence: i.e. mere inadvertence which would attract liability in a civil action was insufficient".

The court held that negligence for a manslaughter conviction is a matter of degree. Although the defendant only became aware after the incident that there was rust on the inside of the chairoplane that had caused the accident, he was nonetheless aware of it's general decrepit state when he bought it and then permitted members of the public ride on it. However, convictions for manslaughter involving workplace fatalities are also very rare.

3. Manslaughter as a result of an assault

If the defendant killed the victim by an assault that was intended to cause more than a trivial injury, but did not intend to cause serious injury, then the proper verdict would be manslaughter and not murder. The prosecution does not have to prove that the defendant foresaw the victim's death. What is required is that the defendant must have intended to cause injury to the victim, such as an assault. It is essential for the prosecution to prove that the defendant intended to perform the unlawful act that caused the victim's death.

The defendant can be convicted of manslaughter as a result of an assault where he did not intend to cause serious injury to the victim, but did, nevertheless, intend to cause some injury. The principal question is what kind of assault or other injury must have been intended. In *R v Holzer* [1968] V.R. 481, the defendant in the course of an argument with the victim, punched him in the face with the result that the victim fell backwards hitting his head on the roadway, from which he suffered fatal injuries and died. The defendant admitted that he had intended to "cut his lip or bruise his lips or something" but that he did not intend to inflict any serious injury to the victim. Smith J. stated:

"... a person is guilty of manslaughter if he commits the offence of [assault] on the deceased and death results directly from the commission of that offence. and the beating or other application of force was done with the intention of inflicting on the deceased some physical harm not merely of a trivial or negligible character, or, it would seem with the intention of inflicting pain, without more injury or harm to the body then is involved in the infliction of pain which is not merely trivial or negligible". [1968] V.R. 481 at 482.

This direction is widely accepted as being the proper direction to the jury as to the occurrence of assault manslaughter. Some cases have extended this principle of criminal liability to include a psychic assault. In *R v Hayward* (1908) 21 Cox C.C. 692, a man chased his wife into the street shouting threats and kicked her. She collapsed and died from a thyroid condition which made her peculiarly susceptible to physical exertion and fear. The trial judges' direction to the jury was that "no violence need be visited upon the victim" and that as in this case, the death of the victim caused by fright alone would be sufficient for a manslaughter conviction.

4. Wilful refusal to perform a legal duty

A failure to perform a positive duty with the result that the victim dies may result in a manslaughter conviction. The policy underlying a conviction in these circumstances is the failure to perform a legal duty. It is generally accepted that murder or manslaughter may be committed by omission, such as intentionally failing to feed a child or other person in one's care. However, the courts have been very reluctant to extend this principle to other forms of harm against the person, notably assault. The circumstances in which criminal liability will attach for a wilful refusal to perform a legal duty are divided into four broad categories: duty arising from contract; duty arising from a relationship; duty arising from the assumption of care of the helpless and infirm; and duty arising from the creation of a dangerous situation. These are discussed in Ch.2 Actus Reus. In each of these categories it is the failure by the defendant to perform a legal duty that is the cause of death; consequently, the charge is manslaughter rather than murder. Naturally, in any of these cases, if the omission was deliberate with the intention of causing death or serious injury, the defendant will be charged with murder as opposed to manslaughter.

Merging the Offences of Murder and Manslaughter

The problematic issue pertaining to the meaning of intention in the construction of criminal responsibility typically relates to the offence of murder. In many cases the jury in a murder trial may return a guilty verdict for the lesser-included offence of manslaughter, thus providing the trial judge with a wide measure of discretion as to the appropriate sentence to be imposed. A conviction for murder carries a mandatory life sentence. In view of the fact that there are various types of murder, the imposition of the same indeterminate sentence on every defendant convicted for this offence, notwithstanding mitigating factors, undoubtedly causes injustice for many defendants.

The dichotomy between the offences of murder and manslaughter was alluded to in *Hyam v DPP* [1975] A.C. 55. Lord Kilbrandon proposed that the offences of murder and manslaughter should be abolished and substituted by a single offence of unlawful homicide. The variation of sentences up to and including life imprisonment for manslaughter would then reflect the culpability of the defendant. A mandatory life sentence is imposed for murder. Further, Lord Kilbrandon pointed out that murder is not per se the most heinous classification of unlawful homicide (at 98). Likewise, in *People (DPP) v Conroy (No. 2)* [1989] I.R. 160 at 163, Finlay C.J. for the Irish Supreme Court, stated that the offence of manslaughter could in many cases, from a sentencing point of view, be more serious than an instance of murder.

The uncertainty of the judicial guidelines pertaining to what constitutes intention in criminal law may lead to inconsistencies of outcome. It may very well be the case that the defendant should have been convicted of manslaughter (recklessness) rather than murder (intent). A conviction for manslaughter would be more appropriate in many cases. The offences of manslaughter and murder should be merged into a single offence of unlawful homicide with intention and recklessness constituting the mens rea requirement for different degrees of culpability. This could serve to resolve the problematic issue in marginal cases.

The Law Reform Commission's *Report on Homicide: Murder and Involuntary Manslaughter* (LRC 87–2008) recommends that the murder/manslaughter distinction should be retained (para.1.24), but that the mandatory life sentence for murder should be abolished and replaced with a discretionary maximum sentence of life imprisonment (para.1.66).

Infanticide

The common law regarded the unlawful killing of a child by the child's mother as murder, notwithstanding the fact that she was suffering from a mental disability. No concession was made for post-natal depression and other pre-

and post-natal effects of childbirth. If the prosecution could not establish the mens rea for murder, the jury could return a manslaughter verdict. The only concession afforded by common law was the punishment imposed; the mandatory death sentence for murder was commuted to life imprisonment.

The Royal College of Psychiatrists in England has propounded the following guidelines that may justify an infanticide verdict, based on the physical, emotional and psychological effects of pregnancy and childbirth:

- Overwhelming stress from the social environment being highlighted by the birth of a child, with the emphasis on the unsuitability of the accommodation and related issues.
- Overwhelming stress from an additional member to a household struggling with poverty.
- Psychological injury, and pressures and stress from a husband or other member of a family from the mother's incapacity to arrange the demands of the extra member of the family.
- Failure of bonding between mother and child through illness or disability, which impairs the development of the mother's capacity to care for the infant.

If, at the time of committing the offence, the mother was suffering from the effects of pregnancy, childbirth or lactation then criminal law should take into consideration the state of mind of the mother.

The position in England was ameliorated somewhat by the Infanticide Act 1922 which was repealed by the Infanticide Act 1938. The apparent reason for the introduction of this legislation was the difficulty in securing convictions in the face of public opinion that opposed the murder conviction of mothers in these circumstances. There was, however, an anomaly in the legislation in that it referred to the unlawful death of "newly-born" children. The question was, how old did a child have to be to be outside the category of a "newly-born" child. For instance, in *R v O'Donoghue* (1927) 28 Cox C.C. 461, the Court of Criminal Appeal held that a child unlawfully killed by its mother 32 days after giving birth to the child was outside the category of a newly-born child; therefore, the child's mother was convicted of murder. Decisions like this led to the enactment of the Infanticide Act 1938 to ameliorate the harshness of the "newly-born" criteria. The Irish Infanticide Act 1949 (the "1949 Act") is effectively a carbon copy of the English 1938 Act. Section 1(1) of the 1949 Act provides that:

> On the preliminary investigation by the District Court of a charge against a woman for the murder of her child, being a child under the age of twelve months, the Justice may, if he thinks proper, alter the

charge to one of infanticide and send her forward for trial on that charge.

Section 1(2) provides that:

> Where, upon the trial of a woman for the murder of her child, being a child under the age of twelve months, the jury are satisfied that she is guilty of infanticide, they shall return a verdict of infanticide.

The mother's conduct would otherwise be murder.

The 1949 Act provided that an infanticide verdict could be returned if the balance of the mother's mind was disturbed by reason of "the effect of lactation consequent upon the birth of the child". This outdated formulation has now been amended by s.22 of the Criminal Law (Insanity) Act 2006 (the "2006 Act") which amends s.1(3) of the 1949 Act in the following terms:

> At the time of the act or omission the balance of her mind was disturbed by reason of her not having fully recovered from the effect of giving birth to the child or by reason of a mental disorder (within the meaning of the Criminal Law (Insanity) Act 2006) consequent upon the birth of the child.

In such cases, the mother will be dealt with under s.6(3) of the 2006 Act, as if she is found guilty of manslaughter on grounds of diminished responsibility. Prior to the provisions of the 2006 Act, the court dealt with this issue on the basis of a manslaughter conviction (under the provisions of the 1949 Act) and the sentence was at the discretion of the court. Naturally, if someone other than the child's mother kills the child, or where the child's mother had the intention to kill the child, then the appropriate charge and conviction would be murder.

ASSISTED SUICIDE

The common law regarded suicide as a felony on the basis that it constituted self-murder (*felonia de se*). The law also imposed criminal liability in the form of transferred malice where the individual who attempted to kill himself, but instead killed another; in these circumstances, he was guilty of murder because the intention to kill was present. In effect, this resulted in an accidental killing occasioned in the course of attempted suicide to be classified as murder. Perhaps a more appropriate charge would be manslaughter, given that the person who accidentally kills another while attempting to commit suicide would not have the moral culpability normally associated with murder.

The Criminal Law (Suicide) Act 1993 Act is almost a carbon copy of the English Suicide Act 1961. Section 2(1) of the 1993 Act provides that, "suicide shall cease to be a crime". With the abolition of suicide as a criminal offence, it follows that the doctrine of transferred malice no longer applies. The policy behind the decriminalisation of the offence of suicide was to remove the social stigma attached to this "offence." Instead, where the individual unsuccessfully attempted to commit suicide, it came to be accepted that treatment rather than punishment was the preferred option. Indeed, "attempted suicide" has also been repealed because one cannot be convicted of an attempt where the act is not an offence.

AIDING AND ABETTING SUICIDE

Section 2(2) of the 1993 Act provides that:

> A person who aids, abets, counsels or procures the suicide of another, or an attempt by another to commit suicide, shall be guilty of an offence and shall be liable on conviction on indictment to imprisonment for a term not exceeding fourteen years.

The reason for the severity of punishment imposed for the commission of this offence is to criminalise situations where the defendant has "engineered" the suicide of another for his own personal gain to act as a deterrent against those who would take advantage of another's suicide.

In *AG v Able* [1984] Q.B. 795, the defendant was a member of a society that advocated both euthanasia and suicide. The society published a booklet which provided advice to people who were intent on committing suicide, as to painless and swift methods for achieving their objective. For the purposes of aiding and abetting, the Court of Criminal Appeal held that this did not in law amount to an offence under English legislation. The prosecution must establish that: the defendant intended the booklet to be used by, and be of assistance to, someone contemplating suicide; with this intention, he circulated the booklet; and the individual(s) who received the booklet actually gained assistance from the contents of the booklet in attempting to commit suicide. Woolf J. refused to grant a declaration that the circulation of the booklet was unlawful. In *Dunbar v Plant* [1997] 3 W.L.R. 1261, a woman and her fiancé decided to commit suicide by hanging. The woman failed and was charged with aiding and abetting the suicide of her fiancé. The Court of Appeal held that since the defendant and her fiancé had agreed to commit suicide and the defendant had participated in each of the three attempts at suicide, there could be no doubt of her criminal complicity and liability in his suicide.

The issue of assisted suicide arose for consideration by the English House of Lords in *R (Pretty) v DPP* [2002] 1 A.C. 800. The applicant suffered from motor neurone disease, with the result that she was paralysed from the neck down, unable to speak and was fed through a tube. She petitioned the English superior courts to provide immunity for her husband if he would help her to commit suicide. The House of Lords held that assisted suicide is a criminal offence, and accordingly, the courts of law did not have the power/authority to suspend or abandon laws without parliamentary consent. She claimed that this subjected her to inhuman and degrading treatment which was in breach of her human rights. The ECtHR held that since assisted suicide is a criminal offence under English law, the refusal by the English courts to grant her husband immunity from prosecution did not breach her human rights. Therefore, her husband would not be immune from prosecution if he would help his wife to commit suicide (cf. *R (Purdy) v DPP* [2010] 1 A.C. 345).

Section 2(3) of the 1993 Act provides that:

> If, on the trial of an indictment for murder, murder to which section 3 of the Criminal Justice Act, 1990 applies or manslaughter, it is proved that the person charged aided, abetted, counselled or procured the suicide of the person alleged to have been killed, he may be found guilty of an offence under this section.

The effect of this provision is that it provides for an alternative sentence in circumstances where it is unclear whether the defendant committed murder or manslaughter, or was a secondary participant in the suicide of the deceased.

Consent of the DPP

Section 2(4) of the 1993 Act provides that:

> No proceedings shall be instituted for an offence under this section except by or with the consent of the Director of Public Prosecutions.

The consent of the DPP is required before a prosecution may proceed. This is to ensure that s.2(2) is applied consistently.

Survivor of a Suicide Pact

The survivor of a suicide pact will be guilty of murder of the other member(s) of the suicide pact who actually die. This may be contrasted with the position in England where the defendant will be guilty of manslaughter (Homicide Act 1957, s.4(1)).

Euthanasia

More commonly referred to as "mercy killing", this involves the bringing about of a gentle and easy death in the case of an individual suffering from an incurable and painful disease. Section 2(1) of the Criminal Law (Suicide) Act 1993 decriminalised suicide. Accordingly, one cannot be convicted of aiding, abetting counselling or procuring the offence of suicide in accordance with the provisions of s.7 of the Criminal Law Act 1997. In order to circumvent this lacuna in criminal law, s.2(2) of the 1993 Act provides that:

> A person who aids, abets, counsels or procures the suicide of another, or an attempt by another to commit suicide, shall be guilty of an offence and shall be liable on conviction on indictment to imprisonment for a term not exceeding fourteen years.

Thus, where the defendant has been charged with murder, he cannot plead consent on the part of the deceased as a defence. Naturally, a defendant who intentionally kills another will be liable to conviction for murder, as consent by the deceased is not a defence.

Euthanasia generally involves some active participation on the part of the person who assisted the deceased in bringing about an end to his life. Does this apply to situations where medical personnel withdraw life-saving treatment? It is not a criminal offence to withdraw or withhold medical treatment where this will result in the death of the patient. Furthermore, if a patient refuses medical treatment or requests that such treatment be discontinued, and has full capacity to make that decision, then medical personnel must accede to that request and will not be criminally liable for the resultant death of the patient. This issue was addressed by the Irish Supreme Court in *In Re a Ward of Court (Withdrawal of Medical Treatment No. 2)* [1996] 2 I.R. 79, where the court was asked by the parents of the young woman (the Ward of Court) to allow medical personnel to withdraw life-support and allow the woman to die a natural death. The Supreme Court held that the right to life implied the right to die naturally and with dignity, which included the withdrawal of medical treatment that artificially kept the woman alive. However, the Supreme Court stressed that this decision is not to be interpreted as legalising euthanasia (cf. *JM v St. Vincent's Hospital* [2003] 1 I.R. 321; *In Re K (Ward of Court)* [2001] 1 I.R. 338; *North Western Health Board v HW* [2001] 3 I.R. 622). The court followed an earlier, and similar, House of Lords ruling in *Airedale NHS Trust v Bland* [1993] A.C. 789, which described euthanasia as the taking of a positive step towards causing the death of the deceased. However, in both *In Re a Ward of Court* and *Bland*, there was no positive step taken towards the causing of death, rather, what was involved was the withdrawal of treatment which had artificially maintained the life of the deceased. Indeed, in *Re a Ward of Court*, Hamilton C.J., at 120, stated that, "[i]t is important to emphasise that the court can never sanction steps to terminate life". The right to die a natural death does not include the right to have life terminated or death accelerated, but it is confined to the natural process of dying. Hamilton C.J. explained that:

> "As the process of dying is part, and an ultimate, inevitable consequence, of life, the right to life necessarily implies the right to have nature take its course and to die a natural death and, unless the individual concerned so wishes, not to have life artificially maintained by the provision of nourishment by abnormal artificial means, which have no curative effect and which is intended merely to prolong life. This right, as so defined, does not include the right to have life terminated or death accelerated and is confined to the natural process of dying. No person has the right to terminate or to have terminated his or her life, or to accelerate or have accelerated his or her death." [1996] 2 I.R. 79 at 124

Thus, the defendant will be charged with murder, as consent by the deceased will not be a valid defence to a murder charge, even where the deceased had requested, for example, that the doctor administer a fatal dose of morphine. If the defendant has caused the death of the deceased, even with the consent of the deceased, with the intention to kill, then he will be charged with murder.

ABSENCE OF A VICTIM

It appears that a prosecution for homicide might succeed even in the absence of a body. In *People (AG) v Ball* (1936) 70 I.L.T.R. 202, the defendant was charged with the murder of his mother, against which he argued that she had committed suicide and that he had merely placed her body in the sea so as to prevent any embarrassment. However, the police had found a bloodstained hatchet together with large amounts of blood in the house, which contradicted the defendant's account of the events. This circumstantial evidence was sufficient to secure a conviction, even in the absence of a body. It was emphasised by the Court of Criminal Appeal in *People (AG) v Cadden* (1957) 91 I.L.T.R. 97, that in these circumstances where a murder conviction is based on circumstantial evidence, that the trial judge must have directed the jury that they must be satisfied, beyond reasonable doubt,

> "that the circumstances of the incident were not only consistent with the defendant having committed the act, but also that they were inconsistent with any conclusion other than his guilt."

Unworthiness to Succeed

A person convicted of murder, attempted murder or manslaughter is debarred on grounds of public policy from benefiting under the victim's will, as provided for by s.120 of the Succession Act 1965 (*In the Goods of Martin Glynn* [1992] I.L.R.M. 582). A convicted murderer whose crime accelerated succession will not be permitted to be an executor.

Proposed Law Reform

The Law Reform Commission's *Report on Homicide: Murder and Involuntary Manslaughter* (LRC 87–2008) made the following recommendations for reform. The label "murder" pertains to the most heinous killings and it should continue to be murder where the defendant intended to kill or cause serious injury to the deceased. The mental element (mens rea) in murder should be broadened to include reckless killings manifesting an extreme indifference to human life, such that, for instance, a defendant who planted a bomb in a busy office block could be convicted of murder if someone dies in the blast, even if his main purpose was to cause criminal damage, rather than to kill or seriously injure anyone in the office at the time the bomb exploded. The mandatory life sentence for murder should be replaced in order to take account of variations in moral culpability in different types of murder.

With regard to unlawful and dangerous act manslaughter, the Law Reform Commission recommends that the existing key elements of the offence should be retained, that is to say, that the act that caused death constitutes a criminal offence and created a risk of bodily harm to another, and the act was such that an ordinary reasonable person would consider to be dangerous and highly likely to cause bodily harm. However, low levels of deliberate violence should be removed from the scope of unlawful and dangerous act manslaughter and be prosecuted with the creation of a new offence of "assault causing death".

The main elements of gross negligence manslaughter test should be retained, that is, the negligence that caused the death of the victim was of a very high degree, together with a high degree of risk or likelihood of substantial personal injury being caused to others. However, a defendant should only be held criminally liable if he was mentally and physically capable of averting to, and avoiding the risk of death at the time that the offence was committed.

The Commission also recommends that dangerous driving causing death should continue to exist alongside the more serious offence of manslaughter. Drivers should be prosecuted for manslaughter for road deaths only where there is very high culpability, such as joy-riding, high alcohol levels, and speeding. The Commission also recommends that a new offence of "careless driving causing death" should be introduced to cover fatalities caused by careless driving.

FURTHER READING

Beaumont, "The Unborn Child and the Limits of Homicide" (1997) 60 J.C.L. 86.

Brennan, "Beyond the Medical Model: A Rationale for Infanticide Legislation" (2007) 58 N.I.L.Q. 505.

Campbell, Kilcommins and O'Sullivan, *Criminal Law in Ireland: Cases and Commentary* (Dublin: Clarus Press, 2010), Ch.17.

Carolan, "US Supreme Court Rules: No Constitutional Right to Physician Assisted Suicide" (1997) 3 M.L.J.I. 43.

Carey, "The Year and a Day Rule in Homicide" (2001) 11(1) I.C.L.J. 5.

Mr Justice Paul Carney, "Decriminalising Murder?" (2003) 8(6) B.R. 254.

Charleton, "Causation in the Law of Homicide" (1991) 1(1) I.C.L.J. 68.

Costello, "The Terminally Ill: The Law's Concerns" (1986) 21 Ir. Jur. (N.S.) 35.

Cox, "Causation, Responsibility and Foetal Personhood" (2000) 51 N.I.L.Q. 579.

Feenan, "Death, Dying and the Law" (1996) 14 I.L.T. 90.

Hanly, *An Introduction to Irish Criminal Law*, 2nd edn (Dublin: Gill & Macmillan, 2006), Ch.18.

Holt, "A Matter of Life and Death: Intimate Partner Homicide in Ireland" (2007) 10 I.J.F.L. 12.

Heaton, "Dealing in Death" (2003) 13(4) I.C.L.J. 18.

Law Reform Commission, *Consultation Paper on Homicide: the Mental Element in Murder* (LRC CP 17–2001).

Law Reform Commission, *Report on Homicide: Murder and Involuntary Manslaughter* (LRC 87–2008).

Law Reform Commission, *Consultation Paper on Involuntary Manslaughter* (LRC CP 44–2007).

McAuley, "Abortion and the Law" (1983) 1 I.L.T. 8.

Mulcahy, "Involuntary Manslaughter: Part I" (2007) 25 I.L.T. 251.

Mulcahy, "Involuntary Manslaughter: Part II" (2007) 25 I.L.T. 265.

O'Connor, "Physician-Assisted Suicide: The Way Forward? — Part I" (2004) 22 I.L.T. 182.

O'Connor, "Physician-Assisted Suicide: The Way Forward? — Part II" (2004) 22 I.L.T. 204.

O'Donnell, "Unlawful Killing Past and Present" (2002) 37 Ir. Jur. (N.S.) 56.

Heaton, "Dealing in Death" (2003) 13(4) I.C.L.J. 18.

17. Non-Fatal Offences Against the Person

INTRODUCTION

The Non-Fatal Offences Against the Person Act 1997 (the "1997 Act") was enacted to repeal most provisions of the Offences Against the Person Act 1861 (the "1861 Act") and to modernise the law governing non-fatal offences against the person, such as false imprisonment and endangerment, and created new offences, including harassment. The 1997 Act implements many of the reforms recommended by the Law Reform Commission's *Report on Non-Fatal Offences against the Person* (LRC 45–1994). The 1997 Act was considered by some commentators as a political response to public concerns regarding the increasing number of robberies committed by offenders using syringes as weapons. However, the 1997 Act replaced offences that lie at the core of criminal law with offences that are more responsive to the demands of contemporary society and the scope of the legislative provisions extends beyond the criminalisation of syringe attacks. Thus, the 1997 Act constitutes an extensive reform of the law governing non-fatal offences against the person.

OMISSION OF A SAVING CLAUSE

Section 28(1) abolished the common law offences of assault and battery, assault occasioning actual bodily harm, kidnapping, and false imprisonment. However, the legislation omitted to include a "saving clause" to deal with transitional provisions as there were many cases pending before the courts based on the pre-existing common law offences. The judicial response endeavoured to grapple with this dilemma. In *People (DPP) v Kavanagh*, Special Criminal Court, October 29, 1997, a charge of false imprisonment that had commenced prior to 1997 could not proceed due to the omission of a transitional provision. Conversely, in *Quinlivan v Governor of Portlaoise Prison* [1998] 2 I.R. 113, the High Court held that the abolition of common law offences did not apply in respect of charges of false imprisonment pending at the time of the abolition. Likewise, in *Mullins v Harnett* [1998] 4 I.R. 426, the High Court held that the abolition of common law offences effected by s.28(1) did not apply in respect of charges of common assault pending before the courts at the time of the abolition. Ultimately, the Interpretation (Amendment) Act 1997 was enacted to remedy the procedural dilemma created by s.28(1), by providing that the abolition, abrogation or repeal of an offence that was an offence at common law shall not affect any pending proceedings (cf. *Cummins v McCartan* [2005] 3 I.R. 559; *Grealish v DPP* [2001] 3 I.R. 144).

ASSAULT

Section 2 replaced the common law offences of assault and battery, generally referred to as "common assault", with the new offence of assault. This combines, in one offence, the element of inflicting personal violence, as formerly in the common law offence of "battery", together with the element of causing another to apprehend the immediate infliction of personal violence, as formerly in the common law offence of "assault".

This provision creates a new offence of assault, thus replacing the pre-existing offences of assault and battery under the 1861 Act. At common law, the term assault meant causing a person to apprehend the infliction of immediate force to their person, whereas the term "battery" meant the application of such force. The term "battery" gradually fell into disuse, and "assault" at common law was understood to mean both assault and battery. The offence of common assault could be committed either by threats of immediate force, or through the physical infliction of force.

Assault under s.2 is committed where the defendant "without lawful excuse" intentionally or recklessly, directly or indirectly, applies force to, or causes an impact on the body of a person, or causes that person to believe on reasonable grounds that he or she is likely immediately to be subjected to any such force, without the consent of the person assaulted. Words may constitute an assault (cf. *Tubberville v Savage* (1669) 1 Mod. Rep. 3). The mens rea is intention or recklessness, which follows the common law definition of assault established by the Court of Appeal in *R v Venna* [1976] Q.B. 421, applied in *R v Spratt* [1990] 1 W.L.R. 1073, and confirmed by the Irish Court of Criminal Appeal in *People (DPP) v McBride* [1996] 1 I.R. 312.

This summary offence will cover most types of minor assaults. The punishment on conviction is a maximum of six months' imprisonment and/or a €1,900 fine.

WITHOUT LAWFUL EXCUSE

The words "without lawful excuse", although taken from the common law definition of assault, must be read in light of s.18 of the 1997 Act, which provides that the use of reasonable force by a person could be justifiable, depending on the circumstances, such as where the person is seeking to protect himself or a member of his family from injury, or to protect his property.

The test for determining whether the force used in the circumstances was "reasonable" is subjective in that it must be judged according to the circumstances as the defendant believed them to be.

CONSENT

Section 2(1) provides that the assault must be committed "without the consent" of the person assaulted, and consequently, the absence of consent is an essential element of the offence. The meaning of consent at common law has been problematic, especially in relation to whether the absence of consent is an essential element of the actus reus of assault, or alternatively whether consent is a defence to the charge. In *R v Brown* [1994] 1 A.C. 212, the House of Lords held that consent does not constitute a defence to a charge of assault causing actual bodily harm. In that case, a group of men that had participated in consensual sado-masochistic sexual activities were convicted of assault under ss.47 and 20 of the 1861 Act. The House of Lords held that consent was not available as a defence to such activities, albeit in private, because they served no valid social purpose, nor was there good reason to exempt such activity from the normal rule of criminal law in respect of consent.

There are exceptions to this general rule where the application of force is justifiable by the purpose of the act involving the risk. For instance, a patient can lawfully consent to a surgical procedure that would otherwise constitute an assault causing serious harm. However, it seems that if the application of force has a valid social purpose, then the degree of harm that may be caused by the application of force will be balanced against the social value of that purpose. For instance, professional and amateur boxers and competitors in other contact sports are deemed to have consented to the application of force in the course of participating in their respective sporting activities, despite the high risk of serious injury that could be inflicted. People may also consent to the application of force through activities such as body-piercing and tattooing. These activities are deemed to have a valid social purpose that justifies the risks of injury involved. Although the risk of bodily injury is apparent, the dilemma for the courts is to determine the validity of the social purpose involved, as the House of Lords considered in *Brown*.

The Law Reform Commission *Report on Non-Fatal Offences Against the Person* (LRC 45–1994, p.333), completed before the House of Lords' decision in *Brown*, made recommendations with regard to the issue of consent. The Commission recommended that although consent should be a defence to assault, it should also be available as a defence, even where serious bodily harm is caused in cases where the harm is inflicted either with the purpose of benefiting another person, or "in pursuance of a socially beneficial function or activity", and where its infliction is reasonable with regard to the intended beneficial purpose, function or activity. Although the Commission recommended that a statutory definition of consent should be adopted, the 1997 Act did not provide any statutory definition of consent in s.2.

Section 2(1) provides that the absence of consent is an element of the actus reus of assault, and s.22 preserves the common law defences, including the rules on consent in relation to sporting activities or medical treatment. While the absence of consent is an essential element of the actus reus, the presence of consent can be a defence to a charge of assault. Since absence of consent is an element of the offence under s.3 (assault causing harm) the consent threshold is one of "serious harm." Section 2(2) provides that the meaning of "force" includes the, "application of heat, light, electric current, noise or any other form of energy," and "application of matter in solid liquid or gaseous form". This clarifies the definition of "force" by providing that it includes the application of various forms of energy. Section 2(3) provides a general defence where the force is "generally acceptable in the ordinary conduct of daily life", such as queuing for a bus and contact sports. Trivial everyday contact such as jostling in a crowd will not constitute an assault. Section 4(4) provides that the maximum penalty on summary conviction is a €1,900 fine and/or six months' imprisonment.

ASSAULT CAUSING HARM

Section 3(1) provides that "a person who assaults another causing him or her harm shall be guilty of an offence". Section 1 defines harm to mean "harm to the body or mind and includes pain and unconsciousness". In *R v Donovan* [1934] 2 K.B. 498, the Court of Criminal Appeal per Swift J. held:

> "... 'bodily harm' has its ordinary meaning and includes any hurt or injury calculated to interfere with the health or comfort of the prosecutor. Such hurt or injury need not be permanent, but must, no doubt, be more than merely transient and trifling". [1934] 2 K.B. 498 at 509

Section 3(2)(a) provides that the maximum punishment on summary conviction is 12 months' imprisonment and/or a €1,900 fine. Section 3(2)(b) provides that where the defendant is convicted on indictment, the maximum punishment is an unlimited fine and/or five years' imprisonment.

This provision creates a new offence of assault causing harm, which replaces the offence of assault causing actual bodily harm in s.47 of the 1861 Act. Consent is a defence to simple assault (s.2) and will also be available as a defence where actual bodily harm is caused, but this excludes serious harm provided for by s.4. Section 3 is framed in reference to s.2, and therefore the principles as to lawful excuse and consent would also apply to a charge of assault causing harm.

The defendant must have committed an assault (as defined in s.2) that caused harm to the victim. This offence would conceivably include psychological trauma as, for instance, in *R v Ireland*; *R v Burstow* [1998] A.C. 147, where the House of Lords held that with regards to contemporary knowledge covering recognisable psychiatric injuries, and taking into consideration the current scientific appreciation of the link between the body and psychiatric injury, recognisable psychiatric illnesses fell within the phrase "bodily harm" in ss.20 and 47 of the 1861 Act. Also, "inflict" included the infliction of psychiatric injury on another and did not mean that whatever caused the harm had to be applied directly to the victim.

Causing Serious Harm

Section 4(1) provides that "a person who intentionally or recklessly causes serious harm to another shall be guilty of an offence". Section 1 defines serious harm as "injury which creates a substantial risk of death or which causes serious disfigurement or substantial loss or impairment of the mobility of the body as a whole or of the function of any particular bodily member or organ".

The actus reus of this offence is causing serious harm. A conviction does not require an assault, because the harm need only be "caused" by the defendant, either intentionally or recklessly. Thus, acts that would not amount to an assault might come within s.4 where serious harm is caused, and this offence can be committed through a wider range of conduct compared to the less serious offence in s.3. Examples of the circumstances where this offence might be committed include causing panic in a theatre by turning out the lights and placing an iron bar across the door, so that those present were caused to crush each other (*R v Martin* (1881) 8 Q.B.D. 54), or chasing a victim so that he put his hand through a glass door (*Cartledge v Allen* [1973] Crim. L.R. 530). This offence would also include serious bodily harm caused by the transmission of an STD where the offender withheld this fact from his or her sexual partner (cf. *R v EB* [2006] EWCA Crim. 2945).

The mens rea is subjective recklessness as to dangerous conduct and the likelihood as to whether serious harm would be caused by the defendant's conduct.

Although consent is not a defence to a charge of causing serious harm, s.22 provides that existing common law defences continue to apply. Therefore, the common law rules under which bodily harm arises in the course of sports, dangerous exhibitions or medical procedures, continue to apply (so as to exempt the defendant's conduct from criminal liability in the appropriate circumstances).

Section 4(2) provides that the maximum punishment on conviction on indictment is life imprisonment and/or an unlimited fine.

THREATS TO KILL OR CAUSE SERIOUS HARM

Section 5(1) is a broadly defined offence that covers threats by any means and extends to threats to cause serious injury as well as to threats to kill:

> A person who, without lawful excuse, makes to another a threat, by any means intending the other to believe it will be carried out, to kill or cause serious harm to that other or a third person shall be guilty of an offence.

The offence must be committed with the intention that the victim should believe that the threat will be carried out. Some threats would in themselves constitute an assault, where they induce in the victim a fear of suffering the immediate application of force.

The actus reus of this offence is a threat to kill or cause serious harm, and the mens rea is the intention to make that threat in addition to an intention that the intended victim would believe that the threat would be carried out.

Section 5(2) provides that the punishment for this offence on summary conviction is a maximum €1,900 fine and/or 12 months' imprisonment. Conviction on indictment carries an unlimited fine and/or 10 years' imprisonment.

SYRINGE ATTACKS

Section 6(1) creates the offence of injuring another by piercing the skin of the victim with a syringe or threatening to do so with the intention of causing the other person to believe that he or she may become infected with disease. This offence also prohibits spraying, pouring or putting onto another, blood, or any fluid or substance resembling blood, or threatening to do so with the intention of causing the other person to believe that he or she may become infected with disease. This offence provides for the core offence of syringe attacks, which involves intentionally injuring another by piercing the skin with a syringe that contains, or has on it, contaminated blood or a contaminated fluid. The offence created by s.6(1) can be committed with a mens rea of objective recklessness, that is, where there is a probability that the victim would be caused to believe that he or she might become infected. The maximum penalty on summary conviction is 12 months' imprisonment and/or a €1,900 fine. Conviction on indictment carries a maximum 10 years' imprisonment and/or an unlimited fine.

Section 6(2) provides that it is an offence to intentionally spray, pour or put onto another contaminated blood. Section 6(2) also stipulates that objective recklessness is the mens rea for this offence. On summary conviction the maximum penalty is 12 months' imprisonment and/or a €1,900 fine.

Section 6(3) provides that in the course of an attempt to commit an offence under ss.6(1) or (2) the doctrine of transferred intent applies where the actual victim is a third party.

Section 6(4) prescribes a maximum penalty of 10 years' imprisonment for offences under ss.6(1), 6(2) and 6(3).

In relation to offences under ss.6(1) and (2), there is no requirement to prove the fact of infection, or risk of infection, nor is it necessary to prove that the syringe or blood used was in fact contaminated.

Section 6(5) creates separate offences, triable only on indictment, relating to the use of contaminated syringes or blood. These aggravated forms of syringe offences can only be committed intentionally and are punishable by a maximum sentence of life imprisonment. Where a person recklessly injures another with a contaminated syringe, or recklessly sprays the other with contaminated blood, they would only be liable under ss.6(1) or (2), as they would lack the requisite mens rea to be convicted under s.6(5). Even if the offender had foreseen the consequences of his action he would only be subject to the same penalty as a person who committed an offence under ss.6(1), (2) or (3) with a non-contaminated syringe, or non-contaminated blood, and without foreseeing the consequences of their action.

These offences can result in great suffering for victims who have been wounded with a syringe and subsequently face a long and agonising wait pending the outcome of medical tests to determine if he or she has contracted a life-threatening disease.

POSSESSION AND ABANDONMENT OF SYRINGES

Section 7 provides that a person who has, in any place, a syringe or any blood in a container intended to cause or threaten injury to or intimidate another, is guilty of this offence. This provision will not make innocent people in possession of a syringe guilty of a criminal offence. People who carry syringes for legitimate purposes, such as diabetics, will not commit an offence by mere possession. The possession must be with the intention of causing or threatening injury or intimidating another. To ensure that the courts will be able to apply a common sense approach to whether this offence has been committed, the court or the jury may regard possession of syringes or containers as sufficient evidence of intent, in the absence of any adequate explanation by the defendant, if it is reasonable to do so in all the circumstances of the case at issue.

The Gardaí have the necessary powers to enforce this provision in that they have powers of stopping, questioning and searching any person suspected of this offence and also have the power to seize any syringe or container with blood in it. The Gardaí may arrest without warrant a suspect who does not co-operate with them and it will be made an offence for a person to fail to so co-operate.

Section 7(1) covers possession of a syringe or of blood in a container in "any place". This section will not make innocent possession of a syringe a criminal offence, but rather will only criminalise possession when there is intention of causing or threatening injury or intimidating another. This offence cannot be committed recklessly. Section 7(5) provides that the court or the jury shall, where reasonable, regard the possession of a syringe or container as sufficient evidence of intent in the absence of any adequate explanation by the defendant.

Section 7(2) gives power to the Gardaí to stop, question and search a person whom they have reasonable cause to suspect may be in unlawful possession of a syringe or container in a public place. This provision also obliges the person to give a "reasonable excuse" for having the syringe or container. Section 7(3) authorises the Gardaí to arrest without warrant where a person fails to stop, give their name and address where required, or obstructs the Gardaí in performing their duties and powers under s.7(2). The effect of these provisions might be to criminalise addiction which might constitute an encroachment on civil liberties.

Sections 7(2) and (5) effectively reverse the burden of proof by obliging the suspect to justify their possession of syringes to the Gardaí. In *O'Leary v AG* [1993] 1 I.R. 102 at 110, the High Court per Costello J. affirmed that while Art.38.1 of the Constitution mandates that all criminal trials are conducted in accordance with the presumption of innocence, a "reverse-onus" presumption was not necessarily unconstitutional as "the Oireachtas is permitted in certain circumstances to restrict the exercise of the right [presumption of innocence] because it is not to be regarded as an absolute right whose enjoyment can never be abridged" (cf. *Hardy v Ireland* [1994] 2 I.R. 550).

PLACING OR ABANDONING SYRINGES

Section 8(1) deals with the serious problem caused by people who intentionally, recklessly or otherwise, leave or abandon syringes in places so that they injure or are likely to injure, cause a threat to or frighten others. This type of behaviour can be engaged in to wound an unsuspecting Garda or prison officer or to wound an unsuspecting member of the public who, for instance, sits on a seat in a café or cinema or on a bus or train where a syringe has been left on the seat.

Section 8(2) creates a separate offence of intentionally placing a contaminated syringe in such a manner that it injures another. The maximum penalty for a section (1) offence is seven years' imprisonment, and the section (2) offence is punishable by a maximum sentence of life imprisonment. The offence created by s.8(1) appears to be a strict liability offence because there is no mens rea requirement stipulated for in this provision, unless the superior courts interpret the phrase "in such a manner that it is likely to" as requiring mens rea.

COERCION

This offence pertains to the intimidation of a victim in order to compel the individual to do some act against his or her will by the use of psychological pressure, physical force, or threats. Section 9 provides that:

> A person who, with a view to compel another to abstain from doing or to do any act which that other has a lawful right to do or to abstain from doing, wrongfully and without lawful authority.

Section 9 updates the law on coercion by replacing s.7 of the Conspiracy and Protection of Property Act 1875 and increasing the penalty on conviction on indictment to a maximum of five years. The previous section offence of "watching and besetting" was particularly contentious in a labour relations dispute context, where it was frequently used by employers to prevent lawful pickets by striking employees. The issue was that the words "wrongfully and without lawful authority" were interpreted to restrict this application of the offence, since peaceful picketing confined to persuasion or the communication of information was not held to be unlawful at common law (*R v Hibbert* (1875) 13 Cox 82; *Ward, Lock & Co v Operative Printers' Assistants' Society* (1906) 22 T.L.R. 327). The circumstances in which picketing is considered lawful is now governed by s.11 of the Industrial Relations Act 1990, which provides that peaceful picketing is lawful.

Section 9(2) of the 1997 Act provides that attendance at or near premises, merely to obtain or communicate information, will not constitute watching or besetting. Accordingly, the right to engage in peaceful picketing is protected.

The maximum sentence for this offence is 12 months' imprisonment and/or a €1,900 fine. Conviction on indictment carries a maximum term of five years' imprisonment and/or an unlimited fine.

HARASSMENT

Section 10 creates the new offence of harassment which criminalises what is generally referred to as "stalking". This offence is committed when the defendant by any means, harasses another by persistently following, watching, pestering, besetting or communicating with that person and can have a profoundly detrimental effect on the life of the victim. The basic element of the offence is that the offender intentionally or recklessly interferes with the peace and privacy of another person or causes them alarm, distress or harm. His or her conduct is such that a reasonable person would realise that it would have such an effect. A typical example of the circumstances for which this offence was created to deal with is where a person becomes obsessed with another. That person is then subjected to sustained harassment and intimidation by the stalker in a perverted attempt to gain the attention or affection of the person.

Section 10(1) provides that such conduct must be "without lawful authority or reasonable excuse." Therefore, surveillance by the Gardaí under the provisions of the Criminal Justice (Surveillance) Act 2009 would not infringe this provision.

The mens rea of this offence is dubious. Under s.10(2)(a) it is not clear whether the prohibited conduct must be committed intentionally or recklessly, or whether the prosecution must prove that the defendant acted intentionally or recklessly as to the consequence of his conduct. That is to say, that the person interfered with the victim's peace and privacy and caused alarm, distress or harm to the victim. However, in consideration of the subjective nature of Irish criminal law, the mens rea for this offence is to be evaluated subjectively (cf. *People (DPP) v Murray* [1977] I.R. 360). The practical implications of the mens rea for this offence are vital as the defendant will typically have engaged in stalking out of a perverted sense of love and affection for the victim and might have been unaware of the effect which their conduct was having on the victim.

Section 10(2)(b) clarifies the mens rea requirement by introducing an additional objective test, which stipulates that the defendant's conduct must be such that a reasonable person would realise their consequences upon the victim. Sections 10(3) and 10(5) provide that the court can make a "non-contact order" prohibiting contact by the defendant (stalker) with the victim and not to communicate in any way with the victim for such period as may be specified by the court or to approach within a specified distance of the victim's residence or place of employment. This is in addition to or as an alternative to any other sanction, and can be imposed on an offender even where the evidence is not sufficient to secure a conviction (cf. *People (DPP) v Ramachchandran* [2000] 2 I.R. 307).

The maximum penalty on summary conviction is 12 months' imprisonment and/or a €1,900 fine. Conviction on indictment carries a maximum of five years' imprisonment and/or an unlimited fine.

Demands for Payment of Debt

Section 11 creates a particular type of harassment offence associated with persistent demands by a creditor for payment of a debt. It is an offence for a person to subject a debtor to demands which, by reason of their frequency, cause the person or his or her family alarm, distress or humiliation, or amounts to misrepresentation or fraud. Other behaviour that would constitute an offence includes falsely representing that criminal proceedings would follow for non-payment of the debt or that the creditor has the official capacity to enforce payment.

This is a summary offence with a maximum fine of €1,900.

Poisoning

Section 12 replaces the offence of administering poison with intent to injure, aggrieve or annoy, contained in the 1861 Act, with a new offence of poisoning. At common law the administration of poison was deemed an assault for the reason that someone can be poisoned without the application of force, and the resulting harm is caused by a biochemical reaction. A separate offence of criminalising poisoning was necessitated, although where serious harm is caused through poisoning, this might also be prosecuted under s.4 (causing serious harm). Section 12(1) provides that a person will be guilty of this offence if:

> ... knowing that the other does not consent to what is being done, he or she intentionally or recklessly administers to or causes to be taken by another a substance which he or she knows to be capable of interfering substantially with the other's bodily functions.

Section 2(2) provides that, "a substance capable of inducing unconsciousness or sleep is capable of interfering substantially with bodily functions".

It is not necessary to prove any injury to secure a conviction for this offence. In the absence of consent to the administration of the substance, provided that it was administered by a person with the knowledge that it is capable of interfering substantially with the other's bodily functions, the offence is complete whether or not the substance does in fact interfere with the other's bodily functions. If the poisoning results in serious harm or death, more serious charges would be proffered against the defendant.

The maximum penalty on summary conviction is 12 months' imprisonment and/or a €1,900 fine. Conviction on indictment carries a maximum of three years' imprisonment and/or an unlimited fine.

Endangerment

Section 13 creates a general endangerment offence where a person intentionally or recklessly engages in conduct that creates a substantial risk of death or serious harm. The essence of the offence is the creation of a dangerous situation that might result in death or serious injury but the actual causing of death or injury is not necessary. Other more serious charges would be proffered against the defendant where death or serious harm results. In *People (DPP) v McGrath and Cagney* [2008] 2 I.R. 111, the Supreme Court upheld convictions for endangerment where *McGrath* chased the victim threatening to kill him and *Cagney* struck the victim, with the result that he fell and sustained injuries. The court stated that in order to secure a conviction for the offence of endangerment, there had to be an intentional or reckless engagement in conduct which created a substantial risk of death or serious harm to another.

The common law rules on consent under s.2 of the 1997 Act might also be relevant when determining the scope of the offence created by s.13. For instance, participants in contact sports like boxing, fencing, rugby and ice hockey might attract criminal liability under this section.

The maximum penalty on summary conviction is a €1,900 fine and/or 12 months' imprisonment, and on indictment the maximum penalty is an unlimited fine and/or seven years' imprisonment.

Endangering Traffic

Section 14 creates a specific offence of endangering traffic on land and water. It is an offence for any person to intentionally place a dangerous obstruction in a railway, street, road; interfere with any device for the control or direction of traffic; to throw anything at any conveyance being aware that injury to the person or damage to property might be caused, or is reckless in that regard. This can have very serious results, for example, where objects are thrown from motorway bridges at moving traffic with disastrous consequences or where somebody knowingly moves a diversion sign on a road and causes traffic to drive into a dangerous area.

Although in some situations conduct that endangers traffic will also constitute an offence under s.13, the offence created by s.14 is aimed at a wider range of risks, including the risk of injury to the person that is not limited to death or serious harm, or the risk of damage to property.

The maximum penalty on summary conviction is a €1,900 fine and/or 12 months' imprisonment. Conviction on indictment carries an unlimited fine and/or seven years' imprisonment.

False Imprisonment

Section 15 gives statutory expression to the common law offence of false imprisonment. Section 15(1) provides a definition taken from the common law offence, which provides that anyone who takes or detains, or causes to be taken or detained, or otherwise restricts the personal liberty of another person, shall be guilty of the offence.

Absence of consent by the victim is an element of the actus reus. Section 15(2) provides that if the victim's consent has been obtained by force, threat of force or deception, causing the victim to believe that he or she is legally obliged to consent, this will not constitute a valid consent. Section 15(2) extends the offence to cover circumstances where the false imprisonment is brought about by deception causing the victim to believe that he or she is under legal compulsion to consent.

As with the common law offence, the essential element of s.15 remains the unlawful detention of the victim or the unlawful restraint on his or her liberty (cf. *R v Rahman* (1985) 81 Cr. App. R. 349). Furthermore, a detention that was initially lawful may become unlawful in certain circumstances, e.g. where a term of imprisonment has expired or a prisoner that was subject to remand has been acquitted (cf. *Mee v Cruikshank* (1902) 20 Cox C.C. 210). A lawful imprisonment may become unlawful if a defendant is detained in a Garda station but is refused private access to a legal adviser (see e.g. *State (Harrington) v Garvey*, unreported, High Court, December 14, 1976), or is denied access to medical attention (*Re The Emergency Powers Bill 1976* [1977] I.R. 159), or indeed was subjected to serious mistreatment while in custody (*People (DPP) v Kelly (No.2)* [1983] I.R. 1).

If a suspect, while at liberty, had been kept under close Garda surveillance this will not constitute false imprisonment since the essential feature of the offence, the unlawful detention of the victim, was absent (*Kane v The Governor of Mountjoy Prison* [1988] 1 I.R. 757).

While there is no provision in s.15 for a defence of lawful authority or reasonable excuse, the provisions in ss.18 to 20 dealing with the justifiable use of force are applicable to a charge of false imprisonment.

Section 15(3) provides that the offence of false imprisonment can be tried either summarily (in which case the maximum penalty is 12 months' imprisonment and/or a €1,900 fine) or on indictment where the maximum punishment is life imprisonment. This provision, and alternative mode of trial, recognises the fact that there may be very different ways in which the offence can be committed, some of which are clearly more serious than others.

Abduction of Children by Parents

The Irish State ratified the Hague Convention on International Child Abduction and the Council of Europe Convention on Recognition and Enforcement of

Decisions concerning Custody of Children and on Restoration of Custody of Children. In view of this, s.16 of the 1997 Act creates a new offence of abduction of a child by his or her parent or guardian out of the jurisdiction in defiance of a court order or without the other parent or guardian's consent. It is also an offence to arrange to have a child removed from the jurisdiction. This pertains to so-called tug-of-love cases and makes abduction out of the State an offence. In circumstances where a child is not taken out of the jurisdiction, then *the* criminal law will not become involved and the matter will be dealt with through the usual custody proceedings.

Section 16(3) provides for a defence where the defendant was unable to communicate with those whose consent is required but believed that they would have consented if they had been aware of the relevant circumstances. It also provides a defence where the defendant did not intend to deprive others of their rights in respect of the child.

Section 16(4) provides that the maximum penalty on summary conviction is a €1,900 fine and/or 12 months' imprisonment. Conviction on indictment carries an unlimited fine and/or a maximum of seven years' imprisonment. Proceedings under this section shall not be instituted except by or with the consent of the Director of Public Prosecutions (s.16(5)).

ABDUCTION OF CHILDREN BY OTHER PERSONS

Section 17 creates the offence of abduction of a child by persons other than the child's parent or guardian. The offence is punishable by up to seven years' imprisonment. This section applies to the taking of a child by a person to whom the offence created by s.16 does not apply. It effectively replaces the common law offence of kidnapping, which had less frequently been used by the prosecution because of the vague elements of the common law offence (see *People (AG) v Edge* [1943] I.R. 115). The prosecution could alternatively rely on the offence of false imprisonment (see e.g. *People (DPP) v Prunty* [1985] I.L.R.M. 716).

Section 17(1) incorporates a defence of "lawful authority or reasonable excuse" which is absent from the offence created by s.16. This would conceivably include a situation where the Gardaí lawfully arrest a child. Section 17(2) incorporates an express defence of mistake, which is clearly based on the defendant's own (subjective) belief, and there is no requirement that there be reasonable (objective) grounds for that belief. The defendant would also have a defence if he believed that the child was over the age of 16 years.

Section 17(3) provides that the maximum punishment on summary conviction is a €1,900 fine and/or 12 months' imprisonment. Conviction on indictment carries an unlimited fine and/or seven years' imprisonment.

JUSTIFIABLE USE OF FORCE

Section 18 specifies the purposes for which reasonable force may be lawfully used (cf. *People (DPP) v McCormack* [2004] 4 I.R. 333). The force used must be reasonable in the circumstances as the defendant believed existed, including the protection of the person or his family or another person from bodily injury, assault or detention caused by a criminal act and to prevent the commission of a criminal offence or a breach of the peace. Where force is used to protect against trespass on another person or another person's property, the force must be with the authority of that other person.

Sections 18, 19 and 20 place legislative provisions governing the use of reasonable force in public or private defence on a statutory footing. At common law, reasonable force could lawfully be used in circumstances where it was deemed necessary to defend oneself, another or one's property against an attack (see *People (AG) v Keatley* [1954] I.R. 12). Reasonable force might also have been used in order to effect a lawful arrest or to prevent the commission of a serious offence and the force used must be proportionate to the injury sought to be prevented. In *People (AG) v Dwyer* [1972] I.R. 416, the Supreme Court held that in homicide cases where self-defence fails because the force was excessive in light of the circumstances, but the force used was no more than the defendant honestly believed to be necessary in the circumstances, then he will be convicted of manslaughter and not murder. However, s.18 is silent as to whether this common law excessive force defence has survived its enactment.

Section 18(1) provides for a range of circumstances, based on common law, in which reasonable force may lawfully be used. It lists these circumstances as follows:

> ...
> (a) to protect himself or herself or a member of the family of that person or another from injury, assault or detention caused by a criminal act; or
> (b) to protect himself or herself or (with the authority of that other) another from trespass to the person; or
> (c) to protect his or her property from appropriation, destruction or damage caused by a criminal act or from trespass or infringement; or
> (d) to protect property belonging to another from appropriation, destruction or damage caused by a criminal act or (with the authority of that other) from trespass or infringement; or
> (e) to prevent crime or a breach of the peace.

If, however, the force is used to protect against trespass on another person or another person's property, the force must then be used with the authority of that other person. Section 18(1) and (5) provide that the circumstances in which the force is used must be judged according to the subjective belief of the defendant.

Section 18(3) is concerned with cases in which the behaviour of the person against whom force is used is criminal, although, if it were the subject of a criminal charge, that person would be acquitted on one of the five listed grounds.

Section 18(6) preserves a common law rule in *R v Fennell* [1971] 1 Q.B. 428, where the Court of Appeal upheld the conviction of a man for assaulting a police officer who was attempting to arrest his son, notwithstanding any honest or reasonable belief on his part that the arrest was unlawful. However, in *People (DPP) v Murray* [1977] I.R. 360, the Supreme Court held that in a prosecution for assaulting a police officer in the course of his duty, the defendant must have been aware of the status of the victim.

Section 18(7) provides that the defence does not apply to a person who causes conduct or a state of affairs with a view to using force to resist or terminate it. In *R v Browne* [1973] N.I. 96 at 107, the Court of Criminal Appeal (Lowry L.C.J.) held,

> "[t]he need to act must not have been created by the conduct of the accused in the immediate context of the incident which was likely or intended to give rise to that view."

JUSTIFIABLE USE OF FORCE IN EFFECTING OR ASSISTING LAWFUL ARREST

Section 19 provides that a person may, in effecting or assisting in a lawful arrest, use such force as is necessary in the circumstances. The issue as to the reasonableness of the force used and consequently, whether the arrest is lawful is determined according to the circumstances as the defendant believed them to be. The common law position was that reasonable force could be used to effect an arrest or to terminate violence subsequent to an arrest (see *Dowman v Ireland* [1986] I.L.R.M. 111). Reasonable force could also be used to suppress an unlawful assembly, although the Supreme Court has held that the use of force must always be reasonable and proportionate to the circumstances (*Lynch v Fitzgerald (No. 2)* [1938] I.R. 382).

MEANING OF "FORCE"

Section 20 defines the meaning of "use of force" for the purposes of ss.18 and 19, and must be read as ancillary to those provisions. With regard to the duty to retreat, s.20(4) reaffirms the common law position on this issue (see *R v McInnes* [1971] 1 W.L.R. 1600). Although there were technical rules pertaining to the duty to retreat before using force to repel an assailant, or at least fatal force, an opportunity to retreat is now simply a factor for the court or jury to take into account in deciding whether it was necessary to use force, and whether the force used was reasonable in the circumstances of the case under consideration.

AMENDMENT OF THE CRIMINAL DAMAGE ACT 1991

Section 21 amends s.6(2) of the Criminal Damage Act 1991 so that the applicable test in relation to damaging property is the same as the test set out in s.18, that is, the conduct of the defendant must be reasonable in the circumstances that he believed to exist. This is a subjective test.

GENERAL DEFENCES

Section 22 preserves defences available under the common law or statute law in relation to conduct that might otherwise attract criminal liability under the provisions of the 1997 Act.

CONSENT BY MINORS TO SURGICAL, MEDICAL AND DENTAL TREATMENT

Section 23 provides that a minor aged over 16 years can consent to surgical, medical or dental treatment. Without consent, such procedures would constitute a trespass to the person. Prior to this, whether consent by a minor to medical treatment was effective depended on whether the minor was deemed to have understood the purpose and implications of the medical treatment. This provision inserts an element of clarity in the law pertaining to the issue of consent in the case of older minors.

ABOLITION OF CORPORAL PUNISHMENT

Section 24 abolishes the common law rule of teachers' immunity from criminal liability in respect of physical chastisement of pupils, which reinforces the Department of Education's policy on the prohibition of corporal punishment in schools.

EVIDENTIAL VALUE OF CERTIFICATES SIGNED BY MEDICAL PRACTITIONERS

Section 25 provides that a doctor's certificate can be accepted in proceedings relating to offences alleging the causing of harm or serious harm as proof of such harm.

FURTHER READING

Bacik, "Striking a Blow for Reform? A Note on the Non-Fatal Offences against the Person Act 1997 and its Effect on the Law of Assault" (1997) 7(1) I.C.L.J. 48.

Byrne, "Non-Fatal Offences against the Person Act 1997" (1998) 16 I.L.T. 245.

Campbell, Kilcommins and O'Sullivan, *Criminal Law in Ireland: Cases and Commentary* (Dublin: Clarus Press, 2010), Ch.15.

Foley, "Boxing, the Common Law and the Non-Fatal Offences against the Person Act 1997" (2002) 12(1) I.C.L.J. 15.

Hanly, *An Introduction to Irish Criminal Law*, 2nd edn (Dublin: Gill & Macmillan, 2006), Ch.19.

Law Reform Commission, *Report on Non-Fatal Offences against the Person* (LRC 45–1994).

McCutcheon, "Sports, Violence, Consent and the Criminal Law" (1994) 45 N.I.L.Q. 267.

White, "The Present Prosecution of Abolished Offence" (1998) 8(2) I.C.L.J. 196.

18. Sexual Offences

Introduction

Irish criminal law provides for various sexual offences including: rape, sexual assault, and sexual offences against children. The punishments on conviction for these offences include: imprisonment, being placed on the sex offenders register, and post-release supervision by the Probation Service. Furthermore, individuals convicted of sexual offences are obliged to inform certain prospective employers of the fact that they have been convicted of such offences.

Rape

The offence of rape is provided for by the Criminal Law (Rape) Act 1981 (the "1981 Act") as amended by the Criminal Law (Rape) (Amendment) Act 1990. The circumstances of the case, age of the victim and evidence against the defendant will determine the offence for which the defendant is charged and convicted. The maximum sentence on conviction for rape is life imprisonment. An offender may also be charged with attempted rape or aiding and abetting a rape.

Actus reus

The actus reus of "common law rape", as provided for by s.2(1) of the 1981 Act, consists of sexual intercourse between a man and a woman, to which the woman does not consent. This is a gender specific offence in that it can only be committed by a man against a woman.

The first element of the actus reus is that sexual intercourse must have taken place. Intercourse for this purpose means vaginal intercourse only and a minimal degree of penetration will suffice, i.e. the offence of rape is complete on penetration. In *People (AG) v Dermody* [1956] I.R. 307, the victim, a young girl, gave evidence that her assailant's male organ "went a wee bit into" her female organ, coupled with the medical evidence that the girl's hymen was intact. The Court of Criminal Appeal held that the offence of rape could be proved by proof of penetration, even though emission could not be proved.

The offence of rape as defined by s.2 of the 1981 Act referred to "unlawful" sexual intercourse which was interpreted to mean sexual relations outside marriage and husbands were effectively granted a "marital rape exemption." This lacuna was ameliorated by s.5(1) of the Criminal Law (Rape) (Amendment) Act 1990, which abolished the marital exemption, although the consent of the DPP is required before a prosecution for rape within marriage can proceed (see s.5(2)).

MENS REA

The mens rea for rape consists of knowledge on the part of the defendant that the victim was not consenting, such as where he forced himself upon the victim, or recklessness as to whether or not the victim was consenting and such as where the victim was under the influence of drugs or alcohol. The mens rea of rape is contained in s.2(1)(b) of the 1981 Act, which provides that:

> ... if at the time [of the intercourse] he knows that she does not consent to the intercourse or he is reckless as to whether she does or does not consent to it, and references to rape in this act or any other enactment shall be construed accordingly.

The mens rea of rape has proven to be the most controversial element of the offence. The present law is contained in s.2 of the Criminal Law (Rape) (Amendment) Act 1990. Essentially, the controversy was whether the test of knowledge should be subjective or objective. In other words, should the question be whether the defendant honestly, though perhaps unreasonably, believed the complainant was consenting or did the defendant have reasonable grounds for believing that the complainant was consenting? The present Irish and English case law requires an honest and reasonable belief by the defendant that the complainant did not consent. If the defendant genuinely believed that the victim had consented, even though this was a mistaken belief, then he may be acquitted depending of the factual circumstances of the case. The legal basis for permitting a mistaken belief, even if this is unreasonable, is that the mens rea for the offence of rape is that the defendant either knew that the victim was not consenting, or he was reckless as to whether or not she was consenting, at the time of the intercourse.

If the defendant honestly believed that the victim was consenting but his belief was unreasonable in the circumstances, the dilemma is whether he should be convicted. If the objective test is applied then he would most likely be convicted where he had an honest belief in circumstances where there were no reasonable grounds justifying an honest belief that the victim was consenting. If the subjective test is applied, it is likely that the defendant would be acquitted as the subjective test concentrates on the defendant's belief at the time of the intercourse, and not whether the reasonably prudent person would have thought that the victim was consenting. This dilemma was considered by the House of Lords in *DPP v Morgan* [1976] A.C. 182. The victim's husband had invited three men to have sexual intercourse with his wife and told them that if she seemed to resist this was merely her way of getting more enjoyment. The defendants argued that they had an honest (but as it transpired unreasonable) belief that the victim was consenting at the time of the intercourse. They were convicted on the basis of the trial judges' direction to the jury that the defendants' honest belief that the victim had consented would not be a defence to a charge of rape unless they could establish reasonable grounds for this belief. In other words, the defendants must not have been reckless as to whether or not the victim actually consented. On appeal, the House of Lords held that the defendants should not have been convicted of rape if they had an honest belief that the victim was consenting to the intercourse. Lord Hailsham stated:

> "Once one has accepted ... that the prohibited act in rape is non-consensual sexual intercourse, and that the guilty state of mind is an intention to commit it, it seems to me to follow as a matter of inexorable logic that there is no room either for a 'defence' of honest belief or mistake, or of a defence of honest and reasonable belief or mistake. Either the prosecution proves that the accused had the requisite intent, or it does not. In the former case it succeeds, and in the latter it fails. *Since honest belief clearly negatives intent, the reasonableness or otherwise of that belief can only be evidence for or against the view that the belief and therefore the intent was actually held* ..." (emphasis added). [1976] A.C. 182 at 214

Naturally, this decision resulted in public outrage and academic commentators argued to change the law on the mens rea for rape to an objective test, since the application of the subjective test in these circumstances was effectively a license to commit rape. The *Heilbron Committee (Report of the Advisory Group on the Law of Rape* 1975 Cmnd. 6352) was established to examine the law governing the mens rea for rape and recommended that the *Morgan* ruling should be placed on a statutory footing. This was done in England by the Sexual Offences (Amendment) Act 1976, and in Ireland, in virtually identical language, by s.2(2) of the Criminal Law (Rape) Act 1981. Section 2(2) of the 1981 Act provides that:

> It is hereby declared that if at a trial for a rape offence the jury has to consider whether a man believed [subjective] that a woman was consenting to sexual intercourse, the presence or absence of

reasonable grounds [objective] for such a belief is a matter to which the jury is to have regard, in conjunction with any other relevant matters, in considering whether he so believed.

This was effectively a compromise between the subjective and objective tests. In other words, the defendant could assert that he had an honest belief that the victim was consenting (subjective test), but the jury will consider whether this belief was reasonable in determining whether the defendant's belief was an honest belief in the entirety of the circumstances (objective test). It may be clearly evident from the circumstances of the case that the victim was not in fact consenting at the time of the intercourse, such as where the defendant forced himself on the victim. In *People (DPP) v McDonagh* [1996] 1 I.R. 565, the Supreme Court held that s.2(1) of the 1981 Act codified the common law governing the actus reus and the mens rea of rape, while s.2(2) dealt with the circumstances in which a defendant might have held a belief which, if the jury accepted that it was so held, could negative the mens rea specified in section 2(1). The court also stated that s.2(2) contained principles to be applied only when an issue of mistaken belief arose in a trial.

There is at present no firm authority in Ireland on the test of recklessness in rape, but it is generally believed to be a subjective test, which pertains in Irish criminal law. This is also the test adopted by the English superior courts. In *R v Satnam and Kewel* (1984) 78 Cr. App. R. 149, the Court of Criminal Appeal per Bristow J. held that recklessness in the offence of rape means:

> "... the prohibited act is and always has been intercourse without consent of the victim and the mental element is and always has been the intention to commit that act, or the equivalent intention of having intercourse willy-nilly not caring whether the victim consents or no". (1984) 78 Cr.App.R. 149 at 153

In other words, the defendant should be found guilty of rape only if he knows that the victim is not consenting, or he had no genuine belief that the victim was not consenting and nevertheless continued. The jury determined from the entirety of the evidence that he "could not have cared less" whether the victim was consenting or not. If the defendant had a genuine belief that the victim was consenting, regardless of the existing circumstances to the contrary, then he would probably be acquitted. English criminal law seems more concerned with the defendant's attitude rather than his state of mind and the approach in that jurisdiction would appear to be whether the defendant cared one way or the other if the complainant was actually consenting to sexual intercourse.

The leading case on recklessness in Irish criminal law is *People (DPP) v Murray* [1976] I.R. 360, where the Supreme Court adopted the subjective test of recklessness which applied to the offence of rape and meant that the defendant must have consciously been aware of the possibility that the complainant was not consenting.

SECTION 4 RAPE

The common law definition of rape as codified by s.2(1) of the 1981 Act did not make provision for anal or oral rape, nor indeed penetration of the victim by an object. Thus, penetration of a female, or male, person other than within the definition in s.2(1) of the 1981 Act, did not constitute the offence of rape. In order to remedy this lacuna in the law of rape, the new offence of rape contrary to s.4 of the Criminal Law (Rape) (Amendment) Act 1990, includes other forms of penetration:

(1) In this Act, 'rape under section 4' means a sexual assault that includes:
  (a) penetration (however slight) of the anus or mouth by the male organ, or
  (b) penetration (however slight) of the vagina by any object held or manipulated by another person.
(2) A person guilty of rape under section 4 shall be liable on conviction on indictment to imprisonment for life.
(3) rape under section 4 shall be a felony.

In essence, this offence is a sexual assault with the additional elements of penetration. It is a gender neutral offence, in that it can be committed by a man against a woman or a man and vice versa. The offence as described in para.1(b) may obviously be perpetrated only on a female victim but the principal may be either a man or a woman. Furthermore, there is no rule of law that restricts the secondary parties to the male sex because a man or woman can aid, abet, counsel or procure the commission of this. As with the offence of rape defined under s.2(1) of the 1981 Act, rape under s.4 stipulates that the degree of penetration need only be slight.

Rape under s.4 does not state the mens rea for this offence, but since this is effectively a sexual assault involving penetration of the victim, it is reasonable to assume that the mens rea for sexual assault would apply.

A conviction for the offence of rape under s.4 is punishable by a maximum sentence of life imprisonment (s.4(2)). A person convicted of this offence may be convicted of aggravated sexual assault or sexual assault as an alternative (s.8).

Sexual Assault

At common law, the offence of indecent assault was an aggravated sexual assault involving any unwanted sexual behaviour or touching that was forced upon a male or female against their will. Section 2 of the Criminal Law (Rape) (Amendment) Act 1990 codified the old common law offence of indecent assault. This provision did not abolish the offence of indecent assault, but as an alternative renamed this offence under the new title of "sexual assault". Section 2 provides that:

(1) The offence of indecent assault upon any male person and the offence of indecent assault upon any female person shall be known as sexual assault.

(2) A person guilty of sexual assault shall be liable on conviction on indictment to imprisonment for a term not exceeding 5 years.

(3) Sexual assault shall be a felony [arrestable offence]

The offence is gender neutral. A sexual assault is essentially an indecent assault on a male or a female. The maximum sentence on conviction for sexual assault is five years' imprisonment (s.2(2)).

The defendant may alternatively be charged with aggravated sexual assault, which is, a "sexual assault that involves serious violence or the threat of serious violence or is such as to cause injury, humiliation or degradation of a grave nature to the person assaulted" (s.3(1)). The maximum sentence for aggravated sexual assault is life imprisonment (s.3(2)).

As stated above, this offence was formerly known as the common law offence of "indecent assault" on a male or female. In *S O'C v Governor of Curragh Prison and the DPP* [2002] 1 I.R. 66, the Supreme Court held that the net effect of s.2(1) of the 1990 Act with respect to the original offence of indecent assault was simply to change the name of the offence while leaving its nature and constituent elements unaltered. The court also held that although the Non-Fatal Offences Against the Person Act 1997 abolished certain common law assaults, this did not include sexual or indecent assault, which are a different category of offences. The offence of indecent assault had always been legislated for separately from the type of offences with which the 1997 Act was concerned—which did not purport to replace common law sexual assault with a statutory equivalent as it did with other common law assaults.

In 2006, the Department of Health and Children published a report entitled *Sexual Assault Treatment Services: A National Review*, which identified some key areas for the development of sexual assault treatment services. The Health Service Executive, in conjunction with the Department of Health and Department of Justice, Equality and Law Reform, will henceforth work to ensure implementation of the recommendations in the report.

Actus Reus

In view of the fact that the offence constitutes an assault, the actus reus is the same as s.2 of the Non-Fatal Offences Against the Person Act 1997, with the additional element that the assault was committed in circumstances of indecency. The offence of assault is committed where the defendant intentionally or recklessly, directly or indirectly, applies force to the victim, and the absence of consent by the victim is a key element of this offence. The elements of indecency are considered below.

Mens Rea

The word "assault" includes both assault in its strict legal sense and battery. In addition to the application of force without consent, the offence of sexual assault can also be committed where the defendant causes the victim to reasonably fear an immediate physical contact to which the victim does not consent. In this context, a sexual assault is an assault accompanied by circumstances which are objectively indecent. In *R v Court* [1989] A.C. 28, the House of Lords per Lord Ackner identified the following three elements of the offence:

"(a) the defendant intentionally assaulted the victim
 (b) the assault or the assault and the circumstances accompanying it, are proved to be indecent according to the contemporary standards of right-thinking people
 (c) the defendant intended to commit the assault in (b)."

It is not essential that there was some physical force or that the defendant acted with aggression or hostility towards the victim. In *Faulkner v Talbot* [1981] 1 W.L.R. 1528, the Divisional Court per Lord Lane L.J. explained that:

"An assault is any intentional touching of another person without the consent of that person and without lawful excuse. It need not necessarily be hostile or rude or aggressive, as some of the cases seem to indicate." [1981] 1 W.L.R. 1528 at 1534

The assault component in the offence of sexual assault is derived from the absence of consent in relation to the non-consensual touching of the complainant. The type of force used may be a factor in determining whether the defendant's conduct had sexual connotations.

Meaning of "sexual"

The meaning of "sexual" was considered in *R v Barnier* (1980) 51 CCC(2d) 193, where the Quebec Court of Criminal Appeal stated that for the purposes of sexual assault, it is only necessary to prove a general intent on the part of the defendant:

> "As the evidence of the agressor's desire for sexual gratification is not an essential element of the offence, to require proof of sexual motivation has the effect of transforming the offence of sexual assault into a specific intent offence. Whether the aggressor's motivation is a desire for sexual pleasure, a desire to inflict suffering on another person, to humiliate or ridicule the victim, does not at all change the criminal nature of his conduct."

In other words, if the defendant touched the victim in a sexual manner, knowing that the victim was not consenting, or was unable to consent, then he is guilty of sexual assault.

In *Fairclough v Whipp* [1951] 2 All E.R. 834, the King's Bench Division held that the word assault in the context of the common law offence of indecent assault could extend to a man inviting a girl to touch his exposed body even though there was no actual contact. In *R v Rolfe* (1952) 36 Cr. App. R. 4, the complainant was travelling on a train in a compartment in which she was the only passenger when the defendant joined her. While the train was in motion, the defendant undid his trousers and, with his person exposed, moved towards her, inviting her "to have connection with him". Lord Goddard C.J. said:

> "The first thing to observe is this: one can very seldom take some rule which has been laid down in another case and apply it to the case under consideration, irrespective of the facts of that particular case. Secondly, the offence of assault is often confused with the offence of battery. An assault can be committed without touching a person. One always thinks of an assault as the giving of a blow to somebody, but that is not necessary. An assault may be constituted by a threat or a hostile act committed towards a person, and if a man indecently exposes himself and walks towards a woman with his person exposed and makes an indecent suggestion to her that, in the opinion of this court, can amount to an assault." (1952) 36 Cr. App. R. 4 at 5–6

The defendant's conduct in exposing himself (indecent conduct) and then moving towards the victim constituted an assault.

ELEMENT OF INDECENCY

The second element in the actus reus of sexual assault is that the assault was committed in circumstances of indecency. In *R v Leeson* (1968) 52 Cr. App. R. 185, the Court of Appeal held that kissing a girl with an overt suggestion of sexual activity constituted an indecent assault. For the assault or other conduct by the defendant to be deemed indecent there must be circumstances of indecency. The specific elements and general meaning of indecency were considered in *R v Court* [1989] A.C. 28, where the House of Lords held that the spanking of a clothed 12-year-old girl could amount to an act of indecency. An infringement of the standards of decent behaviour of right thinking members of society in regard to sexual modesty or privacy is required to prove the element of indecency in this offence. This is a very broad test and could apply to petting a young girl or the examination of a child by someone pretending to be a doctor, but would conceivably exclude removing a girls shoe from her foot or to touch the end of a girl's skirt. Lord Ackner noted that there were three types of behaviour that generally constituted an indecent assault: behaviour that is inherently not indecent; behaviour that is inherently indecent; and behaviour that could be indecent or not depending on the factual circumstances of the case under consideration. It follows that if the circumstances are incapable of being regarded as indecent by the test of the standards of decent behaviour of right thinking members of society, then the defendant's behaviour should not be deemed indecent merely because of a secret indecent purpose by the defendant.

There must be some overt circumstances of indecency (cf. *R v Kilbourne* [1972] 1 W.L.R. 1365). While consent is a defence to the offence, it will not be available as a defence if any actual bodily harm was intended or caused, nor indeed will consent be a defence if it was obtained by fraud as to the defendant's identity or fraud concerning the nature of the act, such as where the defendant is pretending to perform a medical procedure.

AGGRAVATED SEXUAL ASSAULT

Aggravated sexual assault is sexual assault involving serious violence or the threat of serious violence. Section 3 of the 1990 Act provides that:

(1) In this Act "aggravated sexual assault" means a sexual assault that involves serious violence or the threat of serious violence or is such as is to cause injury, humiliation or degradation of a grave nature to the person assaulted.

(2) A person convicted of aggravated sexual assault shall be liable on conviction on indictment to imprisonment for life.

(3) Aggravated sexual assault shall be a felony [arrestable offence].

Whether the aggravating circumstances of the offence are present will be determined by an objective test, and it will be irrelevant that the defendant himself did not think that the circumstances of the assault included an aggravating factor.

The maximum penalty on conviction for aggravated sexual assault is life imprisonment (s.3(2)).

SEXUAL OFFENCES AGAINST CHILDREN

In Irish criminal law there is no specific offence pertaining to child sex abuse. A defendant can be charged with rape, sexual assault, aggravated sexual assault, or alternatively with one of the specific offences relating to children.

STATUTORY RAPE

While the term "statutory rape" was not used in the relevant legislative provisions it has traditionally been used to describe unlawful sexual relations with a person aged less than 17 years of age. Prior to 2006, a defendant could be charged with the offence of statutory rape under the provisions of s.1(1) of the Criminal Law (Amendment) Act 1935 (the "1935 Act"). However, in *CC v Ireland* [2006] 4 I.R. 1, the Supreme Court held that this provision was unconstitutional and declared void ab initio. The issue with s.1(1) of the 1935 Act was that it was deemed a strict liability offence, notwithstanding the fact that the maximum penalty for that offence was life imprisonment. However, the defence of bona fide mistake as to the age of the person with whom he had sexual relations was not provided for in the impugned provision. Consequently, this provision was struck down as being unconstitutional in that it infringed the defendant's right to a trial in due course of law in accordance with Art.38.1 of the Constitution.

In *A v Governor of Arbour Hill Prison* [2006] 4 I.R. 88, the applicant had been convicted and sentenced under s.1(1) of the 1935 Act and challenged the legality of his continued detention following the *CC* judgment. The Supreme Court held that it was not a principle of constitutional law that cases which have been finally decided and determined based on a statute that was subsequently found to be unconstitutional, must invariably be set aside as null and of no affect. The reasoning of the court was that once finality had been reached and the parties had in each case exhausted their actual or potential remedies, the judicial decision must thereafter be deemed valid and lawful. The court also held that the approach to be taken to the application of retrospectivity was to assess whether the compulsion of public order and the common good would allow an applicant to succeed.

To remedy this lacuna, the Oireachtas enacted the Criminal Law (Sexual Offences) Act 2006 (the "2006 Act") to replace the unconstitutional provisions of the 1935 Act with new statutory offences of defilement. The primary purpose of the 2006 Act is to restore and modernise the offence of sexual acts with children and to protect children against sexual abuse. The provisions creating the new offences contain a defence of honest belief by the defendant that the child had attained 15 years (s.2) or 17 years (s.3), in accordance with the Supreme Court judgment in *CC*. The jury must then consider whether that belief was reasonable based on the entirety of the facts of the case under consideration. Consent by the child to sexual relations is not a defence to a charge of defilement if the child was under the legal age of consent.

DEFILEMENT OF A CHILD AGED UNDER 15 YEARS OF AGE

Section 2 of the 2006 Act provides that it is an offence to engage, or attempt to engage, in a sexual act with a child under the age of 15 years. A sexual act for the purposes of the offence of defilement includes: sexual intercourse and buggery between people who are not married to each other, and any sexual act which could constitute aggravated sexual assault. The maximum sentence on conviction where a person engages (s.2(1)), or attempts to engage (s.2(2)), in a sexual act with a child under the age of 15 years, is life imprisonment.

It shall be a defence for the defendant to prove that he or she honestly believed that, at the time of the commission of the offence, the child had attained the age of 15 years (s.2(3)). This is a subjective test. However, the jury shall have regard to the presence or absence of reasonable grounds for the defendant's so believing and all other relevant circumstances of the case under consideration (s.2(4)). This incorporates an objective element in determining whether or not the defendant can avail of the defence of honest mistake as to the age of the child.

It shall not be a defence for the defendant to prove that the child consented to the sexual act (s.2(5)).

DEFILEMENT OF A CHILD AGED UNDER 17 YEARS OF AGE

Section 3(1) of the 2006 Act, as amended by s.5 of the Criminal Law (Sexual Offences) (Amendment) Act 2007, states that it is an offence to engage, or attempt to engage, in a sexual act with a child under 17 years. The maximum sentence for this offence is five years' imprisonment or 10 years if the defendant is a person in authority. The maximum sentence for attempting to engage in a sexual act with a child under 17 years is two years' imprisonment or four years' imprisonment if the defendant is a person is in authority (s.3(2)). A person in authority means: a parent, step-parent, guardian, grandparent, uncle or aunt of the victim; any person acting in loco parentis (that is, in place of a parent or parents) to the victim; and any person responsible for the education, supervision or welfare of the victim (s.1).

A subsequent conviction on indictment under s.3(1) carries a maximum of 10 years' imprisonment or 15 years' imprisonment if the defendant was a person in authority (s.3(3)). A subsequent conviction on indictment under s.3(2) carries a maximum of four years' imprisonment or seven years' imprisonment if the defendant was a person in authority (s.3(4)).

The defendant may assert that he or she honestly believed that the child was aged 17 years of age or over (s.3(5)), but the jury shall have regard to the presence or absence of reasonable grounds for the defendant's belief s.3(6)). Consent by the child is not a defence (s.3(7)).

Where the defendant is aged 17 years of age, or less, then the consent of the DPP is required for any prosecution (s.3(9)). If a defendant who has been convicted for this offence is not more than two years older than the victim (complainant), he is not subject to the requirements of the Sex Offenders Act 2001 (s.3(10)).

A girl aged under 17 years of age who has sexual intercourse may not be convicted of an offence on that ground alone.

INCEST

The offence of incest, which is provided for by the Punishment of Incest Act 1908 (the "1908 Act") as amended by the Criminal Law (Incest Proceedings) Act 1995, prohibits sexual intercourse between close relatives, which includes a child, a sibling or a parent. Sexual intercourse for the purposes of this offence means vaginal intercourse only. While there are no age limits to the commission of this offence, a girl under 17 years of age cannot be prosecuted for incest based on policy considerations. The maximum sentence on conviction for the offence of incest is life imprisonment for males and seven years for females.

Incest was an offence only in the church courts until 1908 when it was made a criminal offence with the enactment of the Punishment of Incest Act. Marriages are forbidden within a wide range of relationships but sexual intercourse is restricted within a much narrower range. The purpose of the offence is to prohibit sexual intercourse between persons of defined close degrees of consanguinity (blood relatives) as opposed to affinity. The justification for the offence is the protection and prevention against exploitation (social and psychological) and eugenic reasons (risks of genetic defects of children born from such unions). Most cases of incest involve acts of violence or abusive behaviour, although this is not a requirement of the offence, with the result that consensual intercourse between close blood relatives is an offence. Typically, the offence of incest is committed where a father sexually abuses his children. Sexual abuse by adoptive parents is not incest because of the absence of a blood relationship, but would constitute a different sexual offence, such as defilement.

INCEST BY A MALE

Section 1(1) of the Punishment of Incest Act 1908, as amended by s.12 of the Criminal Law (Amendment) Act 1935, provides that:

> Any male person who has carnal knowledge of a female person, who is to his knowledge his grand-daughter, daughter, sister, or mother, shall be guilty of an offence ...

A male who has sexual intercourse with a woman who is to his knowledge, his mother, sister, daughter or granddaughter commits incest. Brother and sister include half-brother and half-sister (one parent in common) but not step-brother and step-sister (no blood relationship).

INCEST BY A FEMALE

Section 2 of the 1908 Act provides that:

> A female person of or above the age of seventeen years, who with consent permits her grandfather, father, brother or son to have carnal knowledge of her (knowing him to be her grandfather, father, brother or son, as the case may be) shall be guilty of an offence.

A female of or above the age of 17 years, who with consent, permits her father, grandfather, brother or son to have sexual intercourse with her commits incest, provided she is aware of the relationship between herself and the male. Incest by a female is the same offence as incest by a male with one exception—the female is not criminally liable until she reaches the age of 17 years.

Section 3 provides that the expressions "brother" and "sister" respectively include half-brother and half-sister. Section 4(3) provides that a verdict of guilty of incest is an alternative verdict on an indictment for rape.

CONSENT

Section 1(2) provides that, "it is immaterial that the carnal knowledge was had with the consent of the female person". If a woman is over the age of 17 years and consents to incest, she will be guilty of an offence under s.2, provided she was aware of the relationship between them at the time. Therefore, apart from the age restriction, the elements of the offence are the same as those applying to incest by a male. If a girl under the age of 17 consents to sexual relations within the definition of the offence of incest, she will not be criminally liable for any offence, because the purpose of the 1908 Act was to protect vulnerable children.

Relationship

The relationship of the parties may be proved by an admission or by a certificate of birth coupled with identification of the child and her father by someone who knew them at the time of her birth. It is clear from s.3 that the legislation applies equally to marital and non-marital children, but incest cannot be committed in the absence of a blood relationship, with an adopted child.

Mens rea

Under ss.1 and 3, the mental element of the offence is an intention to have sexual intercourse and knowledge of the relationship between the parties. Recklessness would not appear to be a sufficient fault element (mens rea) for this offence. Intent to have sexual intercourse may not be an issue but knowledge of the blood relationship can be of practical importance in the prosecution of this offence. It will be difficult for the defendant to prove that he was unaware of the blood relationship where the parties were separated at birth. Because the state of the defendant's mind is central to the offence, statements by him to others as to the paternity of his child do not infringe the hearsay rule but are admissible within the category of admissible evidence.

In *R v Carmichael* [1940] 1 K.B. 630, the Court of Criminal Appeal quashed the conviction for incest because the trial judge had refused to admit evidence about the defendant's belief that the woman with whom he had sexual intercourse was not his daughter. The defendant was entitled to give evidence to the effect that he had been told by his first wife, the victim's mother, that the victim had been begotten by another man and that he believed that statement to be true; he had told his second wife that he was not the father of the victim. In *R v Whitehouse* [1977] Q.B. 868, the defendant pleaded guilty to a charge of inciting his daughter, then aged 15 years, to have sexual intercourse with him. Under the relevant English law, a girl under the age of 16 years could not be convicted of incest. The Court of Criminal Appeal quashed the conviction because at common law the act incited must be a criminal offence committed by the person incited. Consequently, the defendant had not in law incited his daughter to commit an offence.

Punishment

Where the incest has been committed by a male the punishment is life imprisonment and if committed by a female the maximum penalty is seven years' imprisonment. The Criminal Law (Incest Proceedings) Act 1995 increased the maximum sentence from seven years' imprisonment (as provided for by the 1908 Act) to life imprisonment where the female is under the age of 15 years. Where the female is of 17 years or over the penalty is still a maximum of seven years' imprisonment. In law, permission does not constitute consent and whether there is consent is a matter for the jury.

If there is evidence that the woman consented, the jury must be cautioned that if they find her to have consented, she then becomes an accomplice and the judge must warn the jury of the dangers of convicting her on uncorroborated testimony.

PROCEDURE

A prosecution for incest requires the consent of the DPP. Section 5 of the 1908 Act provides that all proceedings for incest are to be held in camera; there is no discretion in this as there is in other cases involving indecent acts. In *People (DPP) v WM* [1995] 1 I.R. 226, the High Court per Carney J. questioned the constitutionality of s.5 requiring entire secrecy given that all proceedings were to be held in private.

Section 2 of the Criminal Law (Incest Proceedings) Act 1995 now provides that verdict and sentence are pronounced in public. Under s.3 it is an offence to publish any matter which would identify a person charged with an incest offence or a person against whom the offence is alleged to have been committed. The punishment on conviction on indictment for infringing this provision is a maximum of three years' imprisonment and/or a €12,700 fine, and on summary conviction 12 months' imprisonment and/or a €1,900 fine.

SEXUAL OFFENCES AGAINST PEOPLE WITH DISABILITIES

There are specific provisions for sexual offences involving victims with disabilities. A person who engages in unlawful sexual activity with a person with a disability may, in the alternative, be charged with one of the sexual offences outlined above. Section 5(1) of the Criminal Law (Sexual Offences) Act 1993 provides for the following offences involving people with disabilities:

- Sexual intercourse or buggery with a mentally impaired person (other than a spouse), for which the maximum penalty is ten years' imprisonment.
- Gross indecency by a male with a male who is mentally impaired, for which the maximum penalty is 3 years in the case of a first conviction, and in the case of a second or any subsequent conviction, imprisonment for a term not exceeding 5 years' imprisonment.

It is an offence for a male person to commit, or attempt to commit, an act of gross indecency with another male person who is mentally impaired; the punishment on conviction on indictment is a maximum of two years' imprisonment (s.2(2)). It shall be a defence for the defendant to show that when the offence was allegedly committed, they did not know and had no reason to suspect that the person in respect of whom they were charged and prosecuted was suffering from a mental impairment (s.5(3)). A prosecution under this provision shall not be taken except by or with the consent of the DPP (s.5(4)). A mental impairment pertains to a disorder of the mind, whether through mental disability or mental illness, which is of such a nature or degree as to render a person incapable of living an independent life or of guarding themselves against serious exploitation (s.5(5)).

CONSENT

The absence of consent or the lack of capacity by the victim to give consent is the most problematic element of sexual offences, with particular reference to the offence of rape. In *R v Dee* (1884) 15 Cox C.C. 579, Palles C.B. opined:

> "Consent ... must proceed from the will, not when such will is acting without the control of reason, as in idiocy or drunkenness, but from the will sufficiently enlightened by the intellect to make such consent the act of a reasoning being."

Consent must be voluntarily and freely given. It must also be an informed consent in that the victim knew exactly what she was consenting to. In *Kaitamaki v R* [1985] A.C. 147, the Privy Council held that the offence of rape is a continuing act and the defendant would be convicted of that offence if, having become aware that the woman was not consenting, then failed to desist.

Despite a recommendation from the Law Reform Commission's *Report on Rape and Allied Offences* (LRC 24–1988), the Criminal Law (Rape) (Amendment) Act 1990 Act does not provide any definition of what exactly constitutes consent. Instead, it provides that failure to offer resistance shall not in itself amount to consent as the victim may be submitting to the inevitable. Section 9 provides that:

> It is hereby declared that in relation to an offence that consists of or includes the doing of an act to a person without the consent of that person any failure or omission by that person to offer resistance to the act does not of itself constitute consent to the act.

SEXUAL OFFENCES

In other words, where the victim does not struggle or put up a fight it does not necessarily follow that she did in fact consent. The jury may infer consent from the absence of evidence that the victim resisted. The obvious vitiating factors are fear and fraud. In *R v Clarence* (1888) 22 Q.B.D. 23 at 27, Willis J. explained, "[t]hat consent obtained by fraud is no consent at all is not true as a general proposition either in fact or in law". Stephens J. stated:

> "... the only sorts of fraud which so far destroy the effect of a woman's consent as to convert a connection consented to in fact into a rape are frauds as to the nature of the act itself, or as to the identity of the person who does the act consent in such cases does not exist at all because the act consented to is not the act done". (1888) 22 Q.B.D. 23 at 44

The question then arises as to what else may vitiate consent.

FEAR

If the victim submits to an act of sexual intercourse, this will not necessarily imply consent. The victim may have submitted to the intercourse out of fear, but this will not in law amount to a valid consent. In *R v Olugboja* [1982] Q.B. 320, two teenage girls were offered a lift home from a discotheque by the defendant and his friend. Instead of bringing them home, the defendant brought them to a house, but the girls refused to enter. After an argument during which the girls tried to get away, the defendant's friend eventually got both girls back to the house, raping one of them on the way. Inside, the defendant told the other girl that he was going to rape her and ordered her to undress. She did so because she was frightened and the room was in darkness. He pushed her onto a settee and had intercourse with her. She did not struggle or offer resistance nor did she cry for help, but merely submitted to the inevitable. Having been convicted of rape, the defendant appealed to the Court of Appeal on the ground that in the absence of a threat of violence to the victim her consent had not been vitiated. Dunn L.J. dismissed this argument stating that in a case like this the jury:

> "... should be directed to concentrate on the state of mind of the victim immediately before the act of sexual intercourse, having regard to all the relevant circumstances; and in particular, the events leading up to the act and her reaction to them showing their impact on her mind". [1982] Q.B. 320 at 332

The trial court must consider the entirely of the circumstances. The threat must be an imminent threat of immediate personal violence, although some feminist writers argue that any threat should suffice. The meaning of consent should not be equated with submission, and while every consent involves submission, every submission does not involve consent. Therefore, submitting to the inevitable and consent are not the same. From the limited facts given in *People (DPP) v Reid* [1993] 2 I.R. 186, it would appear that the rape occurred in circumstances somewhat similar to those in *Olugboja*, insofar as the victim's reaction was concerned. The conviction was upheld by the Court of Criminal Appeal, although the issue of consent was not raised on appeal.

The question that the meaning of consent raises is what kind of threat must the defendant make to the complainant before her consent can be said to have been vitiated? The conventional view is that there must be a threat of death or violence to either herself or somebody close to her, such as her child, capable of being carried out immediately. One of the important policy questions in this area is whether the fear should be judged subjectively from the standpoint of the complainant. Other policy issues on the meaning of consent relate to whether the concept of threat should be broadened out, e.g. if the victim has only one copy of a thesis and "consents" to intercourse so that the assailant will not destroy it.

FRAUD: IDENTITY OF THE ACTOR

At common law, fraud as to the nature of the act or the identity of the actor vitiated consent. If the actor misrepresents himself to be somebody with whom the woman would be agreeable to have sexual relations, does this vitiate her consent? Originally, the impersonation had to be of the victim's husband, but now this has been extended to the victim's partner.

It has been held that fraud as to the identity of the actor or the nature of the act will suffice. Under the Criminal Law (Amendment) Act 1885 and the Criminal Law (Amendment) Act 1935, rape is committed by a man who tricks a woman into having intercourse by impersonating her husband. In *R v Dee* (1884) 15 Cox C.C. 579, the Irish Court of Crown Cases Reserved held that where a married woman consented to the defendant having sexual intercourse with her under the impression that he was her husband, the defendant was guilty of rape. Late one evening, the victim's husband had gone out to fish so she went upstairs to her bedroom, lay down on the bed without undressing and fell asleep. She felt someone throw himself on her, whom she thought was her husband. When he came into the room she said to him in his presence and hearing "you came in very soon". He made no answer and had sexual intercourse with her. She then put up her hand and felt the man's hair and knew that it was not her husband. She did not consent after she discovered that the man was not her husband.

It is likely that an Irish court would hold that a mistake as to the identity of a (unmarried) sexual partner does vitiate consent to sexual intercourse. The choice of a partner, even outside marriage, is the predominant factor which determines whether the act of sexual intercourse takes place at all. A mistake as to the identity of that person is fundamental to the consent given. In *Papadimitropoulos v R* [1957] 98 C.L.R. 249, the High Court of Australia held that in determining whether an apparent consent is valid, it is the mistake or misapprehension that makes it so, and it is not the fraud producing the mistake that is material, so much as the mistake itself. Suppose, however, that a woman had intercourse with a man believing him to be her husband, although he had made no effort to deceive her in that regard, would the man be guilty of rape? It is not entirely clear if, in Ireland, the impersonation of somebody other than the complainant's husband amounts to rape. In *R v Elbekkay* [1995] Crim. L.R. 163, the Court of Appeal held that such impersonation did amount to rape. It is likely that the Irish superior courts will follow this line of reasoning.

Fraud: nature of the act

A person who procures sexual intercourse with a woman by fraudulently misrepresenting the nature of the act is guilty of rape. In *R v Flattery* (1877) 2 Q.B.D. 410, the Court of Crown Cases Reserved upheld a conviction where a man who had intercourse with a woman on the pretence that he was performing a surgical operation was convicted of rape. Likewise, in *R v Williams* [1923] 1 K.B. 340, the Court of Criminal Appeal upheld a conviction for rape where a singing teacher had intercourse with one of his pupils on the pretence that is would improve her breathing (a sham voice improvement operation). In both of these cases the victim had no idea that the act performed on them was sexual intercourse.

The limits on this principle became clear in *R v Linekar* [1995] 1 Q.B. 250, in which the defendant had sexual intercourse with a prostitute, having negotiated a fee in advance, and then made off without paying her. He was convicted of rape at first instance, but the Court of Criminal Appeal quashed the conviction on the basis that this type of fraud did not vitiate consent. The complainant knew the nature of the act and the identity of the actor. In other words, the fraud perpetrated as to the collateral issue of payment did not vitiate consent. Although there was evidence that the defendant had no intention of handing over the agreed sum of money, this did not constitute fraud to gain consent as the complainant had consented to the act of sexual intercourse. Thus, it appears that fraud by itself will not vitiate or negative the victim's consent.

SLEEP

Consent will be absent where the victim is asleep or is otherwise unconscious, for example, having taking alcohol. In *R v Mayes* (1872) 12 Cox C.C. 311, the Court of Criminal Appeal held that it was rape to have intercourse with a sleeping woman as she could not consent. A married woman was asleep in bed with her husband. The defendant got into bed and proceeded to have sexual intercourse with her while she was asleep. When she awoke, she at first thought it was her husband, but on hearing him speak, and seeing her husband at her side, she flung the defendant off, and called out to her husband while the accused ran away. He was convicted of the crime of rape. The prosecutrix did not consent before, after, or at the time of the defendant having sexual intercourse with her. It was against her will and the conduct of the prosecutrix did not lend the defendant to the belief that she did consent. Thus, while the victim is asleep she is incapable of consenting and, therefore, the intercourse will amount to an act of rape.

RENDERING THE VICTIM INSENSIBLE

If the victim did not have the capacity to give her consent to the act of intercourse, the perpetrator will be convicted of rape. In *R v Camplin* (1845) 1 Cox C.C. 22, the defendant had plied the complainant with drink in order, he said, to excite her, but in fact he rendered her insensible. Having had intercourse with her, he was convicted of rape, on the basis that she was incapable of giving her consent due to her state of intoxication. Being drunk of itself may not vitiate the victim's consent, unless the complainant was so drunk (intoxicated) that she would not have had the capacity to consent (cf. *R v Fletcher* (1859) 8 Cox C.C. 131). In *R v Lang* (1975) 62 Cr. App. R. 50, the Court of Appeal emphasised that being drunk of itself may not vitiate consent, but what is important is the effect of being drunk on the victim's state of mind at the time of the intercourse. In this case, the fact that the victim could give detailed evidence of the events tended to negate her argument that her state of drunkenness vitiated her consent to intercourse. The courts will be mindful of cases where the intercourse was in fact consensual but a jilted lover subsequently seeks her revenge, although such cases will be rare.

R v Bree [2007] EWCA Crim 256, concerned the issue of consent and intoxication of the complainant, and whether a person can consent to sexual activity when intoxicated. The defendant went to visit his brother. They went out for the evening with his brother's friends, including the complainant. They all drank a considerable amount of alcohol. The complainant remembered little about getting home, but once home remembers being sick and that the defendant and his brother washed her hair. The complainant remembered nothing after this until regaining consciousness and finding the defendant penetrating her sexually. The complainant agreed that she had not said "no", but asserted that she had never consented. The defendant accepted that the complainant was intoxicated but claimed that she was capable of consenting, had undressed herself and appeared willing. The jury convicted the defendant of rape and he appealed on the basis that the trial judge had not made it clear to the jury that a person can consent to sexual activity even when intoxicated. The Court of Appeal held:

> "If, through drink (or for any other reason) the complainant has temporarily lost her capacity to choose whether to have intercourse on the relevant occasion, she is not consenting ... However, where the complainant has voluntarily consumed even substantial quantities of alcohol, but nevertheless remains capable of choosing whether or not to have intercourse, and in drink agrees to do so, this would not be rape." [2007] EWCA Crim 256 at para.34

The appeal was allowed. *Bree* emphasises the importance of "capacity to consent" in cases when it appears that a complainant has been extremely affected by the voluntary consumption of drink and/or drugs.

Under s.3 of the Criminal Law (Amendment) Act 1885, it is an offence carrying a maximum of two years' imprisonment to administer a drug or alcohol "with intent to stupefy her" and then have intercourse with her (cf. Non-Fatal Offences Against the Person Act 1997 s.12 (offence of poisoning)).

REPRESENTATION OF MARRIAGE

Fraud as to the attributes of a partner will not vitiate consent. The attributes of a proposed partner have never been held sufficiently fundamental to vitiate consent; misrepresentations as to status do not alter the nature and quality of the act nor the identity of the partner. In *Papadimitropoulos v R* (1957) 98 C.L.R. 249, the victim, a young migrant speaking no English, had sexual intercourse with the defendant after being duped by him into believing that the notice of intention to marry which they had signed in a Melbourne registry office was, in fact, a marriage ceremony. The High Court of Australia held that the representation by the defendant to the complainant that he was married to her did not vitiate her consent to intercourse, and therefore, he was not guilty of rape. The victim's mistake was not as to the nature and quality of the act (sexual intercourse) or the defendant's identity, but rather as to his status in relation to her which the court held was not sufficiently fundamental to vitiate consent.

CONSENT AND DISCLOSURE

If the defendant has unprotected sex with the victim knowing that he has a sexually transmitted disease, but fails to inform the victim, will this vitiate consent? In *R v Cuerrier* [1998] 2 S.C.R. 371, the Canadian Supreme Court held that the defendant's failure to disclose an STD had vitiated consent to intercourse, because in the absence of disclosure about the STD there could not have been a true consent; in other words, the victim would not have consented to have intercourse with a partner who was HIV positive. The defendant was under a positive duty to disclose this fact because of the consequences of infecting the victim. The court did however, state that the fraud required to vitiate the victim's consent had to include a risk to serious bodily harm, so as to apparently exclude vexatious prosecutions based on fraud, such as in the case of a jilted lover.

R v EB [2006] EWCA Crim 2945, considered whether consent is vitiated and if a person is guilty of rape if he has consensual sex with another without disclosing HIV status. The defendant had sexual intercourse with the claimant. The defendant was HIV positive and failed to disclose this to the complainant. The question for the Court of Appeal was whether the apparent consent given by the complainant was ineffective as a result of the defendant's failure to disclose his status. The court held, at para.17, that a charge of rape could not lie in these circumstances:

> "Where one party to sexual activity has a sexually transmissible disease which is not disclosed to the other party any consent that may have been given to that activity by the other party is not thereby vitiated. The act remains a consensual act."

However, this ruling does not mean that there is a defence to a charge resulting from harm created by the sexual activity, but only relates to consent in sexual offences. It is imperative that consent must be free and informed. Therefore, if a sexual partner fails to disclose the fact that he or she has an STD then this would vitiate consent, as no reasonable person would have consented in those circumstances.

Under Irish criminal law, if a sexual partner failed to disclose the fact that he or she had an STD, this could result in a conviction for "causing serious harm", contrary to s.4 of the Non-fatal Offences Against the Person Act 1997.

DURATION OF CONSENT

Whereas penetration is necessary for sexual intercourse, the ordinary use of language makes it clear that sexual intercourse ceases only on withdrawal. In *Kaitamaki v R* [1985] A.C. 147, the New Zealand Court of Criminal Appeal held that the offence of rape is a continuing offence. If the complainant withdraws her consent at any time during the act of intercourse then the man must desist, otherwise he will be convicted of rape. Sexual intercourse is a continuing act and is only ended on withdrawal. In other words, the act of sexual intercourse was complete upon penetration, in that this is the defined minimum conduct necessary, but continued hereafter by the defendant's failure to withdraw. Therefore, an innocent act of a continuing nature can become criminal during its progress as a result of the change in the state of mind of the defendant. This was followed by the Court of Criminal Appeal in *R v Cooper and Schaub* [1994] Crim. L.R. 531, although the convictions in that case were quashed on other grounds. This has been a controversial aspect of the definition of rape. Some commentators suggest that *Kaitamaki* should no longer be followed, while others maintain that it is consistent with the practice established in *Fagan v Metropolitan Police Commissioner* [1969] 1 Q.B. 439, pertaining to the continuing act theory of the actus reus (see Ch.2).

RECKLESS ENDANGERMENT OF CHILDREN

Section 176 of the Criminal Justice Act 2006 creates a new offence whereby a person who has authority or control over a child, or over a person who has abused a child, intentionally or recklessly endangers the child by causing or permitting the child to be placed or left in a situation which creates a substantial risk to the child of being a victim of serious harm or sexual abuse, or of failing to take reasonable steps to protect a child from such a risk while knowing that the child is in such a situation. This offence is committed by a person who has authority or control over a child, or an abuser, and who intentionally or recklessly endangers a child (s.176(2)). Only the DPP may consent to a prosecution of an offence under this provision (s.176(3)). The punishment for this offence is a maximum of 10 years' imprisonment and/or an unlimited fine (s.176(4)).

CHILD TRAFFICKING AND PORNOGRAPHY

The Child Trafficking and Pornography Act 1998, as amended by s.6 of the Criminal Law (Sexual Offences) (Amendment) Act 2007, provides for several offences involving children under 17 years of age:

- Child trafficking and taking a child for sexual exploitation; the maximum penalty is life imprisonment.
- Meeting a child for the purpose of sexual exploitation; the maximum penalty is 14 years' imprisonment.
- Allowing a child to be used for child pornography; the maximum penalty is a €31,000 fine and/or 14 years' imprisonment.

- Producing, distributing, printing or publishing child pornography; the maximum penalty for a summary offence is €1,900 and/or one year's imprisonment; if convicted on indictment, the maximum penalty is an unlimited fine and/or 14 years' imprisonment.
- Possession of child pornography; the maximum penalty for a summary offence is €1,900 and/or a year's imprisonment; if convicted on indictment, the maximum penalty is €6,350 and/or five years' imprisonment.

The purpose of this legislation is to prohibit trafficking in, or the use of, children for the purposes of their sexual exploitation and the production, dissemination, handling or possession of child pornography.

FURTHER READING

Campbell, Kilcommins and O'Sullivan, *Criminal Law in Ireland: Cases and Commentary* (Dublin: Clarus Press, 2010), Ch.16.

Department of Justice, Equality and Law Reform, *The Law on Sexual Offences: A Discussion Paper* (Dublin: Stationery Office, 1998).

Gillespie, "Tackling Child Grooming on the Internet: The UK Approach" (2005) 10(1) B.R. 4.

Hanly, *An Introduction to Irish Criminal Law*, 2nd edn (Dublin: Gill & Macmillan, 2006), Ch.20.

Hanly, "Corroborating Rape Charges" (2001) 11(4) I.C.L.J. 2.

Law Reform Commission, *Report on Child Sexual Abuse* (LRC 32–1990).

Law Reform Commission, *Consultation Paper on Child Sexual Abuse* (August, 1989).

Law Reform Commission, *Consultation Paper on Rape* (December, 1987).

Law Reform Commission, *Report on Sexual Offences against the Mentally Handicapped* (LRC 33–1990).

Law Reform Commission, *Report on Rape and Allied Offences* (LRC 24–1988).

Leahy, "Hard Cases and Bad Law: An Overview of the Criminal law (Sexual Offences) Act 2006" (2008) 26 I.L.T. 38.

Leahy, "In a Woman's Voice: A Feminist Analysis of Irish Rape Law" (2008) 26 I.L.T. 203.

Ní Raifeartaigh, "Child Sexual Abuse Cases: The Need for Cultural Change within the Criminal Justice System (2009) 14(5) B.R. 103.

Ní Raifeartaigh, "Doctrine of Fresh Complaint in Sexual Cases" (1994) 12 I.L.T. 160.

O'Gara, "Protecting Young Girls from Themselves: The Development of the Mistake as to Age Defence in England, Wales and Canada" (2007) 25 I.L.T. 212.

O'Gara, "Protecting Young Girls from Themselves: Part III: Reform in Ireland" (2007) 25 I.L.T. 221.

O'Malley, *Sexual Offences: Law, Policy and Punishment* (Dublin: Round Hall, 1996).

O'Sullivan, "Protecting Young People from Themselves: Reform of the Age of Consent Law in Ireland" (2009) 31 D.U.L.J. 386.

Ring, "The Criminal Law (Sexual Offences) Act 1993" (1998) 3(7) B.R. 322.

Ryan, "Queering the Criminal Law: Some Thoughts on the Aftermath of Homosexual Decriminalisation" (1997) 7(1) I.C.L.J. 38.

Walsh, "Responding to Sexual Crime: The Need for a New Approach" (1999) 17 I.L.T. 310.

19. Theft and Fraud Offences

INTRODUCTION

The Criminal Justice (Theft and Fraud Offences) Act 2001 (the "2001 Act") modernised and consolidated the Irish criminal law governing theft and fraud offences. The provisions of the 2001 Act are substantially based on the Law Reform Commission *Report on the Law Relating to Dishonesty* (LRC 43–1992) and *Report of the Government Advisory Committee on Fraud* (Dublin: Stationery Office, 1993).

Prior to the 2001 Act, the pre-existing law on dishonesty was found mainly in common law and legislation including the Larceny Acts of 1861, 1916 and 1990, the Forgery Acts of 1861 and 1913, and the Falsification of Accounts Act 1875. The 2001 Act repealed all the major legislation dealing with larceny and related offences up until then. While pre-existing legislation dealt adequately with serious offences of dishonesty, there were difficulties caused by the fact that several different offences existed to deal with comparable dishonest behaviour. Furthermore, the pre-existing law did not always deal adequately with various forms of dishonesty, for instance, false statements as to future intentions.

The 2001 Act modernised the law and made provision for a range of offences dealing with dishonest behaviour and offences of forgery and counterfeiting. It consolidates the law on these offences, as with other offences of dishonesty. The 2001 Act also modified the law governing the investigation of offences and trial procedures.

OVERVIEW OF THE CRIMINAL JUSTICE (THEFT AND FRAUD OFFENCES) ACT 2001

The 2001 Act is a significant piece of legislation with 65 sections divided into nine parts. It was designed to modernise the law governing theft and related offences, their investigation and trial, and to give the force of law to provisions of the Convention on the Protection of the European Communities' Financial Interests 1995 and the Protocols to that Convention.

Part one is introductory and provides a general interpretation of words and phrases used in the definition of offences. It also provides for the abolition of the common law offences of larceny, burglary, robbery, cheating (except in relation to the public revenue), extortion under colour of office and forgery.

Part two provides for the main offences of theft and dishonesty. In addition to stealing, these offences include: deceiving another person or using a computer unlawfully such that the perpetrator makes a gain, receives a benefit or causes another to suffer a loss, failing to pay for goods or services, false accounting, burglary, robbery, and possessing articles for use in committing certain offences under the 2001 Act. Part three creates offences of handling or possessing stolen property and withholding information regarding stolen property. Part four amends the law on forgery and replaces the pre-existing statutory offences contained in the Forgery Acts of 1861 and 1913. It provides for the various offences on forgery and copying and use of false instruments for the purpose of inducing a person to accept these as genuine with consequent prejudice to that person. Part five creates offences against counterfeiting of currency notes and coins, including euro notes and coins, even before these have been issued. Part six contains measures to counter fraud offences affecting the European Communities financial interests and also corruption of or by officials. A significant feature of the 2001 Act is that it also includes measures designed to protect the European Communities' financial interests from fraud and corruption, and also measures for the protection of the euro. Part seven deals with the investigation of offences and provides for the granting of search warrants, forfeiture of property and orders to produce evidential material. Part eight deals with the trial of offences. It provides for summary trial of offences under the 2001 Act and for alternative verdicts pertaining to offences of stealing, handling or possessing stolen or unlawfully obtained property. Provision is also made for the restitution of property to the true owner and for the provision of documents to juries to assist them in their deliberations. Part 9 deals with miscellaneous issues, including: the use of an assumed name to commit an offence, the liability of bodies corporate, admissibility of certain documents as evidence in a criminal trial and amendments to certain legislative provisions.

Many provisions of the 2001 Act are closely modelled on the English Theft Act 1968, as amended, therefore English textbooks and relevant case law are useful for getting an understanding of concepts such as dishonesty, appropriation, deception and so forth.

REPEALS AND TRANSITIONAL PROVISION

When dealing with the offences created by the 2001 Act, it is important to have regard to s.2, which is an interpretation section providing definitions of important terms and concepts found elsewhere in the 2001 Act. Section 3(1) provides that legislation specified in the First Schedule is repealed to the extent set out therein, which includes: the Larceny Acts of 1861 and 1913, Forgery Acts of 1861 and 1916, Coinage Offences Act 1861, and the Falsification of Accounts Act 1875. Section 3(2) provides that the common law offences of larceny, burglary, robbery, cheating, extortion under colour of office and forgery are henceforth abolished. Section 3(3) provides that the abolition of these common law offences shall not affect proceedings for any such offence committed before their abolition. This is a "saving clause" to deal with transitional measures.

THEFT AND RELATED OFFENCES

The 2001 Act sets out the main offences of theft and dishonesty including: stealing, deceiving another person or using a computer unlawfully such that one makes a gain or receives a benefit or causes another to suffer a loss, failing to pay for goods or services, false accounting, burglary, robbery and possessing articles for use in committing certain offences.

THEFT

Section 4(1) provides that a person is guilty of theft where he dishonestly (without a claim of right made in good faith) appropriates property without the consent of its owner and with the intention of depriving (temporarily or permanently) the owner of that property. Section 2(1) defines "property" as including money; real and personal property.

Under s.4(2) no appropriation without consent is deemed to have occurred where the defendant honestly believed that he had consent, excluding consent obtained by deception, or where he honestly believed that the true owner could not be discovered. Section 4(3) pertains to property that is held on trust for, or on behalf of, more than one person by another person acting in the course of business, and where some of the property is appropriated for the latter's benefit without the consent of the owner or owners. Section 4(4) provides for the trial of an offence under s.4 and the matter of reasonable grounds for the defendant's belief that his or her actions do not amount to theft. Section 4(5) defines the words "appropriates" (usurps or adversely interferes with the owner's proprietary rights), and "depriving" (either temporarily or permanently) for the purposes of this offence. Section 4(6) provides that the maximum penalty on conviction for this offence is an unlimited fine and/or 10 years' imprisonment.

1. Actus reus

The actus reus of theft is the dishonest appropriation of property without the consent of its owner. This is a key element of the offence of theft. Section 2 defines "dishonesty" as meaning "without a claim of right made in good faith." Section 4(5) defines "appropriates" as: "in relation to property, means usurps or adversely interferes with the property rights of the owner of the property."

2. Mens rea

One crucial difference between the new offence of theft and the old offence of larceny is that larceny was not committed without intention to "permanently deprive the owner thereof." Intention to deprive permanently as opposed to temporarily deprive was required to prove the old offence of larceny. That is why it was necessary to create a special offence of taking a car without the owner's permission in s.112 of the Road Traffic Act (so-called "joy riding"), because unless the prosecution could prove an intention to deprive permanently, there was no larceny. Under the new offence of theft the mens rea is to permanently, temporarily or dishonestly appropriate property without the consent of the owner. However, there must be a dishonest appropriation in every case.

3. Appropriation

The Larceny Act 1916 defined the offence of larceny (the forerunner of theft) in terms of asportation (unlawful removal of goods from where they are deposited or stored). The defendant had to be proved to have taken and carried away the property that was the subject of the larceny. Appropriation is a much broader concept and it means that a theft of property may occur even though the property was originally obtained with the consent of the owner. Appropriation has proven to be a controversial concept in English law where it is also a key element of the Theft Act 1968. However, an important difference between the English and Irish legislation is that the latter expressly requires that the taking must be without the consent of the owner. The following cases illustrate the confusion caused in England by the absence of any requirement of consent from the definition of theft. In *Lawrence v Commissioner of Metropolitan Police* [1972] A.C. 626, an Italian national, who had little English, arrived in London and took a taxi to a particular address. The true fare was 52 pence, but the taxi driver told the passenger that it was £1. When they arrived at the address, the driver told the passenger that the fare was more than he had indicated. The passenger held out his open wallet and the driver took a further £6 from it. The question for the House of Lords was whether there was appropriation, notwithstanding the apparent consent of the victim. The House of Lords said that the concept of appropriation did not require the absence of consent. In *R v Morris* [1984] A.C. 320, the defendant had taken goods from a supermarket shelf and replaced their price tags with tags bearing lower prices. He then took them to the checkout and bought them at the lower prices. He was convicted of theft and the House of Lords upheld the conviction. However, the House of Lords gave a more restricted definition of appropriation, saying that it involved, "an act by way of adverse interference with or usurpation of" the owner's rights, and that this will generally involve some unauthorised act. In *R v Gomez* [1993] A.C. 442, the House of Lords was called upon to resolve the obvious tension between *Lawrence* and *Morris*. In other words, how necessary, if at all, was absence of consent in order to constitute appropriation? In *Gomez*, an employee of a store persuaded his manager to sell goods to a friend for a cheque which he (Gomez) knew to be worthless. The House of Lords followed *Lawrence* and held that whether the act was done with the owner's consent or authority was immaterial. In *R v Hinks* [2001] 2 A.C. 241, the defendant befriended a man of limited intelligence and received substantial gifts of money (£60,000) from him. She was convicted of theft and the question for the House of Lords was whether this conviction could stand. Surprisingly, the House of Lords, by a majority of four to one, held that this amounted to an appropriation. The expression "appropriation" as used in the Theft Act and explained in *Gomez* was "value neutral" involving any assumption by a person of the rights of the owner. The problem with this decision is that the gift in question was a perfectly valid gift under the private law of personal property.

The true significance of the position in Irish criminal law would probably come to light in a *Hinks*-type scenario. If such a case arose in Ireland, the question would be whether the transfer of the money amounted to an act which usurped or adversely interfered with the property rights of the owner. Crucially, also, the question would be whether the money was obtained without the consent of the owner. Needless to say, in all such cases, it is not enough that there be appropriation, but such appropriation must also have been dishonest.

4. Dishonestly

As noted above, the word "dishonest" is defined to mean, "without a claim of right made in good faith." Take, then, the situations in *Lawrence, Morris* and *Gomez*. Did any of them involve a claim of right made in good faith? In the vast majority of cases, dishonesty, or the lack of it, will be patently obvious. In this respect, the cases decided under s.1 of the Larceny Act 1916 may still be of relevance, because under that section it was necessary that the property be taken and carried away, "without a claim of right made in good faith." In *People (AG) v Grey* [1944] I.R. 326, the defendant was entitled to free fuel and gas from his employer under his conditions of employment. In wartime conditions, it was not possible for the employer to supply this, so the defendant took some batteries from his employer. He believed that he was entitled to do this in lawful substitution for the other fuel and the Court of Criminal Appeal held that he was entitled to raise this as a defence. In *People (DPP) v O'Loughlin* [1979] I.R. 85, the Court of Criminal Appeal held that the defendant's belief that he was entitled to take certain goods belonging to another to enforce a debt due to him constituted a claim of right on good faith.

The leading English case on the meaning of dishonesty under the Theft Act 1968 is *R v Ghosh* [1982] Q.B. 1053, where two basic principles were laid down. First, dishonesty is a matter for the jury to decide. Secondly, dishonesty is something in the mind of the defendant. The Court of Appeal held that the jury should decide whether the defendant was acting dishonestly in two stages. First, the jury must first decide whether, according to the ordinary standards of reasonable and honest people, what was done was dishonest. If it was not dishonest by those standards, then that is the end of the matter and the prosecution fails. Secondly, if it was dishonest by those standards, then the jury must decide if the defendant himself had realised that what he was doing was dishonest by those standards.

5. Exceptions to theft

Section 5(1) provides for several exceptions to the offence of theft:

> Where property or a right or interest in property is or purports to be transferred for value to a person acting in good faith, no later assumption by that person of rights which that person believes himself or herself to be acquiring shall, by reason of any defect in the transferor's title, amount to theft of the property.

This covers a situation where a person buys property in good faith from a person who does not in fact have title to it. It may be that the property is stolen. Suppose the buyer later finds out that this is the case, but continues to hold on to the property. Under the basic definition of theft in s.4, he would be guilty of theft, but he is saved by s.5(1). However, it is essential that he should be acting in good faith in the first place when he acquired the property. Note that all this does is to protect the innocent purchaser from liability for theft. The title to the property under civil law might well be a different matter. Thus, under s.5(1) a transfer of property will not constitute the offence of theft where the defendant obtained property for value and in good faith but it subsequently transpires that the property had been stolen.

Other exceptions are set out in s.5(2). It is not possible to steal land or things forming part of land and severed from it. However, a defendant can be convicted of theft if he was a trustee or company liquidator, then sells or disposes of land or appropriates it for personal benefit. Likewise, a defendant can be convicted where, although not in possession of the land, nevertheless dishonestly appropriates anything forming part of the land by severing it. Similarly, a defendant can be convicted of theft if he was a tenant or licensee of property and dishonestly appropriates anything in breach of the tenancy or license agreement. Section 5(3) defines the meaning of land, tenancy and license for the purposes of the offence of theft. Sections 5(4) and 5(5) exempt the picking of wild flowers, fruit, and the taking of wild creatures not already in another's possession from the offence of theft.

Section 5 lists particular circumstances in which theft does not take place and also certain forms of property which cannot be stolen. As to the latter, land cannot be stolen, nor can anything forming part of the land. There are certain exceptions to this. A trustee (who holds the title of property for the benefit of another) can be responsible for stealing land. Also, a person not in possession of land may be held guilty of theft by appropriating something forming part of the land by severing it, or causing it to be severed, or taking it after it has been severed. This would apply, for instance, to cutting down trees or taking crops growing on the land. It is further provided that a person does not commit theft by picking mushrooms or other fungus growing wild on land or by picking wild flowers, fruit or foliage growing wild unless he does so for reward or for sale or for other commercial purposes. Suppose a person goes on to somebody else's land, uproots a tree or shrub growing wild on that land and plants it in their own garden; is such a person guilty of theft? Suppose someone picks blackberries growing along the side of a field, makes blackberry jam with them and sells that jam at the English Market on a Saturday; would they be guilty of theft? Should the outcome be different if that person gave the jam as a present to their aunt Sally?

Wild creatures, tamed or untamed, are regarded as property, but a person cannot steal a wild creature that is not tamed or ordinarily kept in captivity, or the carcass of such a creature, unless it has been reduced into possession by, or on behalf of, another person, and possession of it has not since been lost or abandoned. Would a person be guilty of theft if he stole a snake from Dublin zoo and sold it to a pet shop? Should the answer be different if he kept it as a pet? Suppose a person happened to meet a penguin that had clearly escaped from Dublin zoo sauntering along a pathway in the Phoenix Park, and kept it; would they be guilty of theft? Would a person be guilty if he shot a pheasant on a neighbour's land, or took a dead rabbit from a trap which had been set by a neighbour on his own land? Suppose a neighbour had a shooting party, several pheasants were shot and bagged, but none of the party noticed that one dead pheasant remained uncollected. The next day, after all members of the shooting party had gone home, someone went on to the land, found the dead pheasant, and kept it; are they guilty of theft?

MAKING GAIN OR CAUSING LOSS BY DECEPTION

Section 6 provides that it is an offence to dishonestly induce another person to do, or not to do, some act with the intention of making a gain for oneself or some other person or causing a loss to another. This offence might be committed where an employer dishonestly induces employees to agree to have their salary deducted for a pension scheme but the employer fails to pay the monies received to that scheme. Another example could be where people are dishonestly induced to pay a deposit and subsequently purchase a house at the advertised price on the premise that this is the last house available, whereas in fact there are many houses still available to be purchased (perhaps at a lower price) in that particular building development scheme. The maximum penalty on conviction on indictment is an unlimited fine and/or five years' imprisonment.

OBTAINING SERVICES BY DECEPTION

Section 7(1) provides that it is an offence for a person by any deception to dishonestly obtain services with the intention of making a gain, either personally or for another, or causing loss to any person. Obtaining services from another arises where that other is induced to confer a benefit on the understanding that it will be paid for. Examples of this offence might include failing to pay a tradesman once the agreed work has been completed, or obtaining a loan that is never repaid in breach of an agreement. The maximum penalty on conviction on indictment is an unlimited fine and/or five years' imprisonment (s.7(4)).

MAKING OFF WITHOUT PAYMENT

Section 8(1) provides that it is an offence for a person, knowing that payment on the spot is required or expected, to dishonestly make off without paying for the goods or services received with the intention of avoiding payment on the spot. An exception to this is where the payment would not be legally enforceable (s.8(2)). Section 8(3) permits any person to arrest without warrant an offender in the act of committing the offence of making off without payment. A Garda is permitted to arrest without warrant a person whom they, with reasonable cause, suspect has committed an offence under this provision (s.8(4)). Under ss.8(5) and 8(6) where a person other than a Garda effects an arrest under this provision, there must be reasonable grounds to suspect that the arrested person is attempting to avoid, or is avoiding, arrest by a Garda and that the arrest is for the purpose of handing the person over to the Gardaí as soon as possible. Examples of this offence include failing to pay for a meal consumed at a restaurant, or failing to pay for petrol at a self-service petrol station. Section 8(7) provides that the maximum penalty on conviction on indictment is a €3,800 fine and/or two years' imprisonment.

Unlawful use of a computer

Section 9(1) provides that it is an offence to dishonestly, within the State or outside the State, operate or cause to be operated, a computer within the State with the intention of making a gain for oneself or for another or causing a loss to another. This offence amplifies and is a more serious offence than s.5 of the Criminal Damage Act 1991, which created the offence of unauthorised accessing of data, also known as computer hacking. The maximum penalty on conviction on indictment is an unlimited fine and/or 10 years' imprisonment (s.9(2)).

False accounting

Section 10 provides that the offence of false accounting is committed where a person, intending to make a gain for oneself or another or to cause loss to another, does any of the following:

(a) destroys, defaces, conceals or falsifies any account or any document made or required for any accounting purpose;
(b) fails to make or complete any account or any such document; or
(c) in furnishing information for any purpose produces or makes use of any account, or any such document, which to his or her knowledge is or may be misleading, false or deceptive in a material particular.

Falsifying accounts or documents is committed where a person makes, or concurs in making, an entry that is or may be misleading, false or deceptive in a material particular, or omits, or concurs in omitting, a material particular there from.

The maximum penalty on conviction on indictment is an unlimited fine and/or 10 years' imprisonment (s.10(3)).

Suppression of documents

Section 11 criminalises the dishonest use of valuable securities and other documents for the purpose of realising a benefit or causing loss. Section 11(1) provides that it is an offence to dishonestly destroy, deface or conceal certain documents, including valuable securities, wills or other testamentary documents, with the intention of making a gain for oneself or another or causing a loss to another. It is also an offence to dishonestly, by any deception, procure the execution of a valuable security with the intention of making a gain for oneself or another or causing a loss to another (s.11(2)). Section 11(3) defines what is meant by "valuable security", which includes any document creating, transferring, surrendering or releasing any right to, in or over property; authorising the payment of money or delivery of any property; or the payment of money or delivery of any property or the satisfaction of any obligation. The maximum penalty on conviction on indictment is an unlimited fine and/or 10 years' imprisonment (s.11(4)).

Burglary

Section 12(1) provides that a person is guilty of burglary if they enter a building (including inhabited vehicles or vessels or other structures) as a trespasser intending to commit an arrestable offence or, being present as a trespasser, commits or attempts to commit an arrestable offence, which is an offence carrying a penalty of at least five years' imprisonment upon conviction (Criminal Law Act 1997, s.2(1)). The maximum penalty on conviction on indictment under s.12 is an unlimited fine and/or 14 years' imprisonment (s.12(3)).

The actus reus of burglary is entering a premises as a trespasser to commit an arrestable offence or being on the premises as a trespasser to commit or attempt to commit such an offence. An effective entry does not have to be complete or substantial. In *R v Brown* [1985] Crim. L.R. 212, the defendant was seen leaning through a broken shop window with the top half of his body inside the shop premises as though he was rummaging around. His feet were on the ground outside the shop and he claimed that he could not be said to have entered a building if only part of his body had been inside. The Court of Appeal held that it was not necessary for the entry to be complete or even substantial, so long as the entry was effective for the defendant to commit the ulterior offence. The fact that the defendant had partially entered the shop through a broken window was sufficient to constitute an effective entry.

The mens rea has two elements: first, entering a premise as a trespasser or being reckless as to whether the defendant was trespassing; secondly, the defendant must have the mens rea for the arrestable offence committed.

Section 13 provides that aggravated burglary consists of burglary committed in circumstances where the perpetrator has with him, when the offence is committed, a firearm, imitation firearm, weapon of offence or explosive. The maximum penalty on conviction on indictment for aggravated burglary is imprisonment for life (s.13(3)).

Robbery

Section 14(1) provides that a person who steals (theft) will be guilty of robbery if he steals from another person, at the time of committing the offence or immediately before the stealing, and in order to do so, he uses force on any person or puts or seeks to put any person in fear of being subjected to force. The use of, or threatened use of, force is intended to facilitate the stealing. The threat of force does not have to be directed at the owner of property and could, for instance, be directed at a family member, official or employee. The maximum penalty upon conviction on indictment is imprisonment for life (s.14(2)).

Possession of certain articles

Section 15(1) provides that it is an offence for a person to have in his possession any article, when not at his or her own residence, with the intent that it be used in the course of or in connection with certain offences including: theft, burglary, offences involving deception, blackmail, extortion and unauthorised taking of a vehicle. Section 15(2) provides that it is also an offence to possess, without lawful authority or reasonable excuse, any article made or adapted for use in the course of or in connection with the commission of any of the above offences. An example of this offence might include possession of an ATM skimming device or housebreaking implements. Provision is made for the forfeiture and destruction of such articles following conviction, final appeal or the expiry of the time for appeal (ss.15(3) and (4)). The maximum penalty on conviction on indictment is an unlimited fine and/or five years' imprisonment (s.15(5)).

Handling Stolen Property and Other Proceeds of Crime

Section 16(1) defines words and phrases used for these offences, including: the "principal offender", "reckless" and "substantial risk" in regard to handling stolen property. "Principal offender" means the person who has stolen or otherwise unlawfully obtained the property alleged to have been handled or possessed. A person is "reckless" if he or she disregards a substantial risk that the property handled is stolen. "Substantial risk" means a risk of such a nature and degree that, having regard to the circumstances in which the person acquired the property and the extent of the information then available to him or her, its disregard involves culpability of a high degree.

Handling stolen property

Section 17(1) provides that the offence of handling stolen property consists of dishonestly receiving, arranging to receive, undertaking or assisting in, its retention or removal (other than in the course of stealing), knowing it was stolen, or being reckless as to whether it was stolen. Section 17(2) provides that a person is guilty of handling stolen property if (otherwise than in the course of the stealing) he, knowing that the property was stolen or being reckless as to whether it was stolen, dishonestly receives or arranges to receive it, or undertakes, or assists in, its retention, removal, disposal or realisation by or for the benefit of another person, or arranges to do so. Where a person handles stolen property in circumstances where it is reasonable to conclude that he knew, or was reckless as to whether it was stolen, he will be taken to have known or to have been reckless, unless the court is satisfied that there is a reasonable doubt on this issue.

Section 17(3) provides that a person may be charged, prosecuted and convicted of handling stolen property even if the principal offender (who could be convicted of theft if tried and convicted) has not been convicted. Thus, a pawnbroker could be convicted in circumstances where the perpetrator has not been detected, charged, prosecuted and convicted of theft. Under s.17(4) the maximum penalty on conviction on indictment is an unlimited fine and/or 10 years' imprisonment. However, this penalty is subject to the proviso that the defendant will not be liable to have a penalty imposed greater than that permitted for the principal offence (theft).

Possession of stolen property

Section 18(1) provides that it is an offence for a person, without lawful authority or excuse, to possess stolen property, other than in the course of stealing, knowing, or being reckless as to whether, the property was in fact stolen. Section 18(2) provides that a person who has stolen property in his possession in such circumstances that it is reasonable to conclude that he knew or was reckless as to whether the property was stolen, will be taken to have known or been reckless unless the court or jury, depending on whether the offence is tried summarily or on indictment, is satisfied that there is a reasonable doubt. Section 18(3) provides that a person may be charged and convicted of possessing stolen property even if the principal offender has not been previously convicted. Section 18(4) provides that the maximum penalty on conviction on indictment is an unlimited fine and/or five years' imprisonment. However, this is subject to the proviso that the defendant will not have a sanction imposed greater than that permitted for the principal offence (theft).

Withholding information regarding stolen property

Section 19(1) provides for where a Garda has reasonable grounds for believing that an offence consisting of stealing property or of handling stolen property has been committed. If he finds any person in possession of any property, and has reasonable grounds for believing that the property includes, or may include, stolen property, or the whole or any part of the proceeds of that property or part, and informs the person of his or her belief, the Garda is empowered to require any person to account for how he came by any property in his possession. Section 19(2) provides that failure or refusal, without reasonable excuse, to give such account, or give false information, is an offence. The penalty on summary conviction is a maximum fine of £1,500 and/or 12 months' imprisonment. However, this will only apply where the person was told in ordinary language of the consequences of failure or refusal to provide the information (s.19(3)).

Section 19(4) provides that any information given in compliance with a demand under this section shall not be admissible in evidence against the person providing such information, or his or her spouse, in any criminal proceedings, except in relation to the offence of failure or refusal to give the account when requested.

SCOPE OF OFFENCES RELATING TO STOLEN PROPERTY

Section 20 provides that the offences of handling stolen property and other proceeds of crime apply whether the stealing occurred before or after the commencement of the 2001 Act, and also to stealing outside the State. For this purpose, stolen property also includes the proceeds of the disposal of stolen property, such as monies received from the sale of stolen paintings or other artefacts. Property that has been returned to its rightful owner will no longer be considered as stolen (s.20(3)).

AMENDMENT OF SECTION 31 OF THE CRIMINAL JUSTICE ACT 1994

Section 21 of the 2001 Act substitutes a new s.31 of the Criminal Justice Act 1994 act which deals with money laundering. The new s.31 provides that it is an offence for a person to do any of a number of things in relation to property without lawful excuse, knowing or believing, or being reckless as to whether, that property is or represents the proceeds of criminal conduct. This offence includes: converting, transferring, handling or removing the property from the State intending to conceal its true nature, source, location, disposition, movement or ownership or any rights with respect to it; assisting another person to avoid prosecution for criminal conduct concerned; or avoiding the making of a confiscation order. Other offences covered include concealing or disguising its true nature, or acquiring or possessing the property. The maximum penalty for this offence is an unlimited fine and/or 14 years' imprisonment. Other provisions in the new s.31 relate to knowledge or recklessness in respect of the source of the property, assumptions in relation to the intention of persons in connection with the property, definitions of words and phrases used in s.31, and proof of foreign law where criminal activity allegedly occurred outside the Irish State (cf. *Burns v Governor and Company of the Bank of Ireland* [2008] 1 I.R. 762).

Amendment of section 56A of the Criminal Justice Act 1994

Section 22 is a technical amendment to s.56A of the Criminal Justice Act 1994, in consequence of the new s.31 of the 1994 Act. This provides that in relation to an offence under the law of a country or territory, other than the Irish State references in Pt IV of the 1994 Act, dealing with money laundering shall be construed as including references to revenue offences.

Amendment of the Criminal Justice Act 1994

Section 23 amends s.57 of the Criminal Justice Act 1994 by the insertion of a new s.57A. This new section governs the designation of certain states or territorial units, which in the opinion of the Minister for Justice, after consultation with the Minister for Finance, has not put in place adequate procedures for the detection of money laundering.

Forgery and Related Offences

Section 24 Act sets out definitions of words and phrases used in relation to forgery and related offences, including the meaning of instrument as including: any document, disc, tape, postage stamp, revenue stamp, social services card, cheque card, credit card and admission tickets.

Forgery

Section 25(1) provides that a person who makes a false instrument intending it to be used to induce another person to accept it as genuine, resulting in prejudice to the person accepting it, will be guilty of forgery. The maximum penalty on conviction on indictment is an unlimited fine and/or 10 years' imprisonment (s.25(2)).

Using a false instrument

Section 26(1) provides that it is an offence to use a false instrument, knowing or believing it to be a false instrument, intending to induce a person to accept it as genuine and thereby causing that person to do some act, or to make some omission, or to provide some service, to the prejudice of that person or any other person. The maximum penalty on conviction on indictment is an unlimited fine and/or 10 years' imprisonment (s.26(2)).

Copying a false instrument

Section 27(1) provides that it is an offence for a person to make a copy of an instrument, knowing or believing it to be a false instrument, intending that it shall be used to induce another person to accept it as a copy of a genuine instrument and, by reason of so accepting it, to do some act, or to make some omission, or to provide some service, to the prejudice of that person or any other person that it should pass to as genuine, and thereby causing loss to any person accepting it as genuine. The maximum penalty on conviction on indictment is an unlimited fine and/or 10 years' imprisonment (s.27(2)).

USING A COPY OF A FALSE INSTRUMENT

Section 28(1) provides that it is an offence for a person to use a copy of a false instrument, knowing or believing it to be false, with the intention of inducing another person to accept it as a copy of a genuine instrument. The maximum penalty on conviction on indictment is an unlimited fine and/or 10 years' imprisonment (s.28(2)).

CUSTODY OR CONTROL OF CERTAIN FALSE INSTRUMENTS

Section 29(1) provides that it is an offence to have custody or control of certain false instruments with the intention that they shall be used to induce another person to accept them as genuine and, by reason of so accepting them, to do some act, or to make some omission, or to provide some service, to the prejudice of that person or any other person. It is also an offence to have custody or control of such instruments without lawful authority or excuse (s.29(2)). Custody or control of a machine or other apparatus for making false instruments or intending to make such instruments is an offence (s.29(3)), in addition to having custody or control of such machine or other apparatus without lawful authority or excuse (s.29(4)).

Section 29(5) sets out what is meant by machine and includes: any disk, tape, drive or other device on or in which a program is recorded or stored by mechanical, electronic or other means, being a program designed or adapted to enable an instrument to be made or to assist in its making. Those subsections shall apply and have effect accordingly.

Section 29(6) provides that the maximum penalties for offences under the section are an unlimited fine and/or five years' imprisonment for offences under subss.(2) or (4), and an unlimited fine and/or 10 years' imprisonment for offences under subss.(1) or (3).

MEANING OF "FALSE" AND "MAKING"

Section 30 defines the meaning of a false instrument for the purposes of forgery and related offences. A false instrument is one that purports to be something which it is not because, inter alia, it was not authorised by the person who had authority to authorise it. Furthermore, a person will be treated as making a false instrument if that person alters an instrument so as to make it false.

Meaning of "Prejudice" and "Induce"

Section 31 provides that "prejudice" arises where a person loses property, is deprived of an opportunity to earn remuneration, where another is given the opportunity to earn remuneration or gain financial advantage, or where a person accepts a false instrument as genuine. The meaning of "inducing" includes persuading a machine to respond to the instrument as if it were genuine.

Counterfeiting and Related Offences

Section 32 defines currency, note and coin to mean those lawfully issued or customarily used as money in the Irish State or any other state, including euro notes and coins, whether issued or not. A counterfeit includes items that look like genuine currency notes and coins. Items that represent one side only of a currency note or of parts of currency notes are also deemed counterfeits.

Counterfeiting currency notes and coins

Section 33(1) provides that it is an offence to make a counterfeit currency note or coin intending that it shall pass as genuine. The maximum penalty on conviction on indictment is an unlimited fine and/or 10 years' imprisonment (s.33(2).

Passing counterfeit currency notes or coins

Section 34(1) provides that it is an offence for a person to pass or tender as genuine a counterfeit or deliver a counterfeit to another intending it to be passed as genuine; s.34(2). The maximum penalty on conviction on indictment is an unlimited fine and/or 10 years' imprisonment for an offence under s.34(1), and an unlimited fine and/or five years' imprisonment for an offence under s.34(2).

Custody or control of counterfeit currency notes and coins

Section 35(1) provides that it is an offence to have custody or control of counterfeit notes or coins intending to pass them as genuine or to deliver them to another to pass as genuine. Custody or control of such a counterfeit without lawful authority or excuse is also an offence (s.35(2). The maximum penalty on conviction on indictment is an unlimited fine and/or 10 years' imprisonment for an offence under s.35(1), and an unlimited fine and/or five years' imprisonment for an offence under s.35(2).

Materials and Implements for Counterfeiting

Section 36(1) provides that it is an offence to make or have in one's custody or control any thing intending to use it, or to permit another to use it or to make a counterfeit of a currency note or coin intending it to be passed or tendered as genuine. It is also an offence to have custody or control, without lawful authority or excuse, of any thing that has been specially designed or adapted for making a counterfeit of a currency note or coin (s.36(2)). Section 36(3) provides that the maximum penalty on conviction on indictment is an unlimited fine and/or 10 years' imprisonment for an offence under s.36(1), and an unlimited fine and/or five years' imprisonment for an offence under s.36(2).

Import and Export of Counterfeits

Section 37(1) provides that it is an offence for a person, without lawful authority or excuse, to import into or export from a Member State of the European Union a counterfeit of a currency note or coin. The maximum penalty on conviction on indictment is an unlimited fine and/or 10 years' imprisonment (s.37(1)).

Convention on Protection of European Communities' Financial Interests

Section 40(1) sets out the definitions of words and phrases used in relation to offences against the European Communities financial interests, including: the meaning of active corruption, passive corruption, community official, national officials (including Government Ministers), the Attorney General, members of Dáil or Seanad, members of the judiciary, and the Director of Public Prosecutions. Section 40(2) sets out the circumstances in which a person will be deemed to have benefited from, or derived pecuniary advantage from, fraud or money laundering.

Convention and Protocols

Section 41 provides that the Convention on Protection of European Communities' Financial Interests and Specified Protocols, with the exception of certain articles, will have the force of law in the Irish State and judicial notice shall be taken of them. Judicial notice shall also be taken of rulings, decisions and opinions of the Court of Justice of the European Communities on the meaning or effect of the Convention and Protocols.

Fraud affecting European Communities' financial interests

Section 42(1) provides that it is an offence to commit, participate in or obtain benefit or advantage from a fraud affecting the European Communities' financial interests. The maximum penalty is an unlimited fine and/or five years' imprisonment.

Active corruption

Section 43 provides that "active corruption" is an offence. Active corruption pertains to promising or giving an advantage to an official to act, or refrain from acting, in accordance with his duty, or to exercise his functions in breach of duty, which is damaging to or likely to damage the European Communities' financial interests. The maximum penalty on conviction on indictment is an unlimited fine and/or five years' imprisonment.

Passive corruption

Section 44 provides that "passive corruption" is an offence. Passive corruption pertains to an action of an official requesting or receiving advantage, or accepting a promise of advantage, to act or refrain from acting in accordance with his or her duty or to exercise his or her functions in breach of duty, which is damaging to or likely to damage the European Communities' financial interests. The maximum penalty on conviction on indictment is an unlimited fine and/or five years' imprisonment.

Extra-territorial jurisdiction of certain offences

Section 45(1) provides that it is an offence to commit, participate in or instigate any fraud affecting the European Communities' financial interests, or an offence of money laundering outside the Irish State, where a benefit is obtained by a person in the State, or where assistance in their commission is rendered by a person within the State, or where the offender is an Irish citizen or a national or European Community official. Active or passive corruption committed outside the State is also an offence where the offender is an Irish citizen or a national or Community official (s.45(2)). The maximum penalty on conviction on indictment is an unlimited fine and/or five years' imprisonment (s.45(3)).

Restriction on certain proceedings

Section 46(1) provides that proceedings for an offence under s.42 may only be taken by or with the consent of the DPP. The DPP is permitted to cooperate with the appropriate authorities in another Member State with a view to deciding which country is the more appropriate one in which to prosecute a person for such an offence (s.46(2)). Proceedings may be taken anywhere in the State for the offence (s.46(3)). Where the offence is also an offence under s.38 of the Extradition Act 1965, which deals with offences committed abroad by Irish citizens, then proceedings shall not be taken under s.38 of the 2001 Act (s.46(4)).

EXTRADITION FOR REVENUE OFFENCES

Section 47 provides that extradition for fraud against the European Communities' Financial Interests or money laundering will not be refused solely on the ground that the offence constitutes a revenue offence, as defined in the Extradition Act 1965.

INVESTIGATION OF OFFENCES

The 2001 Act also deals with the investigation of offences, including the granting of search warrants, forfeiture of property and orders to produce evidential material.

SEARCH WARRANTS

Section 48 provides that search warrants shall only be granted in the case of offences under the 2001 Act that carry a penalty of at least five years' imprisonment. A District judge may grant a search warrant where evidence is given on oath by a Garda that there are reasonable grounds to suspect that evidence relating to such an offence is to be found in a specified place (s.48(2)). A search warrant will authorise the Gardaí to enter, within seven days of its issue, to search the place and any persons found therein and to examine or seize anything reasonably believed to be evidence relating to the offence (s.48(3)). It shall also authorise the copying of documents or records, the seizure of computers containing records and the operation of a computer by the Gardaí, including: the provision of passwords and copies of records and other pertinent information (ss.48(4) and (5)). However, items subject to legal privilege shall not be seized (s.48(6)). The power to issue search warrants under s.48 is in addition to any other power to issue such warrants.

Obstruction of Garda acting on warrant

Section 49(1) provides that it is an offence for a person to obstruct a Garda executing a search warrant, to refuse to identify oneself to the Garda if found on premises being searched, or to fail to provide computer passwords or computer records or other pertinent information when requested. The maximum penalty on summary conviction is a maximum €635 fine and/or six months' imprisonment. Section 49(2) provides that a Garda may arrest without warrant any person who is committing an offence under this section or whom the member suspects, with reasonable cause, of having done so.

Forfeiture of seized property

Section 50(1) applies to property seized by the Gardaí (whether the seizure was effected by virtue of a warrant under s.48 or otherwise), which they suspect is being used in connection with forgery or counterfeiting. Where property has been seized, the Gardaí can apply to the District Court for an order for the forfeiture and destruction of that property (s.50(2)). Where a defendant has been convicted of an offence of forgery or counterfeiting, the court may order the forfeiture and destruction of property used in the commission of the offence (s.50(3)). However, before making an order for the forfeiture of property under this section, the court may hear submissions from the owner of the seized property (s.50(4)).

Concealing facts disclosed by documents

Section 51(1) provides that it is an offence for a person, knowing or suspecting that the Gardaí are investigating an offence under the 2001 Act, to falsify, conceal or destroy any document relevant to the investigation of offences. Where a person falsifies, conceals, destroys or otherwise disposes of a document, in circumstances where it is reasonable to conclude that he knew or suspected an investigation was being carried out and that the document was relevant to it, the person will be taken to have known or suspected the investigation was being carried out, unless the court or jury having considered the evidence, is satisfied otherwise (s.51(2)). The maximum penalty on conviction on indictment is an unlimited fine and/or five years' imprisonment (s.51(3)).

Order to produce evidential material

Section 52 applies to offences under the 2001 Act that carry a penalty of at least five years' imprisonment (subs.(1)). Section 52(2) provides that where a Garda gives evidence on oath and the District Court is satisfied that the Gardaí are investigating an offence where a person has possession or control of particular material, and there are reasonable grounds for suspecting that it is evidence of the offence, the court may order that the material be produced to the Gardaí. Material contained on computer must be provided in legible form (s.52(3)). Under s.52(4) an order made in accordance with s.52 also empowers the Gardaí to take copies of documents, but there is no right to produce documents that are subject to legal privilege. Section 52(5) provides that material taken away following a production order may be used in evidence in any criminal proceedings. Section 52(6) pertains to the use of such documents in criminal proceedings. However, it excludes their use where the document is subject to legal privilege or was provided by a person who may not be compelled by the prosecution to give evidence or was compiled for the purpose of or in contemplation of court or other proceedings. Section 52(7) provides that an order to produce material may be varied by the District Court. The penalty for failure to comply with a production order is a maximum fine of €1,900 and/or 12 months' imprisonment (s.52(8)).

Trial of Offences

The 2001 Act also deals with the trial of offences and provides for summary trial of offences and for alternative verdicts pertaining to offences of stealing, handling or possessing stolen property or unlawfully obtained property. It also provides for the restitution of property to the true owner and for the provision of documents to juries to assist them in their deliberations.

Summary trial of indictable offences

Section 53 provides that the District Court may summarily try a person charged with an indictable offence under the 2001 Act, where the court considers that the facts disclose a minor offence fit to be tried summarily. The defendant agrees to summary disposal of the offence and the DPP consents to this process. Partly for this reason, there is a dearth of case law from the superior courts on the meaning and scope of principal offences created by the 2001 Act.

Trial procedure

Section 54(1) provides that in proceedings for offences under ss.6, 7, 9, 10 and 11 it shall be sufficient for the prosecution to prove that the defendant acted dishonestly with the intention of causing a loss or making a gain. Section 54(2) provides that any number of persons may be charged in the same indictment with having, at different times or at the same time, handled or possessed all or any of the stolen property, and the persons so charged may be tried together. Under s.54(3), a partner or part beneficial owner of property may be charged with stealing where he steals any property belonging to the partnership or other beneficial owners. Where a person is charged with stealing property and it appears that the property was stolen at different times, s.52(4) permits up to three separate charges to be tried together, unless the trial judge directs otherwise, provided those takings occurred within a six-month period. Section 54(5) provides that charges of stealing, handling or possessing any property or any part thereof may be included in separate counts of the same indictment and such counts may be tried together. Section 54(6) provides that any person or persons charged in the same indictment with separate counts of stealing may be found guilty of stealing, handling or possessing the property or any part thereof. Where more than one person is charged with jointly handling or possessing stolen property, s.54(7) allows the court (summary trial) or jury (trial on indictment) to find any of them guilty of handling or possession based on the evidence.

ALTERNATIVE VERDICTS

Section 55(1) provides that a person charged with theft may be found guilty of handling or possession if the facts prove the alternative verdict. If the defendant is charged with handling or possession he may be found guilty of theft, if the facts prove theft (s.55(2)).

ORDERS FOR RESTITUTION

Section 56(1) provides that where a defendant is convicted of a theft of property offence, the court may order restoration of the stolen property to the rightful owner, or the delivery to the person of property representing the proceeds of the stolen property, or the payment of a sum representing the value of the stolen property, provided that the person does not recover more than the value of the stolen property (s.56(2)). Where a person has bought the stolen property in good faith or has lent money on the security of it in good faith, the court may order that the purchaser or lender shall be entitled to recover the sums paid or lent (s.56(3)). An order under this section will only be made where the court is of the opinion that the evidence tendered at trial would warrant it (s.56(4)).

PROVISION OF INFORMATION TO JURIES

Section 57(1) provides that where a person is charged on indictment with an offence under the 2001 Act, the trial judge may order that the jury be provided with certain documents, including: any document admitted in evidence, transcripts of statements or evidence, charts, diagrams and any other document, which the judge considers would be of assistance to the jury in its deliberations. Where an affidavit sworn by an accountant is to be made available at trial, the person who swore it may be required to explain to the jury any relevant accounting procedures or principles (s.57(3)).

MISCELLANEOUS MATTERS

The 2001 Act also deals with miscellaneous matters, including the use of an assumed name to commit an offence, the liability of corporations, admissibility of certain documents as evidence and amendments to certain pieces of legislation.

LIABILITY FOR OFFENCES BY BODIES CORPORATE AND UNINCORPORATED

Section 58(1) provides that where an offence under the 2001 Act is committed by a body corporate or unincorporated, with the consent or connivance of a director, manager, secretary or other officer of the body corporate, or a person purporting to act in any such capacity of the body, the person, as well as the body, will be guilty of the offence. Similar provisions apply where the affairs of a body corporate are managed by its members (s.58(2)).

REPORTING OF OFFENCES

Section 59(1) provides that a relevant person (who audits the firm or accountant providing professional services) shall report to the Gardaí any suspected offence by the firm or a partner, director, manager, secretary or other officer of the body corporate indicated by the firm's accounts. This duty would arise in circumstances where information or documents indicate that certain offences under the 2001 Act may have been committed by a client entity, or by its management or employees. Failure to do so will render the person liable, on summary conviction, to a maximum fine of €1,900 and/or 12 months' imprisonment (s.59(4)).

EVIDENCE IN PROCEEDINGS

Section 60(1) makes provision for the use in proceedings of a document and the translation of such a document, provided by a lawyer practising in another state or a territorial unit about comparable offences under the law of that state or territorial unit. In relation to proceedings under s.45, evidence that a person is an Irish citizen may be provided in a document signed by an officer of the Department of Foreign Affairs (s.60(2)).

JURISDICTION OF THE DISTRICT COURT IN CERTAIN PROCEEDINGS

Section 61 provides that for the purpose of the exercise of jurisdiction by the District Court in cases where an offence was committed aboard a vessel or hovercraft or on an installation in the territorial seas or in a designated area in the territorial seas, the offence can be treated as having been committed in any place in the Irish State.

AMENDMENT OF SECTION 9 OF THE MARRIED WOMEN'S STATUS ACT 1957

Section 62 amends s.9 of Married Women's Status Act 1957 by the substitution for subs.(3) of the following subsection: (3) No criminal proceedings referred to in subsection (1) or (2) shall be taken by a spouse against the other spouse except by or with the consent of the Director of Public Prosecutions.

AMENDMENT OF THE DEFENCE ACT 1954

Since the 2001 Act repeals earlier larceny legislation, and creates new theft and fraud offences, it was necessary to substitute a new section in place of s.156 of the Defence Act 1954 dealing with larceny and related offences by persons subject to military law. The new section 156 provides that it is an offence, triable before courts-martial, for a person to steal, handle or possess stolen property belonging to another such person or any public service property.

EFFECT OF THE 2001 ACT AND TRANSITIONAL PROVISIONS

Section 65 deals with the arrangements to apply when the 2001 Act provisions came into operation. The legislation will only apply to offences committed wholly or partly after the appropriate provisions are commenced and that proceedings in being before such commencement will be unaffected by that commencement. This is a saving clause to deal with transitional provisions. There is also provision concerning the correspondence of offences for the purposes of the Criminal Law (Jurisdiction) Act 1976. The offences created by the 2001 Act do not have retrospective effect.

FURTHER READING

Ashe and Reed, "Money Laundering: An Overview" (2000) 7 (8) C.L.P. 183.
Byrne, "The Theft and Fraud Offences Act 2001" (2002) 20 I.L.T. 213.
Campbell, Kilcommins and O'Sullivan, *Criminal Law in Ireland: Cases and Commentary* (Dublin: Clarus Press, 2010), Ch.18.
Griffin, "The Irish Briber Abroad: The Bribery of Foreign Public Officials in International Business Transactions" (2007) 14 (6) C.L.P. 115.

Hanly, *An Introduction to Irish Criminal Law*, 2nd edn (Dublin: Gill & Macmillan, 2006), Chs 22–27.

Law Reform Commission, *Report on the Law Relating to Dishonesty* (LRC 43–1992).

Law Reform Commission, *Report on Receiving Stolen Property* (LRC 23–1987).

Maher, "Handling Stolen Property" (2009) 14(2) B.R. 48.

McGreal, *Criminal Justice (Theft and Fraud Offences) Act 2001* (Dublin: Round Hall, 2003).

McIntyre, "Computer Crime in Ireland: A Critical Assessment of the Substantive Law" (2005) 15(1) I.C.L.J. 13.

McMullan, "The Criminal Justice (Theft and Fraud Offences) Act 2001: An Overview" (2003) 13(1) I.C.L.J. 8.

Murray, "The Criminal Justice (Theft and Fraud Offences) Bill 2000 and the Internet" (2001) 19 I.L.T. 143.

O'Neill, "Money Laundering and the Criminal Justice Act 1994" (1996) 2(3) B.R. 112.

Report of the Government Advisory Committee on Fraud (Dublin: Stationery Office, 1993).

Wade, "Stolen Moments" (2002) 96 (8) L.S.G. 10.

Walsh, "The Enforcement of Money Laundering Legislation" (1999) 9(2) I.C.L.J. 204.

20. Public Order Offences

Introduction

The Criminal Justice (Public Order) Act 1994 and the Criminal Justice (Public Order) Act 2003 govern the law on public order offences. The 1994 Act repealed and modernised most of the common law offences. This legislation deals with the regulation of behaviour by people in public places, although some offences can be committed in public or private places.

Meaning of a Public Place

For most offences created by the 1994 Act, if a Garda suspects that an individual has committed an offence, the offender is obliged to provide his name and address if asked by the Garda, and failure to do so is an offence. A suspect can be arrested without warrant for failing to provide his name and address when requested to do so and a maximum fine of €1,000 may be imposed for that offence on summary conviction.

While most offences can be committed in a public place only, the definition of what constitutes a public place has been extended under s.3 of the Criminal Justice (Public Order) Act 1994. This defines a public place to include: roads; public parks or recreational areas; cemeteries; churchyards; trains; and buses and other public transport vehicles. Notwithstanding the specific definitions of "public place", the courts have experienced difficulty in distinguishing public places from private places in marginal cases. For instance, if an offender commits a public order offence while sitting in his private car on a public road, there appears to be a lacuna in the case law as to whether he could then claim sanctuary to avoid prosecution and conviction for a public order offence, e.g. "threatening, abusive or insulting behaviour" in a public place, contrary to s.6 of the 1994 Act (see below).

Intoxication in a Public Place

Section 4 creates the offence of being intoxicated in a public place. It is an offence for someone to be so intoxicated in a public place that they could reasonably be presumed to be a danger to themselves or to anyone else in the surrounding area. This provision empowers the Gardaí to confiscate intoxicating substances in circumstances where they have reasonable suspicion that an offence under ss.4, 5 or 6 of the 1994 Act is or has been committed. The Gardaí must have "reasonable cause" for suspecting that a bottle, other container, or its contents, "is relevant to the offence under section 5 or 6 which the member suspects is being committed" (s.4(3)).

Section 23B of the 1994 Act, as inserted by s.184 of the Criminal Justice Act 2006, provides for a fixed charge fine instead of District Court proceedings for being intoxicated in a public place. The fine is currently set at €100 and can be varied by the Minister for Justice, Equality and Law Reform. The advantage of this procedure for the offender is that he will not have a conviction recorded against him and the District Court may not have to deal with an increasing number of these offences, which in recent decades have come before the courts more frequently.

While there is no legislation per se criminalising drinking in public places, each local authority area is empowered to regulate or prohibit the consumption of alcohol in public places. Under the provisions of the Intoxicating Liquor Act 2008, the Gardaí are empowered to confiscate alcohol that is in the possession of a child under 18 years of age where they have reasonable cause to believe that the alcohol will be consumed by such a child in a public place.

Disorderly Conduct in a Public Place

Under s.5(1) it is an offence to engage in offensive conduct in a public place between 12am and 7am, or at any time after having been requested to desist from such behaviour by a Garda. Offensive conduct is defined in s.5(3) as:

> ... any unreasonable behaviour which, having regard to all the circumstances, is likely to cause serious offence or serious annoyance to any person who is, or might reasonably be expected to be, aware of such behaviour.

The purpose of this offence is to deal with types of disorderly behaviour that fall short of threatening behaviour, but nevertheless adversely affect the quality of people's lives. Typical examples include people shouting in public streets, playing loud music late at night, and pulling over bins in circumstances where this would cause serious annoyance to local residents. The punishment on summary conviction for this offence is a maximum fine of €1,000.

Section 23A was inserted by s.184 of the Criminal Justice Act 2006 and permits the Gardaí to impose a fixed charge fine for disorderly conduct in a public place instead of District Court proceedings. The offender must give his name and address to the Garda, and failure to do so means that the offender can be arrested without warrant and convicted of a summary offence. If the Gardaí decide to proceed with the imposition of a fixed-charge fine, they may serve notice on the offender that he will not be charged with the offence if the fine is paid within 28 days. The fixed charge is currently €140, and may be amended by ministerial regulation.

THREATENING, ABUSIVE OR INSULTING BEHAVIOUR IN A PUBLIC PLACE

Under s.6(1) it is an offence to use threatening, abusive or insulting words or behaviour in a public place, with the intention of causing a breach of the peace or being reckless as to whether a breach of the peace occurs. Typical examples of this offence include circumstances where an offender, by his words or actions, is likely to cause a fight with the person or persons whom he was insulting, or where groups of youths are seeking to create trouble by their threatening behaviour towards other people. The Gardaí are also empowered to confiscate alcohol from the offender.

The maximum penalty on conviction for this offence is a fine of up to €1,000 and/or a maximum three months' imprisonment (s.6(2)).

In *Clifford v DPP* [2008] IEHC 322, the defendant was convicted under s.6 of the 1994 Act due to the fact that he had entered the public office of Kilmainham Garda Station and had threatened and been abusive to Gardaí. No members of the public that were present attempted to become involved and shied away from any confrontation. The defendant argued that there was no evidence that he had intended to breach the peace or was reckless as to whether or not a breach would occur. The District Court stated a case to the High Court on the issue as to whether or not the court was entitled to infer an intention to breach the peace in such circumstances. The High Court held that it was possible for the court to infer such an intention or recklessness if the evidence of the conduct of the defendant was sufficient to support that inference (cf. *Thorpe v DPP* [2007] 1 I.R. 502; *Murphy v DPP* [2004] 1 I.R. 65).

DISTRIBUTION OR DISPLAY OF THREATENING, ABUSIVE, INSULTING OR OBSCENE MATERIAL

Section 7(1) prohibits the distribution or display of offensive material. Although the distribution or display of material might be obscene to one person, it might not be to another person. In *Müller v Switzerland* (1991) 13 E.H.R.R. 212, the ECtHR considered the issue of sensitivity in the context of a conviction for displaying obscene paintings that depicted sexual relations between men and animals. The court held that the paintings were liable or likely to grossly offend persons of ordinary sensitivity. Therefore, it is likely that the courts in signatory states to the ECHR, including Ireland, will apply the objective or "reasonable person" test when deciding if the impugned distribution or display of material is abusive, insulting or obscene.

The penalty on conviction for this offence is a maximum €1,000 fine and/or a maximum three months' imprisonment (s.7(2)).

FAILURE TO COMPLY WITH THE DIRECTION OF A GARDA

Section 8(1) provides that it is an offence to fail to comply, without reasonable excuse or lawful authority, with a direction given by a Garda in circumstances where the Garda has a reasonable apprehension for the safety of persons or property or for the maintenance of public peace. This provision grants powers of enforcement to the Gardaí where the offence under ss.4, 5, 6, 7, or 9 has been committed, or where a person is deemed to be loitering in a public place and the Gardaí have reasonable suspicion that the safety of persons or property in a public place is threatened. This provision empowers the Gardaí to disperse people so as to prevent any disturbances in public places and a Garda can direct people to "move on" without having to arrest, charge and prosecute individuals. The difficulty in prosecuting this offence is that some defendants might claim to have been so intoxicated at the time and consequently did not understand that the Garda was instructing them to "move on".

The penalty on conviction for this offence is a maximum fine of €1,000 and/or six months' imprisonment (s.8(3)).

WILFUL OBSTRUCTION

Under s.9 it is a summary offence for a person without legal authority or reasonable excuse to wilfully prevent or interrupt the free passage of any person or vehicle in any public place. While the Gardaí have no power of arrest under this provision, they can invoke the powers of ss.7 or 8 to direct any person to desist from the obstruction in question, and failure to comply with such direction is an offence.

This offence was created with the purpose of protecting the constitutional rights of individuals to pass and re-pass in public places. To constitute an offence under this provision, the interruption of the right of free passage must be without lawful authority or reasonable excuse and the prevention or interruption must be wilful, which imports a mens rea element into this offence. Despite the fact that the Gardaí do not have a power of arrest under this provision, if the conduct of the persons obstructing the right of free passage constitutes a breach of the peace, then the Gardaí could arrest without warrant under the common law power of arrest. Section 25 of the 1994 Act provides that the powers conferred on Gardaí are in addition to, and not in substitution for, "any other power" exercisable by the Gardaí, and the words "other power" would suggest common law powers together with other statutory powers and regulations.

The maximum penalty on conviction for this offence is a €400 fine.

ENTERING A BUILDING WITH INTENT TO COMMIT AN OFFENCE

Section 11(1) provides that it is an offence to enter a building or the vicinity of a building (cartilage) as a trespasser "in circumstances giving rise to the reasonable inference that such entry or presence was with intent to commit an offence or with intent to unlawfully interfere with any property situate therein." In *Adler v George* [1964] 2 Q.B. 7 at 9, Lord Parker C.J. said that the natural meaning of vicinity was "the state of being near in space". It is not necessary for the offender to have entered a building to commit an offence under this section and merely being present on the property, such as the back garden or the driveway of a house, may suffice to justify a conviction under this provision. The prosecution will have to prove that the defendant was present in the building or on the property with the intention of committing an offence, or with intent to interfere with any property.

The maximum penalty on conviction for this offence is a €2,500 fine and/or six months' imprisonment (s.11(2)).

TRESPASS ON A BUILDING

Section 13(1) provides that it is an offence for any person, without reasonable excuse, to trespass on a building or the curtilage thereof, "in such a manner as causes or is likely to cause fear in another person." This offence is complementary to that provided for in s.11. Unlike s.11, it is not necessary for the prosecution to establish any intent to commit an offence or to interfere with property. A Garda may direct any person trespassing on a building or the curtilage, in such a manner as causes or is likely to cause fear in another, to desist from acting in such a manner and to leave the vicinity or area of the place concerned immediately in a peaceable and orderly manner. It is an offence to fail or refuse, without reasonable excuse or lawful authority, to comply with the direction of the Garda in these circumstances. The penalty on conviction for this offence is a maximum fine of €1,270 and/or 12 months' imprisonment (s.13(3)(a)).

Section 13(2) empowers the Gardaí who find any person in a place to which s.13(1) relates, and have a reasonable suspicion "that such person is or has been acting in a manner contrary to the provisions of [s.13(1)]", to direct that person to desist from acting in such a manner and to immediately leave the vicinity of the place concerned "in a peaceable and orderly manner". Failure to comply with this direction in the absence of "lawful authority or reasonable excuse" is an offence punishable with a maximum €635 fine and/or six months' imprisonment (s.13(3)(b)).

RIOT

The offence of riot is one of the most serious public order offences. Section 14(1) defines this offence in the following terms:

> Where 12 or more persons who are present together as any place (public or private) use or threaten to use unlawful violence for a common purpose, and
>
> The conduct of these persons, taken together, is such as would cause a person of reasonable firmness present at that place to fear for his or another person's safety,
>
> then, each of the person's using unlawful violence for the common purpose shall be guilty of the offence of riot.

This section replaced the common law offence of riot (s.14(4)).

Section 14(2) adds a number of important explanations to the definition of this offence: it is immaterial that not all 12 persons use or threaten to use violence simultaneously; the common purpose may be inferred from the defendant's conduct; and no person of reasonable firmness need actually be, or be likely to be, present at that place.

This offence is distinguished from other public order offences because it can be committed in a public or private place while most other offences that can only be committed in public places. Where large groups of people assemble for a common purpose, such as a peaceful protest which turns into unlawful violence, the Gardaí may arrest and charge the participants with the offence of riot.

This is an indictable offence carrying a maximum penalty of 10 years' imprisonment and/or an unlimited fine (s.14(3)).

VIOLENT DISORDER

Section 15(1) creates the offence of violent disorder, which is similar to the offence of riot, although it is a less serious type of that offence:

(a) three or more persons who are present together at any place (whether that place is a public place or a private place or both) use or threaten to use unlawful violence, and
(b) the conduct of those persons, taken together, is such as would cause a person of reasonable firmness present at that place to fear for his or another person's safety,

then, each of the persons using or threatening to use unlawful violence shall be guilty of the offence of violent disorder.

This section parallels the offence of riot with the exception that the number of participants required is a minimum of three and not 12, as stipulated for in the offence of riot. The offences of riot and violent disorder are distinguished by the fact that there is no requirement for the group to share a common design or purpose to secure convictions for violent disorder.

The mens rea for this offence is intention or subjective recklessness. Section 15(3) provides that a defendant shall not be convicted of violent disorder unless the defendant intends to use or threatens to use violence or is aware that his conduct may be violent or threatens violence.

This is an indictable offence carrying a maximum penalty of 10 years' imprisonment and/or an unlimited fine (s.15(4)).

AFFRAY

Section 16(1) defines the offence of affray in the following terms:

(1) Where
(a) two or more persons at any place (whether that place is a public place or a private place or both) use or threaten to use violence towards each other, and
(b) the violence so used or threatened by one of those persons is unlawful, and
(c) the conduct of those persons taken together is such as would cause a person of reasonable firmness present at that place to fear for his or another person's safety,

then, each such person who uses or threatens to use unlawful violence shall be guilty of the offence of affray.

This offence is distinguished from riot and violent disorder by the fact that the violence involved in affray must be directed towards each of the participants and not innocent parties. It can also be committed in a private place. An example of this offence is where a group of people fight against each other in a public street, or some private place, e.g. a theatre, cinema, or restaurant. Section 16(5) provides that the common law offence of affray is abolished and replaced by this statutory offence.

In *People (DPP) v Reid and Kirwan* [2004] 1 I.R. 392, the defendants were convicted of affray, but acquitted of the charge of assault on a police officer (contrary to s.19 of the 1994 Act). They sought leave to appeal on the following grounds: the trial judge should have withdrawn the count of affray from the jury when requested to do so by counsel for the defendants; the convictions for affray were inconsistent with the acquittals on the counts of assault; and the trial judge should have instructed the jury that, if the defendants were acquitted of assault, there would be no case against them for affray. The Court of Criminal Appeal allowed the appeal and quashed the convictions on the grounds that the actual or threatened use of violence for the purpose of the offence of affray must be violence "towards each other". There was no evidence of the first defendant using or threatening to use violence towards any other person, and specifically towards any member of a group of two or more people. There was no prima facie case of affray against the first defendant and that count should have been withdrawn from the jury. It was unnecessary for the purposes of the offence of affray that each defendant at the joint trial should have used violence against the other co-accused. However, the court queried whether the new statutory offence of affray is broad enough to include a person using violence (not necesssarily unlawful) against a person using unlawful violence, on the basis that the conduct of persons taken together, "is such as would cause a person of reasonable firmness present at that place to fear for his or another person's safety", contrary to s.16(1)(c) of the 1994 Act.

The penalty on conviction on indictment is an unlimited fine and/or five years' imprisonment, and on summary conviction the maximum penalty is a €635 fine and/or 12 months' imprisonment (s.16(4)).

BLACKMAIL, EXTORTION AND DEMANDING MONEY WITH MENACES

Section 17(1) provides that, "[i]t shall be an offence for any person who, with a view to gain for himself or another or with intent to cause loss to another, makes any unwarranted demand with menaces." The exception to this offence is that if the person making the demand with menaces honestly believes that he has reasonable grounds for making the demand, then the use of menaces is a proper means of reinforcing the demand (s.17(2)).

The offence is somewhat vague in that the 1994 Act does not define the meaning of "menaces." In view of this lacuna, judicial guidance on the meaning of the word may be derived from *Thorne v Motor Trade Association*

[1937] A.C. 797, where the House of Lords considered the meaning of the word as defined in case law under the old Larceny Act 1916. Lord Wright stated:

> "... the word 'menace' is to be liberally construed and not as limited to threats of violence but as including threats of any action detrimental to or unpleasant to the person addressed." [1937] A.C. 797 at 817

This might include threats to publish embarrassing photographs on the internet.

The punishment on conviction on indictment for this offence is an unlimited fine and/or 14 years' imprisonment, and on summary conviction to a maximum fine of £1,270 and/or 12 months' imprisonment (s.17(3)).

Assault with Intent

While the Non-fatal Offences Against the Person Act 1997 deals with assault and related offences against the person, s.18(1) of the 1994 Act creates a additional offence of assault with intent to cause bodily harm to some person, or to commit an indictable offence:

> Any person who assaults any person with intent to cause bodily harm or to commit an indictable offence shall be guilty of an offence.

This is effectively an aggravated form of assault with intent to cause bodily harm or to commit an indictable offence. It is regrettable that the various types of assault offences were not consolidated and placed on a statutory footing. The common law offence of assault was abolished by s.28(1) the 1997 Act, but s.18 of the 1994 Act fails to provide a definition of assault. Furthermore, the 1997 Act did not repeal the definition of assault in the 1994 Act, so it appears that the offence of assault under s.18 is available to the prosecution in addition to the hierarchy of assault offences created by the 1997 Act.

The penalty on summary conviction is a maximum fine of €1,270 and/or 12 months' imprisonment, and a conviction on indictment carries an unlimited fine and/or five years' imprisonment (s.18(2)).

Assault or Obstruction of a Peace Officer

The key elements of this offence are that the assault is on a peace officer acting in the execution of his duty, or that the assault was on any other person that was aiding or assisting the peace officer, or that the assault on any other person was to prevent the lawful arrest or detention of himself or of any other person for any offence (s.19(1)). The mens rea for this offence is intention or subjective recklessness (s.19(1)(a)). Section 19(2), as amended by s.185 of the Criminal Justice Act 2006, provides that the maximum punishment for assault is seven years' imprisonment and/or a €5,000 fine.

A person will also commit this offence if they wilfully obstruct a peace officer acting in the course of their duty or obstruct any person who is assisting or helping the peace officer in the course of their duty (s.19(3)). Section 19(4), as amended by s.185 of the Criminal Justice Act 2006, provides that the maximum punishment for wilful obstruction is six months' imprisonment and/or a €2,500 fine.

Section 19(6) defines a "peace officer" as a member of An Garda Síochána, a Prison Officer or a member of the Defence Forces. Section 185 of the Criminal Justice Act 2006 has extended this definition to include those providing emergency services, including ambulance and fire brigade personnel. Accordingly, this provision creates new offences of assaulting or obstructing emergency service personnel engaged in providing emergency services. This also includes people working in accident and emergency departments of hospitals.

With regard to the prosecution of this offence, the defendant may elect to have his case dealt with summarily in the District Court or alternatively on indictment in the Circuit Criminal Court (s.19(2)). However, this procedure could potentially deprive the defendant of his right to a jury trial for what is essentially an indictable offence (cf. *DPP (Travers) v Brennan* [1998] 4 I.R. 67; *State (O'Hagan) v Delap* [1982] I.R. 213; *State (Clancy) v Wine* [1980] I.R. 228).

CROWD CONTROL AT PUBLIC EVENTS

The purpose of crowd control by An Garda Síochána at public events, such as festivals, concerts and sporting events, is to maintain public peace and order and ensure the safety of all those who attend all such public events. Article 40.6.1°.ii of the Constitution guarantees "the right of the citizens to assemble peaceably and without arms." This is a qualified constitutional right and can be limited by legislation in the interests of public order and morality. Certain offences under the 1994 Act were created to prevent and control meetings that are calculated or designed to cause a riot or breach of the peace. Part III of the 1994 Act, which is substantially based on the recommendations of the Hamilton Committee on Public Safety and Crowd Control, established in the wake of the Hillsborough disaster in 1989, governs crowd control at public events.

CONTROL OF ACCESS TO CERTAIN EVENTS

Section 21(1) empowers the Gardaí to place barriers on roads for up to one mile (1.6 km) from where a public event is taking place. The decision on the placing of barriers is made by a Garda who is of Superintendent rank or higher. The decision by the Superintendent is amenable to judicial review and may be quashed on grounds of procedural impropriety if it is not shown to be bona fide, factually sustainable and not unreasonable in the circumstances of the case under consideration (see *Kiberd v Hamilton* [1992] 2 I.R. 257).

The Gardaí are empowered to prohibit people from crossing or passing a barrier if the person does not have a valid ticket for the event. The Gardaí may also confiscate any alcohol or disposable drinks containers or any offensive articles in the possession of a person at the barrier before allowing that person to proceed to the event (s.21(2)).

Section 21(3) allows people to pass the barriers if they are going home, to a place of work or going for any other lawful purpose "to any place in the vicinity of the event other than the place where the event is taking place or is about to take place."

Failure to obey the direction given by a Garda at a barrier constitutes an offence (s.21(4)) and is punishable on summary conviction by a maximum €1,000 fine (s.21(5)).

SURRENDER AND SEIZURE OF INTOXICATING LIQUOR

Section 22(1) gives the Gardaí the power to search people going to an event where a barrier has been erected and provides that the Gardaí can seize intoxicating liquor or any disposable container or any other article which could be used to cause injury. The Gardaí may also refuse to allow people to proceed to the event where they refuse to surrender or give up the intoxicating liquor, disposable container or other article concerned. The Gardaí may also require that people leave the area in an orderly and peaceful manner as directed (s.22(2)). Failure to comply with such a request by the Garda without lawful authority or reasonable excuse constitutes an offence (s.22(3)), and the maximum fine on conviction is €1,000 (s.22(4)).

GARDA POWERS OF ARREST WITHOUT WARRANT

Section 24(1) of the 1994 Act provides that the Gardaí can arrest without warrant any person committing an offence under a relevant provision. The Gardaí are given a power of arrest without warrant for most offences created by the 1994 Act, including: being intoxicated in a public place (s.4); threatening or abusive behaviour in a public place (s.6); distributing or displaying threatening, obscene or insulting material in a public place (s.7); failing to comply with the direction of a Garda (s.8); entering a building with intent to commit an offence (s.11); trespassing on a dwelling (s.13); riot (s.14); violent disorder (s.15); affray (s.16); blackmail and demanding money with menaces (s.17); assault with intent to cause bodily harm or to commit an indictable offence (s.18); and assaulting or obstructing a peace officer (s.19).

Section 24(2) provides that:

> Where a member of the Garda Síochána is of the opinion that an offence has been committed under a relevant provision, the member may:
> (a) demand the name and address of any person whom the member suspects, with reasonable cause, has committed, or whom the member finds committing, such an offence, and
> (b) arrest without warrant any such person who fails or refuses to give his name and address when demanded, or gives a name or address which the member has reasonable grounds for believing is false or misleading.

Section 24(3)) provides that it is an offence to fail or refuse to give one's name and address or give a false name or address when demanded by a Garda pursuant to s.24(2). This offence is punishable on summary conviction with a maximum €635 fine and/or six months' imprisonment (s.24(4)).

In *DPP (Ryan) v Mulligan* [2009] 1 I.R. 794, the defendant was prosecuted in the District Court for an offence contrary to s.24, because he failed to provide his name and address to a Garda upon request. The prosecuting Garda was the sole prosecution witness. The defendant sought a direction as no evidence had been adduced that the Garda had made a demand for the defendant's name and address in the exercise of her powers under s.24(2) Also, even if such a demand had been made, it would have to be proven that the defendant was informed that failure to comply with such demand constituted an offence. The defendant was convicted as the District Court judge having heard the evidence was satisfied that the offence had been proven. On appeal to the High Court, Charleton J., allowing the appeal, held that a lawful demand for a name and address under s.24(4) was made where the Garda specified that he or she had power under the legislation to demand such particulars and that if they were not given, an offence was committed. Where a power of compulsion, enforceable by statutory provision, was exercised by a Garda, the person to whom it was directed should be informed of this power and also of the consequence of a refusal to comply. Charleton J. also held that a person was not obliged to submit to a demand pursuant to police powers unless information was provided to that person that such a power existed. An arrest is lawful only where the reason for the arrest was stated, and, further, that a person who refused to comply with an informal request did not commit an offence.

Exclusion and Closure Orders

The Criminal Justice (Public Order) Act 2003 provides that on conviction for certain offences under the 1994 Act, the defendant may be excluded from entering or being in the vicinity of specified catering premises for up to a year. This is in addition to the penalty under the 1994 Act. Section 3(1) of the 2003 Act provides that a conviction under ss.4, 5, 6, 7, 8 or 9 of the 1994 Act may be subject to an "exclusion order". Section 3(2) provides that the maximum period of an exclusion order shall not exceed 12 months and shall commence:

(a) in case the person has been sentenced to imprisonment or detention for the offence, on the date of his or her release therefrom, or
(b) in any other case, on the date of the order.

A person who, without reasonable excuse, does not comply with an exclusion order is guilty of an offence punishable on summary conviction by a maximum €650 fine and/or three months' imprisonment (s.3(4)).

The 2003 Act provides that a Garda of the rank of Inspector may apply to the District Court for a "closure order" in respect of catering premises. Section 4(1) provides that there must have been disorder on the premises or in its vicinity, or there must have been excessive noise emanating from the premises or its vicinity (not exceeding a distance of 100 metres from the premises) and that such disorder is likely to recur. The disorder or noise must involve persons who were on the premises, and reasonable noise is excluded from the scope of this provision. A Garda not below the rank of Inspector can make an application for a closure order to the District Court.

The closure order will be for a period not exceeding seven days in the case of the first such order, or not less than seven and not exceeding 30 days in the case of a second or subsequent order (s.5(2)).

Begging in Public

In *Dillon v DPP* [2008] 1 I.R. 383, the applicant challenged the constitutionality of s.3 of the Vagrancy (Ireland) Act 1847. Prosecutions for begging had been brought under that provision but the High Court found it to be unconstitutional on the basis that the section was too vague and unspecific. Moreover, it held that the constitutional right to freedom of expression and communication in accordance with Art.40 of the Constitution was being unreasonably curtailed (cf. *King v AG* [1981] I.R. 233). Since this judgment there has been a lacuna in criminal law with regard to begging in public places. The Criminal Justice (Public Order) Bill 2010 arose as a direct result of the High Court judgment and seeks to rectify this situation. The Bill proposes to prohibit harassment or intimidation of members of the public by persons who engage in begging in public places, and also to empower the Gardaí to direct persons to desist from begging. The Gardaí will be empowered to arrest without warrant any person whom a Garda suspects, upon reasonable grounds, of having committed an offence under the proposed legislation.

IMPACT OF THE CONSTITUTION

The constitutionality of ss.5, 6, and 7 of the 1994 Act might be questionable based on the overarching presumption of constitutionality in statutory interpretation. Article 40.6.1°.ii of the Constitution is the constitutional guarantee of the, "right of the citizens to assemble peaceably and without arms", but this is a qualified right.

> Provision may be made by law to prevent or control meetings which are determined in accordance with law to be calculated to cause a breach of the peace or to be a danger or nuisance to the general public and to prevent or control meetings in the vicinity of either House of the Oireachtas.

It does not automatically follow that legislation which is designed to prevent breaches of the peace is exempt from constitutional scrutiny. However, any such legislation must not be designed to, "ignore the fundamental norms of the legal order postulated by the Constitution" (*King v Attorney General* [1981] I.R. 233 at 257, per Henchy J.).

ADULT CAUTIONING SCHEME

Under the provisions of the Adult Cautioning Scheme that was introduced in February 2006, certain public order offences are included in the list of offences that may be dealt with by the Gardaí by way of caution under this Scheme. If an offender is cautioned under the provisions of this Scheme he is not brought into the court system and will not be required to attend the District Court. The scheme is an alternative to prosecuting adults for the following public order offences: intoxication in a public place (s.4); disorderly conduct in a public place (s.5); threatening, abusive or insulting behaviour in a public place (s.6); failing to comply with a direction of a Garda (s.8); committing wilful obstruction (s.9); entering a building with intent to commit an offence (s.11); surrender and seizure of intoxicating liquor (s.22). If the offender complies with the terms of the caution he will not have a conviction recorded against him.

FURTHER READING

Campbell, Kilcommins and O'Sullivan, *Criminal Law in Ireland: Cases and Commentary* (Dublin: Clarus Press, 2010), pp.775–809.

Carey, "*Mens Rea* and the Irish Riot" (2000) 10(4) I.C.L.J. 4.

Carey, "The Rule of Law, Public Order Targeting and the Construction of Crime" (1998) 8(1) I.C.L.J. 26.

Hanly, *An Introduction to Irish Criminal Law*, 2nd edn (Dublin: Gill & Macmillan, 2006), Ch.28.

National Crime Council, *Public Order Offences in Ireland* (Dublin: Stationery Office, 2003).

Index

Abduction see **Child abduction**
Abortion
  conspiracy, 209
  constitutional amendment, 10
  incitement, 214
  life or health of pregnant woman, 153
Absolute liability, 34, 99–100
Accessories
  acquittal of principal, 185
  after the fact, 185–186
  aiding and abetting, 176
  conduct element, 175
  counselling, 176–177
  extent of participation, 178–180
  failure to exercise control, 180–181
  knowledge of principal offence, 183–185
  mens rea, 181–183
  mere presence, 178–180
  principal offence, 174–175
  procuring, 177–178
  recklessness, 182–183
  statutory provisions, 174
Actus reus
  definition, 36
  attempt, 196–198
  burglary, 291
  causation see Causation
  causing serious harm, 243
  coincidence with mens rea
    continuing act, 96–98
    in law, 94
    in time, 94–96
    requirement for liability, 93
  conduct crimes, 36
  conspiracy, 37, 208–210
  construction of, 37–38
  crimes of circumstance, 37
  element of criminal offence, 34–35
  incitement, 213–215
  murder, 219
  omissions, 51–58

  possession as, 43–51
  rape, 257–258
  result crimes, 36–37, 58
  sexual assault, 263
  state of affairs or status offences, 38–39
  theft, 284
  threat to kill or cause serious harm, 244
  voluntary conduct, 38–43
Adult Cautioning Scheme, 320
Adverse inferences from silence, 27
Affray, 313–314
Age of criminal responsibility, 119, 219
Aggravated murder, 221
Aggravated sexual assault, 262, 265–266
Aiding and abetting, 176
Appeals
  Court of Criminal Appeal, 22
  insanity finding, 122–123
  Supreme Court, 23
  "without prejudice", 23
Arrest
  justifiable use of force, 254
  without warrant, 317–318
Arrestable offences, 33, 194–195
Assault
  causing harm, 242–243
  consent, 241–242
  former assault and battery, 240
  intent, with, 315
  manslaughter as a result, 228–229
  medical treatment, 241–242
  mens rea, 240
  peace officer, 315–316
  psychological trauma, 243
  sport, 241–242
  use of reasonable force, 240–241
  without lawful excuse, 240–241
  words constituting, 240

Assisted suicide, 232–236
Attempt
  definition, 195
  abandonment, 206
  actus reus, 196–198
  criminal liability, 194
  equivocality approach, 201–202
  impossibility
    generally, 203–204
    inadequate means, 205
    legal impossibility, 205–206
    physical impossibility, 204–205
  last act theory, 198–199
  mens rea, 202–203
  murder
    duress no defence, 149–150
    mens rea, 203, 220
  preparation distinguished, 195–196, 197–202
  proposed law reform, 216
  proximity test, 199–201
Automatism
  definition, 126
  defence, as, 126
  degree of consciousness, 129–130
  insane automatism, 128, 130–131
  internal and external factors, 128–129
  psychological blow, 131–134
  self-induced through drugs or alcohol, 131
  sleep-walking, 128, 130–131
  sleeping or unconscious while driving, 41–43
  voluntariness of conduct, and, 41–43, 126–128

Bail, refusal of, 27
"Balance of probabilities", 14
Begging in public, 319–320
"Being found", 38–39
"Being in possession", 38
"Beyond reasonable doubt", 13–14
Binding over, 17–18
Blackmail, 314–315
Blasphemy, 106

Body corporate
  liability for theft and fraud offences, 304
  reporting of suspected offences, 304
Burden of proof, 13, 117–118
Burglary, 291

Causation
  "but for" test, 59
  conduct or condition of victim, 64–67
  drug overdose, 67–69
  "eggshell skull" cases, 64–65
  factual causation, 59–60
  "flight" cases, 67
  legal causation, 60–61
  medical negligence, 61–64
  medical treatment shortening life, 60
  natural consequences of criminal act, 64
  novus actus interveniens, 60–61
  operating and substantial cause, 62–63
  problematic sets of facts, 58–59
  victim refusing medical treatment, 66–67
  voluntary intervening act, 61
Central Criminal Court, 21
Child abduction
  Council of Europe Convention, 251–252
  Hague Convention, 251
  other persons, by, 252
  parents, by, 251–252
Children
  abduction *see* Child abduction
  age of criminal responsibility, 119, 219
  child trafficking and pornography, 279–280
  corporal punishment, 255
  Garda duty where believed to have committed offence, 120
  HSE custody, 120
  reckless endangerment, 279
  sexual offences against, 266–268

INDEX

Circuit Court, 20–21
Circumstance, crimes of, 37
Classification of criminal offences
    arrestable and non-arrestable offences, 33
    Irish Crime Classification System, 33
    minor and non-minor offences, 32–33
    offences triable either way, 32
    serious and non-serious offences, 33
    summary and indictable offences, 31–32
Closure order, 319
Coercion, 247
Common design
    doctrine of, 186–187
    murder, 187–189
    particular offence or consequences, 187–189
    withdrawal from, 189–193
Community service order, 16
Compensation order, 19
Computer
    hacking, 290
    unlawful use, 290
Concealing facts disclosed by documents, 301
Conduct crimes, 36
Conspiracy
    definition, 206–207
    abandonment, 212
    acquittal of co-conspirator, 211
    actus reus, 37, 208–210
    boycotting, 207
    co-conspirators' knowledge, 210–211
    husband and wife, 209–210
    impossibility, 211–212
    mens rea, 210
    proposed law reform, 216
    punishable per se, 207–208
    secrecy not required, 210
    types of, 208
Constitution of Ireland
    amendment, 26
    declaration of unconstitutionality, 29–30

    jury trial, 19
    legislative power of Oireachtas, 9, 10
    non-retroactivity of penal provisions, 9, 11, 25, 26
    presumption of innocence, 26–27
    refusal of bail, 27
    rights under
        due process, 30
        equality, 15
        fair trial, 27
        marital privacy, 29–30
        personal liberty, 27
        silence, 27
    source of law, 11
Constructive possession, 43–46
Contaminated blood offences, 244–245
Corporal punishment, abolition, 255
Corruption, 299
Counselling, 176–177
Counterfeiting and related offences
    counterfeiting currency notes and coins, 297
    custody or control of counterfeit currency notes and coins, 297–298
    import and export of counterfeits, 298
    materials and implements for counterfeiting, 298
    passing counterfeit currency notes and coins, 297
Court of Criminal Appeal, 22
Court poor box, 17
Courts of Justice Complex, 24
Criminal Assets Bureau, 19
Criminal damage, 255
Criminal justice, 1
Criminal negligence, 88, 226–228
Criminal procedure, 1
Criminology, 1

Dangerous driving
    automatism, 41–43
    proposed law reform, 237–238

Death penalty, 218
Debt demands, 249
Declaration of unconstitutionality, 29–30
Defences
  absence, as element of criminal offence, 34–35
  automatism, 126–134
  burden of proof, 116, 117–118
  diminished responsibility, 121, 123
  due diligence, 113–114
  duress, 141–150
  infancy, 119
  insanity, 121–123
  intoxication, 135–139
  justification and excuse distinguished, 116–117
  necessity, 150–154
  proposed law reform, 118
  provocation, 165–173
  self-defence, 155–163
  standard of proof, 118
Demanding money with menaces, 314–315
Diminished responsibility, 121, 123
Director of Public Prosecutions (DPP), 2
Disorderly conduct in public place, 308–309
Distribution or display of offensive material, 309–310
District Court, 20
Doli capax, 119
Double effect, principle of, 91
Drugs
  causation in overdose cases, 67–69
  possession, mandatory minimum sentence, 15
Due diligence, 113–114
Due process rights, 30
Duress
  attempted murder, no defence to, 149–150
  burden of proof, 141
  circumstances, of, 150
  defence, as, 141
  murder, no defence to, 147–149
  per minas, 141
  threats, by
    family or others, to, 142
    generally, 141–142
    immediacy, 144–146
    limits on defence, 142, 147–150
    nature of threat, 142
    objective or subjective test, 143–144
    relevant characteristics of defendant, 144
    violent association voluntarily joined, 146–147

"Eggshell skull" cases, 64–65
Electronic monitoring, 18
Elements of criminal offences
  actus reus *see* Actus reus
  defence, absence of *see* Defences
  mens rea *see* Mens rea
  overview, 34
Emergency services personnel
  assault or obstruction, 315–316
Endangering traffic, 250
Endangerment, 250
European Convention on Human Rights, 12, 114
European Union law, 11–12
Euthanasia, 235–236
Exclusion order, 16–17, 319
Extortion, 314–315
Extradition for revenue offences, 300

Fair trial, right to, 27
False accounting, 290
False imprisonment, 251
Firearms offences, 15
Force
  definition, 254
  arrest, effecting or assisting, 254
  assault *see* Assault
  self-defence, 253–254
Forfeiture of property, 19, 301

INDEX

Forgery and related offences
copying false instrument, 295–296
custody or control of false instrument, 296
false instrument: definition, 296–297
forgery, 295
induce: definition, 297
making a false instrument: definition, 297
prejudice: definition, 297
using copy of false instrument, 296
using false instrument, 295
Fraud see **Theft and fraud offences**
Functions of criminal law
generally, 1–2
maintains order in society, 2–3
protects individuals and property, 3
resolves disputes, 3–4

Gardaí
arrest without warrant, 317–318
crowd control at public events, 316–317
duty as to child offender, 120
obstruction where executing search warrant, 300–301
omission to act on complaint, 57
surveillance powers, 212

Handling stolen property, 292–293
Harassment, 247–248
Harm principle, 4, 5
Hart-Devlin debate, 4–5
High Court, 21
Homicide
absence of body, 236
assisted suicide, 232–236
infanticide, 230–232
lawful killing, 218
manslaughter see Manslaughter
murder see Murder
offences, 218
proposed law reform, 237–238
Homosexuality, decriminalisation, 4, 5, 30

Incest
definition, 268
adoptive parents, 268
consent, 269
female, by, 269
half-brother and sister, 269
in camera proceedings, 271
justification for offence, 268
legislation, 268
male, by, 269
maximum sentence, 268
mens rea, 270
non-marital children, 270
proof of relationship, 270
publication restrictions, 271
sentencing, 270–271
Inchoate offences
attempt see Attempt
conspiracy see Conspiracy
generally, 194
incitement see Incitement
proposed law reform, 216–217
Incitement
definition, 212–213
actus reus, 213–215
communication to those being incited, 214–215
impossibility, 215–216
Incitement to Hatred Act 1989, 213
mens rea, 215
person incited underage, 215
proposed law reform, 216–217
whether substantive offence committed, 213
Indicia of criminal offences, 6–8
Indictable offences, 31–32
Infanticide, 230–232
Insanity
appeals, 122–123
automatism, and, 128, 130–131
conditional discharge, and recall under 2010 Bill, 123–125
defence, 121–122
fitness to be tried, 122, 125

Insanity *(continued)*
   Mental Health (Criminal Law)
      Review Board, 123
   review of detention, 123–124
   temporary release, 124
   time for raising, 121
   transfer of prisoners, 124
   verdict, 122

Intention
   direct (purpose) intent, 71–72
   English case law, 72–77
   Irish case law, 77–82
   Law Reform Commission guidelines, 81–82
   oblique (foresight) intent, 71–72

International Criminal Court, 12
International law, 12
Intoxication
   aggravating factor in sentencing, 135
   defence
      Dutch courage, 138–139
      involuntary, 137–138
      offences of specific and basic intent, 135–137
      proposed law reform, 139
      voluntary, 137
   public place, in, 307–308

Joint enterprise *see* **Common design**
Joy riding, 285
Jurisdiction
   Central Criminal Court, 21
   Circuit Court, 20
   Court of Criminal Appeal, 22
   District Court, 20
   High Court, 21
   Special Criminal Court, 21–22
   Supreme Court, 23
   working group, 23–24

Jury nullification, 14
Jury trial
   Central Criminal Court, 21
   Circuit Court, 20–21
   constitutional right, 19
   majority verdict, 21

Kidnapping, 252
Knowledge and belief, 88–89

Larceny, old offence, 93, 282, 284, 285
Legality, principle of
   criminal offences must be clear and precise, 25, 28–29
   non-retroactivity, 25
   nullum crimen sine lege, 24
   nulla poena sine lege, 24
   strict construction of penal provisions, 25–26

Literal rule of statutory interpretation, 105

Making gain or causing loss by deception, 288–289
Making off without payment, 289
Manslaughter
   definition, 222
   assault, 228–229
   criminal and dangerous act, 223–226
   criminal negligence, 88, 226–228
   involuntary, 223
   maximum life sentence, 222
   merging with murder, 230
   proposed law reform, 237–238
   succession debarred, 237
   voluntary, 222–223
   wilful refusal to perform legal duty, 229

Medical certificate
   evidential value, 255
Medical treatment
   consent by minor, 255
Mens rea
   accessories, 181–183
   assault, 240
   attempt, 202–203
   burglary, 291
   causing serious harm, 243
   coincidence with actus reus
      continuing act, 96–98
      in law, 94
      in time, 94–96
      requirement for liability, 93

INDEX

conspiracy, 210
criminal negligence, 88
double effect, principle of, 91
element of criminal offence, 34–35, 70
harassment (stalking), 248
incest, 270
incitement, 215
intention, 71–82
knowledge and belief, 88–89
motive distinguished, 70–71
murder, 219–220
offences of specific and basic intent, 135–137
rape, 258–261
recklessness, 82–87
sexual assault, 263
theft, 285
threat to kill or cause serious harm, 244
transferred malice, 89–91
types of, 70
violent disorder, 313
Mental Health (Criminal Law) Review Board, 123
Mentally impaired person
sexual offences against, 271–272
Mill, John Stewart, 1–2, 4, 5
Minor see also **Children**
consent to medical etc treatment, 255
Minor offences, 20, 32–33
Miscarriage of justice, 22
Misprision of felony, 58, 193
Money laundering, 294–295
Morality and criminal law, 4–6
Motive, 70–71
Murder
definition, 218
abandonment of child, 219
absence of body, 236
actus reus, 219
aggravated, 221
alternative verdict, 222
attempt

duress no defence, 149–150
mens rea, 203, 220
causation, 222
commutation and remission of sentence, 220–221
diminished responsibility, 123
duress no defence, 147–149
mandatory life sentence, 15, 123, 220
mens rea, 219–220
merging with manslaughter, 230
necessity no defence, 152–154
proposed law reform, 237
provocation, 165–173
succession debarred, 237
year and a day rule, 218

Necessity
abortion, 153
conjoined twins, 153–154
defence, as, 141, 150–151
duress by circumstances, as, 150
limits on defence, 152
murder, no defence to, 152–154
proposed law reform, 154
Non-fatal offences against the person
abolition of common law offences without saving clause, 239
assault, 240–243
causing serious harm, 243–244
child abduction, 251–252
coercion, 247
debt demands, 249
endangering traffic, 250
endangerment, 250
false imprisonment, 251
harassment (stalking), 247–248
justifiable use of force, 253–254
effecting or assisting arrest, 254
legislation, 239
poisoning, 249
syringe offences, 244–247
threat to kill or cause serious harm, 244

Non-retroactivity of penal provisions, 9, 11, 25, 26

Obstruction of Garda executing search warrant, 300–301
Obtaining services by deception, 289
Offences triable either way, 32
Omissions
close personal relationship, 52–53
contractual duty to act, 52
creation of perilous situation, 56
failure to comply with statutory duty, 58
failure to report commission of offence, 58
failure to rescue, 51
general rule as to liability, 51–52
public duty, 56–57
refusal of medical treatment on religious grounds, 53
voluntary assumption of care, 53–56

Peace officer
definition, 316
assault or obstruction, 315–316
Perjury, 37
Picketing, 247
Point of law of exceptional public importance, 23
Poisoning, 249
Possession
definition, 43
actus reus, as, 43
constructive possession, 43–46
control element, 46–47
knowledge element, 47–51
Possession of certain articles, 292
Possession of stolen property, 293
Presumption of innocence, 13, 26–27
Probation order, 17
Proceeds of crime
forfeiture order, 19
Procuring, 177–178
Prohibited publications
confiscation, 19

Property, offences against *see* **Theft and fraud offences**
Prosecution of offences, 2
Protection of European Communities' financial interests
active corruption, 299
Convention and Protocols, 298
extra-territorial jurisdiction, 299
extradition, 300
fraud, 299
passive corruption, 299
restriction on proceedings, 299–300
Provocation
definition, 165
battered woman syndrome, 171–172
cumulative, 171–172
English law, objective test, 165
evidence of, 167–168
Irish law, subjective test, 166–167, 169–171
partial defence to murder, 165
proposed law reform, 173
rationale for, 166
self-induced, 169
third party, 168–169
words or conduct, 166
Public and private law distinguished, 1
Public events
access control, 316–317
legislation, 316
right of peaceful assembly, 316
surrender and seizure of alcohol, 317
Public order offences
Adult Cautioning Scheme, 320
affray, 313–314
arrest without warrant, 317–318
assault or obstruction of peace officer, 315–316
assault with intent 315
begging, 319–320
blackmail or extortion, 314–315
closure order, 319
constitutionality of provisions, 320

crowd control at public events, 316–317
disorderly conduct, 308–309
distribution or display of offensive material, 309–310
entering building with intent to commit offence, 311
exclusion order, 16–17, 319
failure to comply with Garda direction, 310
intoxication, 307–308
legislation, 3, 307
name and address, failure to provide, 307, 318
public place: definition, 307
riot, 312
threatening, abusive or insulting behaviour, 309
trespass on a building, 311–312
violent disorder, 312–313
wilful obstruction, 310–311
Punishment *see* **Sentencing**

Rape
actus reus, 257–258
continuing act, 98, 272, 278–279
failure to offer resistance, 272–273
fear vitiating consent, 273–274
fraud vitiating consent
identity of actor, 274–275
nature of act, 275
free and voluntary consent, 272
HIV status, 278
honest belief in consent, 258–260
informed consent, 272
intoxication and consent, 276–277
legislation, 257
marital, 258
marriage representation, 277
maximum sentence, 257
mens rea, 258–261
recklessness, 260–261
rendering victim insensible, 276–277
s.4 rape, 261
sexually transmitted disease, 277–278

sleeping victim, 276
statutory rape, 266–267
Recklessness
English approach
objective *(Caldwell)* recklessness, 83–85
return to subjective test, 85–86
subjective *(Cunningham)* recklessness, 82–83
Irish subjective test, 86–87
mens rea, as, 82
Recognisances, 18
Reporting criminal activity, 193
Restriction of movement order, 18–19
Result crimes, 36–37, 58
Riot, 312
Robbery, 291–292

Scheduled offences, 21–22
Search warrant, 300–301
Secondary participation
accessories *see* Accessories
common design *see* Common design
Self-defence
burden of proof, 117–118
burglar, by, 161–162
excessive force, 159–161
imminent danger, 156
justifiable use of force, 253–254
mistake as to threat, 158
occupier of dwelling, 161, 163
preparation for attack, 156–157
proposed law reform, 162–163
requirement to retreat, 155, 157–158, 254–255
statutory provisions, 155
subjective or objective test, 159
Sentencing
aggravating factors, 14
binding over, 17–18
community service order, 16
compensation order, 19
concurrent sentences, 14
consecutive sentences, 14
court poor box, 17

Sentencing *(continued)*
  curfew, 16
  exclusion order, 16–17
  fine, 14
  forfeiture and confiscation of
    property, 19
  imprisonment, 14
  life sentence, 15
  mandatory minimum sentence, 15
  mandatory sentence, 15
  maximum sentence, 15
  mitigating factors, 14
  orders for sex offenders, 18
  probation order, 17
  proportionality, 14
  restriction of movement order,
    18–19
  suspended sentence, 15–16
Serious offences, 33
Sexual assault
  actus reus, 263
  aggravated, 262, 265–266
  former indecent assault, 262
  gender neutral, 262
  indecency element, 265
  mens rea, 263
  sexual: definition, 264
  statutory provisions, 262
Sexual offences
  children, against
    child trafficking and pornography,
      279–280
    defence of honest belief, 266–268
    defilement of child under 15 years,
      267
    defilement of child under 17
      years, 267–268
    reckless endangerment, 279
    statutory rape, 266–267
  incest, 268–271
  legislation, 3
  mentally impaired person, against,
    271–272
  orders on conviction, 18
  rape, 257–261

  registration of sex offenders, 18
  sexual assault, 262–266
Silence, right to, 27
Social contract theory, 3
Sources of criminal law
  common law, 10
  Constitution, 11
  European Convention on Human
    Rights, 12
  European law, 11
  generally, 8
  institutional writers, 11
  international law, 12
  legislation, 9–10
  scholarly writings, 11
Special Criminal Court, 21–22
**Spouse, criminal proceedings
  against**, 305
Stalking, 247–248
Standard of proof, 13–14, 118
State of affairs or status offences,
  38–39
Statutory rape, 266–267
Stolen property
  handling, 292–293
  possession, 293
  restitution order, 303
  retrospective effect of offences, 294
  stealing outside State, 294
  withholding information, 293–294
Strict liability
  definition, 34, 37, 99
  absolute liability distinguished, 99–100
  classification of offences, 99
  common law, 104–106
  constitutionality, 114–115
  criteria for, 108–109
  defence of due diligence, 113–114
  enforceability, 111–112
  European Convention on Human
    Rights, 114
  general principles, 102–104
  gravity of punishment, 112
  historical background, 99
  presumption of innocence, and, 114

presumption of mens rea, 109–110
rationale, 100–101
social context, 101–102
statutory offences, 106–108
"truly criminal" offences, 109
wording of statutory provision, 110–111
Suicide
accidentally killing another while attempting, 232
aiding and abetting
consent of DPP to prosecution, 234
criminal liability, 233–234
decriminalisation, 233
euthanasia, 235–236
survivor of suicide pact, 234
Summary offences, 20, 31–32
Suppression of documents, 290–291
Supreme Court, 23
Surveillance powers of Gardaí, 212
Syringe offences
placing or abandoning, 246–247
possession, 245–246
reasons for legislation, 9, 239
syringe attack, 244–245
use of contaminated syringe or blood, 245

Teleological approach to statutory interpretation, 105
Theft and fraud offences
alternative verdicts, 303
burglary, 291
concealing facts disclosed by documents, 301
corporate liability, 304
corruption, 299
counterfeiting see Counterfeiting and related offences
Defence Forces, 305
District Court jurisdiction, 304–305
false accounting, 290
foreign law, evidence of, 304
forfeiture of seized property, 301
forgery see Forgery and related offences
fraud affecting European Communities' financial interests, 299
handling etc stolen property see Stolen property
information to juries, 303
Irish citizenship, evidence of, 304
legislation
background, 282
overview of provisions, 282–283
repeals and transitional provisions, 283–284, 305
making gain or causing loss by deception, 288–289
making off without payment, 289
money laundering, 294–295
obtaining services by deception, 289
partner or part beneficial owner, by, 302
possession of certain articles, 292
production of evidential material, 301–302
reporting of offences, 304
restitution order, 303
robbery, 291–292
search warrant, 300–301
separate charges tried together, 302–303
several persons tried together, 302–303
spouse, proceedings against, 305
summary trial of indictable offences, 302
suppression of documents, 290–291
theft
actus reus, 284
appropriation, 284, 285–286
claim of right on good faith, 286
cutting trees or taking crops, 288
dishonesty, 284, 286–287
exceptions, 287–288
mens rea, 285
purchaser in good faith, 287

Theft and fraud offences *(continued)*
    statutory provisions, 284
    trustee, tenant or licensee, 287–288
    wild flowers, fruit and creatures, 288
    trial procedure, 302–303
    unlawful use of computer, 290
Threat to kill or cause serious harm, 244
Threatening, abusive or insulting behaviour in public place, 309
Torture, 12
Transferred malice, 89–91
Trespass on a building, 311–312

Vagueness, offences void for, 25, 28–29
Valuable securities
    definition, 290–291
    destruction, dishonest use etc, 290–291
Violent disorder, 312–313
Voluntary assumption of care, 53–56
Voluntary conduct
    automatism, 41–43, 126–128
    mens rea distinguished, 40
    physical force, and, 40–41
    requirement for actus reus, 39–40
    state of affairs, whether, 38–39

Wild flowers, fruit and creatures, 288
Wilful obstruction of free passage, 310–311
Withdrawal of life-support, 235–236
Withholding information as to stolen property, 293–294
Wolfenden Report, 4